# TRAINING TO BE A PRIMARY SCHOOL TEACHER: ITT & BEYOND

EDITED BY
# MEGAN STEPHENSON & ANGELA GILL

# TRAINING TO BE A PRIMARY SCHOOL TEACHER: ITT & BEYOND

1 Oliver's Yard
55 City Road
London EC1Y 1SP

2455 Teller Road
Thousand Oaks
California 91320

Unit No 323-333, Third Floor, F-Block
International Trade Tower
Nehru Place, New Delhi – 110 019

8 Marina View Suite 43-053
Asia Square Tower 1
Singapore 018960

Editor: Amy Thornton
Senior project editor: Chris Marke
Cover design: Sheila Tong
Typeset by: C&M Digitals (P) Ltd, Chennai, India

Editorial arrangement, Megan Stephenson and Angela Gill, 2024.

Chapter 1 Megan Stephenson and Angela Gill; Chapter 2 Michaela Oliver; Chapter 3 Charlotte Wright and Samantha Wilkes; Chapter 4 Kirsty Ross; Chapter 5 Jo Smith; Chapter 6 Sarah Cummins and Diana Mann; Chapter 7 Lewis Morgan and Anna Park; Chapter 8 David Waugh and Rebecca Linfield; Chapter 9 Zoe Proctor and Melanie Moore; Chapter 10 Sophie Nelson and Louise Brooke; Chapter 11 Alison Griffiths; Chapter 12 Jonathan Glazzard; Chapter 13 Mahnaz Siddiqui; Chapter 14 Rachel Simpson; Chapter 15 Amanda Nuttall; Chapter 16 Leigh Hoath; Chapter 17 Catherine Reading; Chapter 18 Laura Wild.

First published in 2024

Apart from any fair dealing for the purposes of research or private study, or criticism or review, as permitted under the Copyright, Designs and Patents Act 1988, this publication may be reproduced, stored or transmitted in any form, or by any means, only with the prior permission in writing of the publishers, or in the case of reprographic reproduction, in accordance with the terms of licences issued by the Copyright Licensing Agency. Enquiries concerning reproduction outside those terms should be sent to the publishers.

**Library of Congress Control Number: 2024933067**

**British Library Cataloguing in Publication Data**

A catalogue record for this book is available from the British Library

ISBN 978-1-5296-7278-7
ISBN 978-1-5296-7277-0 (pbk)

The editors would like to dedicate this book to all the students past, present and future who choose to join teacher education.

This book will help you learn from the most experienced and dedicated experts in ITT.

Well done for choosing the most inspiring profession in the world.

Keep with it, you can do it, it is worth it.

# CONTENTS

*Acknowledgements* ix
*About the editors and contributors* xi
*Editor's preface* xviii
*Foreword by Aimee Quickfall* xix
*Foreword by Lynn Newton* xxi

    Introduction 1
    *Megan Stephenson and Angela Gill*

## Section 1: Preparing for initial teacher training    7

1  An introduction to the ITT curriculum    9
   *Megan Stephenson and Angela Gill*

2  Learning about your teaching    30
   *Michaela Oliver*

3  Developing a teacher identity and creating professional relationships    47
   *Charlotte Wright and Samantha Wilkes*

4  Learning in context: Tracking your knowledge, understanding and progress    62
   *Kirsty Ross*

5  Your wellbeing and self-care    78
   *Jo Smith*

6  Safeguarding and wellbeing of pupils    95
   *Sarah Cummins and Diana Mann*

## Section 2: Initial teacher training: Knowledge and understanding    113

7  The curriculum in the primary school    115
   *Anna Park and Lewis Morgan*

8   The importance of early reading and Phonics        131
    *David Waugh and Rebecca Linfield*

9   Pupil behaviour                                     148
    *Zoe Proctor and Melanie Moore*

10  Delivering sequences of learning: Understanding
    the principles of planning                          167
    *Sophie Nelson and Louise Brooke*

11  Adaptative teaching                                 185
    *Alison Griffiths*

12  Inclusive education: Working with pupils who have special
    educational needs and/or disabilities (SEND)        203
    *Jonathan Glazzard*

13  Diversity and inclusive teaching                    222
    *Mahnaz Siddiqui*

14  Assessment and progression                          241
    *Rachel Simpson*

15  Education, social justice and disadvantage          257
    *Amanda Nuttall*

16  Teaching children sustainability                    273
    *Leigh Hoath*

17  Making the most of professional networks and your next steps   289
    *Catherine Reading*

18  Getting your first teaching post and the ECT programme    310
    *Laura Wild*

    Conclusion                                          333
    *Megan Stephenson and Angela Gill*

*Appendix*                                              337
*Index*                                                 355

# ACKNOWLEDGEMENTS

Megan and Angela would like to thank Andrew Murray for support with designing their diagrams and Ed Podesta for underpinning the academic knowledge and understanding in the book. They would also thank to thank all the academic and professional service teams across Leeds Trinity University (LTU) and Durham University ... They know why.

Chapter 2: Michaela would like to thank Nicole McIlvaney, Catherine Taylor and Peter Mason for contributing to case studies in this chapter. Nicole has recently completed a three-year undergraduate BA Honours degree in Primary Education with QTS at Durham University. Catherine and Peter are both directors for the Advance Learning Partnership multi-academy trust in County Durham. The experiences shared offer real examples of ways to learn about your teaching and greatly enhance this chapter.

Chapter 4: Kirsty would like to thank Lucie Forsyth for her case study contribution. Lucie, as a former student at Durham University, was recognised for her notable performance as a trainee teacher over the course of her programme. She built upon and developed her practice during her school experiences, successfully achieving QTS and securing employment in her final placement school.

Chapter 5: Jo would like to thank Chris, Francesca and Charlie for their support, positivity and proof-reading.

Chapter 6: Sarah and Diana would like to thank Rebecca Ingram-Lacey for writing the vignette case studies within this chapter, for her long-lasting faith in the editors and her level-headed approach to teacher education.

Chapter 7: Lewis and Anna would like to thank Emily Newell and Jonny Davies, art lead and headteacher respectively of St Oswald's school in Guiseley, for providing them with such a rich seam of practice and provision to use as a case study. Their energy, ideas and focus are an inspiration.

Chapter 9: The authors would like to thank each other. Working and learning together is what we do best.

Chapter 10: Sophie and Louise would like to thank Normanton Junior Academy and St Mary's Horsforth Catholic Voluntary Academy. Both schools are an inspiration to the staff and provide aspiration for all the pupils within them.

Chapter 11: Alison would like to thank all the students she has worked with over the years. They have provided her with the evidence base needed to create the chapter and to be able to reflect on how best to support students and how pupils learn through adaptive teaching.

Chapter 12: Jonathan would like to express his thanks to the many students and colleagues who have, throughout his career, consistently inspired him and shaped his values in relation to inclusive education.

Chapter 13: Mahnaz would like to sincerely thank David Waugh for mentoring her throughout the writing of this chapter; Ruth Lilly and Graham Downes for support and encouragement; and Lizzie Yeoman for sharing her expertise in religion and worldviews. She would also like to thank Amy and Martha (aliases) for their time and their case studies. Both trainees are White British, which was relevant for their case studies and experiences.

Chapter 14: Rachel would like to thank Charlotte Lam for her contribution of the examples in the case study. Thank you to the Schools Partnership Team in the School of Education, Durham University, for providing the assessment-related task list in the case study.

Chapter 15: Amanda would like to thank her work colleagues at Leeds Trinity University for their patience and support in completing the chapter. She'd especially like to thank Megan Stephenson for sharing office and head space over the years.

Chapter 16: Leigh would like to thank Heena Dave for her unfaltering support and expertise.

Chapter 17: Cath would like to thank Marc Hayes from Roundhay School for the thoughtful reflections on his pathway to leadership and Claire Walker from Gosforth Middle School for her case study and insightful commentary.

Chapter 18: Laura would like to thank Hannah Williamson for designing the Interview Triangle model to support trainees with their responses in interview and Dan Wheadon for sharing his valuable insight into subject leadership and his experience in how to prepare for this role.

# ABOUT THE EDITORS AND CONTRIBUTORS

**Megan Stephenson** is an Associate Professor in Professional Practice at Leeds Trinity University and is currently leading the ITT reaccreditation. Her roles at LTU have included Primary PGCE programme lead, Academic Early Reading and Phonics Curriculum Director and Academic Partnership Coordinator. Megan has contributed to several published works across her field of expertise. Prior to working in higher education institutions (HEIs) Megan taught for over 20 years in primary and special provision across the North of England, where she led on phonics and early reading and trained as a reading recovery teacher and trainer. She has presented at national conferences in the UK on her approach to developing 'inspirational teacher education', and has most recently published research into the impact on early career teachers (ECTs) who graduated throughout the Covid-19 pandemic.

**Angela Gill** is an Associate Professor at Durham University. She is the Director of ITT Programmes, leading both UG and PGCE programmes in the School of Education. She is the subject lead for Primary English and her areas of interest include phonics and writing. She is currently researching how play-based approaches can support the writing process in the primary school. She has written and edited books and articles about many aspects of primary English and the wider curriculum, and her recent publications include the fourth edition of *Teaching Systematic Synthetic Phonics in Primary Schools* (with Wendy Joliffe and David Waugh, 2022) and the second edition of *Mastering Writing at Greater Depth* (with Adam Bushnell and David Waugh, 2020). She has presented at national conferences in the UK and has organised conferences for trainees related to key aspects of the curriculum, such as phonics and employability. For more than 20 years, Angela taught in primary schools in Durham and Somerset, during which time she was subject lead for English and phonics.

**Michaela Oliver** is Assistant Professor in the School of Education at Durham University. She currently teaches across undergraduate and postgraduate modules and on initial teacher education (ITE) programmes. She is Programme Director for the BA (Hons) Primary Education undergraduate degree. Michaela's research focuses on discipline-specific reasoning in primary English. Her Economic and Social Research Council (ESRC)-funded PhD explored reasoning styles important in primary English and ways to promote these in the classroom. She is currently involved in funded research projects exploring ways to improve the teaching of crucial digital literacies in primary and secondary education. She is particularly interested in the roles of pedagogical task design, dialogic and collaborative teaching and learning approaches and their role in promoting reasoning. Michaela has published and presented at national and international conferences in these areas. She is on the editorial panel for the British Educational Research Association's (BERA's) *Curriculum Journal* and *Enhancing Teaching and Learning in Higher Education* journal. A former primary school teacher and subject lead, Michaela is passionate about ensuring that academic research is accessible and meaningful to school practitioners.

**Charlotte Wright** is a Senior Lecturer in Education and Programme Coordinator for the MA in Education at Leeds Trinity University. She has taught English for three decades in a range of schools, and trains new teachers and researchers. She is currently engaged in a doctorate in Education, looking at the theorising practice of English teachers.

**Samantha Wilkes** is a Senior Lecturer in Primary Education, across both undergraduate and postgraduate programmes. She has extensive experience in the Early Years and KS1 curricula, with a particular focus on language development and acquisition, systematic synthetic phonics and early reading and writing development. She is currently completing her MA in Education focused on research around teacher retention and career progression. Her role in ITT and mentoring ECTs as a previous headteacher has driven an interest in this area of research.

**Kirsty Ross** completed a PGCE following a change of career, taught and led in several education settings over a 20-year period before moving to a trainee teacher educator role at Durham University. Currently, she is the Director of Professional Practice across the ITT undergraduate and postgraduate programmes and teaches on a number of modules at the School of Education. Her research interests relate to the contribution a creative art curriculum makes to social and emotional wellbeing through the deepening understanding of personal identity, and how this can be an influencing and motivating factor for pupils to learn across all subjects. She is also interested in examining the relationship between centre-based and school-based experts in supporting and developing beginning teachers including how mentors strengthen and build on approaches that help trainees make sense of educational research and pedagogies in practice on school placements. Kirsty, as a passionate supporter of schools and children in the North East region, is also chair of governors at a local primary school.

**Jo Smith** is an Assistant Professor at Durham University's School of Education. She is the Deputy Director of ITT Wellbeing and teaches science across UG and PGCE programmes. She has a keen interest in the underrepresentation of minority groups in STEM; first generation students; social mobility; and wellbeing.

She has written chapters and articles about primary science and teaching pedagogy and presented at UK conferences. Jo has taught in both large and small primary schools from mixed-age EYFS/KS1 classes to readying her Y6s for SATs at KS2. She has led science, arts and early years across a federation of schools. Jo has taught science at secondary school, specialising in physics to A-Level. In her earlier career, Jo used her physics degree as a semiconductor engineer, travelling the world to buy multi-million-pound pieces of equipment to manufacture microchips. You can engage with her using her social media handle: @jojophysicsgirl.

**Sarah Cummins** is a Senior Lecturer at Leeds Trinity University and is currently undertaking her PhD at Anglia Ruskin University. Prior to working in higher education, she spent 20 years working in early years and primary education around the globe, with her last role being headteacher of a Montessori nursery and primary school. Sarah specialises in Montessori education and is currently the chairperson for the Montessori Society UK. Her research interests include examining the dichotomy of play and work in early years; the impact of adult perceptions of play on the child's experience of play; and Montessori education for sustainability. Her PhD work is examining the impact of trauma (domestic violence) in early childhood and the education outcomes. Her work is influenced by her experiences in educational settings and working with families.

**Diana Mann** is a Senior Lecturer in Primary Education in the School of Education at Leeds Trinity University, where she leads Professional Studies across all UG and PG routes. Prior to working in higher education, she had a long and successful career as a primary school teacher and then, latterly, headteacher, working primarily in schools where there was a degree of challenge and disadvantage. Diana was instrumental in introducing and promoting *oracy* as a whole-school approach, which led to increased progress and improved standards for children. Diana was one of the first child protection trainers in Leeds, delivering whole-school staff training across the city in response to serious high-profile safeguarding cases. She also worked as a mathematics advisory teacher for the local authority. Diana's particular areas of research include the education of children with English as an additional language (EAL), the focus of her MA, and, more recently, investigating the impact of the Covid pandemic on children's social and emotional wellbeing.

**Lewis Morgan** is a Senior Lecturer in Primary Science at Leeds Trinity University. Following ten years as a primary school teacher and science lead, he now delivers the science content across all undergraduate and postgraduate primary education degrees. Lewis is extremely passionate about introducing children to science and changing the beliefs and opinions children, and adults, have about science. He is also working alongside colleagues from across the university in planning how to embed climate change and sustainability into the primary curriculum.

# About the Editors and Contributors

**Anna Park** is a Senior Lecturer in Primary English at Leeds Trinity University, teaching across undergraduate and postgraduate programmes. She began working as a bookseller and developed a love of children's literature that continues to this day. Anna taught for 20 years in a variety of urban and rural schools and continued to develop her passion for teaching and English and languages teaching. Anna's master's in education dissertation focused on modelled writing, research she has presented at an international conference. She is currently researching students' identities as readers and their knowledge of children's literature.

**David Waugh** is Professor of Education at Durham University. He has published extensively in primary English. He is a former deputy headteacher, was Head of the Centre for Education Studies at the University of Hull and was a Regional Adviser for ITT for National Strategies from 2008 to 2010. As well as his educational writing, David regularly works in schools and has written seven children's novels, including *The Wishroom* (2017), which was written with 44 children from 16 East Durham schools, and *Twins?* (2019), which was written with 12 children in West Durham.

**Rebecca Linfield** is a school Link tutor based at Durham University. She has been a classroom teacher and senior school leader for over 20 years. Rebecca is a former Assistant head teacher specialising in Early Years Leadership, Early Reading, Phonics, Science, Sustainable Education and Curriculum Design. Rebecca supports a range of schools to develop their Curriculum Intent to ensure Phonics and Reading is both prioritised and embedded across the whole school curriculum from Nursery to Year 6. Raising early reading standards for every child in all settings is her main focus.

**Zoe Proctor** is a Senior Lecturer in Primary Education at Leeds Trinity University where she is Level Lead for Level 4 Primary Education and a Professional Studies lecturer. Zoe is an experienced teacher who has worked across the primary age phase and supported teacher development as an advanced skills teacher for Mathematics. Her research interests are metacognition and learning behaviours.

**Melanie Moore** is a Senior Lecturer in Primary Education at Leeds Trinity University, where she is Level Lead for Level 6 Primary Education and Primary Mathematics. Before joining Leeds Trinity University, Melanie worked as a classroom teacher in Key Stage 2 for two decades. Melanie's research interests include primary mathematics and behaviour management.

**Sophie Nelson** is a Senior Lecturer in Primary Education at Leeds Trinity University. She currently leads the second year of the UG primary education programme and teaches across English and Professional Studies. Sophie has had the privilege of working with teachers at all stages of their careers in her roles as a teacher, teaching school director and head of school prior to teaching in higher education. Sophie is passionate about encouraging creativity in the classroom and her areas of interest include philosophy for children, drama for learning and climate change education.

**Louise Brooke** is the Assistant Headteacher at St Mary's Horsforth Catholic Voluntary Academy. In recent years, she has led and taken responsibility for teaching and learning within English, reading and mathematics. Entering her tenth year in the classroom, she is an advocate of developing research-based practice and is committed to securing outstanding results through experience-led learning, enriching and widening the curriculum offer. Her background in coaching and mentoring ITT students led to her taking on the lead mentor role for the Eden Teaching School Alliance with Leeds Trinity University.

**Alison Griffiths** has worked in education since 1992 and during that time has been class teacher and year lead in primary schools in North Wales and London. She is currently Deputy Head of School at Leeds Trinity University with responsibility for the primary PGCE programme. Alison has a master's degree in creative pedagogies and is currently completing her Professional Doctorate in Education, focusing upon the intellectual and academic work of teacher educators, looking to understand how their engagement with research impacts on how they view themselves as part of the wider academic community.

**Jonathan Glazzard** is the Rosalind Hollis Professor of Education for Social Justice at the University of Hull. He is an experienced teacher and teacher educator, and he has published extensively on inclusive education, special educational needs and mental health and wellbeing in education. Jonathan is committed to the principle that education should serve a powerful role in advancing social justice. He is a convenor for BERA's Special Interest Group on Mental Health and Wellbeing in Education and a member of the All-Parliamentary Committee for a Fit and Healthy Childhood.

**Mahnaz Siddiqui** (she/her, mixed heritage Pakistani/White, British) is a Senior Lecturer in ITE at Liverpool John Moores University. Mahnaz is on the strategic board for NWMathsHub3 and engaged in work with their ITT workgroup. She is a trustee for the Association of Teachers of Mathematics and leads a mathematics subject network group with local schools, keeping up to date in the field of primary mathematics. She has a keen interest in dialogic approaches and is Philosophy for Children (P4C) trained. Mahnaz recognises the importance of being mentally healthy and has undertaken mental health first aid (MHFA) training in order to better support training teachers. She advocates outdoor spaces as learning environments to motivate learners. Mahnaz has engaged with training for behaviour management and her most recent interests include trauma-informed practices, which she advocates strongly. Having lived experience of racism and neurodiversity, Mahnaz has always been an advocate for issues of inclusion, diversity and equality/equity and being an anti-racist/anti-prejudice educator; from attending courses and conferences, reading and research, Mahnaz is learning more about how to actively be anti-prejudiced.

**Rachel Simpson** is an Associate Professor at Durham University. She is the Assessment Leader for ITT Programmes in the School of Education and Subject Lead for Primary Science. Rachel is currently researching the potential benefits of using a creative teaching approach and developing associated skills for trainees. She has written book chapters and articles about aspects of primary science, assessment-related pedagogical approaches and creative teaching skills. Rachel has presented at national conferences in the UK. Prior to working in higher education, Rachel was a school leader in primary schools in Cambridgeshire, leading a range of subjects, and a teacher in an international school in Vietnam.

**Amanda Nuttall** is Associate Professor in the School of Education at Leeds Trinity University and has recently completed a DPhil at the Department of Education, University of Oxford. Prior to working in higher education, she spent 13 years teaching in primary schools serving predominantly disadvantaged communities. Her research interests include examining the impact of poverty and disadvantage in education, epistemological conceptions and perceptions of teachers' work, and theorising professional learning and development for educators through a lens of identity. Her doctoral and post-doctoral work is built on co-construction of rich narratives of teachers' experiences of reformation and transformation of multiple dimensions of identity[ies] as they engage in master's level research activity. This work is influenced by her own experiences as a research-active teacher and an interest in transformational professional learning experiences for teachers and teacher educators across initial and continuing teacher education programmes.

**Leigh Hoath** is a Professor of Science Education at Leeds Trinity University and co-founder of CAPE (Climate Adapted Pathways for Education). She has led outreach work for the world's largest chemical company, been a consultant for the BBCTeach Blue Planet and The Regenerators campaigns. Leigh is an author of primary and secondary books, a regular national conference presenter and very actively involved with the Association for Science Education (ASE) where she is co-chair for 2023/4.

**Catherine Reading** is a Professor at Durham University and the Director of Professional Development in the School of Education. At Durham, she contributed to ITE programmes for over 15 years, working with undergraduate and postgraduate students in the primary and secondary phases. Catherine is a chartered science teacher and previously taught in schools in London and the North East. As a science specialist, she has delivered professional development for teachers in science education nationally and internationally. Catherine is passionate about teacher education and professional development; she heads Durham's Centre for Continuing Professional Development and School Engagement.

**Laura Wild** is an Assistant Professor at Durham University. She is the Curriculum, Assessment and Student Experience (CASE) Programme Lead for the UG programme in the School of Education. She is the subject lead for primary mathematics. Her areas of interest include mastery in mathematics, subject leadership, teaching and learning in a mixed-aged classroom and effective continuing professional development (CPD). She is currently researching anxiety in mathematics. For 15 years Laura taught in primary schools in Yorkshire, during which time she was an executive deputy headteacher and achieved her NPQH. Since then, Laura was the Teaching for Mastery lead of a maths hub and was part of a Trust school improvement team. Laura was then sought to be the Curriculum Development Project Lead for a local authority. Throughout this time Laura was an associate member of the primary team for the National Centre for Excellence in the Teaching of Mathematics (NCETM), designing and leading, monitoring and evaluating local and national workshops.

# EDITOR'S PREFACE

This book is a complete guide to your Initial Teacher Training programme and your transition to becoming an early career teacher.

Through a rich variety of themes, the Department for Education (DfE) criteria for teacher training is explored. In January 2024, the DfE announced that the Core Content Framework (CCF) for ITT would be replaced, from September 2025, with the Initial Teacher Training and Early Career Framework (ITTECF). This new framework is a combining of the Core Content Framework and the Early Career Framework. These frameworks have been combined to ensure that trainee and new teachers have a coherent and consistent training programme that bridges their initial teacher training and first two years in teaching. The content of the CCF continues into the ITTECF. We are aware that your training provider may implement ITTECF during the academic year 2024/25 or during the academic year 2025/26. Therefore, this book explores the statutory Initial Teacher Training curriculum expressed in both frameworks, the CCF and the ITTECF.

For Trainee Teachers: This book will help support you with your training whether your provider is structuring your ITT curriculum around the ITT Core Content Framework or the Initial Teacher Training and Early Career Framework.

For ITT Providers: This book is a resource for all primary ITT courses. We have considered both the ITT Core Content Framework and the Initial Teacher Training and Early Career Framework when writing and have included relevant links to both/each document where needed.

# FOREWORD BY AIMEE QUICKFALL

This book is going to change your life – which is not a small claim, but I can defend the assertion.

Becoming a teacher is a complex, sometimes confusing process; it is completely normal to feel like you are on a rollercoaster of emotional highs and lows, elated at 9.02am and feeling crushed by 9.05am. Being on a rollercoaster for days can be really exhausting. At times, the amount that you need to prepare, notice, react to and reflect upon feels unmanageable. Sometimes the joy of working with some of the best people on Earth (children and other educators, of course) makes you feel like you have won the lottery for eight weekends on the bounce. I remember my own teacher training very clearly, and these are some of the most vivid memories I have: the panic at having jammed the staff photocopier at 8.45am on a Monday morning; the elation when my much-dreaded fractions lesson made sense and children progressed before my eyes; the feeling of belonging when my fabulous teaching assistant, Lucy, shared a bar of chocolate with me after a particularly trying afternoon of whole-class D&T (with glue guns).

Any book, blog, article or chat that helps you negotiate that rollercoaster, that supports you in enjoying the ride, is worth hunting for and engaging in. This book does a lot of friendly supporting and advising – not just on the big-ticket items of planning, subject knowledge and assessment, but also on the aspects of teacher training that sometimes get missed out of the advice: how to reflect on what you are experiencing in a positive way; how to make sure your health and wellbeing don't plummet during the loop-the-loop; and how to find your rollercoaster buddies through peer support, networks and professional development. Read this book, read lots – and talk about your experiences, seek out your favourite advisers, listeners and supporters – they will all change your life as a teacher for the better.

*Dr Aimee Quickfall, Head of the School of Education, Leeds Trinity University*

# FOREWORD BY LYNN NEWTON

Nothing is so certain as change. In education, in the early 20th century, we saw school systems and their underpinning curricula reflecting the needs of 19th- and early 20th-century industrial society. By the late 20th century, that heritage became history. We saw technology and computing bringing change to industries, businesses, societies and environments, with greater national and global mobility. Teachers needed to be increasingly flexible, adaptable and inclusive. Now, well into the 21st century, we are challenged by artificial intelligence and its growing impact on lives, including the working lives of teachers. What it means to be a teacher is changing once again.

Being a primary teacher and having the chance to work with young learners and change lives is a privilege as well as a challenge. Having decided on this career path, the first formal stage is normally the initial teacher training phase. Done well, ITT can begin to develop, consolidate and enhance the breadth and depth of skills, knowledge and understandings necessary to grow as a really effective teacher in a changing 21st-century classroom and nurture appropriate attitudes towards inclusivity and resilience.

Those ITT foundations enable teachers to foster classroom environments in which teachers can engender in learners purposeful, productive thinking, through a curriculum that builds on knowledge, understanding and skills, helping learners to be creative thinkers and solve problems, to be critical and evaluative evidence and to make wise decisions. But this will only happen if the teachers themselves have these firm foundations and that is what this book is about.

The primary children we teach are the adults who will be living and working in a future that is unpredictable and will, without doubt, have changed from what we are currently experiencing. After all, many will still be here to see in the next century.

*Lynn D. Newton, Head of School of Education, Durham University*

# INTRODUCTION

## MEGAN STEPHENSON AND ANGELA GILL

Combining knowledge and application is the 'golden thread' throughout your ITT curriculum. The Knowledge and Application model below shows how this is introduced in the *ITT Core Content Framework* (DfE, 2019b), through 'Learn that' and 'Learn how to' criteria, and how it is woven into the curriculum designed by your provider.

**Learn that and Learn how to –
The Knowledge and Application Model**

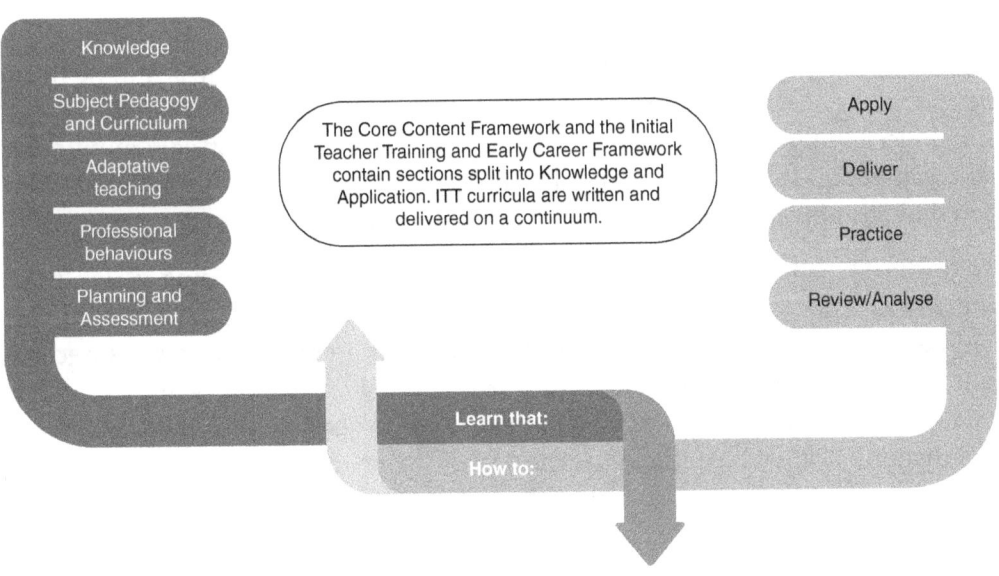

Chapter 1 focuses on how and why knowledge and application are integral to your development as a trainee teacher. It will identify the origins of the *Core Content Framework* (CCF) and the Initial Teacher Training Early Career Framework (ITTECF) and introduce you to the phrasing used across your initial teacher training (ITT) curriculum. It defines the key terminology that will form the basis of your ITT programme. It explores how the CCF/ITTECF have been used to create an ITT curriculum and identifies and exemplifies the importance of receiving carefully crafted, logically sequenced training.

In Chapter 2 you will discover the importance of both teaching and learning about your teaching to ensure that you continually provide high-quality learning experiences for all pupils. It will explore the concept of reflective practice, and the values, attributes and competencies required to engage in this process. There will be consideration about what reflective practice might look like for trainees and teachers, in both centre-based and school-based settings. The chapter provides practical scaffolding to support trainees to embark on their reflective journey.

Chapter 3 will encourage you to develop your sense of yourself as a developing professional in an education setting, and help you to build bridges to and from curriculum learning centres and school-based learning centres. You will explore what the term 'professionalism' means and guidance is offered about how to conduct yourself in school, and how to seek help from your mentor. The chapter will also help you find ways to reflect on your emerging teacher identity and to navigate between your ideals about teaching and the practical constraints that might challenge them. You will be asked to think about yourself as a role model, and ways to look at your practice as a teacher but also as a learner yourself.

Learning in context and an appreciation of learning through practical application and experience are the focus in Chapter 4. Introducing what it means to be in the classroom as a teacher, the chapter will explore the significance of secure knowledge and understanding to ensure good teaching and learning, and consider monitoring, observation and feedback on school-based practice. The content is intended to support and promote personal growth, professional identity and efficacy.

By reading Chapter 5 you will begin to understand why wellbeing is important and where it sits within the CCF/ITTECF. By working through the activities, you will be introduced to the benefits of journalling and creating a personalised pep talk in the form of a letter addressed to the future you. You will gain insight into what you can and cannot control and know who to approach for help in a variety of situations. You will explore what makes you happy and identify your stress triggers and indicators. You will be advised to reframe stress positively to increase your resilience and your wellbeing and reassure you that a little stress can be good for you, increasing blood flow and performance. Careful planning and time management are key to ensuring a good work–life balance and a high level of wellbeing.

Chapter 6 will clearly identify that ensuring the safety, security and wellbeing of pupils and educators is of paramount importance in any educational setting. The chapter addresses the comprehensive approach that primary schools must adopt to safeguard their pupils and educators, creating an environment conducive to learning, growth and development. Prioritising safeguarding and promoting wellbeing within your environment will not only foster a positive and nurturing community, but also enable pupils and educators to thrive within a secure environment. The chapter will also review how we create a safe and secure environment for all children while protecting the trainee's own self and sense of wellbeing throughout training and early career.

In Chapter 7, we will be developing your understanding of what a curriculum is, what it is for and how we arrived at the National Curriculum that has been in use since 2014. Using case studies and examples, you will learn that schools take the content of the National Curriculum and use this as a minimum entitlement for all children. In this chapter we demonstrate how schools bring this curriculum to life in a way that offers all children deep and rich learning experiences. By the end of the chapter, you will have a greater understanding of whole-school planning and a child's overall learning experience.

In Chapter 8, you will be introduced to some of the key considerations related to early reading and phonics and why teaching these aspects of the curriculum is so important. The chapter explores why phonics is the chosen method for teaching early reading and some of the challenges that phonics can pose. You will explore how you might ensure children make progress in phonics to develop their reading and how you can support parents when reading with their children at home.

Chapter 9 will set out where *managing behaviours* is positioned within the *ITT Core Content Framework* Standard 7. It will discuss how many common strategies to support behaviour have evolved from evidenced-informed research and how each approach connects to create a cohesive whole picture, which you can begin to apply in your practice in the classroom. It will also encourage you to think about your own values and the educational philosophy you hold with regards to managing behaviour.

Whether you are teaching from pre-prepared resources or creating your own sequences of learning from scratch, Chapter 10 will explore the vital thinking process which must take place when preparing your lessons to ensure effective teaching and learning in your classroom. While planning is a complex process, the steps within the chapter offer considerations which will support you to sequence learning episodes over varying periods of time and ensure that the learning reflects the unique context and needs of the pupils in your setting.

By reading Chapter 11 you will learn that, as a teacher, you are a role model who can influence the way that children view themselves as learners. Learning is built from a foundation of high expectations; the way that you view your children is central to the way you adapt your teaching. You will begin to understand that teaching is an iterative process and as a teacher you will be required to constantly assess, reflect and adapt both in planning and in the moment to respond the needs of your learners. Learning is cumulative and you need to be aware of the prior learning that your pupils bring with them and build from this. You will learn that adaptive teaching asks you to teach to the top, ensuring there is sufficient challenge for all.

Chapter 12 focuses on inclusive education for pupils with special educational needs and/or disabilities (SEND). It directly addresses the concept of adaptive teaching and contrasts this with traditional approaches to differentiation. The chapter covers the *SEND Code of Practice* (DfE/DoH, 2015) and consider the implications of this for trainee teachers, teachers and early career teachers (ECTs). The chapter outlines some important adaptive teaching strategies and considers how to work effectively with teaching assistants, the special educational needs coordinator (SENCO), external professionals and parents and carers.

By reading Chapter 13 you will learn that becoming an anti-prejudiced educator will support schools in diversifying and decolonising their curriculums for inclusion, as well as why this is important and the impact that curriculum design has on achievement, inclusion (sense of belonging), motivation; it is the duty of every teacher. The chapter demonstrates that being a diverse and inclusive educator takes time, effort and commitment. There is not a simple tick list to becoming and being anti-discriminatory; it is a constant part of a teacher's practice. The chapter emphasises the importance of self-reflection and awareness development which will help you to actively consider some solutions with regards to your classroom practices.

Chapter 14 will help you to develop your knowledge and understanding of assessment in primary education, and its place in enabling pupils' progression in their learning experiences. The crucial role of assessment regarding pupil progress will be considered by exploring different types of assessment, according to different purposes. The chapter aims to equip you as a trainee to make the most effective decisions about assessment. Therefore, the discussion of different assessment strategies alongside reflective tasks will enable you to develop assessment skills as a trainee and apply these to your teaching context.

In Chapter 15, we will unpack some of what is meant by *poverty* and *disadvantage* and go on to examine the distinct relationship between family income and educational attainment. The chapter will conjoin these relationships with notions of social justice and consider what this means for you in your role as a primary teacher.

Chapter 16 will outline some tricky conversations around sustainability and climate change education. Although this is not a mandatory element of the curriculum, CCF/ITTECF or any other aspect of education, it is one with a growing agenda and prevalence within schools. The purpose of this chapter is to draw upon many of the other learnings from previous chapters and demonstrate that sustainability and climate change education demands the same consideration. The content within this will position the difficulties to be overcome, the need to think carefully about how and who you are teaching and explore a lot of the existing literature in this area.

The diverse nature of career development and progression in the teaching profession will be explored in Chapter 17. It will emphasise the role and the importance of continuing professional development (CPD) for a practising teacher and explore the key elements that ensure effective delivery. The construct of a professional learning network (PLN) will be introduced, and examples of developing this effectively will be given. The chapter explores how to make the most of a PLN and to use it effectively for your professional growth and progression.

Chapter 18 will provide an insight into the path that lies ahead for you in the early stages of your teaching career. It will explain what the DfE *Teachers' Standards* are and will provide an understanding of how the CCF/ITTECF and the *Early Career Framework* (ECF) (DfE, 2019a, 2019b and 2024) are used to support trainees and ECTs in the achievement of these standards. The chapter aims to equip you with an understanding of the application and interview process, including ideas on how to stand out from the crowd to secure your first teaching post. The chapter moves from the CCF/ITTECF, beyond the ECF, to encourage you to begin to consider the role of subject leadership and what it takes to prepare to be successful in that role.

# REFERENCES

Department for Education (DfE) (2019a) *Early Career Framework*. Available at: https://assets.publishing.service.gov.uk/government/uploads/system/uploads/attachment_data/file/978358/Early-Career_Framework_April_2021.pdf [accessed August 2023].

DfE (2019b) *ITT Core Content Framework*. London: DfE. Available at: https://assets.publishing.service.gov.uk/government/uploads/system/uploads/attachment_data/file/974307/ITT_core_content_framework_.pdf [accessed November 2023].

DfE (2024) *Initial teacher training and early career framework* Available at: https://www.gov.uk/government/publications/initial-teacher-training-and-early-career-framework [Accessed March 2024].

Department for Education and Department of Health (DfE/DoH) (2015) *Special Educational Needs and Disability Code of Practice: 0 to 25 Years. Statutory Guidance for Organisations Which Work with and Support Children and Young People who Have Special Educational Needs or Disabilities*. London: DfE/DoH.

# SECTION 1
## PREPARING FOR INITIAL TEACHER TRAINING

# 1

# AN INTRODUCTION TO THE ITT CURRICULUM

## MEGAN STEPHENSON AND ANGELA GILL

**Learn that and Learn how to –
The Knowledge and Application Model**

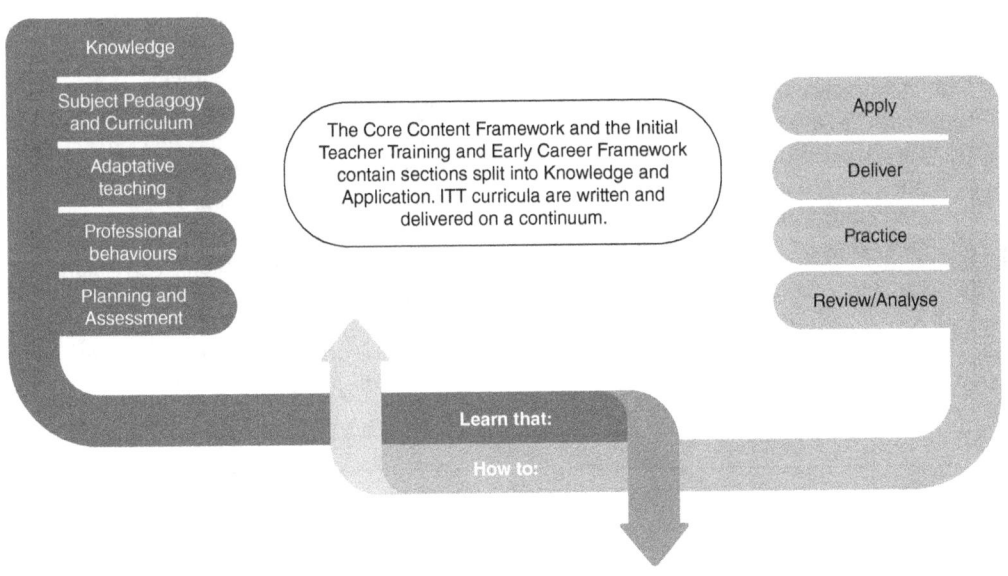

## FRAMED BY THE CCF - FOR FULL LINKS TO THE ITTECF, SEE PAGE 337

| How Pupils Learn | |
|---|---|
| (Standard 2 – 'Promote good progress') | |
| Learn that … | Learn how to … |
| 1. Learning involves a lasting change in pupils' capabilities or understanding.<br>2. Prior knowledge plays an important role in how pupils learn; committing some key facts to their long-term memory is likely to help pupils learn more complex ideas. | Avoid overloading working memory, by:<br><br>• Receiving clear, consistent and effective mentoring in how to take into account pupils' prior knowledge when planning how much new information to introduce. |
| Subject and Curriculum | |
| (Standard 3 – 'Demonstrate good subject and curriculum knowledge') | |
| Learn that … | Learn how to … |
| 2. Secure subject knowledge helps teachers to motivate pupils and teach effectively.<br>3. Ensuring pupils master foundational concepts and knowledge before moving on is likely to build pupils' confidence and help them succeed.<br>10. Every teacher can improve pupils' literacy, including by explicitly teaching reading, writing and oral language skills specific to individual disciplines. | Deliver a carefully sequenced and coherent curriculum, by:<br><br>• Receiving clear, consistent and effective mentoring in how to identify essential concepts, knowledge, skills and principles of the subject.<br>• Observing how expert colleagues ensure pupils' thinking is focused on key ideas within the subject and deconstructing this approach.<br>• Discussing and analysing with expert colleagues the rationale for curriculum choices, the process for arriving at current curriculum choices and how the school's curriculum materials inform lesson preparation. |

## CHAPTER OBJECTIVES

On reading this chapter you will consider:

- how the change in the educational landscape brought about the introduction of the CCF/ITTECF;
- the key terms and phrases used in all ITT curricula;
- what a well-sequenced, coherent ITT curriculum looks like (including intensive training and practice);
- how ITT curricula demonstrate fidelity between centre-based and school-based training.

# 1 AN INTRODUCTION TO THE ITT CURRICULUM

> **KEY VOCABULARY**
>
> Initial teacher training (ITT)
>
> Initial Teacher Training and Early Career Framework (ITTECF)
>
> Core Content Framework (CCF)
>
> Qualified teacher status (QTS)
>
> Spiral curriculum
>
> Curriculum learning centres (CLCs)
>
> School-based learning centres (SBLCs)
>
> Intensive training and practice (ITaPs)
>
> Expert colleagues
>
> Expert mentors

# INTRODUCTION

Combining knowledge and application is the *golden thread* throughout your initial teacher training (ITT) curriculum. The Knowledge and Application model at the top of this chapter shows how this is introduced in the *ITT Core Content Framework* (DfE, 2019b), through 'Learn that' and 'Learn how to' criteria, and how it is woven into the curriculum designed by your provider. This chapter focuses on how and why knowledge and application are integral to your development as a trainee teacher.

## HOW THE CHANGE IN THE EDUCATIONAL LANDSCAPE BROUGHT ABOUT THE INTRODUCTION OF THE *CORE CONTENT FRAMEWORK*

In 2019, the government commissioned an independent consultative review of all the initial teacher training providers (ITTPs) in England. This became known as the Market Review. The outcome of the consultation led to all ITT providers in England being required to apply for reaccreditation in order to be able to continue to offer qualified teacher status (QTS). The institution where you are training to become a teacher may be an accredited or lead provider, both of which provide a rich ITT curriculum for trainees. In the same year, the Department for Education (DfE) published a document that replaced the previous *Framework of Core Content for Initial Teacher Training* (2016) that had been created by experts in the ITT field. The new publication is known as the *Core Content Framework* (CCF) (DfE, 2019b).

The CCF was to provide the framework (or building blocks) from which all providers designed their excellent ITT provision: 'In designing their curricula, providers should carefully craft the experiences and activities detailed in the *ITT Core Content Framework* into a coherent sequence that supports trainees to succeed in the classroom' (DfE, 2019b, p. 4).

This chapter will introduce you to the phrasing and criteria used across the CCF/ITTECF and help you to unpick the key terminology that forms the basis of your initial teacher training programme. It will explore how the CCF is used to create an ITT curriculum and identify and exemplify the importance of delivering carefully crafted, logically sequenced training, both within your provider, the curriculum learning centres (CLCs), and within school-based learning centres (SBLCs).

The CCF/ITTECF is designed to support trainee development in five core areas or domains:

- behaviour management;
- pedagogy (teaching);
- curriculum (subject knowledge and planning);
- assessment (assessing pupils' knowledge and progress);
- professional behaviours.

(DfE, 2019b and 2024)

Each domain is presented in eight sections, and these provide a context and congruence for the *Teachers' Standards* (DfE, 2021). These standards set the minimum requirements for teachers' practice and conduct that have to be met by the end of an ITT programme, in order for a trainee to gain QTS.

The eight sections of the CCF/ITTECF, with the Teachers' Standard that the section relates to, are as follows:

1. High Expectations (Standard 1 – 'Set high expectations')
2. How Pupils Learn (Standard 2 – 'Promote good progress')
3. Subject and Curriculum (Standard 3 – 'Demonstrate good subject and curriculum knowledge')
4. Classroom Practice (Standard 4 – 'Plan and teach well structured lessons')
5. Adaptive Teaching (Standard 5 – 'Adapt teaching')
6. Assessment (Standard 6 – 'Make accurate and productive use of assessment')
7. Managing Behaviour (Standard 7 – 'Manage behaviour effectively')
8. Professional Behaviours (Standard 8 – 'Fulfil wider professional responsibilities').

(DfE, 2019b)

Each of the eight areas is divided into sets of key evidence – 'Learn that' – and practice – 'Learn how to' – statements, outlining two types of content. Within each area, these statements are clearly used to indicate 'what makes great teaching' (DfE, 2019b).

Figure 1.1 shows an example taken from the CCF, showing the 'Learn that' and 'Learn how to' statements related to Section 1: High Expectations. Some criteria are slightly amended within the ITTECF (DfE, 2024).

| High Expectations (Standard 1 - 'Set high expectations') ||
|---|---|
| **Learn that** | **Learn how to …** |
| 1. Teachers have the ability to affect and improve the wellbeing, motivation and behaviour of their pupils. | **Communicate a belief in the academic potential of all pupils, by:**<br><br>• Receiving clear, consistent and effective mentoring in how to set tasks that stretch pupils, but which are achievable, within a challenging curriculum. |
| 2. Teachers are key role models, who can influence the attitudes, values and behaviours of their pupils. | **And – following expert input – by taking opportunities to practise, receive feedback and improve at:**<br><br>• Using intentional and consistent language that promotes challenge and aspiration.<br><br>• Creating a positive environment where making mistakes and learning from them and need for effort and perseverance are part of the daily routine. |
| 3. Teacher expectations can affect pupil outcomes; setting goals that challenges and stretch pupils is essential. | • Seeking opportunities to engage parents and carers in the education of their children (e.g. proactively highlighting successes) with supports from expert colleagues to understand how this engagement changes depending on the age and development stage of the pupil. |
| 4. Setting clear expectations can help communicate shared values that improve classroom and school culture. | **Demonstrate consistently high behavioural expectations, by:**<br><br>• Receiving clear, consistent and effective mentoring in how to create a culture of respect and trust in the classroom that support all pupils to succeed (e.g by modelling the types of courteous behaviour expected of pupils). |
| 5. A culture of mutual trust and respect supports effective relationships. | **And – following expert input – by taking opportunities to practise, receive feedback and improve at:**<br><br>• Teaching and rigorously maintaining clear behavioural expectations (e.g. for contributors, volume level and concentration). |
| 6. High-quality teaching has a long-term positive effect on pupils' life chances, particularly for children from disadvantaged backgrounds. | • Applying rules, sanctions and rewards in line with school policy, escalating behaviour incidents as appropriate.<br><br>• Acknowledging and praising pupil effort and emphasising progress being made. |
| **Notes**<br>Learn that … statements are informed by the best available educational research; references and further reading are provide below.<br>Learn how to … statements are drawn from the wider evidence base including both academic research and additional guidance from expert practitioners.<br>Other key definitions can be found in the introduction ||

*Figure 1.1 ITT Core Content Framework (DfE, 2019b)*

The statements underpin the expectations of the whole CCF/ITTECF, encompassing all aspects required across the above key domains or areas. The domains define an entitlement for you as an ITT trainee, as you begin to learn key subject knowledge and applied pedagogy.

The delivery of an ITT curriculum and opportunities to review and 'have a go at practising' in school are carefully crafted so that they occur simultaneously. A deep knowledge of the content of the ITT curriculum and the CCF/ITTECF is therefore essential for all those involved in the training of teachers, including the trainee themselves. This also includes expert colleagues within ITT providers and in all partner schools, where school practice takes place as part of your ITT programme. The CCF/ITTECF does not provide your full ITT curriculum, and it is up to individual providers to design their curriculum to suit the needs of trainees, specifically related to age phases and subjects that are offered.

### EVIDENCE-INFORMED RESEARCH: USING EVIDENCE-INFORMED RESEARCH

In each chapter of this book, you will be introduced to key pieces of evidence-informed research related to the chapter theme. In the first of these sections, we will share some key sources of evidence to support you in your development as a trainee.

The CCF (DfE, 2019b) provides a suggested list of reading for trainees, with recommendations for each of the eight sections in the framework. The Education Endowment Foundation (EEF) is an independent charity that focuses on education achievement. It delivers research around key educational themes, and its *Teaching and Learning Toolkit* (EEF, 2021) is recognised as an informative and accessible summary of education evidence. The *Teacher Training Survival Toolkit* (Sage, n.d.) is a collection of useful resources and extracts from teacher training publications. Ofsted have published a series of *Curriculum Research Reviews* (www.gov.uk/government/collections/curriculum-research-reviews), covering the breadth of the primary curriculum. It would also be useful for you to familiarise yourself with other key DfE and Ofsted publications, such as the *Education Inspection Framework* (Ofsted, 2023).

### ACTION LEARNING SET

Find the CCF or the ITTECF on the DfE website, part of www.gov.uk

What does the CCF or the ITTECF say about Part 2 of the *Teachers' Standards*?

How might the CCF or the ITTECF support you when considering SEND, disadvantage and mental health?

# KEY TERMS AND PHRASES USED IN THE CCF/ITTECF AND YOUR ITT CURRICULUM

Throughout the CCF/ITTECF, key phrases and terminology are used repeatedly. You will be introduced to these terms along with the *subject-specific* and *age-specific* content of the ITT curriculum. The following terms and the supporting statements will be used across all of your curriculum materials.

> **Expert colleagues**: Professional colleagues, including subject and age phase specialists, at your curriculum learning centre and in school (experienced and effective teachers, mentors, lecturers and tutors).
>
> **Observing** how expert colleagues deliver knowledge.
>
> **Deconstructing** these approaches. Working with expert colleagues – using *in-class observation, modelling, or analysis of video and mixed media* will support your understanding of what might make a particular technique successful or unsuccessful.
>
> **Practise**: Opportunities to use approaches defined in the 'Learn how to' column of the CCF.
>
> **Receiving clear consistent and effective mentoring**: Receiving *structured feedback* from expert colleagues on a *particular approach* – using the best available evidence to provide a *structured process* for *improving your practice*.
>
> (DfE, 2019b, p. 5)

Throughout your training, you will have many opportunities to rehearse and refine particular approaches, possibly beginning outside the classroom and perhaps using *digital approximations* or *micro-teaching* before then adapting ideas and approaches and *enacting* (demonstrating) what you have observed, practised and learned.

## DIGITAL APPROXIMATIONS

Digital approximation is grounded in a theory of practice-based teacher education, in which teachers learn from engaging in and reflecting on their practice in several ways, including engagement in approximations of practice (Grossman et al., 2009) using video and other digital media. Approximations 'include opportunities to rehearse and enact discrete components of complex practice in settings of reduced complexity' (Howell and Mikeska, 2021, p. 283). This work includes teaching practices such as eliciting student thinking, analysing student work, or leading discussions (Howell and Mikeska, 2021).

Digital approximations enable trainees to develop a deep understanding of the link between educational research and effective classroom practice and help to bridge the gap between theory and practice. Trainees can experiment and make mistakes outside the classroom, enabling them to make the most of precious time with mentors during school-based practice. ITT providers are able to deliver high-quality training, without compromise, to all trainees.

## MICRO-TEACHING

Micro-teaching is a scaled down teaching encounter where a trainee teaches a single concept of content, using a specified teaching skill for a short time (five to ten minutes), to a very small group of participants (five to ten members) in a mock classroom situation. Micro-teaching might take place in your curriculum learning centre or in school. Your participants might be your peers or pupils. Research by Remesh (2013) found that micro-teaching can help in eliminating errors and in building stronger teaching skills. Micro-teaching can increase self-confidence, improve in-class teaching performance and develop classroom management skills.

## ROLES AND RESPONSIBILITIES

You will work collegiately with a range of expert colleagues in both curriculum centres and schools. *Expert colleagues* and *expert mentors* will ensure you have access to the full ITT curriculum throughout your programme.

### TRAINEE

As a trainee teacher, you will be expected to gain secure subject knowledge, to practise key skills and apply your knowledge and understanding of evidence in the classroom. Reflecting on how approaches should be integrated into your own practice and identifying targets, with support from your expert colleagues and expert mentors, will be an important aspect of your development.

### EXPERT COLLEAGUES

You will receive multiple opportunities to rehearse and refine teaching and learning approaches, building on and revisiting areas of the ITT curriculum; this will support and aim to build your confidence, depth of knowledge and refine skills. You will receive support from your expert colleagues in building your subject knowledge across the primary curriculum and in understanding a wide range of educational themes.

### EXPERT MENTORS

Receiving clear consistent and effective mentoring in school is key. You should receive structured feedback from expert colleagues on a particular approach using the best available evidence to provide a process for improving your practice throughout their training.

# A WELL-SEQUENCED, COHERENT ITT CURRICULUM

> **REFLECTIVE QUESTIONS**
>
> How might you define *curriculum* and what types of curricula are you already aware of?
>
> Find the curriculum designed by your provider. How are the 'Learn that' and 'Learn how to' criteria addressed?

The sequencing, progression and alignment of the theoretical and practical aspects of your ITT programme are key to its success. A programme map (see example below) can illustrate how the curriculum has been devised, with information and learning introduced gradually and logically, building upon specific subject and age phase knowledge and skills. Aspects of learning will be revisited, repeated and reviewed many times, and each time you revisit an aspect further learning will take place (this is known as a *spiral curriculum*). Throughout the programme, progressive, staged expectations support you and develop your expertise and confidence as you progress.

Revisiting key concepts and ideas supports the expansion of knowledge and a depth of understanding that would not be achieved by adopting a linear-cumulative approach. Careful sequencing ensures a coherent, layered spiral curriculum, which research evidence indicates is important in securing your progress (e.g., Bruner, 1960; Biesta, 2019). This avoids you, as a trainee, being 'overloaded' with masses of information at once and your ability to understand and process this information being hindered through *cognitive overload* (Coe et al., 2020).

Coe et al. (2020) emphasised that the main goal for all those involved in education (including you from your first days as a trainee) should be to improve the lives and life chances of children and young people. The quality of such teaching, and therefore the delivery of a high-quality curriculum, is the most effective mechanism for achieving this outcome (Wiliam, 2018). Coe et al. (2020) concluded that your understanding of not only the content but also the order and organisation of how the curriculum is taught is what makes 'great teaching'. Knowledge of the primary curriculum and how children learn best needs to be delivered in a clear and coherent, sequential order across the year/years. Figure 1.2 shows an example of an ITT provider programme map.

## Stage One

| Learning weeks | CCD | Subject |
|---|---|---|
| 1 | Curriculum and Subject (1) | PE |
| 2 | | English, Maths, Science and Introduction to *Broad and Balanced Curriculum (BB) |
| 3 | Curriculum and Subject (2) | English, Maths, Science, BB |
| 4 | | English, Maths, Science, BB |
| 5 | Professional Behaviours (1) | English, Maths, Science, BB |
| 6 | | History |
| 7 | Behaviour Management (1) | Music |
| 8 | Half term | |
| 9 | ITaP | |
| 10 | | |
| 11 | Assessment (1) | MFL |
| 12 | | |
| 13 | Adaptive Teaching (1) | Design Tech |
| 14 | | |
| 15 | Planning and Teaching (1) | Geography |
| 16 | | |
| 17 | Christmas holidays | |
| 18 | | |

## Stage Two

| Learning weeks | CCD | Subject |
|---|---|---|
| 19 | ITAP | |
| 20 | Planning and Teaching (2) | Maths |
| 21 | | |
| 22 | Professional Behaviours (2) | |
| 23 | Assessment (2) | PE |
| 24 | | Science |
| 25 | Half term | |
| 26 | ITaP | |
| 27 | Adaptive Teaching (2) | Computing |
| 28 | | PSHE/SMSC |
| 29 | Behaviour Management (2) | |
| 30 | | |
| 31 | Adaptive Teaching (3) | English |
| 32 | | |
| 33 | Easter holidays | |
| 34 | | |

## Stage Three

| Learning weeks | Domains | Subject |
|---|---|---|
| 35 | Planning and Teaching (3) | Trainees continue to review and evaluate their knowledge, with their mentors, and: |
| 36 | | |
| 37 | Curriculum and Subject (3) | • update knowledge audits |
| 38 | | • access online resources |
| 39 | Half term | • review textbooks and other sources |
| 40 | Behaviour Management (3) | • attend 1:1 subject knowledge sessions where intervention is needed |
| 41 | Assessment (3) | |
| 42 | Professional Behaviours (3) | |

> ### ACTION LEARNING SET
>
> Find your programme handbook/website and identify the programme map.
>
> Identify the five core areas or domains of the CCF.
>
> Choose one area, for example 'Adaptive Teaching', and highlight where this learning takes place across the year/s.
>
> - Why do you think this domain is repeated?
> - What learning do you anticipate will be introduced across this domain?

> ### EVIDENCE-INFORMED RESEARCH: PEDAGOGY IN TEACHING
>
> Pedagogy refers to the method and practices of a teacher. It's how they approach their teaching style, and relates to the different theories they use, how they give feedback and the assessments they set. When referring to the pedagogy of teaching, it means how the teacher delivers the curriculum to the class.
>
> Carefully sequenced curricula that incorporate both theory- and evidence-informed research, and opportunities for trainees to 'practise' in context, are well established within the fabric of high-quality teacher education and other graduate professions. Developing a common understanding of the most frequently used and successful teaching techniques and strategies across the programme can be defined as common or *signature pedagogy* (Shulman, 2005).
>
> Coherent signature pedagogies for teacher education programmes allow accredited providers and their partners the autonomy to create intellectualised and rigorous approaches to delivering initial teacher training. Active student teacher engagement is crucial. High 'buy in' and motivation is required from trainees. Signature pedagogies acknowledge an affective or emotional dimension to professional learning: they have an influence on the values, disposition and character of the learner (Falk, 2006; Shulman, 2005).

All of the curriculum materials in your ITT programme should be viewed collectively, and interweaving is integral to the model as a whole. No aspect of training should be viewed in isolation but as part of an integrated, deliberate, coherent sequence of learning. What you learn within your curriculum learning centre relates directly to what you observe, review and begin to deliver in school.

# THE GOLDEN THREAD: MAINTAINING FIDELITY BETWEEN CENTRE-BASED LEARNING AND SCHOOL-BASED LEARNING IS ESSENTIAL WITHIN AN EFFECTIVE ITT CURRICULUM

Communities of practice (CoPs) were identified by Lave and Wenger (1991); they refer to the stakeholders who support the delivery and operation of ITT, such as universities, multi-academic trusts, local education authorities, faith schools and so on. For fidelity to be achieved these establishments and the expert colleagues who work within them all must have a common goal and a full understanding of projective common goals and objectives in order to maintain fidelity across the training.

Moreover, fidelity refers to how closely the curriculum is aligned in centre and in school, and the degree to which your provider and the lead school partners co-create, implement/deliver and assess your progress as intended. In practice, this means that all those involved in the delivery of the ITT curriculum have a full understanding of the materials and how to best support you as a trainee in internalising and interpreting it to develop your knowledge, understanding and practice. Figure 1.3 demonstrates how fidelity between centre-based and school-based learning works in practice.

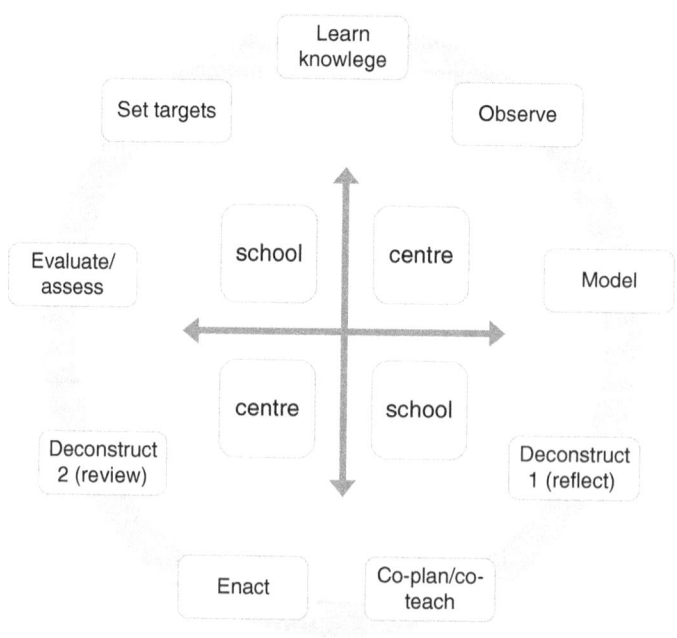

Figure 1.3 A carefully sequenced knowledge- and application-based curriculum

The model shows how centre-based and school-based practice aligns to provide fidelity. Table 1.1 provides you with further detail about each section of the model.

Table 1.1 A carefully sequenced knowledge- and application-based curriculum: An explanation of the model

| Term | Definition | Explanation |
|---|---|---|
| Learn knowledge | Delivered at curriculum learning centre or in school learning centre by expert colleagues | New or revisited content in the ITT curriculum |
| Observe | Observe this knowledge being delivered | This could be at the centre of learning or in a school environment |
| Model | Expert colleagues model behaviours and language of this knowledge while being observed by trainee | This could be at the centre of learning or in a school environment. This may also be through approximations |
| Deconstruction part 1 (reflect) | Expert colleagues review the modelled behaviours that have been observed and reflect on the learning that took place | This could be at the centre of learning or in a school environment. The learning could be that of the trainees or the pupils or both! |
| Co-plan/ co-teach | Student and expert colleagues analyse learning and plan next steps together | Based on what trainee has learned from observation and modelling |
| Practise/ enactment | Student practises/enacts behaviours and delivers knowledge based on co-planning | This could be at the centre of learning or in a school environment. If enacting at the centre, student could micro-teach to peers |
| Deconstruction part 2 (review) | Expert colleagues review delivery of knowledge to pupils, reflecting on evidence-informed practice | Look at the learning and review what worked and what might be improved |

# CASE STUDY: JO AND ELLIS

Jo and Ellis are both in their final-stage school placement, as part of their three-year BA Undergraduate Honours degree in Primary Education (with a three to seven age phase specialism). They have returned to the same school where they completed successful eight-week placements in their second year, and this year they are in a different age phase. Returning to the same school across the second and third stages of the programme can support trainees in many ways; namely, it provides consistency for the pupils, trainees and staff. The school is a two-form entry primary school in the centre of Wakefield in West Yorkshire. The lead mentor in the school has worked with their

(Continued)

provider for several years and has close links to the university. She has attended both mandatory mentor training and top-up training prior to the placement starting, so she is fully conversant with all the necessary expectations.

On their second-year placement, Jo and Ellis were both in parallel reception classes. They were able to share the planning of the core subjects and across the provision. This offered them the opportunity to operate within an Early Years unit. This year, to support their understanding and experience across their specialised age phase, Jo is in Year 1 and Ellis in Year 2.

The lead mentor in the placement school uses the provider's website and online platform to review what training the trainees have had prior to the placement. All the information regarding their ITT curriculum is clearly displayed and she can see what additional training they have received in subject knowledge in their final year. She also encourages them to complete an 'audit' of subject knowledge in phonics, so that she can support them in identifying any gaps or misconceptions before they start delivering within this new age phase.

The lead mentor then supports the trainees in setting targets on 'next steps' when preparing to deliver phonics in KS1. She also encourages both trainees to observe expert colleagues across the school. Post observations, the expert colleagues, trainees and lead mentor join a meeting to *deconstruct* the lesson and reflect together on the strengths in pedagogy. This also provides the trainees with the opportunity to ask questions of experts in school.

Week by week, both trainees gain further knowledge and are able to apply this to their practice. They are observed and receive expert, deliberate feedback for their taught episodes of learning. Both trainees complete the final eight weeks of school placement knowing far more about the curriculum and with an understanding of the pedagogy within school. This is a direct result of expert colleagues at the university ensuring that expert mentors and colleagues in school understand and can follow the ITT curriculum. Expert colleagues in school then embed the knowledge further by providing opportunities to observe, review and practise in context.

## INTENSIVE TRAINING AND PRACTICE

Intensive training and practice (ITaP) experiences are focused learning opportunities that are designed to support trainees during their ITT programme, to develop skills and knowledge in foundational areas of the curriculum.

Building on knowledge and theory, and how such is applied in practice in school, is also the focus of intensive periods of training or 'spotlights' in training across the programme. Theoretical perspectives introduced by expert colleagues, usually at the curriculum learning centre, are combined with practical application in school placements during planned episodes of ITaP.

ITaPs are integral to all ITT programmes and should be of the following length:

One-year programme: 20 days (four weeks)

Three-year programmes: 30 days (six weeks)

This element of the programme does not need to take place in one block and can be divided across the programme. Some elements of the ITaP can be held in the training centre or virtually – for example as digital approximations and/or recorded lesson observations. The learning should then be applied across the centre and school throughout the ITaP weeks. The provider has control over the specific foci for these ITaP experiences.

### EVIDENCE-INFORMED RESEARCH: MODELS AND FRAMEWORKS

When formulating ITaPs across the programmes, your provider will have used evidence-informed research to plan, conceptualise and devise a model of practice. 'At its heart, practitioner enquiry rests on the proposition that those in practice are able to take informed intentional actions, explore their effects and form judgements of their value' (Lofthouse, 2014, p. 15).

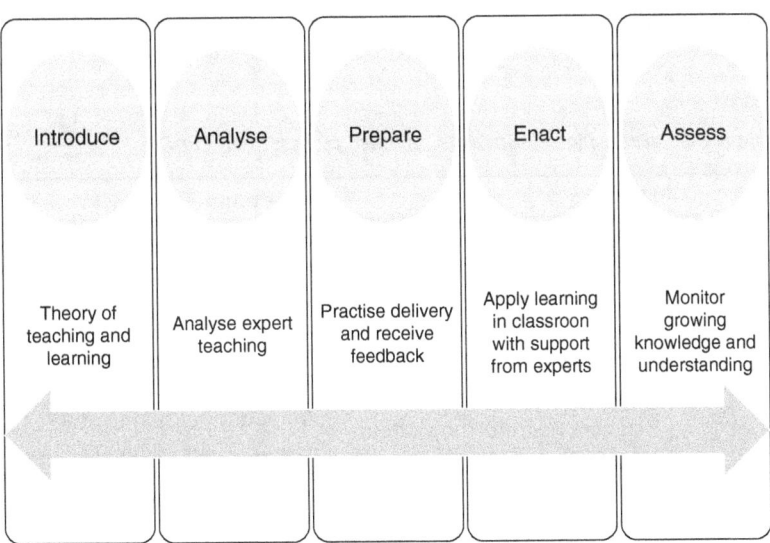

*Figure 1.4 Designing an ITaP (adapted from Grossman, 2018)*

(Continued)

> Clarke and Hollingsworth (2002) identified the complexities and multiple mechanisms involved in developing trainee teachers' understanding of learning within the classroom. The impact of prior learning, experience and beliefs can impact and *skew* the learner's view of what is happening within any given context (classroom). Only by using a consistent and sustained process or cycle of reflection and review that considers trainees' cultural and developmental experiences can learning, change and personal and 'professional growth' be effectively developed.
>
> Grossman (2018) devised a practice-based teaching model that identified key aspects for trainees to experience in order to understand how theory and practice meet. Figure 1.4 exemplifies these key requirements and provides an example of how an ITaP has been designed to deliver the experiences across both the curriculum learning centre and in school.
>
> The key requirements are non-linear and should not be ordered sequentially and chronologically but used interchangeably and, when appropriate, during episodes of intensive training.

The following model of practice is an example week of ITaP taken from a PGCE Primary 5–11 curriculum. The work of Grossman (2018) was used as a starting point by expert university tutors and adapted to construct and integrate the theoretical framework within an intensive week of training. The university combined the expertise of colleagues, digital approximations and expert mentors in school to create fidelity with the ITT curricula for one example programme. Curated readings with scaffolded questions support reflection and the evaluation of effectiveness of the intensive week.

Table 1.2 Example ITaP weekly plan: Framework informed by Grossman (2018)

| Day | Morning | Afternoon |
| --- | --- | --- |
| Monday<br>Introduce<br><br>*lectures, seminars, assigned readings<br><br>Takes place at: Curriculum learning centre (CLB) | **Lecture**: Input from expert college to introduce the focus for the ITaP and the structure and organisation of learning for this ITaP module.<br><br>**Indicative theme**: What do teachers need to know about learning?<br><br>**Workshop: Micro-teach** Teach a skill to your peers. What does this activity tell us about structuring learning? | **Individual reading**: Time allocated for individual engagement with evidence base (4-5 texts identified)<br><br>**Tutor-supported reciprocal reading groups:**<br>Workshop session to share insights across all the readings. Making connections between the evidence base and current experience |

# 1 AN INTRODUCTION TO THE ITT CURRICULUM

| Day | Morning | Afternoon |
|---|---|---|
| Tuesday<br>Prepare<br>*instructional rehearsal, scenario planning<br><br>Takes place at: CLB | **Workshop**: Groups review planning pro-forma from across the curriculum.<br>Trainees bring such from lead placement school<br><br>Consideration of what these tell us about how learning is structured. How does this relate to principles of cognitive science?<br><br>**Peer-supported learning**: Using learning from across the sessions so far in this module, create an observation scaffold timetable that will take in placement school and will support focused observations against this domain of learning. How will they know how expert colleagues structured learning?<br><br>**Workshop**: Sharing and collating observation schedules with expert colleagues and peers | |
| Wednesday<br>Prepare and analyse<br><br>*role play, digital approximations<br><br>Takes place at: CLB | **Digital approximation:**<br><br>Immersion experiences using digital approximations to analyse modelling of delivery and enacting questioning | |
| Thursday<br>*Instructional coaching, teach teaching, co-planning<br><br>Enact<br>Takes place:<br>In school (SBLC) | **Lead placement school experience day:**<br><br>Practice delivering sets of questions adapted from digital approximation from Wednesday<br><br>Takes place:<br>Across ages/classes in lead placement school with associated school-based tasks | |
| Friday<br><br>*Lesson observations, classroom resources, portfolios<br>Evaluate and assess<br><br>Takes place:<br>Online | AM<br><br>Deconstruct effectiveness of questioning with lead mentor<br><br>(MS Teams meeting); summary of ITaP | PM<br><br>Workshops to reflect upon learning from analysis sessions in school, presentation of initial findings |

\* Teaching strategies used to demonstrate and develop understanding of knowledge and skills

> **ACTION LEARNING SET**
>
> Consider the importance of intensively studying an aspect of the curriculum in detail.
>
> List five benefits of conducting ITaP across the curriculum learning centre and in school.

# MEASURING THE IMPACT OF ITAP ON YOUR DEVELOPING PROFESSIONAL PRACTICE

The impact of ITaP is tracked by the curriculum learning centre in the short term, through an assessment and evaluative process in the form of a peer-to-peer presentation at the end of the two-week unit. For example, this could take the form of a poster/display that provides evidence of what trainees have taken from their experience and looks ahead to future practice. Longer-term impact is reviewed through tracked assessment against the *core aspects* or *domains* across the CCF/ITTECF, with feedback from the expert mentor, in line with exiting assessment processes being completed in school.

## LEARNING: KNOWLEDGE AND SKILLS

Throughout the chapters in this book, you will be provided with clear instruction and information that supports your growing understanding of the key principles behind building deep learning and knowledge of skills.

Supporting all learners to succeed is important and understanding the key fundamentals of practice will help you to do this as a trainee. The following aspects of practice were exemplified in a report from EEF: The five-a-day approach (EEF, 2022).

These include:

1. explicit instruction;
2. cognitive and metacognitive strategies;
3. scaffolding pupils' learning (and skilfully and gradually reducing scaffolding);
4. flexible grouping;
5. using technology.

The EEF's research evidence suggests there is a set of five core practices that can support all pupils, including those with special education needs, to learn more and know more.

Each of these principles, along with others, will be exemplified across the book. Explicit examples of how you as a trainee will be able to develop expertise within the classroom as a result of excellent modelling and deconstruction of such teaching pedagogy can be found throughout.

# CONCLUSION

This chapter identified the origins of the CCF/ITTECF and introduced you to the phrasing used across your ITT curriculum. It defined the key terminology that will form the basis of your ITT programme. It explored how the CCF/ITTECF has been used to create an ITT curriculum and identified and exemplified the importance of delivering carefully crafted, logically sequenced training, both within your provider, the CLCs, and within SBLCs. Maintaining fidelity between your CLC and SBLCs is known as the *golden thread*, and it plays a crucial role in ensuring that the knowledge and application across your programme are interwoven expertly by all the professionals delivering your training.

> ### REVIEW OF CHAPTER OBJECTIVES
>
> Within this chapter you have considered:
>
> - how the change in the educational landscape brought about the introduction of the CCF/ITTECF;
> - the key terms and phrases used in all ITT curricula;
> - what a well-sequenced, coherent ITT curriculum looks like (including ITaPs);
> - how ITT curricula demonstrate fidelity between centre-based and school-based training.

# FURTHER READING AND RESOURCES

Department for Education (DfE) (2019b) *ITT Core Content Framework*. London: DfE. Available at: https://assets.publishing.service.gov.uk/government/uploads/system/uploads/attachment_data/file/974307/ITT_core_content_framework_.pdf [accessed November 2023].

Education Endowment Foundation (EEF) (2021) *Teaching and Learning Toolkit*. Available at: https://educationendowmentfoundation.org.uk/education-evidence/teaching-learning-toolkit [accessed 19 December 2023].

EEF (2022) The five-a-day approach: How the EEF can support (educationendowmentfoundation.org.uk) [accessed November 2023].

Sage (n.d.) *Teacher Training Survival Toolkit*. Available at: https://us.sagepub.com/en-us/nam/teacher-training-survival-toolkit [accessed 19 December 2023].

# REFERENCES

Biesta, G. (2019) Teaching for the possibility of being taught: World-centred education in an age of learning. *English E-Journal of the Philosophy of Education*, 4, pp. 55–69.

Bruner, J. (1960) *The Process of Education*. Cambridge, MA: Harvard University Press.

Clarke, D. and Hollingsworth, H. (2002) Elaborating a model of teacher professional growth. *Teaching and Teacher Education*, 18(8), pp. 947–967.

Coe, R., Rauch, C., Kime, S. and Singleton, D. (2020) *Great Teaching Toolkit: Evidence Review*. Cambridge: Cambridge Assessment International Education. Available at: https://evidence-based.education/great-teaching-toolkit-evidence-review/ [accessed 19 December 2023].

Department for Education (DfE) (2016) *Framework of Core Content for Initial Teacher Training (ITT)*. Available at: https://assets.publishing.service.gov.uk/government/uploads/system/uploads/attachment_data/file/536890/Framework_Report_11_July_2016_Final.pdf [accessed November 2023].

DfE (2019a) *Early Career Framework*. Available at: https://assets.publishing.service.gov.uk/government/uploads/system/uploads/attachment_data/file/978358/Early-Career_Framework_April_2021.pdf [accessed August 2023].

DfE (2019b) *ITT Core Content Framework*. London: DfE. Available at: https://assets.publishing.service.gov.uk/government/uploads/system/uploads/attachment_data/file/974307/ITT_core_content_framework_.pdf [accessed November 2023].

DfE (2021) *Teachers' Standards: Guidance for School Leaders, School Staff and Governing Bodies*. London: DfE. Available at: https://assets.publishing.service.gov.uk/media/61b73d6c8fa8f50384489c9a/Teachers__Standards_Dec_2021.pdf [accessed 19 December 2023].

DfE (2024) *Initial teacher training and early career framework* Available at: https://www.gov.uk/government/publications/initial-teacher-training-and-early-career-framework [Accessed March 2024].

Education Endowment Foundation (EEF) (2021) *Teaching and Learning Toolkit*. Available at: https://educationendowmentfoundation.org.uk/education-evidence/teaching-learning-toolkit [accessed 19 December 2023].

Falk, B. (2006) A conversation with Lee Shulman – signature pedagogies for teacher education: Defining our practices and rethinking our preparation. *The New Educator*, 2, pp. 73–82.

Grossman, P. (Ed.) (2018) *Teaching Core Practices in Teacher Education*. Cambridge, MA: Harvard Education Press.

Grossman, P., Compton, C., Igra, D., Ronfeldt, M., Shahan, E. and Williamson, P. W. (2009) Teaching practice: A cross-professional perspective. *Teachers College Record*, 111(9), pp. 2055–2100.

Howell, H. and Mikeska, J. M. (2021) Approximations of practice as a framework for understanding authenticity in simulations of teaching. *Journal of Research on Technology in Education*, 53(1), pp. 8–20, doi: 10.1080/15391523.2020.1809033.

Lave, J. and Wenger, E. (1991) *Situated Learning: Legitimate Peripheral Participation.* Cambridge: Cambridge University Press.

Lofthouse, R. M. (2014) Engaging in educational research and development through teacher practitioner enquiry: A pragmatic or naive approach? *Education Today*, 64(4), pp. 13–19.

Ofsted (2023) *Education Inspection Framework.* London: Ofsted. Available at: www.gov.uk/government/publications/education-inspection-framework/education-inspection-framework-for-september-2023 [accessed 21 December 2023].

Remesh, A. (2013) Microteaching: An efficient technique for learning effective teaching. *Journal of Research in Medical Science*, 18(2), pp. 158–163. PMID: 23914219; PMCID: PMC3724377.

Sage (n.d.) *Teacher Training Survival Toolkit.* Available at: https://us.sagepub.com/en-us/nam/teacher-training-survival-toolkit [accessed 19 December 2023].

Shulman, L. (2005) Signature pedagogies in the professions. *Daedalus*, 134(3), pp. 52–59.

Wiliam, D. (2018) *Creating the Schools our Children Need: Why What We're Doing Now Won't Help Much (And What We Can Do Instead).* Blairsville, PA: Learning Sciences in International.

# 2

# LEARNING ABOUT YOUR TEACHING

## MICHAELA OLIVER

**Learn that and Learn how to –
The Knowledge and Application Model**

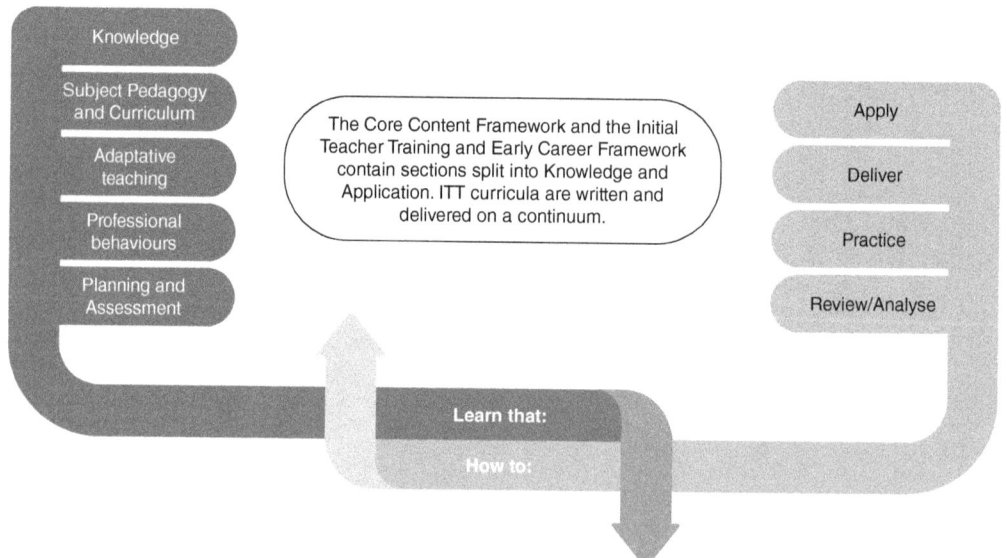

## FRAMED BY THE CCF – FOR FULL LINKS TO THE ITTECF, SEE PAGE 337

| Professional Behaviours | |
|---|---|
| (Standard 8 – 'Fulfil wider professional responsibilities') | |
| Learn that … | Learn how to … |
| 2. Reflective practice, supported by feedback from and observation of experienced colleagues, professional debate, and learning from educational research, is also likely to support improvement. | Develop as a professional, by: <br>• Reflecting on progress made, recognising strengths and weaknesses and identifying next steps for further improvement. <br>• Engaging critically with research and using evidence to critique practice. |

## CHAPTER OBJECTIVES

On reading this chapter you will:

- learn what is meant by reflective teaching;
- consider ways that you can develop reflective practice;
- learn how to engage with a range of evidence to inform your teaching;
- consider why learning about your teaching is as important as learning how to teach.

## KEY VOCABULARY

Initial teacher training (ITT)

Initial Teacher Training and Early Career Framework (ITTECF)

Core Content Framework (CCF)

Reflective practice

Research-informed practice

Research-informed decision-making

Artificial intelligence (AI)

Evidence

# INTRODUCTION

Chapter 1 outlined the *Core Content Framework* (CCF/ITTECF) and ITT curriculum requirements. It also introduced the importance of intensive training and practice

(ITaP). ITT criteria set out by the DfE (2022) includes a compulsory ITaP element. This element foregrounds the importance of evidence-informed practice, aiming to consolidate trainees' understanding of how to engage with a range of evidence when developing their teaching practice.

As part of ITaP, trainees can expect:

- input from experts related to theory and practice;
- support to access and critically analyse research literature;
- modelling and demonstrations within subject teaching which include critical reflection and deconstruction of approaches;
- a range of opportunities to develop, practise and rehearse classroom practice (including outside the classroom, e.g. through micro-teaching or virtual approximations);
- opportunities to reflect on own practice, critique approaches, adapt and refine practice;
- feedback on teaching from expert colleagues which also prompts reflection;
- opportunities to respond to feedback and develop practice in subsequent teaching.

This chapter focuses on the importance of both teaching and *learning about your teaching* to ensure that you continually provide high-quality learning experiences for all pupils. While ITT periods require a substantial amount of learning (incorporating dimensions of 'Learn that' and 'Learn how to'), this learning does not end upon the award of qualified teacher status (QTS). Rather, to ensure sustained effective teaching, teachers must engage in a continual process of learning and reflection.

## REFLECTIVE TEACHING

Deciding how best to support pupil learning is underpinned by a commitment *to reflective practice*. The concept of reflective practice is associated with John Dewey, and requires 'active, persistent and careful consideration of any belief or supposed form of knowledge in the light of the grounds that support it' (1933, p. 9). Donald Schön (1983, 1987) developed ideas about reflective practice, distinguishing between the importance of *reflection in action* and *reflection on action*. This is important in education, since it recognises the role of reflection both in situations where action is required immediately (as in situations where teachers must think and act 'on their feet'; see Chapter 11 on Adaptive Teaching) and in situations where it is important to reflect on action already taken, which can be used to inform future practice. This chapter will mainly focus on reflection on action, but developing these processes will also support teachers' capacity to reflect in action.

Reflective practice in education involves consideration of your own teaching practices and the practices of others, open-minded critique and a commitment to adapt your approaches following reflection. Reflective practice includes analysis and evaluation of teaching methods, instructional strategies and classroom interactions, and clear justification of these (Pollard, 2019). As part of this process, teachers must look inwards, exploring and questioning their own beliefs, values and biases. This constitutes reflexivity, an important part of reflective practice. During ITT, reflective practice plays a crucial role in developing as a professional. It encourages trainees to think deeply about their approaches and the effects these have on their pupils (in terms of engagement, learning outcomes and so on). By committing to reflective practice, trainees can identify their areas of strength, as well as aspects to develop further in their teaching.

### REFLECTIVE QUESTIONS

What does reflective practice mean?

Why is it important?

## WHAT DOES REFLECTIVE PRACTICE LOOK LIKE?

For many trainees enrolled on ITT courses, requirements for reflection will be built into programmes (e.g. through reflective assignments, required lesson planning reflections etc.). These formal mechanisms induct trainees into processes of reflection. Yet reflection should be continued beyond early career teacher (ECT) years, becoming part of a teacher's approach to everyday practice to ensure sustained improvements in teaching quality (Pollard, 2019). For more about your ECT years, see Chapter 18.

There are numerous ways to demonstrate and engage in reflective practice. Figure 2.1 shows a possible cycle of reflective practice; each section is explained below.

### SOURCE OF FEEDBACK

Feedback can be obtained from a number of sources. *Peer/expert feedback* can be gained from other trainees/ECTS or from expert teachers. Peer feedback may be based on lesson observations, but could also focus on other aspects of practice (e.g.

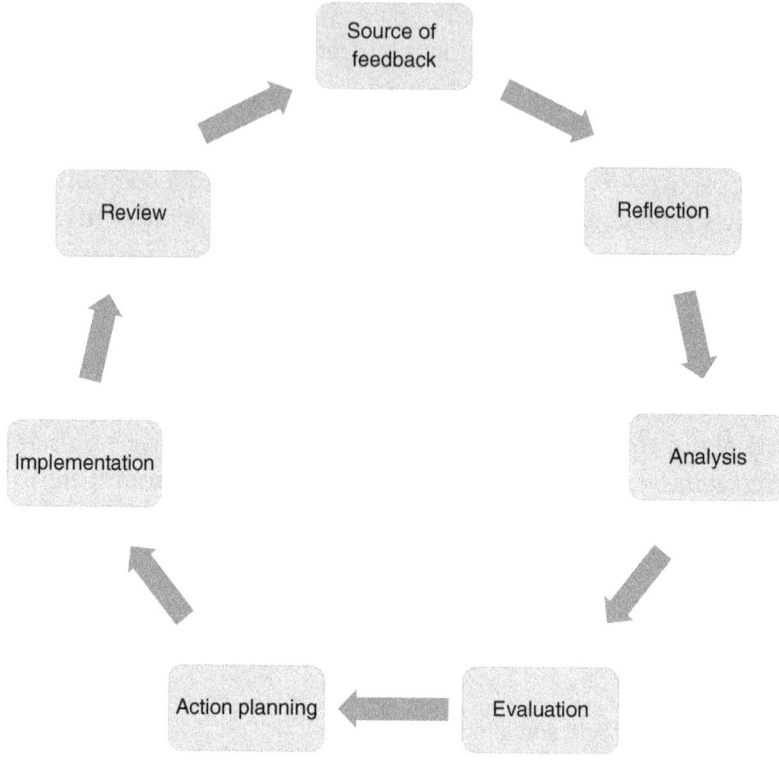

*Figure 2.1 Cycle of reflective practice*

feedback on planning, marking or assessment practices). Other sources of feedback include *summative sources* (such as pupil assessment results, school performance data); *feedback from pupils*; and other *external stakeholder feedback* (e.g. from parents, governors). Feedback may also come from *self-reflections* (e.g. a teacher may observe a video recording of their own teaching).

## REFLECTION

Reflection includes consideration of feedback received. Teachers reflect on their practices, thinking deeply about the impacts these had on pupils and their learning. This might be facilitated by keeping a reflective journal (Farrell, 2013; see also case study below). Reflection is important even before the teaching has happened. Thinking about what you will teach, why you are teaching it and how you will deliver should prompt a range of considerations which will help you to justify your approach and consider whether alternatives might be more effective.

## ANALYSIS

Teachers critically analyse the effectiveness and consequences of their teaching practices, considering aspects such as pupil learning and engagement. Consideration is made about what has been achieved in the class and by whom.

## EVALUATION

Teachers evaluate the strengths and weaknesses of their practice, identifying areas requiring development. Judgements are made about the consequences of the practices reflected upon.

## ACTION PLANNING

Teachers use evaluative judgements to develop clear action plans supporting them to implement changes required. Action planning sets goals and identifies strategies required to achieve these.

## IMPLEMENTATION

Teachers implement the actions needed to develop and enhance their practice. This may include adapting teaching strategies, incorporating new approaches, adjusting approaches to classroom management and so on.

## REVIEW

Teachers review the changes made, considering impacts of these changes (e.g. to pupil engagement, learning outcomes, the classroom environment etc.). This prompts new feedback (including self-reflection) and the reflective cycle begins again, with new goals set to continue the process of improvement.

Through processes of reflective practice, teachers continually monitor and improve their practice, adapting to pupil needs and fostering an effective, positive learning environment. Reflective practice develops self-awareness and prompts a much deeper understanding of one's own practices. This can support teachers to make informed decisions which have a positive impact in their classrooms.

The reflective cycle complements Stephenson and Gill's Knowledge and Application model, introduced earlier in the book.

All elements of 'Learn that' and 'Learn how' should be subject to reflection and continual improvement. Indeed, reflective practice is a key component of the 'Learn how to: review/analyse' component. An example of reflective practice is shared in the case study below.

## CASE STUDY: NICOLE

Nicole McIlvaney has recently completed a three-year undergraduate BA Honours degree in Primary Education with QTS at Durham University.

*During my teacher training, reflective practice supported me in developing my teaching expertise. One strategy I adopted was journalling my observations from my class teacher's practice.*

*Throughout teacher training, there are abundant opportunities to journal experienced teachers' practices across the entire curriculum. I found this particularly useful when working with a new key stage or year group. On one occasion, I was preparing to teach a Year 4 class, after only having Key Stage 1 experience. In preparation, I used a journal to record the observations I made from a highly experienced Key Stage 2 teacher. To record my observations, I would write down explicit pedagogy the teacher used during their lessons. For example, while observing a maths lesson, the teacher provided each child with a whiteboard to write down and hold up their answers. In my journal, I would record the procedure and relevant information the teacher gave during the activity which provided me with an in-depth example of the practice.*

*Following the journalling of my observations, I would read my journal prior to planning my lessons. I would integrate the practices the teacher used into my planning. For example, when teaching my first maths lesson to the Year 4 class, I included a whiteboard starter activity. I utilised my journal to follow the steps the teacher completed to support my planning.*

*Once I had taught my lessons, I would reflect on whether the practice I had implemented was useful. First, I would consider if the practice was helpful for me as the teacher. During this process, I would examine if the practice supported me in ensuring the children met the learning objective. In addition, I reflected on if the practice helped me achieve additional benefits, such as assessment for learning. Second, I would consider if the practice benefitted the children. Within this, I would contemplate if this practice was a more appropriate method of teaching than another to support the children's knowledge and understating. Once I had reflected on the practice, if I found the method helpful, I would continue to integrate this into my lessons with any adaptations I considered during the reflective process. For instance, I found the whiteboard starter in maths benefitted me as the teacher as I was able to quickly identify misconceptions; it also supported the children by providing them with the opportunity to trial and error the questions. After I had reflected upon the practice, I later added a responsive teaching approach. Responsive teaching involves using evidence from formative assessment to consolidate your class's knowledge and understanding. In maths, I addressed the misconceptions I observed during the whiteboard activity to the whole class. This approach further supported my lessons as I was able to respond to the learners' needs in order to prepare them with the relevant knowledge and understanding for the lesson ahead.*

*Overall, during my teacher training, I found this reflective practice strategy was significant in guiding and developing my practice. This strategy allowed me to discover a number of techniques taught by experienced teachers while the reflection process provided me with the time to consider further practice adaptations and developments. I will continue to use this when opportunities arise during my teaching career.*

### ACTION LEARNING SET

Choose a particular aspect of your teaching (you could focus on a specific subject, or on a particular aspect of teaching, such as assessment, or classroom management).

Gather some feedback about this aspect of teaching (see the various forms of feedback discussed in the section above).

Move through the cycle of reflective practice described above. Use the outcomes to inform your next steps.

How did these stages help to develop your reflective practice?

# ENGAGING WITH EVIDENCE

The section above has mainly focused on the reflective processes involved after some action has been taken (i.e. after teaching in a particular way). Yet reflection is also important when deciding how to approach teaching during the planning stages. Reflective practitioners should also incorporate a range of evidence sources when deciding and then justifying the approaches used in their practice.

### REFLECTIVE QUESTIONS

- What forms of evidence can be used to inform teaching?
- Why is it important to engage with evidence in your teaching practice?
- What considerations need to be made before using evidence?

The importance of engaging with evidence to inform teaching practice is recognised across the ITT curriculum, and is incorporated in the *Teachers' Standards* (DfE, 2021) and the '(CCF/ITTECF) (DfE, 2019 and 2024). Engaging with evidence supports teachers in making informed decisions to promote high-quality learning environments. Teachers have a duty to ensure that what they do in the classroom is based on knowledge of the best available evidence. This represents an aspect of professionalism, as well as accountability. It is important that any resource spent (including time) is focused on approaches which are likely to be met with success (Gorard, 2020) and which take account of the specific school context. By engaging with evidence, teachers will be in a much stronger position to justify and articulate the foundations underpinning their teaching practice and instructional decision-making. Engaging with evidence is therefore a source of empowerment for teachers (DfE, 2017).

## TYPES OF EVIDENCE

There are many types of evidence which support teachers in developing their practice.

Evidence can be taken at school level, as in the case of school performance data generated through assessment and inspection. Engagement with school-level data may involve analysing pupil attainment or progression data, and using this to inform what you do in the classroom. Individual pupil-level data (e.g. SEND categories, pupil premium information and other biographical details) should also be drawn on. Such data can illustrate where additional support may be needed and where instruction may need to be adapted to meet the needs of all pupils (see Chapter 12 on Inclusive Education). More informal sources of school-based evidence can also be used. For example, pupil work is a valuable source of information which teachers can use to support reflection upon both teaching and pupil learning, and to plan next steps.

Educational research represents another major type of evidence. Types and forms of research are varied; there is not one form of research which is always 'better' than another (Biesta, 2007). Nevertheless, it is important to develop a critical awareness of strengths and limitations of various forms of research. This will allow you to critically consider research findings, and to decide whether to use them to inform your teaching practice.

Professional literature is another useful form of evidence. This differs to research literature in that it is not solely based on evidence gathered during a study (e.g. an empirical investigation), but is focused instead on sharing pedagogical expertise from professionals in that area. Pedagogical literature may draw upon research evidence and may summarise findings and recommendations in an accessible way to teachers.

Some teachers may also participate in classroom-based research. This may take the form of action research, where teacher-researchers engage in multiple cycles of enquiry to help them to improve practice in their own context (see e.g. Pring, 2010).

Ideally, multiple sources of evidence will be used to make informed decisions about classroom practice and instructional design. Teachers need to develop skills necessary to be able to critically evaluate evidence, to assess the reliability and validity of this and to consider applicability to their own context.

# EVALUATING THE QUALITY OF EVIDENCE

If evidence is to inform what you do in your class, it is important to develop skills needed to be able to assess the quality of this evidence. No form of research is without criticism, and developing an awareness of the strengths and limitations of various forms is important in the journey to becoming a reflective and research-informed practitioner. There are several aspects to consider when you are assessing evidence quality. Some of these can be captured by the 'Five Ws plus How' mnemonic.

Table 2.1 'Five Ws plus How' mnemonic

| | |
|---|---|
| What? | What are the main claims made? What does the evidence suggest? |
| Who? | Who wrote the piece of evidence/conducted the research? What are their credentials? What expertise do they have? |
| Where? | Where is the evidence taken from (i.e. in which educational context or geographical area)? Will this affect how applicable the evidence is to your setting? Where is the evidence published? Is this a reputable place? Is the publication peer-reviewed or quality-controlled prior to publication? |
| When? | When was the evidence gathered/reported? Does this affect the relevance to your present context? |
| Why? | Why was the evidence gathered? Are reasons reported or obvious? Does this affect your evaluation of the evidence? |
| How? | What were the methods used to collect the evidence? Are these appropriate? Do they allow the authors to make the claims they have made? |

These considerations apply to a range of evidence types. There are additional factors to consider when appraising the quality of educational research.

Table 2.2 Evidence type factors to consider

| | |
|---|---|
| Type of research | Is the evidence based on empirical or non-empirical research? Is the evidence reporting findings from one study or bringing together evidence from multiple studies (e.g. as in a meta-analysis or systematic review)? |
| Research question | What does the study ask? Is the research question 'answerable' using the chosen research design and methods? |

(Continued)

*Table 2.2 (Continued)*

| Research design and methods | Do the research design and chosen methods fit with the research question? Are the design and methods justified? What are the main strengths and limitations of the design and methods used? Do these affect decisions and judgements about application to your context? |
|---|---|
| Sample | Who are the sample participants? How many were involved? Does the sample size affect confidence in claims that can be made? (Appropriate sample size depends on the type of research question asked and is informed by fitness for purpose, e.g. it could be too small to make the claims generalisable to other contexts; or it could be too large to allow for in-depth description of particular experiences.) |

# ENGAGING WITH EVIDENCE: WHERE TO BEGIN

For many ITT trainees, engaging with evidence is a requirement of their programme. This requirement continues throughout a teaching career, where the importance of evidence-informed practice is now widely acknowledged (e.g. see Education Endowment Foundation (EEF), National Foundation for Educational Research (NFER)). This does not mean this process is always easy though. There are issues of finding and accessing evidence to begin with, followed by concerns over how this evidence should be used. For many teachers, it is useful to access sources which consider a large body of evidence in one place, and which treat this evidence critically and with a concern for quality. Research reviews and summaries are useful in that they bring together bodies of research and interpret this in accessible and practice-focused ways.

## EVIDENCE-INFORMED RESEARCH LITERATURE

The EEF's (2021) *Teaching and Learning Toolkit* summarises a range of research evidence related to many key teaching and learning approaches. The *Toolkit* represents an accessible way of accessing high-quality evidence and is designed to support teachers and school leaders to make decisions about how to ensure their practice improves learning experiences and outcomes for all pupils. The *Toolkit* provides a systematic synthesis of findings from high-quality studies related to different approaches. Useful graphic summaries of average impact on attainment, strength of evidence and likely costs are also provided. These support teachers in making decisions about approaches to use in their classrooms. The *Toolkit* provides an indication of what is likely to be beneficial to pupils based on existing evidence. It therefore provides 'best bets' for educational improvement. The *Toolkit* also provides support to schools who might be considering implementing an approach in their own setting, recognising that all schools are different and acknowledging the importance of considering context before investing time and resources into new approaches. Links to key readings and other EEF research findings are also included. The *Toolkit* therefore represents a way of accessing high-quality, relevant research which has been evaluated and synthesised by expert academics.

## ACTION LEARNING SET

Access the *Teaching and Learning Toolkit* online (EEF, 2021).

Watch the Toolkit Explainer video and/or read the Guide to Using the Toolkit.

Select one of the Toolkit Strands. This might be a strand relevant to what you've seen in your school-based practice, or something you want to explore further.

Read the summary of the approach and the available evidence.

Explore the evidence basis drawn upon, and links to other sources of evidence (e.g. other relevant EEF studies).

Consider the implications for your own setting.

- Is the approach appropriate/feasible?
- How might evidence sources like the *Toolkit* support you to make research-informed decisions in your practice?
- How might engagement with evidence promote your reflective practice?

## CASE STUDY: ADVANCE LEARNING PARTNERSHIP LITERACY PROJECT

Advance Learning Partnership is a not-for-profit multi-academy Trust consisting of a mix of primary and secondary academies. Catherine Taylor is a School Improvement Partner and Peter Mason is Director of Research and Development for the Trust.

> Our case study focuses on a project to increase staff knowledge and awareness of key issues impacting on literacy outcomes, before and during Year 6-7 transition. Evidence suggests that a lack of parental agency in supporting children's reading is consistently linked with underperformance of pupils and low levels of reading engagement (Loera et al., 2011). We recognised that these findings (among others) would help to support development in our Trust. It was hoped that by disseminating research, teachers would become empowered to make evidence-informed decisions in their own setting.
>
> Our next step was to decide the format of professional development and to identify which staff cohort to target. Evidence suggested the benefits (in terms of knowledge

*(Continued)*

and practice improvement) of delivering CPD to a network of staff who could collaborate across the organisation rather than focused on an individual school (Malouf and Taymans, 2016). First, it was essential to involve literacy leaders in our primary and secondary schools because they are tasked with increasing teacher knowledge about barriers to literacy. We also engaged headteachers, given that research tells us that their influence and support is essential for the successful delivery and adoption of changes in practice (Farley-Ripple et al., 2018; Moonen and Voogt, 1998).

Research also informed our consideration of the best format for transferring new knowledge to staff and stimulating reflective and collaborative practice. Colleagues were invited to a termly conference-workshop. This followed a set format of delivery:

- dissemination of new knowledge including academic research via a mini lecture;
- reflection activity involving delegates from other settings;
- takeaway task to stimulate follow-up activity in school;
- reading list to promote further exploration of the field.

Within the workshops, we blended knowledge from research papers alongside contextualised data from our schools. New knowledge disseminated in the literacy-focused conference-workshop included information about home literacy environments (Bennett et al., 2002), types of reading interventions (Merga and Mat Roni, 2018) and school communication and interaction with parents (Compton-Lilly et al., 2016). Our internal Trust evidence base for reading performance included historic reading data from SAT papers, NFER reading scores and Year 7 GL reading tests. Professional feedback from teachers and literacy leaders across the Trust relating to low pupil reading engagement during transition from Year 6-7 and low levels of parental agency was also shared.

Our evaluation of the literacy project demonstrates that staff knowledge and confidence has increased (based on staff feedback about the quality of the conference-workshop, changes of practice within individual schools and the implementation of a long-term project funded by SHINE, an education charity). A commitment to engaging with research is at the heart of our endeavours. This has been developed through the collaborative conference-workshop format for sharing and developing evidence-informed practice within our Trust.

## EVALUATING TEACHING RESOURCES

### REFLECTIVE QUESTIONS

How do you select teaching resources?

How can you ensure they are high quality and effective?

The *Teaching and Learning Toolkit* (EEF, 2021) and other forms of large-scale evidence summaries are valuable when making judgements about teaching approaches to be used in schools. These decisions are often made at the whole-school level (e.g. decisions about whether to 'stream' pupils according to ability). Such evidence is therefore crucial for those in school leadership positions (see Chapters 17 and 18 for focus on next steps in your teaching career). Yet even on an individual, lesson-by-lesson basis, teachers engage in decision-making. Lesson objectives are selected, teaching materials are prepared, activities are selected. These decisions and choices should become increasingly research-informed. They should be supported by rigorous reflection and should therefore be justifiable.

The critical capacities and reflective competencies developed when reflecting on a range of evidence sources also apply when evaluating the quality of teaching resources to use in practice. It is not feasible for trainees and teachers to create every teaching resource needed themselves. A wealth of high-quality materials is available to support teachers in their practice. Using previously developed materials as a basis also means that time is freed to focus on other aspects of teaching. Despite the benefits of using existing resources, there are also issues to consider. There is an obvious need to ensure that resources are of high quality and will support teachers to promote learning objectives derived from the national curriculum. Issues related to quality control are of growing concern in the context of artificial intelligence (AI) development. Increasing numbers of teachers are relying on AI software to support them in their planning. While AI can promote efficiency savings for teachers, concern for quality and rigour must be upheld.

These are some of the considerations teachers should make when deciding on the teaching resources they will use in their lessons. Again, the 'Five Ws plus How' mnemonic is useful.

Table 2.3 'Five Ws plus How' for teaching resources

| | |
|---|---|
| What? | What is the resource? Which aspect of the curriculum does it target? What does it claim to 'teach'? <br> What do I want to achieve in my lesson? Will the resource help me to meet these goals? |
| Who? | Who created the resource? What expertise do they have? <br> Who does the resource target (e.g. which year group)? Is it relevant to all pupils in your class? Who might need adaptations to be made before using the resource? |
| Where? | In which educational context or geographical area was the resource created? Does this affect how relevant the resource is for your setting? <br> Where is the resource published/shared? Is this a reputable place? How accessible is the resource (e.g. free and publicly available, or payment required)? <br> Where might you use the resource? Are there any contexts for which the resource would be more or less relevant? |

*(Continued)*

*Table 2.3 (Continued)*

| When? | When was the resource created? Does this affect the relevance to your present context?<br>When could you use the resource (e.g. as part of a larger sequence of lessons, at a specific point in the pupils' learning journey)? |
|---|---|
| Why? | Why was the resource created?<br>Why might the resource be useful? Does this affect your judgement about its value and utility?<br>Why would you use the resource? What would it support you and your pupils with (e.g. time-savings, learning opportunities etc.)? |
| How? | How will you use the resource in your own practice?<br>What changes/adaptations need to be made? |

Table 2.3 indicates some of the reflective questions which are important when evaluating potential teaching resources. Given the wealth of materials available, the ease with which these can be accessed and the growth in responsive AI, it has never been more important that teachers engage in critical reflection when selecting resources to promote their learning objectives. This will ensure that lessons are both effective and appropriate to the specific context in which you are working. By considering the questions above, teachers can engage in research-informed decision-making.

### ACTION LEARNING SET

When planning your next lesson, choose a particular teaching resource created by someone else (this might be a particular task, or could even be a whole lesson plan).

Answer the questions listed in Table 2.3.

Make any changes necessary after engaging in this reflective process.

- How did these considerations help to develop your reflective practice?
- Would the process lead to any changes in your future classroom practice?

## CONCLUSION

This chapter focuses on the importance of *learning about your teaching* to ensure that you continually provide high-quality learning experiences for all pupils. This chapter has explored the concept of reflective practice, and the values, attributes and competencies required to engage in this process. There has been consideration about what reflective practice might look like for trainees and teachers, in both centre-based and school-based settings. A cycle of reflective practice has been outlined, and advice about ways to evaluate evidence quality and teaching resources has been shared. The chapter provides practical scaffolding to support trainees to embark on their reflective journey. Ultimately, reflective practice encourages teachers to think deeply about their practice, and the range of effects that these have on their pupils. This paves the way for ongoing development and demonstrates a true commitment to developing as a professional ((CCF/ITTECF) Standard 8).

### REVIEW OF CHAPTER OBJECTIVES

Within this chapter you have:

- learnt what is meant by reflective teaching;
- considered ways that you can develop your own reflective practice;
- learnt how to engage with a range of evidence to inform your teaching;
- considered why learning about your teaching is as important as learning how to teach.

## FURTHER READING AND RESOURCES

Chartered College of Teaching (n.d.) Resources and CPD opportunities via membership. Available at: https://chartered.college/ [accessed 19 December 2023].

Education Endowment Foundation (EEF) (2021) *Teaching and Learning Toolkit*. Available at: https://educationendowmentfoundation.org.uk/education-evidence/teaching-learning-toolkit [accessed 19 December 2023].

EEF (n.d) Evidence, resources, summaries and reviews. Available at: https://educationendowmentfoundation.org.uk/ [accessed 19 December 2023].

National Foundation for Educational Research (NFER) (n.d.) Evidence and resources. Available at: www.nfer.ac.uk/ [accessed 19 December 2023].

## REFERENCES

Bennett, K. K., Weigel, D. J. and Martin, S. S. (2002) Children's acquisition of early literacy skills: Examining family contributions. *Early Childhood Research Quarterly*, 17(3), pp. 295–317.

Biesta, G. (2007) Why 'what works' won't work: Evidence-based practice and the democratic deficit in educational research. *Educational Theory*, 57(1), pp. 1–22.

Compton-Lilly, C., Caloia, R., Quast, E. and McCann, K. (2016) A closer look at a summer reading program: Listening to students and parents. *The Reading Teacher*, 70(1), pp. 59–67.

Department for Education (DfE) (2017) *Evidence-informed teaching: An evaluation of progress in England: Research report*. Available at: https://assets.publishing.service.gov.uk/government/

uploads/system/uploads/attachment_data/file/625007/Evidence-informed_teaching_-_an_evaluation_of_progress_in_England.pdf [accessed 19 December 2023].

Department for Education (DfE) (2019) *ITT Core Content Framework*. London: DfE. Available at: https://assets.publishing.service.gov.uk/government/uploads/system/uploads/attachment_data/file/974307/ITT_core_content_framework_.pdf [accessed November 2023].

DfE (2021) *Teachers' Standards: Guidance for School Leaders, School Staff and Governing Bodies*. London: DfE. Available at: https://assets.publishing.service.gov.uk/media/61b73d6c8fa8f50384489c9a/Teachers__Standards_Dec_2021.pdf [accessed 19 December 2023].

DfE (2022) *Initial Teacher Training (ITT) Provider Guidance on Stage 2*. Available at: https://assets.publishing.service.gov.uk/government/uploads/system/uploads/attachment_data/file/1119026/ITT_Provider_Guidance_Stage_2.pdf [accessed 19 December 2023].

DfE (2024) *Initial teacher training and early career framework* Available at: https://www.gov.uk/government/publications/initial-teacher-training-and-early-career-framework [Accessed March 2024].

Dewey, J. (1933) *How We Think: A Restatement of the Relation of Reflective Thinking to the Educative Process*. Chicago: Henry Regnery.

Education Endowment Foundation (EEF) (2021) *Teaching and Learning Toolkit*. Available at: https://educationendowmentfoundation.org.uk/education-evidence/teaching-learning-toolkit [accessed 19 December 2023].

Farley-Ripple, E., May, H., Karpyn, A., Tilley, K. and McDonough, K. (2018) Rethinking connections between research and practice in education: A conceptual framework. *Educational Researcher*, 47(4), pp. 235–245.

Farrell, T. S. (2013) Teacher self-awareness through journal writing. *Reflective Practice*, 14(4), pp. 465–471.

Gorard, S. (Ed.) (2020) *Getting Evidence into Education: Evaluating the Routes to Policy and Practice*. London: Routledge.

Loera, G., Rueda, R. and Nakamoto, J. (2011) The association between parental involvement in reading and schooling and children's reading engagement in Latino families. *Literacy Research and Instruction*, 50(2), pp. 133–155.

Malouf, D. B. and Taymans, J. M. (2016) Anatomy of an evidence base. *Educational Researcher*, 45(8), pp. 454–459.

Merga, M. K. and Mat Roni, S. (2018) Empowering parents to encourage children to read beyond the early years. *The Reading Teacher*, 72(2), pp. 213–221.

Moonen, B. and Voogt, J. (1998) Using networks to support the professional development of teachers. *Journal of In-Service Education*, 24(1), pp. 99–110.

Pollard, A. (2019) *Reflective Teaching in Schools* (5th ed.). London: Bloomsbury Academic.

Pring, R. (2010) *The Philosophy of Educational Research*. London: Continuum.

Schön, D.A. (1983) *The Reflective Practitioner: How Professionals Think in Action*. London: Temple Smith.

Schön, D. A. (1987) *Educating the Reflective Practitioner*. San Francisco: Jossey Bass.

# 3

# DEVELOPING A TEACHER IDENTITY AND CREATING PROFESSIONAL RELATIONSHIPS

## CHARLOTTE WRIGHT AND SAMANTHA WILKES

**Learn that and Learn how to –
The Knowledge and Application Model**

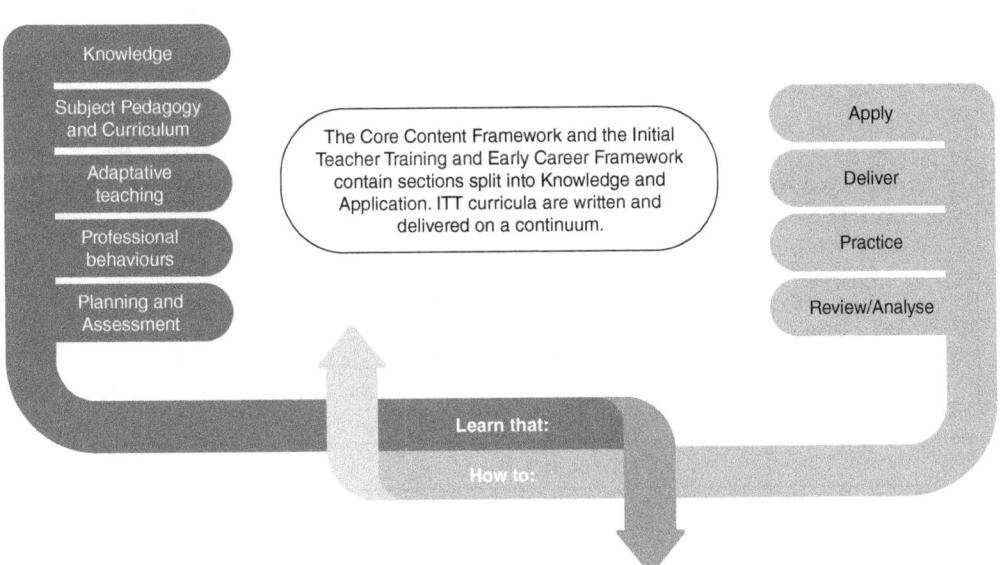

### FRAMED BY THE CCF – FOR FULL LINKS TO THE ITTECF, SEE PAGE 337

| Professional Behaviours | |
|---|---|
| (Standard 8 – 'Fulfil wider professional responsibilities') | |
| Learn that … | Learn how to … |
| 1. Effective professional development is likely to be sustained over time, involve expert support or coaching and opportunities for collaboration.<br>2. Reflective practice, supported by feedback from and observation of experienced colleagues, professional debate, and learning from educational research, is also likely to support improvement.<br>3. Teachers can make valuable contributions to the wider life of the school in a broad range of ways, including by supporting and developing effective professional relationships with colleagues | Develop as a professional, by:<br><br>• Receiving clear, consistent and effective mentoring in how to engage in professional development with clear intentions for impact on pupil outcomes, sustained over time with built-in opportunities for practice.<br><br>And – following expert input – by taking opportunities to practise, receive feedback and improve at:<br><br>• Seeking challenge, feedback and critique from mentors and other colleagues in an open and trusting working environment.<br>• Reflecting on progress made, recognising strengths and weaknesses and identifying next steps for further improvement.<br>• Knowing who to contact with any safeguarding concerns and having a clear understanding of what sorts of behaviour, disclosures and incidents to report.<br>• Collaborating with colleagues to share the load of planning and preparation and making use of shared resources (e.g. textbooks).<br><br>Build effective working relationships, by:<br><br>Discussing with mentor and expert colleagues how to share the intended lesson outcomes with teaching assistants ahead of lessons.<br><br>Manage workload and wellbeing, by:<br><br>• Observing how expert colleagues use and personalise systems and routines to support efficient time and task management and deconstructing this approach. Protecting time for rest and recovery and being aware of the sources of support available to support good mental wellbeing. |

### CHAPTER OBJECTIVES

On reading this chapter you will consider:

- what 'professional' means and how professionalism is conceptualised in key frameworks;
- the relationship between personal and professional identity;

- professional conventions and expectations in placement schools and in your first teaching job;
- being a role model and self-care as a dimension of professionalism;
- developing a sense of agency and working with others.

### KEY VOCABULARY

Initial teacher training (ITT)

Initial Teacher Training and Early Career Framework (ITTECF)

Early career teacher (ECT)

*Core Content Framework* (CCF)

Curriculum-based learning centres (CBCs)

School-based learning centres (SBLCs)

Expert colleagues

Expert mentors

# INTRODUCTION

This chapter will encourage you to develop your sense of yourself as a developing professional in an education setting and help you to build bridges to and from curriculum learning centres and school-based learning centres. You will explore what the term 'professionalism' means and explore the formal professional expectations of a trainee teacher and an early career teacher (ECT). Guidance is offered about how to conduct yourself in school, and how to seek help from your mentor. The chapter will also help you find ways to reflect on your emerging teacher identity, and navigate between your ideals about teaching and the practical constraints that might challenge them. You will be asked to think about yourself as a role model, and ways to look at your practice as a teacher but also as a learner yourself.

# SEEING YOURSELF AS A PROFESSIONAL

As you approach and take up your first teaching post as a qualified teacher, you may feel you are still on the threshold of the profession of teaching. You may feel that you are still learning how to inhabit a new identity – it would not be unusual to find yourself pausing outside the school entrance on the first day of term and taking a breath to prepare yourself to 'step into role' as a 'professional teacher'. You may also compare yourself to other more experienced teachers and wonder how they manage the many demands of the job. Yet, over time, your understanding of and confidence in your professional identity will feel more and more natural, as you set out into training and then live the role of teacher through the weeks and terms and find greater and greater degrees of 'comfortableness' (Paige et al., 2020).

## THE PROFESSIONAL IN THE CORE CONTENT FRAMEWORK, EARLY CAREER FRAMEWORK, THE INITIAL TEACHER TRAINING AND EARLY CAREER FRAMEWORK AND TEACHERS' STANDARDS

The adjective 'professional' is used 18 times in the *ITT Core Content Framework* (CCF) (DfE, 2019b), 21 times in the *Early Career Framework* (ECF) and 25 times in the *Teachers' Standards* (DfE, 2011). These documents in the public domain are one key way in which a common understanding of professionalism might be founded – indeed, the word 'professionalism' comes from the Latin word *profiteri*, meaning 'to declare publicly'. Most obviously, the adjective 'professional' appears in the title of Standard 8 of both frameworks – 'Professional Behaviours' – and in Part 2 of the *Teachers' Standards* – 'Personal and professional conduct'. But it is also coupled in these documents with:

- judgement;
- duties;
- responsibilities;
- bodies (such as the Chartered College of Teaching);
- relationships;
- development.

These frameworks exist in part to help you understand the different dimensions of becoming and being a teacher professional. They will help you conceptualise core elements of the teacher's work, and you will use them with your mentors and trainers to monitor and assess your own progress. Yet, if you look again, you will find there is a strong *interpersonal* emphasis here too: these frameworks encourage you to work on integrating yourself into the professional community of the school, through the forging of beneficial connections with other colleagues and stakeholders. Professionalism here is not just about the idea of having a firm individual knowledge and practice base from which to work, or the display of a set of 'good behaviours', but also about fostering an ongoing commitment to the forging of developmental relationships with pupils, their families and other practitioners. The Organisation for Economic Co-operation and Development (OECD), states that a professional is someone who is able to take autonomous and expertise-based actions and decisions in relation to their work. Their actions and decisions are grounded in a specialised set of knowledge and skills stemming from both quality training and *constant collaboration and dialogue with peers and other stakeholders* (Fraser, 2019, our italics).

The 'Learn how' statements in the CCF/ITTECF underline the importance of these collaborative and dialogic aspects of teaching, with repeated emphasis on the need to build strong bridges between yourself and others – for example, in Standard 5 (Adaptive Teaching): 'Develop an understanding of different pupil needs, by: ... Working closely with the Special Educational Needs Co-ordinator (SENCO) and special education professionals' (DfE, 2019b, p. 20).

It is helpful to see these bridges as important investments in your own development, but also as a way to 'give something back'. By paying attention to these professional relationships, by actively seeking and responding positively to advice and by expressing appreciation of shared knowledge and expertise in your school, you will be both contributing positively to the staff community and strengthening your own sense of yourself as an attentive, respectful and supportive colleague. Losano et al. (2018) remind us that to a large extent our professional identity is developed during social interactions, and that when we reflect on it we do so in relation to how we think we 'fit' with others in the professional community.

Being professional is always going to be more than the disembodied set of standards you see codified in policy: it will also involve interwoven social, emotional, personal and even physical aspects. You will move between many different states and roles, even within a single school day. Eaude (2018) captures something of the rapid gear-shifting required of the primary teacher each day when he describes the teacher who may adopt different personae depending on what, and how, they are teaching. They may be: 'more directive when conducting a physical education lesson with a somewhat unwilling class, and more facilitating when encouraging children to conduct an investigation in maths'; while not actually teaching they might be: 'creative in planning with others; patient in assisting a less experienced member of staff, diplomatic in dealing with an angry parent, forceful when trying to access additional support' for a child (p. 157).

The fast pace of the job of teaching makes it even more important that you take time to pause and to define for yourself what being professional looks like, as your personal definition will affect how you measure your own success and sense of belonging, and the development and achievement of your aspirations.

## ACTION LEARNING SET

Imagine you have been asked at an interview for a teaching job about your understanding of what constitutes 'professional conduct and behaviour'.

- What specific examples of good practice in relation to 'professional conduct and behaviour' could you speak about – either from your experience or that you have observed in others' practice?

- If you were a headteacher interviewing for new staff, *why* might you ask that question? What might the implications be for your pupils, your staff and your school if you appointed someone who did *not* meet professional standards?

## EVIDENCE-INFORMED RESEARCH

The literature around teacher identity often talks about professional identity alongside personal identity (Beauchamp and Thomas, 2011). As a 'person's source of meaning and motive', a sense of personal identity is fundamental in the connection with how practitioners do their job and fulfil their roles and responsibilities (Richards and Malomo, 2022, p. 8). The professional identity element will be influenced and developed by the mentoring and tuition that you receive at both curriculum learning centres and school-based learning centres (Podesta and Hoath, 2023).

There may be times when the two identities seem to differ and could even conflict with each other. Your own memories of teachers' approaches when you were a pupil in school may not align with ways in which you are asked to teach now, for example, and you may have to work on suspending judgement in order to learn more. This is not unusual. Teacher agency can be considered as how you develop your professional autonomy and is a component of your professional identity, taking on board all the coaching and modelling and building your own way of enacting your role as a teacher. Working on your own identity and agency are paramount to building a strong sense of your own self; stay mindful that there are multiple dimensions of professional identity (Beijard, Meijer and Verloop (2004) in Pearce, 2022) and you will review this work at each stage of your career.

The work of Erikson (1959) suggests we have an *ideal* and a *real* identity; as a trainee teacher this might come into focus for you as you move from the curriculum learning centre to the school-based learning centre. The ideal that you construct when at the curriculum base does not always dovetail neatly with the reality of the school-based context, and you may need to come to terms with the fact there may be a boundary space between these two places.

> **REFLECTIVE QUESTION**
>
> - Consider how you will manage to work through differing experiences and ideals from both settings: school-based and curriculum-based learning.
> - Who would you discuss these possible conflicts with?

Your evolving identity will be influenced by the experienced teachers and mentors whom you encounter daily. These relational overlaps may cause you to question your own shifting identity and ask the questions: *Who am I?* and *Who am I as a teacher?* Much research exists into these shifts – for example, in their influential work on identity, Beauchamp and Thomas (2011) discuss the inter-relationships of the concepts of identity and agency and how we ought to be, as opposed to how we naturally are. Our *teacher-self*.

Over time your identity will undergo change. The keeping of a reflective journal in which you note how you deal with scenarios or challenges can help you recognise self-growth and celebrate your own achievements. Sometimes we are so close up to our own development we do not have the luxury of a more objective, distanced viewpoint from which we can observe improvements in ourselves as well as what has stayed the same (Howard and Paige, 2022). A reflective journal may help you see that your teacher identity is not fixed and therefore can be influenced and impacted upon by you and those around you.

It is worth reminding yourself that personal and professional do not always perfectly align; at times you may experience tension between your ideals and the practical constraints of the job, but don't bury any feelings of concern or confusion. You should seek support and advice from your mentor: use this professional dialogue as an opportunity to share your thoughts and be clear what you would like them to help you with. Your mentor will be able to provide support with tackling scenarios – for example, how to respond to a parent/carer's query or whether you contribute to staff meetings and other professional development opportunities. Talking about how you feel can give you some clarity on how you are developing as a professional and how you would like to develop as a practitioner.

> **CASE STUDY: *TEACHER IDENTITY***
>
> Joe is in his third year of a BA (Hons) QTS in Primary Education and is in a two-cohort primary placement. He has both a mentor and class teacher supporting him. He meets weekly with his mentor and recognises that their conversations are instrumental to aid progression and his understanding of the links between curriculum-based learning and school-based learning.
>
> *(Continued)*

(Continued)

During the weekly mentor meetings, Joe is asked to identify areas of development across his practice and pedagogy, evidencing in particular in the early weeks an emphasis on professionalism and behaviour management strategies.

His mentor initially leads these discussions, with a tight focus on the foundational competencies of the CCF/ITTECF, but also makes sure there is time for Joe to talk about the evidence of professional practice that he is gathering – including his online documentation and observations of practice, and how the digital approximations that featured as part of his curriculum-based learning professional studies modules have been applied proactively in school.

Joe shares examples, celebrates his successes and asks for advice. The coaching and mentoring dialogue with both his class teacher and mentor support his development from supported trainee to 'freestanding' qualified teacher. These focused and timely conversations offer Joe a vital opportunity to verbalise his thoughts and concerns over this transitional period, to understand that problem-solving is an inevitable part of the job and that actively tackling doubts or questions is not a sign of weakness but an important aspect of self-care and professional growth.

As you move from the supported environment of training into the more independent space of being a qualified ECT, you will inhabit the *transitional mode* referred to by Beauchamp and Thomas (2011). The space between trainee and qualified teacher, termed 'boundary space' by Beauchamp and Thomas, can be a place of significant learning as well as somewhere where your own agency and individuality can flourish.

## WHAT DOES BEING PROFESSIONAL LOOK LIKE?

When you begin each placement in a school, and your first job, you will be given policies and handbooks for the school; these will contain key information about vital procedures and processes (such as what to do about safeguarding concerns). However, sometimes these documents may not make explicit all the school's conventions and expectations around professional behaviours. To make the best first impression in a new placement or job, you should try to educate yourself about the school's written *and* unwritten rules. In the early days or weeks, find out about the daily expectations of staff through careful reading of documentation and by politely asking your mentor or colleagues, so that you can avoid any inadvertent missteps. Do not rely on informal observation alone in case an example you observe is not representative.

The following list serves as a useful starting point for gathering information about these professional conventions and expectations:

- *Dress code*: What is deemed acceptable workwear and footwear for staff within this school and within the age phase in which you are based?

- *Arrival and departure times for staff*: Is there a time by which you are expected to be in school? On what occasions may you be required to stay later, and is there any expectation on a daily basis about times to leave?
- *Terms of address*: How do your colleagues, mentor and leadership team prefer to be addressed?
- *Protocols for asking for help*: If you are unable to ask your mentor for help (e.g. because they are unavailable or because the issue might relate to a whole-school issue beyond their remit), to whom should you turn?
- *Email protocols*: If staff use email are there standard greetings and/or sign-offs, protocols for length/tone of emails and acceptable limits for sending and responding?
- *Absence*: What are the school protocols for absence? In particular, find out what the expectations are around setting and marking cover work, what to do if your reason for absence means you will be out of school for more than one day and what you are expected to do on your return.
- *Phone usage*: What are the expectations about staff phone usage/visibility/audibility during the school day? This can be linked to safeguarding and thus is worth very careful consideration.
- *Body language*: Are there written or unwritten expectations about body language (e.g. teachers not sitting on desks or yawning)?

If you find you have made a mistake, try not to feel panicked or criticised – all teachers are human! In recognising the error, let your mentor know. Frame the future positively by asking for their guidance, and by telling them how you are going to do things differently and what you have learned from the situation.

## BEING A ROLE MODEL

The point about body language above is a reminder that your pupils will be consciously or unconsciously watching you all the time, and that you will function as a powerful role model in their lives. It is important that they see you as a genuine and approachable person, but you will also need to consider how much of yourself you should share with them. Sometimes new teachers make the mistake of seeking to build relationships with a class by telling lots of personal stories; this can have the unintended effect of undermining their professional authority. Warmth and authenticity are extremely important, but so is a judicious approach to how much of yourself you choose to share. If in doubt, seek counsel from your mentor in the first instance: it is always better to 'try out' an example or story from life with them first if you are unsure about its suitability.

In addition, while you will be building your own unique value set about education and its current manifestations in school, be wary of voicing personal opinions to pupils about the aspects which you would like to question. Professional debate and enquiry have an important role to play in your career and identity development, but could cause distraction and confusion for the pupils.

Third, find out about the way that your school deals with contact with parents/guardians. It will be expected that you will model your professionalism in the mode and manner of any communications. For example, you might be in the playground at home time when a parent or guardian approaches you out of the blue with a question. Your manner of response can set the tone for the immediate or subsequent exchanges, so even if the question comes as a surprise, model the politeness and respect that you would want in return. If in doubt, it is always advisable to buy yourself some time so that you can consult a colleague and frame your response correctly. You might say: 'If you don't mind, I would like to double-check so that I can be sure you are getting the right answer.' If the question relates to safeguarding, follow the school's safeguarding policy and be sure to inform the designated safeguarding lead as soon as possible.

Phone calls and emails home for students also require careful thought. As a trainee or new teacher, you may want to check whether it might be more appropriate to do it in partnership with an experienced colleague.

The management of parent/guardian communications can be a complex acquired skill; if you are worried about this aspect of professionalism, ask your mentor to rehearse sample situations with you so that you can practise using positive and constructive language.

## SELF-CARE AS A DIMENSION OF PROFESSIONALISM

Teaching is a profession which attracts recruits who care about children and education and, naturally, the majority of your work will centre around planning, delivering, evaluating and improving your lessons and activities for your pupils. When you think back to your own schooling, you will remember the importance of having teachers who were passionate, well organised and kind.

However, what will have been less obvious (or indeed invisible) to you as a school child was the importance of the teacher practising *self-care* as a dimension of professionalism. The CCF/ITTECF and ECF both mention the need to 'Learn how to… manage workload and wellbeing' (Standard 8). Remember it is a positive facet of professionalism to:

- recognise the importance of asking for help when you feel you are unsure or struggling;
- block out time every week as time away from work;

- maintain a healthy relationship with pre-made or pre-planned resources;
- make use of support networks and tools within and beyond the school (for example, the Educational Support Partnership or the NHS Every Mind Matters resources).

In fact, looking after yourself is ironically a key aspect of strong *team* play, as it will enable you to make the maximum contribution that you can to the school over the arc of the year. For more information on looking after your self-care see Chapter 5.

# DEVELOPING A SENSE OF AGENCY

All the decisions you make in your practice are small steps to beginning to build your agency as a practitioner. The positive contribution of experienced teachers and expert mentors can have an enormous influence on your development. Sometimes this makes it challenging to develop your own teacher agency when their support is reduced or removed (Podesta and Hoath, 2023). However, all the decisions you make in your practice are small steps to beginning to build your agency as a practitioner. This will have been evolving over time and you will gradually take more of a lead on key elements – for example, the planned curriculum within your classroom or age phase. As your confidence, knowledge and understanding increase, your mentor will help you to plan more independently and this will be an empowering boost and move areas of your practice forward.

## CASE STUDY: ISBAH

Isbah has returned to her placement school for her final placement. Her training pathway is a three-year BA (Hons) Undergraduate degree in Primary Education. She is specialising in the three to seven age phase. Based in a Year 1 class, she has observed experienced expert colleagues deliver a daily sequenced systematic synthetic phonics (SSP) lesson. Through the lectures and seminars at her curriculum base, she understands the teaching of early reading through this approach and has had opportunities to deconstruct digital approximations of lessons. She has also carried out micro-teaching in small groups with her peers.

In her first two placements, she co-planned and delivered lessons from the school's SSP scheme. These developed into weekly sequences of learning; helping her to see how learning builds over time. On the final placement Isbah is planning independently and is adapting the published scheme to the needs of the pupils in her class. As her confidence

*(Continued)*

(Continued)

and subject knowledge have grown, she feels capable and ready to produce a sequence of learning for the needs of the pupils. She is now able to draw on all her previous observations and reflections to plan each week, with a strong understanding of how and why learning is broken down and the need to revisit and review prior learning. Her mentor can see the sequence of learning develop over time and that her planning is adapted for all learners, as well as considering how additional adults will be deployed.

During the weekly mentor meeting, Isbah takes the opportunity to discuss with her mentor why she made the changes to the published scheme. This clearly demonstrates her developing agency through more independent autonomy of knowing her pupils' needs, editing the planning to ensure they make progress.

# WORKING WITH OTHERS (INCLUDING EXPERT COLLEAGUES AND PEERS)

It is worth noting that an important aspect of training is where you are occupying the role of learner *and* teacher. This may be hard work but gives you the advantageous position of viewing the 'learning process from the perspective of the teacher *and* the learner': you operate with a 'vari-focal' lens (Wright and Raheem, in Podesta and Hoath, 2023, p. 16).

The act of teaching does require an ongoing commitment to learning as well as teaching. Here, we are going to consider how working with others, including expert colleagues at centre base and expert mentors and practitioners within your setting, will allow you to reflect on the *teacher–learner* identity.

## REFLECTIVE QUESTIONS

Try asking yourself the following questions.

1. You are at the point in your academic year where you have several assignment submissions and deadlines to meet. How do you manage this alongside the demands of the placement expectations of increasing planning and teaching?

Consider who might support you, what steps can you take to relieve these potential pressure points and how can you ensure your self-care is not compromised.

2. How do you flip between observing the practice of the experienced colleague one lesson, then being the practitioner the next lesson? Does this transition always happen smoothly and how is it managed by the staff in school? Consider and record some of these examples in your journal or development record.

Reflection is a teacher tool used to understand the strengths in your practice and why these exist, as well as to interrogate aspects that need developing. When you are the *learner*, reflect on what ways you can develop targets set and agreed by you and your mentor to evidence and make progress towards meeting the Professional Behaviours Core Content Standard 8 – Fulfil wider professional responsibilities.

As you move between both school and curriculum centres during your training and then into your first appointment as an ECT, you will have the opportunity to work alongside numerous professionals. You will be responsible for deploying other staff members at your placement setting and in your first teaching post. It is critical to remember the value of all interpersonal relations. Success will not come from trying to impersonate the mentors or other colleagues, but more from the way you draw from these coaching and mentoring interactions to enhance and shape your own identity and agency. At times you may experience staff members with differing approaches or values to your own; if this occurs, discussing the matter with your mentor or tutor at centre base can be a good professional dialogue to help see situations through a more objective lens.

## CASE STUDY: ZAIN AND CIARA

Zain and Ciara are studying for a Postgraduate Certificate in Primary Education with QTS. They are in their first school-based training placement in a large three-form entry school in Bradford, in a mixed Year 3 and 4 class. They meet separately each week with their mentor and also have informal ongoing coaching from their class teachers. Within the class there are three additional adults all of whom support the pupils' learning, social and emotional wellbeing, and lead intervention teaching and SSP groups.

With guidance and support from their expert mentor, Zain and Ciara join their team meetings which are scheduled each Tuesday after school. All staff attend these and it offers the opportunity for both trainees to observe professional dialogue, and how the class teacher shares the following week's planning with the additional adults. It is an example of how the team works collaboratively on the planning process; this includes adaptations to stretch, challenge and support all learners and the outlining of clear roles for each adult.

Conversations take place on how to successfully manage behaviour following the school's policy and examples of different groupings and seating plans for improved relationships are put in place. This modelled practice supports Zain and Ciara when they begin to communicate their planning with the staff team. They have seen the need for including details such as resources, questions, support and timings onto the planning pro forma, so that each adult is well-informed ahead of their teaching each day.

## ACTION LEARNING SET

- Reflecting on the case study, consider what you can do to build these crucial professional relationships. You may find yourself feeling a little out of your depth or comfort zone when instructing and deploying additional adults; they will often be more senior and will definitely be more experienced.

- Think of positive ways to foster and nurture the personal, as well as professional inter-relational exchanges which often occur ad hoc before the beginning or at the end of the school day. Take these small but valuable moments to get to know and understand the dynamics of your team and you will reap the benefits that come with this investment.

# CONCLUSION

This chapter clarified what professionalism means in relation to teacher identity and practice. It identified how policy frameworks and standards define professional conduct and behaviours and explored the importance of close observation of and dialogue with your more experienced professional colleagues to help you to 'fit in' with staff and meet school expectations, while also developing your own agency and confidence.

## REVIEW OF CHAPTER OBJECTIVES

Within this chapter you have considered:

- what 'professional' means and how professionalism is conceptualised in key frameworks;
- the relationship between personal and professional identity;
- professional conventions and expectations in placement schools and in your first teaching job;
- being a role model and self-care as a dimension of professionalism;
- developing a sense of agency and working with others.

# FURTHER READING AND RESOURCES

Howard, C. and Paige, R. (2022) *Essential Guides for Early Career Teachers: Professional Behaviours*. St Albans: Critical.

Richards, H. and Malomo, M. (eds.) (2022) *Developing your Professional Identity: A Guide for Working with Children and Families*. St Albans: Critical.

# REFERENCES

Beauchamp, C. and Thomas, L. (2011) New teachers' identity shifts at the boundary of teacher education and initial practice. *International Journal of Educational Research*, 50(1), pp. 6–13.

Department for Education (DfE) (2011) *Teachers' Standards Guidance*. Available at: https://assets.publishing.service.gov.uk/media/61b73d6c8fa8f50384489c9a/Teachers__Standards_Dec_2021.pdf [accessed 5 December 2023].

DfE (2019a) *Early Career Framework*. Available at: https://assets.publishing.service.gov.uk/government/uploads/system/uploads/attachment_data/file/978358/Early-Career_Framework_April_2021.pdf [accessed August 2023].

DfE (2019b) *ITT Core Content Framework*. London: DfE. Available at: https://assets.publishing.service.gov.uk/government/uploads/system/uploads/attachment_data/file/974307/ITT_core_content_framework_.pdf [accessed November 2023].

Eaude, T. (2018) *Developing the Expertise of Primary and Elementary Classroom Teachers*. London: Bloomsbury Academic.

Ensor, P. (2001) From preservice mathematics teacher education to beginning teaching: A study in recontextualizing. *Journal for Research in Mathematics Education*, 32(3), pp. 296–320.

Erikson, E. H. (1959). Identity and the life cycle: Selected papers. *Psychological Issues*, 1, pp. 1–171.

Fraser, P. (2019) What does it mean to think of teachers as professionals? *OECD and Skills Today*. Available at: https://oecdedutoday.com/teachers-professional-school-leaders-principals-talis-oecd/ [accessed 8 July 2023].

Howard, C. and Paige, R. (2022) *Essential Guides for Early Career Teachers: Professional Behaviours*. St Albans: Critical.

Losano, L, Fiorentini, D. and Villarreal, M. (2018) The development of a mathematics teacher's professional identity during her first year teaching. *Journal of Mathematics Teacher Education*, 21(3), pp. 287–315.

Paige, R., Geeson, R. and Lambert, S. (2020) *Building Skills for Effective Primary Teaching*. London: Sage/Learning Matters.

Pearce, A. (2022) *Beacons of Hope: Lessons We Can Learn from Resilient Teachers*. Lausanne: Peter Lang.

Podesta, E. and Hoath, L. (eds.) (2023) *Professional Studies for Secondary Teaching*. London: Sage/Learning Matters.

Richards, H. and Malomo, M. (eds.) (2022) *Developing your Professional Identity: A Guide for Working with Children and Families*. St Albans: Critical.

Ur, P. (2002) The English teacher as professional, in Richards, J. C. and Renandya, W. A. (eds.), *Methodology in Language Teaching: An Anthology of Current Practice*. Cambridge: Cambridge University Press.

Wright, C. and Raheem, N. (2023) Developing knowledge, identity and relationships as a teacher-learner, in Podesta, E. and Hoath, L. (eds.), *Professional Studies for Secondary Teaching*. London: Sage/Learning Matters.

# 4

# LEARNING IN CONTEXT: TRACKING YOUR KNOWLEDGE, UNDERSTANDING AND PROGRESS

## KIRSTY ROSS

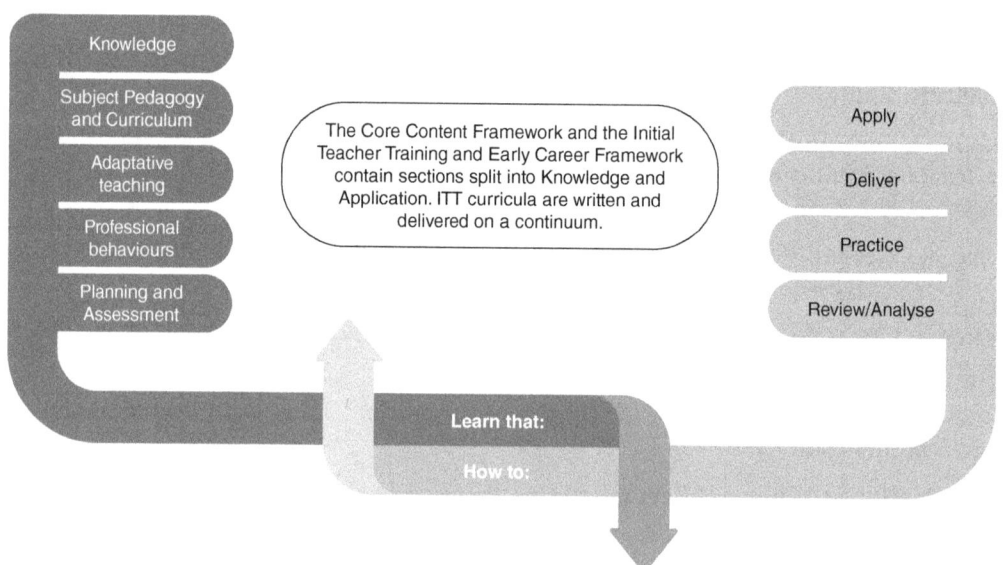

Learn that and Learn how to – The Knowledge and Application Model

## FRAMED BY THE CCF – FOR FULL LINKS TO THE ITTECF, SEE PAGE 337

| Subject and Curriculum | |
|---|---|
| (Standard 3 – 'Demonstrate good subject and curriculum knowledge') | |
| Learn that … | Learn how to … |
| 2. Secure subject knowledge helps teachers to motivate pupils and teach effectively.<br>3. Ensuring pupils master foundational concepts and knowledge before moving on is likely to build pupils' confidence and help them succeed.<br>4. Anticipating common misconceptions within particular subjects is also an important aspect of curricular knowledge; working closely with colleagues to develop an understanding of likely misconceptions is valuable. | Deliver a carefully sequenced and coherent curriculum, by:<br><br>• Receiving clear, consistent and effective mentoring in how to identify essential concepts, knowledge, skills and principles of the subject.<br>• Observing how expert colleagues ensure pupils' thinking is focused on key ideas within the subject and deconstructing this approach.<br><br>And – following expert input – by taking opportunities to practise, receive feedback and improve at:<br><br>• Being aware of common misconceptions and discussing with expert colleagues how to help pupils master important concepts. |
| Professional Behaviours | |
| (Standard 8 – 'Fulfil wider professional responsibilities') | |
| Learn that … | Learn how to … |
| 1. Effective professional development is likely to be sustained over time, involve expert support or coaching and opportunities for collaboration.<br>3. Teachers can make valuable contributions to the wider life of the school in a broad range of ways, including by supporting and developing effective professional relationships with colleagues. | Develop as a professional, by:<br><br>• Receiving clear, consistent and effective mentoring in how to engage in professional development with clear intentions for impact on pupil outcomes, sustained over time with built-in opportunities for practice.<br><br>And – following expert input – by taking opportunities to practise, receive feedback and improve at:<br><br>• Strengthening pedagogical and subject knowledge by participating in wider networks.<br>• Learning to extend subject and pedagogic knowledge as part of the lesson preparation process.<br>• Seeking challenge, feedback and critique from mentors and other colleagues in an open and trusting working environment.<br>• Reflecting on progress made, recognising strengths and weaknesses and identifying next steps for further improvement. |

## CHAPTER OBJECTIVES

On reading this chapter you will:

- learn about the importance of secure knowledge and understanding to ensure good teaching and learning;
- consider strategies and methods to develop your knowledge and understanding;
- consider how progress on school-based practice is evidenced and measured on ITT programmes;
- learn how observation and feedback are critical to the development of teachers.

## KEY VOCABULARY

Adaptive teaching

Content knowledge

Continuous professional development (CPD)

Enactment and micro-teaching

Formative and summative assessment

Intensive training and practice (ITaP)

Pedagogy

Peer review

Pupil misconceptions

Reflective practitioner

# INTRODUCTION

This chapter will focus on *learning in context* and an appreciation of learning through practical application and experience. Introducing what it means to be in the classroom as a teacher, the chapter will explore the significance of secure knowledge and understanding to ensure good teaching and learning, and consider monitoring, observation and feedback on school-based practice. The content is intended to support and promote personal growth, professional identity and efficacy.

# KNOWLEDGE AND UNDERSTANDING

In the *Core Content Framework* (CCF) the Department for Education (DfE, 2019) states that all trainee teachers need to learn that: 'Secure subject knowledge helps teachers to motivate pupils and teach effectively' (p. 13). This section of the CCF aligns with Standard 3 of the *Teachers' Standards* which states that all teachers must: 'Demonstrate good subject and curriculum knowledge'.

## BUT WHAT CONSTITUTES KNOWLEDGE AND HOW DOES IT IMPACT TEACHING AND LEARNING?

Conceptualising teacher knowledge is a complex issue that involves understanding underlying processes. In its broadest sense, it can consist of the information, concepts and skills for each subject and the methods to teach, plan and assess. Teachers should understand the content they are teaching and how it is learned. Introduced below is an interpretation of the foundations which comprise effective knowledge and understanding:

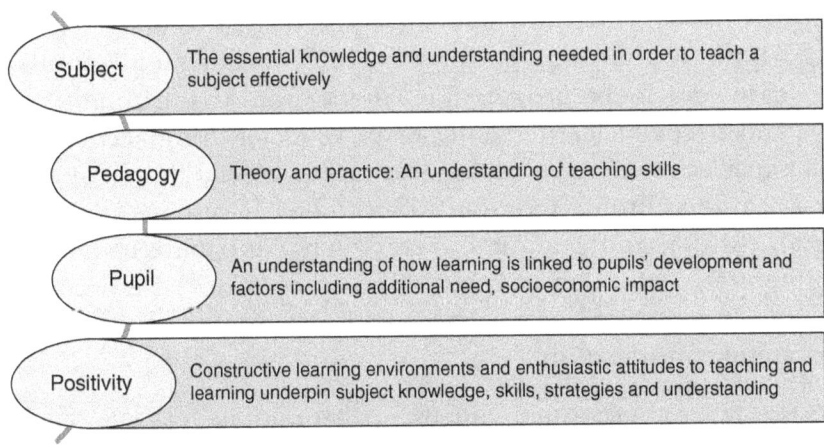

Figure 4.1 An interpretation of the foundations which comprise effective knowledge and understanding

Subject/curriculum knowledge is vitally important and refers to the body of information, facts, theories, principles, ideas and vocabulary. To be a great teacher you should prioritise your own development; you are first a learner before becoming the teacher. Essentially, a subject cannot be taught thoroughly if the teacher is not confident in their own subject knowledge (Ball et al., 2008). To underline the point, 'the ways in which morphemes communicate meaning and govern spelling construction' (Castles et al., 2018, p. 25) requires more than just being able to read well; it also demands a secure knowledge of phonics and the elemental reading process. Teachers with strong subject knowledge can sequence over time, convey information clearly, address pupil need and questions, adapt and innovate instruction. Being secure in the subjects you teach will also give you the ability to address pupil misconceptions by offering alternative explanations and interpretations with confidence. The CCF/ITTECF states that, 'Anticipating common misconceptions within particular subjects is also an important aspect of curricular knowledge' (DfE, 2019, p. 13).

*Pedagogy* is defined simply as the method and practice of teaching. It encompasses teaching skills, strategies, feedback and assessment (formative and summative), referring to the way teachers deliver content to the class. Overarching approaches and theories of learning may underpin pedagogical decision-making. The most effective pedagogies encompass a range of teaching techniques, guided learning, assessment practice and individual activity. These pedagogies develop metacognition, foster higher-order thinking, problem-solving skills and creativity and make good use of questioning and dialogue in doing so. There will always be approaches that best suit the subject and the context in which it is being taught. For instance, an Early Years Foundation Stage (EYFS) teacher may reference cognitive development research in successfully planning the use of guided play.

Knowledge of learners and how pupils learn is related to understanding their needs and how to plan high-quality teaching to enable all pupils to participate, learn and make progress. Teachers should continually assess the strengths and needs of learners and adapt their teaching accordingly so all can meet expectations. This adaptive teaching is crucial in meeting the needs of diverse learners. Bronfenbrenner's bioecological systems theory explores how social, cultural and economic factors may contribute to pupil learning (Bronfenbrenner, 2004). Regarding the influence of social environments on development it is one of the most accepted explanations and highlights the need for careful consideration.

Positivity and a good classroom climate – where pupils feel safe, engaged and inspired to learn – fosters open communication, encourages collaboration and respects diversity. A nurturing atmosphere which promotes active participation and critical thinking where pupils are resilient to failure should not be underestimated in terms of its importance to learning outcomes.

### EVIDENCE-INFORMED RESEARCH

The significance of, and critical need for, knowledge and understanding is also well supported by educational research which consistently concludes that teachers with solid knowledge and deep understanding are more effective in promoting pupil learning and engagement. Below is research literature to explore in more depth; it features in the CCF/ITTECF, Subject and Curriculum (Standard 3 – 'Demonstrate good subject and curriculum knowledge') further reading recommendations list.

Durham University and the Sutton Trust conducted an extensive review of educational research, *What Makes Great Teaching?*, looking to identify the key factors that contribute to great teaching (Coe et al., 2014). Some of the findings from the report that support the need for strong knowledge and understanding include:

*Content knowledge*: The report emphasises that teachers with a strong content knowledge are better at explaining concepts, answering pupils' questions and adapting their teaching to meet pupils' needs.

*Pedagogical content knowledge*: The report also acknowledges the significance of pedagogy – the ability to translate subject matter expertise into effective teaching strategies. This reinforces the idea that subject knowledge alone is not sufficient; teachers need to know how to teach effectively.

*Teacher clarity*: Teacher clarity was identified as a vital component of effective teaching in the report. Teachers with strong subject knowledge are more likely to offer clear explanations and well-structured and coherent lessons.

*High expectations*: Having strong subject knowledge allows teachers to set high expectations based on a deep understanding of what pupils can achieve.

The importance of strong subject knowledge is also evident in a seminal piece of educational guidance, Rosenshine's 'Principles of instruction', which details ten strategies 'all teachers should know' (Rosenshine, 2012).

When evaluating teaching in maths, Rosenshine noted that the 'most effective' teachers displayed strong subject knowledge; a number of his principles align with recognising this as being key to promote learning.

*Daily review*: Rosenshine's principles emphasise the need for teachers to review previous materials regularly. Teachers with strong subject knowledge can review content effectively, reinforcing understanding.

*Clear expectations*: Teachers who thoroughly understand the subject matter can provide clear and concise explanations that help pupils grasp new concepts.

*Active practice*: Rosenshine encourages teachers to provide opportunities for pupils to practice skills. Teachers with a strong knowledge base are best equipped to ensure that activities are designed to be meaningful and aimed at reinforcing learning.

*Feedback*: Providing timely and specific feedback to pupils is crucial. Teachers with strong content knowledge can identify misconceptions and provide guidance for improvement.

*Demonstration*: Teachers with expertise in their subject can model correct techniques and problem-solving strategies.

# DEVELOPING YOUR KNOWLEDGE AND UNDERSTANDING AS TRAINEE TEACHER

Evolving your knowledge, revisiting and revising is part of an ongoing cycle of continuous professional development (CPD). In this section, we shall look at strategies and methods to build upon and deepen your understanding.

> **REFLECTIVE QUESTIONS**
>
> Knowledge acquisition and understanding underpins high-quality teaching and learning.
>
> Reflect on this statement and consider how confident you are in supporting pupil learning in the subject/s you will teach and across the curriculum.
>
> - What aspects do you feel you have most understanding of?
> - What aspects do you feel least prepared for?

## IDENTIFYING KNOWLEDGE GAPS AND AUDITING

The purpose of an audit is to help you to pinpoint strengths and identify areas for development in your knowledge, offering a means to check, update and record current understanding. A knowledge audit should measure your own perceptions of your competence and confidence; it is not intended to be a conclusive directory of what needs to be known, but rather a way to take ownership of your own learning and give clarity. It will prove to be a valuable tool to assist you in your teaching and learning, helping you in enhancing your practice for the benefit of all pupils.

> **ACTION LEARNING SET**
>
> In the audit how can you assess your own knowledge and how do you track your understanding?
>
> - *Unpick the curriculum*: As an initial starting point gather all relevant information including national curriculum documentation and all relevant schemes of learning, going through each one carefully identifying/annotating key points.
>
>   Break down each unit of work into its component parts rather than a more general subject focus. For example, identifying 'algorithms and how they work' as an area of strength or weakness is far more targeted than noting 'computer science'.
>
>   By immersing yourself and exploring in detail you will deepen your understanding and develop a more comprehensive knowledge base.
>
> - *Reflective evaluation of knowledge and understanding*: Consider carefully, the topics you feel confident to teach and which units you are unfamiliar with. Be sure to recognise your strengths alongside the deficits in your understanding and be reassured that no-one knows everything.

> Create and complete an audit template to give yourself an overview of your subject knowledge and to also identify areas to work on. Rather than simply deciding that you either 'know' or 'don't know', look to employ a more specific criteria, such as using traffic light system to colour code your responses or a sliding scale, as below, to assess the certainty of your judgements in each area.
>
> *Self-assessment scale*
>
> 1. Excellent level of knowledge and understanding. Confident and fully prepared to teach.
> 2. Good level of knowledge and understanding. Not fully confident to teach.
> 3. Some knowledge and understanding. Further research and study required before teaching.
> 4. Limited knowledge and understanding. Action required to prepare for teaching.

Mastery of content, themes and topics will only come with time and effort on your part. Sometimes you will learn from expert colleagues, training input, working with peers and by observing experienced practitioners. Other times, you will develop knowledge through research, reading widely, engaging in professional dialogue and reflecting on practices. There are several ways you could consider developing your knowledge and understanding, some of which are explored below.

*Plan in time* to develop your knowledge in the same way you would set aside time to plan lessons and create resources. Little else will develop your teaching as much as time given to reading extensively, reviewing initiatives and building on your expertise by keeping continued learning at the forefront.

*National curriculum appraisal, current research evaluation* and *subject reviews* will support you in becoming an expert on the content you teach. Continue to familiarise yourself with content, stay up to date with amendments to the curriculum and recommendations to ensure cutting edge insights.

*Keep a knowledge notebook* as a way of recording your notes and jotting down ideas for subjects/topics to be added and referred to.

*Engaging in CPD* in-service training (INSET), staff meetings and 'twilight sessions', along with mentorship and involvement with research can all aid and improve your effectiveness as a teacher.

*Peer review and support* promotes reflective conversations; working together with others can help to identify practices to be enhanced and developed (O'Leary, 2020). Peer review differs from observations in that the aim is to give focused feedback that offers ideas and insight to evolve specific skills.

*Enactment and micro-teaching* provide helpful opportunities to rehearse activities and explore teaching strategies. The introduction of intensive training and practice

(ITaP) looks to strengthen the links between evidence and the classroom and will help you embed your learning by practising what would happen in the classroom, supported by feedback. This process of planning, performing, receiving expert input and reflecting as a group in a safe environment is a valuable way of assessing knowledge, supports refinements to practice and builds a sense of efficacy.

*Employ technology and media platforms*, video clips, blogs, BBC Bitesize, YouTube, podcasts ... an endless list of online possibilities that opens up a wealth of information to be used to support both your understanding and learning in the classroom. For instance, in history, if you are teaching lessons on the Great Fire of London, why not immerse yourself in documentaries scrutinising events, life and times.

*Access and enrol with subject-specific associations* to make the most of resources and training opportunities. The National Centre for Excellence in the Teaching of Mathematics (NCETM) provides self-evaluation tools for both subject content and pedagogy; for English teachers, the National Association for the Teaching of English (NATE) is a good platform for current context, subject developments/news and exploring research. There are also an increasing number of subject-specific TeachMeet events being organised nationwide.

*Follow regarded educators and experts on social media* as these communities of teachers generate resources, discuss difficult teaching concepts and share information about the most effective ways to improve practice. On X (formally Twitter) most subjects have their own hashtags, such as #GeographyTeacher, and many dedicated group chats.

## PROGRESSION AND MONITORING ACROSS THE ITT PROGRAMME

All ITT programmes should aim to develop the skills, knowledge, professional values and competencies trainees need to gain at each phase of the teacher journey. There should be a clear and sequenced curriculum that sets out the learning aims, diagnostic assessment to ensure prerequisites are secure, models of excellent performance, scaffolding, guidance, opportunities for practice, observation and, crucially, feedback that guides next steps and indicates progress. The structure and design should also ensure trainees are reflective practitioners and active learners.

Time spent in schools, early years or further education settings should be part of a coherent training programme that enables trainees to meet the *Teachers' Standards*.

All accredited ITT providers must ensure that training programmes are designed to provide trainee teachers with sufficient time being trained in schools, early years and/or further education settings to enable them to demonstrate that they have met all the standards for QTS.

All accredited ITT providers must ensure that each trainee teacher has taught in at least two schools. Trainee teachers need a variety of experience in schools to enable them to meet all the *Teachers' Standards*. They need to teach children and young people in their specified age range, from different backgrounds, as well as gaining experience of different approaches to teaching and to school organisation and management (DfE, 2023).

## CASE STUDY: LUCIE

Lucie Forsyth has recently completed a three-year undergraduate BA Honours degree in Primary Education with QTS at Durham University. In her case study she describes her placement experiences, progress over time and assessment of her developing core competencies as a trainee teacher.

> My course was comprehensively designed to guide trainee teachers on their journey to becoming a fully qualified teacher, developing both the professional and personal skills. With a blend of centre-based learning and school-based training, the structured programme supported and promoted my teaching and learning.
>
> During my training at Durham University, I had the opportunity to observe professionals and teach across all key stages in a variety of primary schools. This allowed me to gain a wide range of knowledge, understanding and experience. Before entering schools, trainees were given extensive training, resources and advice, so were fully prepared to start their school-based training. School experience days complement centre-based tuition, allowing trainees to work with a range of expert colleagues on understanding key elements from knowledge of statutory legislation, to building on their understanding of child development, to exploring research, while also beginning to observe and apply centre-based learning within the school-based setting. Observation is a critical component, in terms of observing expert practitioners and in gaining advice following observed lessons. Detailed reflective discussions and constructive observation feedback with action points aided my development and improved my practice.
>
> In my first year of training at Durham University, I was placed in EYFS. I observed professional teaching staff, completed a wide range of activities and taught a small percentage of the school curriculum. In my second year, I was placed in Year 1. This built on first-year experiences with a series of tasks, structured school days, a longer placement and a higher percentage teaching commitment. In my final year of training, I was placed in Year 5. This included completing school experience days before completing a 12-week block placement – with the expectation that by the end of the block placement, I should be teaching 80 per cent of the timetable (which is reflective of expectations of an ECT). At this end point, I was also expected to display evidence of meeting the Teacher's Standards. This ensured that I was then ready to progress into my ECT years.

*(Continued)*

(Continued)

> As mentioned, activities were set to guide thinking and promote development. Tasks ensured that I gained experience and was able to reflect on elements including the curriculum, lesson planning, behaviour management and meeting individual needs – SEND and EAL. All placement activities were uploaded onto PebblePad, where attendance and feedback were also evidenced. This allowed progress to be effectively tracked by both university tutors and school mentors.
>
> PebblePad is an online learning portal used as a portfolio of evidence. PebblePad can be accessed by the trainee, university staff and school staff. This means that it is continuously monitored, and additional support and advice can be provided from expert colleagues electronically. This is an extremely useful learning platform, which allows yourself as a trainee to review your progress across your training and monitor your development as a trainee teacher. Using PebblePad, I was able to reflect upon my training and highlight areas I would like to continue to develop. This has effectively informed my teaching and training practice.
>
> Both formative and summative assessment tracked progress. Durham University uses 'milestones' linked to the CCF/ITTECF. There are five milestones on which trainee will be asessed. Trainees must achieve each milestone before progressing onto the next. However, it is important that trainees continue to meet each milestone throughout their training. The progress and development were incremental, allowing me to gradually gain confidence and expertise over time. Milestones are easily accessible and understandable. This allows all trainees to have a good understanding of what is expected of them, timeframes and how they will effectively complete their training, leading to a recommendation of QTS.

## OBSERVATIONS

As noted in Lucie's case study, teacher training programmes place a significant emphasis on observation.

As part of your teacher training, you will have the opportunity to observe expert colleagues, watch and learn from your peers, reflect on learning from the pupil perspective and also be monitored as part of the ongoing assessment of your development. Understanding the significance and importance of these observations and how to make them both effective and constructive is critical (O'Leary, 2020).

- *Observing in the classroom*: As a trainee teacher you may ask yourself, 'What am I supposed to be looking for?' when observing in the classroom; it is essential to clearly understand the purpose of all observations and the key aspects to focus on. Seeing what happens in the classroom makes self-reflection, mentoring and sharing practice more effective.
- *Initial exposure*: Early observations serve as a way to acclimatise to the classroom environment, helping you to begin to understand the daily routine

of the classroom and the types of activities pupils engage with in different subjects.

- *Observing expert colleagues*: Experienced teachers' teaching is often so accomplished as to look easy; the skill which might not easily be seen lies in the expert decision-making. Observing expert teachers in the classroom provides opportunities to witness and interpret elements of effective teaching practice employed such as:
    - sound subject/curriculum knowledge and pedagogy
    - classroom and behaviour management techniques
    - teaching strategies – such as questioning, modelling and scaffolding
    - adaptive and inclusive teaching
    - learning activities and resources
    - assessment policy – formative and summative
    - interactions between colleagues and pupils
    - pupil engagement, communication and responses.
- *Identifying knowledge gaps*: Observing others can reveal aspects of teaching you may not fully understand. For instance, you may observe the teacher stopping regularly to conduct a mini plenary and ponder the rationale for this. By reflecting on and engaging in conversations with the expert teacher you can explore how these episodes are a way to encourage the class to evaluate their learning as they go and a tool for the teacher to assess informally during the lesson.
- *Defining your teaching style*: Witnessing different teaching styles and approaches allows you to reflect on the kind of teacher you want to become. Each teacher is unique, and their individuality influences their teaching persona. By observing the approaches of others, you can consider which qualities align with your character, principles and capabilities and which you want to incorporate into your own teaching practice.
- *Tracking individual learners*: Observing the learning journey of individual pupils or small groups can be very enlightening and a way to consider the impact of teaching on the learning taking place. These observations give opportunities to examine how pupils interact with learning activities, respond to questioning and have their needs addressed. Conversations with teachers on aims and objectives and a review of the work produced by individuals will support your evaluation of the learning experience observed.

- *Guided observations*: Over the course of your ITT programme, and on ITaP, aspects of teaching may be considered in detail and intense focus given to specific pivotal areas. Critical analysis and observation of key aspects is an integral element of the model; observing behaviour management, for example, will highlight and provide insight on differing approaches to establishing teacher presence/identity, positive ethos, rewards and sanctions, strategies to promote positive behaviour and the importance of positive relationships in the classroom.

- *Lesson observations and feedback*: Throughout your ITT programme and beyond, assessment and lesson observations will form an important element of your training linked to the evaluation and monitoring process. Lesson observations are powerful tools for development when well done. In most cases this will involve you being observed by an expert colleague in their role as a mentor. Discussion and feedback should highlight specific goals/targets to work on to improve your practice and knowledge – in other words, to show you where you are, where you are heading and how to get there. When feedback is seen as supportive it can also have real benefits for teachers, giving them agency and control over their professional development and satisfaction and engagement in the process (Coe, 1998). However, lessons don't always go to plan. So, be patient with yourself, learn from your experiences and keep striving to be the best teacher you can.

### REFLECTIVE QUESTIONS

Questions to ask yourself after observing a lesson and/or following a formal lesson observation.

- Did learning take place? Did every pupil make progress?
- Evaluate the classroom environment – did it feel purposeful and well managed?
- How do you and the teacher know that the lesson content and teaching was effective?
- How was the learning assessed?

## PROGRESS TRACKING AND MONITORING

The structure of each ITT programme is different. Combining centre-based taught sessions, self-study and school-based practice and placements, programmes are designed to provide trainee teachers with the developmental knowledge and skills required to evolve classroom practice. Through demonstrating progress and meeting the expectations within the curriculum, trainees are expected to have met all aspects of the *Teachers' Standards* by the end of final placement.

Although models differ, all are designed to support trainee development through an incremental, structured approach that builds upon understanding and skill, that sees assessment at regular intervals to ensure progression is evidenced.

Formative feedback on your progress towards gaining the knowledge and skills and applying this to practice is provided through:

- *Evaluation reviews and reflection points*: These reviews are a tool for regular dialogue between trainee and mentor. Focused on self-reflection and achievement, the written records are a useful way of identifying and recording next steps for professional learning. Further discussions may centre on, for example, reviewing school experience files, lesson planning, assessment/record keeping and subject knowledge development.

- *Seminars*: Regular feedback within centre-based subject and school-based seminars aims to ensure curriculum knowledge and skills develop.

- *Electronic record of professional development*: These online e-portfolios/platforms – for example, PebblePad as noted in the case study – are used to monitor, track and record your progress. A professional record accessed by mentors, tutors, school-based and centre-based colleagues provides additional means to enhance learning and offer feedback.

## CONCLUSION

This chapter, about *learning in context*, has explored how to better understand, transfer and apply knowledge to the classroom. It considered how learning to be a great teacher involves building upon skills to ensure secure subject knowledge and a deep understanding of how to deliver the content. Quality teaching should be defined by its impact: a great teacher is one whose pupils learn more and improves outcomes for all. You discovered how the first step to developing was to ascertain what you know and what you don't. The benefit of conducting learning audits was explored and a range of supportive practices highlighted to aid and inform. You reviewed how observation and feedback adds another element to the learning process and considered how progress on school-based practice is evidenced and measured on ITT programmes.

> ### REVIEW OF CHAPTER OBJECTIVES
>
> Within this chapter you have:
>
> - learned about the importance of secure knowledge and understanding to ensure good teaching and learning;
> - considered strategies and methods to develop your knowledge and understanding;
> - considered how progress on school-based practice is evidenced and measured on ITT programmes;
> - learned how observation and feedback are critical to the development of teachers.

## FURTHER READING AND RESOURCES

Creemers, B. P. M. and Kyriakides, L. (2006) Critical analysis of the current approaches to modelling educational effectiveness: The importance of establishing a dynamic model. *School Effectiveness and School Improvement*, 17, pp. 347–366.

Guidance from the National Education Union (NEU):

http://neu.org.uk/advice/social-media-and-online-safety

Traditional and progressive approaches to teaching:

https://teacherhead.com/2014/03/15/the-progressive-traditional-pedagogy-tree/

## REFERENCES

Ball, D. L., Thames, M. H. and Phelps, G. (2008) Content knowledge for teachers: What makes it so special? *Journal of Teacher Education*, 59, p. 389. doi:10.1177/0022487108324554.

Bronfenbrenner, U. (2004) Ecological systems theory (1992), in U. Bronfenbrenner (ed.), *Making Human Beings Human: Bioecological Perspectives on Human Development*. London: Sage, pp. 106–173.

Castles, A., Rastle, K. and Nation, K. (2018) Ending the reading wars: Reading acquisition from novice to expert. *Psychological Science in the Public Interest*, 19(1), pp. 5–51. doi: 10.1177/1529100618772271.

Coe, R. (1998) Can feedback improve teaching? A review of the social science literature with a view to identifying the conditions under which giving feedback to teachers will result in improved performance. *Research Papers in Education*, 13(1), pp. 43–66. doi: 10.1080/0267152980130104.

Coe, R., Aloisi, C., Higgins, S. and Major, L. E. (2014) *What Makes Great Teaching? Review of the Underpinning Research*. Durham University. Available at: https://durham-repository.worktribe.com/output/1607293/what-makes-great-teaching-review-of-the-underpinning-research [accessed 20 December 2023].

Department for Education (DfE) (2022) *Initial Teacher Training (ITT) Provider Guidance on Stage 2*. Available at: https://assets.publishing.service.gov.uk/government/uploads/system/uploads/attachment_data/file/1119026/ITT_Provider_Guidance_Stage_2.pdf [accessed 19 December 2023].

DfE (2023) *Initial Teacher Training (ITT): Criteria and Supporting Advice*. Available at: https://assets.publishing.service.gov.uk/media/64ef61b813ae15000d6e30c1/Initial_teacher_training_criteria_and_supporting_advice_2024_to_2025.pdf [accessed 20 December 2023].

O'Leary, M. (2020) *Classroom Observation: A Guide to the Effective Observation of Teaching and Learning* (2nd ed.). London: Routledge. doi: 10.4324/9781315630243.

Rosenshine, B. (2012) Principles of instruction: Research-based strategies that all teachers should know. *American Educator*, 12–20. doi: 10.1111/j.1467-8535.2005.0057.x.

# 5

# YOUR WELLBEING AND SELF-CARE

## JO SMITH

**Learn that and Learn how to –
The Knowledge and Application Model**

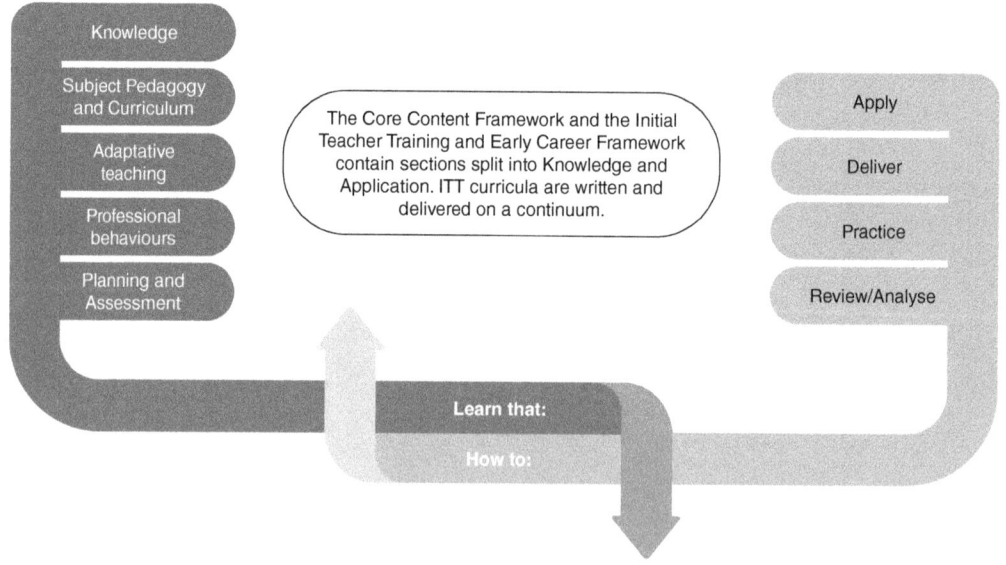

## FRAMED BY THE CCF – FOR FULL LINKS TO THE ITTECF, SEE PAGE 337

**High Expectations**

(Standard 1 – 'Set high expectations')

| Learn that … | Learn how to … |
| --- | --- |
| 2. Teachers are key role models, who can influence the attitudes, values and behaviours of their pupils. | Demonstrate consistently high behavioural expectations, by:<br><br>• Receiving clear, consistent and effective mentoring in how to create a culture of respect and trust in the classroom that supports all pupils to succeed (e.g. by modelling the types of courteous behaviour expected of pupils).<br><br>And – following expert input – by taking opportunities to practise, receive feedback and improve at:<br><br>• Creating a positive environment where making mistakes and learning from them and the need for effort and perseverance are part of the daily routine. |

**Managing Behaviour**

(Standard 7 – 'Manage behaviour effectively')

| Learn that … | Learn how to … |
| --- | --- |
| 3. The ability to self-regulate one's emotions affects pupils' ability to learn, success in school and future lives. | Develop a positive, predictable and safe environment for pupils, by:<br><br>• Receiving clear, consistent and effective mentoring in how to respond quickly to any behaviour or bullying that threatens emotional safety. |

**Professional Behaviours**

(Standard 8 – 'Fulfil wider professional responsibilities')

| Learn that … | Learn how to … |
| --- | --- |
| 1. Effective professional development is likely to be sustained over time, involve expert support or coaching and opportunities for collaboration. | Manage workload and wellbeing, by:<br><br>• Observing how expert colleagues use and personalise systems and routines to support efficient time and task management and deconstructing this approach.<br><br>• Discussing and analysing with expert colleagues the importance of the right to support (e.g. to deal with misbehaviour).<br><br>• Protecting time for rest and recovery and being aware of the sources of support available to support good mental wellbeing. |

*(Continued)*

| Professional Behaviours | |
|---|---|
| (Standard 8 – 'Fulfil wider professional responsibilities') | |
| Learn that … | Learn how to … |
| | And – following expert input – by taking opportunities to practise, receive feedback and improve at: <br><br>• Seeking challenge, feedback and critique from mentors and other colleagues in an open and trusting working environment. <br><br>• Reflecting on progress made, recognising strengths and weaknesses and identifying next steps for further improvement. <br><br>• Collaborating with colleagues to share the load of planning and preparation and making use of shared resources (e.g. textbooks). |

## CHAPTER OBJECTIVES

On reading this chapter you will consider:

- wellbeing, resilience and the culture of teaching;
- what it means to be well;
- resting, recovery and work-life balance;
- time management;
- self-help and external sources of help.

## KEY VOCABULARY

Initial teacher training (ITT)

Initial Teacher Training and Early Career Framework (ITTECF)

*Core Content Framework* (CCF)

Curriculum learning centres (CLCs)

School-based learning centres (SBLCs)

Expert colleagues

Expert mentors

Early career teacher (ECT)

General practitioner (your doctor) (GP)

# INTRODUCTION

Whether you are reading this book in readiness for your ITT course, or dipping in to access support, working through the activities will provide you with the tools you need to help keep you safe and well. The advice applies no matter what stage of your teaching career you are at.

Teachers are told they need to be resilient to thrive, but many find this an elusive quality. Resilience can be improved by having the tools, techniques and resources to hand when needed and by having a positive outlook on life, learning to celebrate achievement. You will be introduced to reflective journalling, explore what being well means for you and become mindful of your health so that you can take appropriate and timely action using one of the self-help strategies taken from a first aid toolkit that you will create.

For good mental and physical health, we need to eat well, exercise and be sufficiently rested, but these are often the first things sacrificed in a busy life. In this chapter we will explore techniques to free up time and learn how to balance our work and personal lives.

Most people choose to become teachers because they want to make a difference in children's lives and, with plentiful altruistic rewards, teaching is a joy. Learning new professional skills while undertaking an academic course and trying to satisfy national standards can be difficult at times. You will have the opportunity to compile a bespoke set of contacts, crewing your support lifeboat should you ever need to reach out; you will also find an emergency contacts list at the end of this chapter.

Be mindful of anxiety in others. Gently probe a peer who tells you that they are fine, especially if you can see they are not. It is the sign of a good friend and colleague. Ask for help when you need it. It demonstrates resilience, strength and commitment, not weakness. Sometimes, just talking can help worries shrink and even evaporate, like magic.

# WELLBEING, RESILIENCE AND THE CULTURE OF TEACHING

> **REFLECTIVE QUESTIONS**
>
> - What is driving you to train as a teacher?
> - What are you most looking forward to?
> - Where do you see yourself in five years?

Teachers often want to make a societal difference or share their subject love, but school environments and an education system influenced by national policy are not always conducive to good mental or physical health. Having a growth mindset (Dweck, 2008) and choosing to react positively to external stressors can minimise the impact on wellbeing. Research shows examining situations through a positive lens builds resilience (Yeager and Dweck, 2020), but that is not always easy to do.

> **ACTION LEARNING SET**
>
> Reflecting and actioning improvement can aid resilience building. If you have not already done so, start journalling or use a diary or planner to record your thoughts and plan in future tasks and activities. You can find out more about journalling in Chapter 2.
>
> Write a letter to yourself in the future, sharing your motivations for teaching and any hurdles that you have already overcome. Try to identify to your future self what excites you most, what your aspirations are and consider what success looks like for you. Remind yourself: you are expecting this to be hard work, but others have managed successfully; to build on your strengths and reflect positively on what you can do to improve; to pause and do things you enjoy too - we forget when we are busy; that it is okay to ask for help.
>
> It is recommended that this is written when you are in a positive frame of mind about teaching. Place the letter in an envelope to retrieve later, should you need it.
>
> You could add your letter into the back of your reflective journal.

If you have a difficult lesson (and every teacher does), read your letter. It may have been uncomfortable to write, but it could be just the tonic you need to pick yourself up and brush yourself down. Even as an ECT or established teacher, it could provide a free boost of positivity.

Formal and informal observations often focus on improvement and can therefore seem negative in nature. Reflect on your actions and ask yourself (and your observer if you feel comfortable in doing so) what went well. Record this in your journal.

Reflecting on teaching positives alongside areas for development is an excellent habit to develop. Continually striving for perfection can lead to burnout. If you met your target to improve questioning techniques, but in doing so forgot to give out homework, don't worry. Give it out next lesson. Teaching involves juggling many roles, actions and emotions simultaneously. As these become instinct and routine, the art of teaching becomes more natural. As an ITT trainee, you are practising. Own, embrace and model how to deal with mistakes. It is difficult to make progress without them.

> **EVIDENCE-INFORMED RESEARCH: SELF-EFFICACY, WELLBEING AND CONTROL**
>
> Good personal and professional relationships are important in teaching. Get to know your pupils by name as soon as possible. You matter, as do your pupils – even the tricky customers. Be genuine, curious and a good listener to create an emotionally positive classroom.
>
> *Every Child Matters* puts pupil wellbeing at the heart of teaching, but every teacher matters too (DfES, 2004; Lovewell, 2012). Wellbeing encompasses more than taking good care of yourself and being happy. Good wellbeing enables you to fulfil your teaching potential. Imagine a world full of flourishing teachers. What that would mean for their pupils?
>
> Last century, Bandura (1977) discussed that teachers who believed in themselves, those with a high self-efficacy for teaching, were more likely to be successful. Since then, research into wellbeing detractors has popped up like field daisies (Zee and Koomen, 2016). In 2017, Helliwell et al. identified a good work-life balance as having the largest positive influence on teacher wellbeing.
>
> Teachers, working 50-hour weeks (56 in Wales), are more at risk of strokes and heart disease (DfE, 2023). When research shows what a huge difference teachers make to young people, gaining life balance for diligent and committed teachers can prove difficult. You are a long time at work once qualified, so it is worth finding a school which is a good match for you, one where your voice can be heard and you feel a sense of belonging and autonomy. This will offer you the freedom to create an emotionally positive classroom (Bethune and Kell, 2021) where cared-for and encouraged children can express themselves appropriately (Smith, 2017), having a positive effect on your own wellbeing.

## WHAT IT MEANS TO BE WELL

> **REFLECTIVE QUESTIONS**
>
> - What people, hobbies or interests help contribute to your wellbeing?
> - Do you recognise your early warning signs for a deteriorating physical or mental health?

To relax, you may like to read, cook, sing, talk to your plants, or climb mountains. It doesn't matter what you do (within the bounds of time and legality), but don't give up everything you love in the pursuit of teaching perfection. Learn how to balance work and home to the benefit of your wellbeing.

A note of warning: overdoing activities may indicate illness. For example, having a glass of wine with friends may be a stress relief, but drinking two bottles while lesson planning is not considered to be healthy.

As no two days are the same and you get to shape the lives of children, teaching is an amazingly rewarding vocation, but responsibility and high-stakes scrutiny can take their toll if you do not have enough resilience. Teachers are more than educators, sometimes giving their all for the benefit of their pupils, but this is unsustainable in the long term. Invisibly reaching into small hearts to make a difference is emotionally intense. To satisfy the CCF/ITTECF, you need to demonstrate how to regulate your emotions, modelling how not to spin out of control. You may have to forget your awful morning at home for the sake of your class's wellbeing, acting as a shock absorber for an often-overwhelmed system (Hochschild, 1983). Remaining in an enhanced state of emotional awareness can be exhausting.

You (teachers) are amazing, but you need to look after yourself. You cannot pour from an empty cup. The next activity is to identify your early warning signs of ill health and explore your stress-busting activities. Counterintuitively, even at your busiest, a 20-minute brisk walk can help you refocus and work more effectively when you return.

> **ACTION LEARNING SET**
>
> Draw a gingerbread person's circular head with a smile.
>
> On the outside jot down your early warning stress signals. Examples might include drinking more alcohol, developing cold sores, not sleeping well, comfort eating, a shorter than usual concentration span. You can always add to this later as things come to mind.
>
> Inside the stress head, note activities that help you relax and that you look forward to doing. Examples might be walking the dog, reading a book, playing the tuba in the brass band ... Be as creative as you like and use colours or symbols to group them. You could highlight quick, easy wins by underlining them, or put a star next to ones you cannot live without.

One of your stress-busting activities might have been to travel around the world, and this may need to wait for the holidays, but plan some time into every day to do a little bit of what you love, guilt-free. You are satisfying the CCF/ITTECF and feeding your mental health and wellbeing.

Being aware of your stress triggers and early warning signs allows you to nip potential problems in the bud, aiding resilience. Stress in any job is unavoidable, but knowing when to act and what to do, develops excellent self-care and a positive mindset.

# CASE STUDY: REGAINING CONTROL

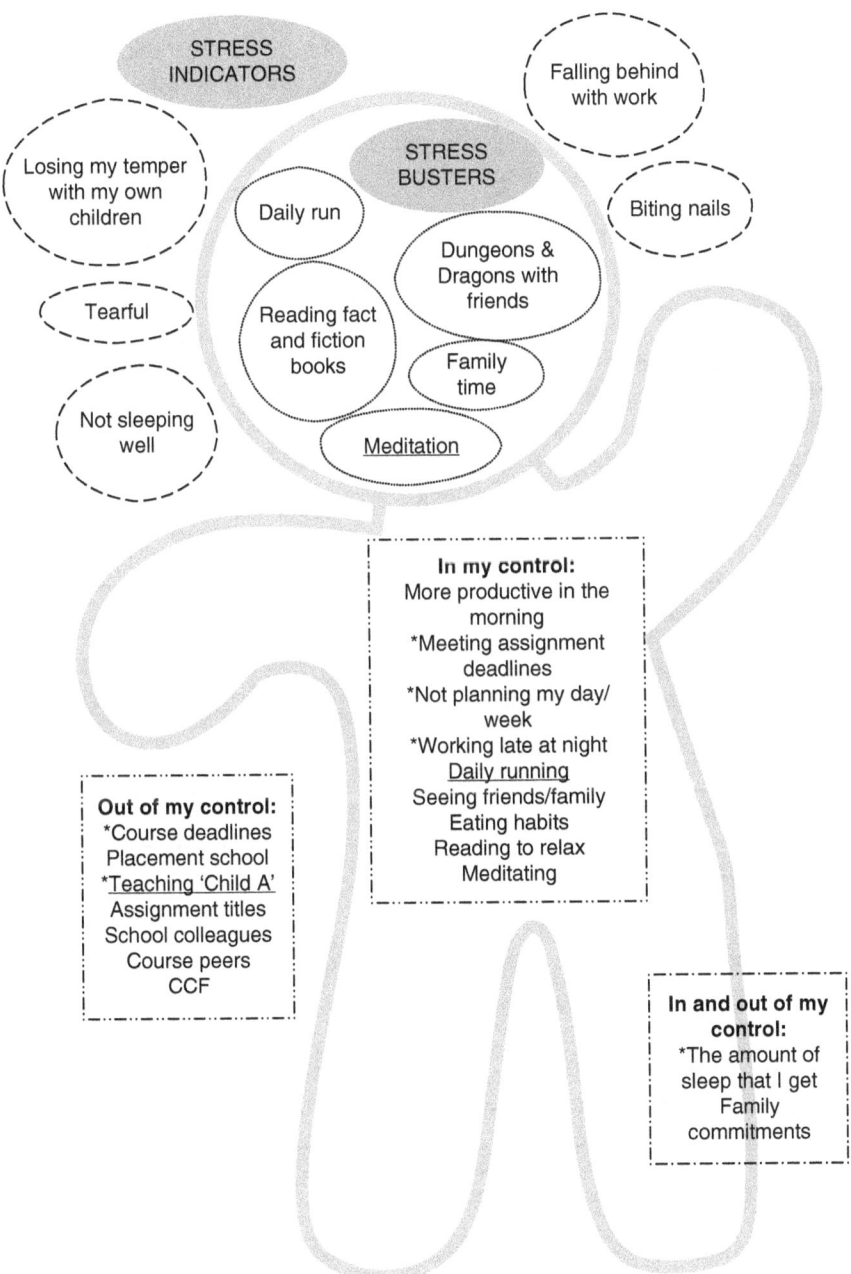

Figure 5.1 Matty's gingerbread stress head and body of control

*(Continued)*

(Continued)

Matty (a pseudonym) drew a gingerbread stress head and shared it with their course mentor as they felt they needed some support. The training course was negatively impacting on their wellbeing.

Matty was asked to draw the accompanying body of a gingerbread person, with those items inside Matty's control being placed inside the body, and those outside Matty's control, placed externally. Some straddled across both Matty's sphere of influence and external control factors. Issues causing the most anxiety were starred and those taking up large amounts of Matty's time underlined.

Following a discussion with their mentor, Matty agreed that focusing on items within their control was a more productive use of time. Matty decided to use their planner, getting up early and going to bed early to make use of their more productive morning time. Matty cut back on their daily run at pinch points in the course, recognising that work-life balance includes making room for academic work. This created more family time, impacting positively on both Matty's wellbeing and that of their young children. Matty felt issues around teaching child A were outside their control, but when they were reassured that reaching out for help was not considered failing, agreed to gather ideas and strategies from the class teacher.

## REFLECTIVE QUESTIONS

Consider the completed gingerbread diagram in Figure 5.1.

If this had been drawn by one of your peers, what advice might you have for them?

## ACTION LEARNING SET

Draw a gingerbread person with areas that you can influence contained within the body.

Jot items outside of your control external to the body, noting who can help if possible.

Add any that straddle both areas.

Reflect, and focus your action where you can make a difference.

## EVIDENCE-INFORMED RESEARCH: DEALING WITH STRESS

In the 1970s, burnout from unrelenting stress was common among professionals such as teachers, who sacrifice some of themselves for the benefit of their pupils (Freudenberger,

1974). Though little has changed in this regard, we now know that teachers need resilience to adapt and overcome adversity, with purpose, positivity in relationships and passion for teaching identified as key (Shields and Mullen, 2020). Those teachers displaying high emotional intelligence calmly take control of difficult situations and are less susceptible to burnout (Corcoran and Tormey, 2012; Greer and Hollis, 2020).

Not all stress is bad. The *eustress* (positive stress) of a pounding heart before teaching increases blood flow, improving confidence and performance. Research indicates that reframing stress positively can reduce the risk of premature death by a staggering 43 per cent (Quigley, 2016; Keller et al., 2012; Holmes, 2018), but first we need to recognise when we are under stress. This can be difficult when we are unwell. HALT and ask yourself whether you are Hungry, Angry, Lonely or Tired as there may be an easy fix for any of these, but they can also be early stress indicators (Quigley, 2016).

Once identified, if stress cannot be reframed in a more positive light, it should not be ignored. Self-help strategies such as controlled breathing can offer relief within seconds.

1. Stop.
2. Breathe in for the count of four.
3. Breathe out for the count of six.
4. Repeat.

Breathing techniques can be employed secretly while teaching or getting feedback to bring calm, help regain control and break the vicious cycle of anxiety. The heart rate lowers, calming the brain, even helping you sleep (Mosley, 2023).

# RESTING, RECOVERY AND WORK–LIFE BALANCE

Teachers often work tirelessly and selflessly in the pursuit of pupil learning and pupil wellbeing. To meet the CCF/ITTECF criteria, you need to protect your rest and recovery time too.

Do you recognise your stress behaviour? Look out for:

1. *excessive tiredness*: frustration, mood swings, lack of concentration, fatigue, headaches;
2. *job detachment*: cynicism, pessimism, avoiding contact with colleagues, no love of the job;
3. *performance drop*: feeling negative, low self-confidence, wasting time, apathy;
4. *personal life*: sickness, lack of sleep, no exercise, poor social/private life, reduced empathy.

> **ACTION LEARNING SET**
>
> Write down a few reflections every day (little and often is most beneficial).
>
> Be mindful of any early signs of stress and highlight them.
>
> Acknowledge negative feelings and try to reframe them in a positive light.
>
> Identify actions to take (see following self-care and time management ideas).
>
> Reflect on the positive elements of your day.

Being aware of your emotions enables you to take timely action. It is okay to say no if you are busy, and reaching out for help is a sign of self-awareness and strength. Improving diet, exercise and sleep regimes may help combat stress.

- *Diet*: Cut back on sugary foods, and plan in regular (healthy) meals. You could take fruit and nuts with you as snacks to replace crisps or chocolate, for example.

- *Exercise*: Continue with any current exercise regimes that you enjoy if time permits. If you do not currently exercise, start small and check with your GP if you have any underlying health issues. Look for a gap in your day. Perhaps peers, colleagues, or pupils (a school club) will join you on a weekly lunchtime walk.

- *Sleep*: Healthy eating and regular exercise can help with sleep but relaxation techniques and introducing bedtime and morning routines may be of additional benefit. Reflect on your evening habits and make any necessary adjustments to wind down before you attempt to sleep.

Remember to do a little of what you love and ensure your work and home life are balanced appropriately. This may need you to reconsider what you can manage to accomplish in the time you have available. Remember your training course may be intensive, but it is not forever.

# TIME MANAGEMENT

As a trainee teacher, juggling life with academic and teaching commitments can be challenging. Doing more does not always mean achieving more if we become overburdened and anxious. If you bounce from activity to activity, accomplishing little, reflect on your time management:

- aim to limit individual lesson planning time to 30 minutes;
- after teaching, make brief notes for the following lesson, while it is fresh in your memory;
- use free time at school wisely; making friends with other members of staff is valuable, but getting a set of books marked may be more beneficial;
- organise work and resources as you go; a 'pile to file' quickly grows beyond control;
- magpie ideas from books, colleagues and websites; teaching is a well-trodden path.

### ACTION LEARNING SET

The 1906 Pareto Principle states that tackling 20 per cent of a 'to-do' list contributes to 80 per cent of the output.

- Make a list in your journal of five urgent and important work-related tasks.
- Action the task that will make the biggest impact on your work.
- Set a dedicated amount of uninterrupted time to focus on this top task.
- If the task is too large, break it into smaller, manageable chunks and apply the Pareto Principle again.
- Repeat for the next task on your list to avoid procrastination (resist cherry picking easy, less impactful tasks – they still eat into valuable time).
- Repeat until you run out of your allotted time.
- Schedule your next task into your diary.
- Cross out any tasks that you do not need to do. Be ruthless.

Do not forget to schedule in non-work goals and activities too. Finish marking early to have dinner with your family, or schedule time off on Sunday morning to lay in bed with coffee. Making space for mindfulness, meditation, or yoga is not wasted time. Exercise. Telephone a friend. Separate work from home if you can, even if that means placing a cover over your work corner when you are done. Take time to reflect. No matter how hard you work, and how much you do, with teaching there will always be more. Decide when enough is enough and stop.

> **CASE STUDY: HARRI**
>
> Harri (a pseudonym) is in the final year of a three-year BA Undergraduate Honours degree in Primary Education, with assignments including a double credit dissertation still to submit and a final school placement to complete. The first two years have been a struggle, but academic grades are high and the end is in sight. Having recently split from their partner, Harri has household debts and rent that can no longer be covered. Petrol costs mean attendance at lectures becomes sporadic and leaving the course feels like the only remaining option. All Harri's peers seem to be working hard and doing well. Unsurprisingly, Harri's mental health deteriorates.
>
> One term into year three, Harri receives an attendance warning, triggering a support meeting with the wellbeing team and course directors. Extensions to deadlines alleviate some stress, but expert help is required. Harri links into university systems and engages with mental health counselling and a financial advisor. It takes time, but, determined to continue, Harri finds cheaper accommodation to rent and attends regular support meetings. Harri completes the course with honours and a strong QTS record, albeit later in the following academic year.

Not all cases will be as complicated as Harri's; everyone's journey through life is different. The resilience and willingness to reach out for and respond positively to offered help was key to their success and stands them up well for their ECT journey. All providers have systems and processes to help.

It is rarely beneficial to compare yourself to peers. They may appear serene and swanlike, but you have no idea how hard they are paddling underneath and the support mechanisms on which they are relying.

Building resilience and managing time efficiently can help but, where self-help is insufficient, reach out. Emergency contact details are in the Further reading section.

# SELF-HELP AND EXTERNAL SOURCES OF HELP

> **REFLECTIVE QUESTIONS**
>
> Who would you approach for help with:
>
> - proofreading an assignment;
> - a physical health-related issue;

- a mental health-related issue;
- an academic aspect of your ITT course;
- the placement aspect of your ITT course?

Who we approach for help depends on the problem(s) that we face. When academic work piles up, you may seek out a tutor at your curriculum learning centre. If you are struggling to manage a pupil's behaviour, your mentor or class teacher in school may be your best source of support. SEND support should be available through your provider. Your GP provides both physical and mental health support. Ensure that you have registered with a GP for term-time if you have moved away from home.

### ACTION LEARNING SET

Complete the table with contact numbers. Some numbers may require an internet search, such as your local NHS mental health line.

Place a copy into the back of your journal and another in a key place, ready to use should you ever need it.

*Table 5.1 Important contact information*

| Name | Contact | Comment |
| --- | --- | --- |
| GP (name if known) Dentist (if you have one) | | Your local GP is usually a first point for non-emergencies |
| NHS mental health line | | A local number (look it up on internet) |
| Local A&E department | | Look up yours |
| Academic contacts | | List who to contact if you:<br>- are ill<br>- require an assignment extension<br>- have questions about a particular aspect of the course |
| Placement contacts | | List who to contact if you:<br>- are absent through illness<br>- need help with classroom teaching<br>- need general placement help |

*(Continued)*

*Table 5.1 (Continued)*

| Name | Contact | Comment |
|---|---|---|
| Peers | | Collect contact details (if they are willing to share) and try to develop a peer-support network |
| Friends and family | | Have their numbers to hand in case you or a flat mate should ever need them |
| Other | | You may have specialist help for several reasons or want the number for a local taxi firm or your favourite treat take-away |

This is not a fully exhaustive list. Edit and add to it, tailoring it to you. The time and effort taken now will be worth every second should you ever need to locate someone in an emergency.

# CONCLUSION

This chapter identified why wellbeing is important and where it sits within the CCF/ITTECF'. By working through the activities, you have been introduced to the benefits of journalling and created a personalised pep talk in the form of a letter addressed to the future you. You have gained insight into what you can and cannot control and know who to approach for help in a variety of situations. You have explored what makes you happy and identified your stress triggers and indicators. You have been advised to reframe stress positively to increase your resilience and your wellbeing and reassured that a little stress can be good for you, increasing blood flow and performance. Careful planning and time management are key to ensuring a good work–life balance and a high level of wellbeing.

While most issues can be solved through self-help, or approaching family and friends, it is okay to reach out externally for help too if needed. Most importantly, take the time to enjoy your journey to being the best teacher you can be and look after yourself.

## REVIEW OF CHAPTER OBJECTIVES

Within this chapter you have considered:

- wellbeing, resilience and the culture of teaching;
- what it means to be well;
- resting, recovery and work–life balance;
- time management;
- self-help and external sources of help.

# FURTHER READING AND RESOURCES

If you are ever in crisis and need urgent support, the following contacts may be of use to you:

| Service | Contact | Comment |
| --- | --- | --- |
| NHS | 111<br>www.nhs.uk<br>www.nhs.uk/service-search/mental-health | In a non-emergency, if the GP surgery closed Offer help if you are stressed, anxious, or depressed. Will answer your mental health questions and find you support locally |
| Emergency services | 999 | 24/7 Use in the event of an emergency |
| Education support | 0800 562561 www.educationsupport.org.uk | 24/7 confidential helpline specifically for school and college staff<br>Resources to help with wellbeing |
| Samaritans | 116 123<br>www.samaritans.org | 24/7 confidential freephone helpline |
| Mind infoline | Text 86463<br>info@mind.org.uk | Mental health support |

Mosley, M. (2023) How to reset your brain with your breathing. *Just One Thing*. BBC Radio 4. Available at: www.bbc.co.uk/programmes/articles/1mW6885X3N2gKnVjXT00KCj/how-to-reset-your-brain-with-your-breathing [accessed 20 December 2023].

Sage (n.d.) *Teacher Training Survival Toolkit*. Available at: https://us.sagepub.com/en-us/nam/teacher-training-survival-toolkit [accessed 19 December 2023].

# REFERENCES

Bandura, A. (1977) *Self Efficacy: The Exercise of Control*. Belper: Worth.

Bethune, A. and Kell, E. (2021) *A Little Guide for Teachers: Teacher Wellbeing and Self-care*. London: Sage

Corcoran, R. and Tormey, R. (2012) *Developing Emotionally Competent Teachers*. Oxford: Peter Lang.

Department for Education and Skills (DfES) (2004) *Every Child Matters: Change for Children*. London: DfES.

DfE (2019) *ITT Core Content Framework*. London: DfE. Available at: https://assets.publishing.service.gov.uk/government/uploads/system/uploads/attachment_data/file/974307/ITT_core_content_framework_.pdf [accessed November 2023].

DfE (2023) *Working Lives of Teachers and Leaders*. London: DfE. Available at: https://assets.publishing.service.gov.uk/media/642b519efbe620000c17db94/Working_lives_of_teachers_and_leaders_-_wave_1_-_core_report.pdf [accessed 20 December 2023].

Dweck, C. S. (2008) *Mindset*. New York: Ballantine.

Freudenberger, H. J. (1974) Staff burn-out. *Journal of Social Issues*, 30(1), pp. 159–165.

Greer, J. and Hollis, E. (2020) *Workload*. St Albans: Critical.

Helliwell, J., Layard, R. and Sachs, J. (2017) *World Happiness Report 2017*. New York: Sustainable Development Solutions Network.

Hochschild, A. R. (1983) *The Managed Heart*. Berkeley, CA: University of California Press.

Holmes, E. (2018) *A Practical Guide to Teacher Wellbeing* (Ready to Teach). Exeter: Learning Matters.

Keller, A., Litzelman, K., Wisk, L. E., Maddox, T., Cheng, E. R., Creswell, P. D. and Witt, W. P. (2012) Does the perception that stress affects health matter? The association with health and mortality. *Health Psychology*, 31(5), pp. 677–684.

Lovewell, K. (2012) *Every Teacher Matters: Inspiring Well-being through Mindfulness*. Mountain View, CA: Ecademy Press.

Mosely, M. (2023) How to reset your brain with your breathing. *Just One Thing*. BBC Radio 4. Available at: www.bbc.co.uk/programmes/articles/1mW6885X3N2gKnVjXT00KCj/how-to-reset-your-brain-with-your-breathing [accessed 20 December 2023].

Pareto, V. (1906) *Cours d'économie politique*. Lausanne: Rouge.

Quigley, A. (2016) *The Confident Teacher: Developing Successful Habits of Mind, Body and Pedagogy*. London: Routledge

Shields, L. and Mullen, C. (2020) *Veteran Teacher Resilience*. New York: Springer.

Smith, M. (2017) *The Emotional Learner: Understanding Emotions, Learners and Achievement*. London: Routledge.

Yeager, D. S. and Dweck, C. S. (2020) What can be learned from growth mindset controversies? *American Psychologist*, 75(9), pp. 1269–1284. doi: 10.1037/amp0000794.

Zee, M. and Koomen, H. M. (2016) Teacher self-efficacy and its effects on classroom processes, student academic adjustment, and teacher well-being: A synthesis of 40 years of research. *Review of Educational Research*, 86(4), pp. 981–1015. doi: 10.3102/0034654315626801.

# 6

# SAFEGUARDING AND WELLBEING OF PUPILS

## SARAH CUMMINS AND DIANA MANN

**Learn that and Learn how to –
The Knowledge and Application Model**

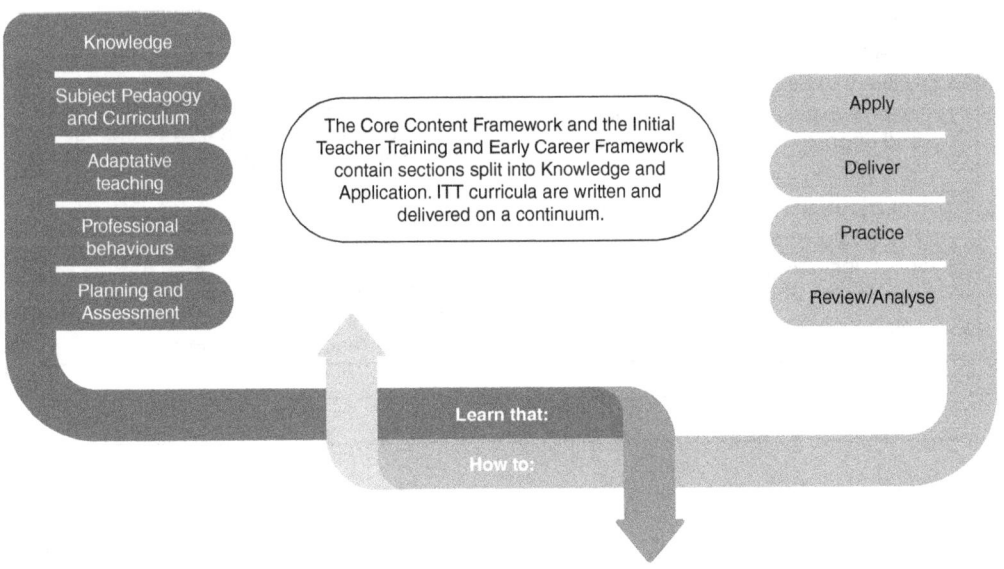

## FRAMED BY THE CCF – FOR FULL LINKS TO THE ITTECF, SEE PAGE 337

| High Expectations | |
|---|---|
| (Standard 1 – 'Set high expectations') | |
| Learn that … | Learn how to … |
| 1. Teachers have the ability to affect and improve the wellbeing, motivation and behaviour of their pupils.<br>2. Teachers are key role models, who can influence the attitudes, values and behaviours of their pupils.<br>6. High-quality teaching has a long-term positive effect on pupils' life chances, particularly for children from disadvantaged backgrounds. | Communicate a belief in the academic potential of all pupils … – following expert input – by taking opportunities to practise, receive feedback and improve at:<br><br>• Seeking opportunities to engage parents and carers in the education of their children (e.g. proactively highlighting successes) with support from expert colleagues to understand how this engagement changes depending on the age and development stage of the pupil. |
| Professional Behaviours | |
| (Standard 8 – 'Fulfil wider professional responsibilities') | |
| Learn that … | Learn how to … |
| 1. Effective professional development is likely to be sustained over time, involve expert support or coaching and opportunities for collaboration.<br>3. Teachers can make valuable contributions to the wider life of the school in a broad range of ways, including by supporting and developing effective professional relationships with colleagues. | Develop as a professional, by:<br><br>• Receiving clear, consistent and effective mentoring in how to engage in professional development with clear intentions for impact on pupil outcomes, sustained over time with built-in opportunities for practice.<br>• Receiving clear, consistent and effective mentoring on the duties relating to Part 2 of the Teachers' Standards. |

## CHAPTER OBJECTIVES

On reading this chapter you will consider:

- what is meant by *safeguarding* and *wellbeing*, as well as highlight the challenges around these terms;
- understand the terms 'safeguarding' and 'child protection';
- understand your role and responsibilities in relation to safeguarding young children;
- the importance of an awareness of current legislation in safeguarding children;

- how to support pupil wellbeing;
- understand that promoting safe environments and opportunities for teacher and student to grow emotionally and mentally will benefit the whole community.

### KEY VOCABULARY

Safeguarding

Child protection

Designated safeguarding lead/officer

Emotional and physical safety

Resilience

# INTRODUCTION

Ensuring the safety, security and wellbeing of pupils and educators is of paramount importance in any educational setting. This chapter addresses the comprehensive approach that primary schools must adopt to safeguard their pupils and educators, creating an environment conducive to learning, growth and development. Prioritising safeguarding and promoting wellbeing within your environment will not only foster a positive and nurturing community but will also enable pupils and educators to thrive within a secure environment.

The chapter will also review how we create safe and secure environments for all children while protecting the trainee's own self and sense of wellbeing throughout the training and early career.

Throughout this chapter you will read extracts and reflections from a trainee across their training year. They review their understanding of safeguarding, procedure and the impact of wellbeing on the children and, at times, themselves. The accounts are interwoven throughout the material as the trainee themselves develops a deeper understanding of what safeguarding involves in school and the importance of recognising the impact of this on all involved.

# HOW DO WE DEFINE SAFEGUARDING?

The definition of safeguarding and promoting the health and wellbeing of children, which we can take from *Working Together to Safeguard Children* (DfE, 2023b, p. 8) is as follows:

- 'protecting children from maltreatment, whether that is within or outside the home, including online
- preventing impairment of children's mental and physical health or development
- ensuring that children grow up in circumstances consistent with the provision of safe and effective care …
- taking action to enable all children to have the best outcomes'.

Achieving all these responsibilities goes beyond the role of the individual teacher or trainee teacher. School staff, practitioners and outside agencies must work effectively together, in partnership with the family, to meet the needs of the child.

## WHAT DOES SAFEGUARDING INCLUDE?

On your journey towards becoming a fully qualified teacher, you will learn many things. These will enable you to teach the children in your care a range of knowledge, skills and understanding which they can utilise in their education and life beyond. There are only a small number of aspects of your training, however, which might help to save a child's life or protect them from harm. This means that having a deep comprehension of safeguarding is crucially important for all school staff, including new and trainee teachers.

Although there has been legislation related to safeguarding and child protection in place since the first act of parliament for the prevention of cruelty to children – commonly known as the 'Children's Charter', which was passed in 1889 – this did not prevent children suffering harm and losing their lives. More recently, in the period of time following the public inquiry into the high-profile case of Victoria Climbié in 2003, there is the hope that lessons have been learned and a further series of reforms and procedures have been put in place, with the intention of protecting children from harm, which necessarily impact upon you as an early career teacher (ECT).

One of the most important messages which new teachers need to learn and adhere to comes from the 2004 Children's Act and it is repeated in the key guidance *Keeping Children Safe in Education* (DfE, 2023a). This is that 'safeguarding is everyone's responsibility'; from the first moment you go into school you must have an awareness of safeguarding and you become part of the team around the child which aims to keep them safe from harm.

It is important to understand that safeguarding and child protection are not the same thing. Safeguarding includes a whole raft of policies, procedures and activities which promote the health and wellbeing of children. Sometimes it is referred to as an *umbrella term*, meaning that it encompasses a range of different aspects. Child protection is just one part of safeguarding.

Those in education who have daily contact with pupils are well placed to identify and recognise when there's a potential issue. Because of this, it is crucial that you understand your responsibilities and the role you play in safeguarding.

# ROLES AND RESPONSIBILITIES

## THE SCHOOL GOVERNING BODY

School governors have a broad range of responsibilities to ensure that the school and staff are protecting the safety and wellbeing of the pupils in the school community. These include:

- safe recruitment of staff;
- school and site security;
- approving policies and procedures;
- monitoring the implementation of the above;
- evaluation of safeguarding in the school;
- monitoring attendance;
- ensuring that staff training is in place.

## THE DESIGNATED SAFEGUARDING LEAD/OFFICER

This role in school was laid out in the 2004 Children's Act. The Act stated that all schools had to have a *named person* who would be responsible for leading and managing safeguarding within the school. It is generally the case that the designated safeguarding lead (DSL) is a senior member of staff who, because they have received additional training and development, is able to make decisions and shape the policy and procedures with authority.

The responsibilities of the DSL include:

- being an advocate for safeguarding in school;
- being a source of support and advice to staff;
- maintaining detailed records of children where there are concerns or where there is a child protection plan;

- ensuring that all staff have appropriate training and induction in safeguarding;
- making referrals as appropriate, e.g. to social care;
- liaising with the local authority and other services;
- working with outside agencies and other professionals;
- working with the families of children.

The short extract from a trainee's ongoing reflective development record below demonstrates how schools share school policies and key documents, including *Keeping Children Safe in Education* (KCSiE, DfE, 2023a) during induction.

*What a busy start! I have completed my induction; I've signed to say I have read this year's KCSiE and lots of other policies including the Child Protection Policy. There are lots of acronyms I don't fully understand, but I do know how to log a cause for concern. I had a meeting with the DSL, about the children on our school's vulnerable children list. In my class I have one child who is in care or CLA (child looked after), one child who lives with grandparents as part of a Special Guardianship Order (SGO), one who has been on a child protection plan but is now on a child in need plan (CIN) and one where the school has offered an early help plan to the parent, but they've refused, so we have to monitor them. It is all a bit overwhelming.*

Extract from ECT's reflective journal, week 2 in the autumn term

### ACTION LEARNING SET

- From the above extract of the case study, consider what the trainee could do about not understanding all the policies they have read and signed. What would you do? Who would you talk to?
- What support might the trainee need at this stage?

## TEACHERS AND OTHER SCHOOL STAFF

Everybody who works in a school has the responsibility to safeguard the children who attend. It is widely recognised that school staff are ideally placed to notice when a child may be vulnerable to significant harm because of the intensive, daily contact they have with the children in their care and the positive relationships which they build over time. Many children who are suffering abuse may be too afraid to disclose this to an adult, or they may not understand that what is happening to them is not the norm, so it is crucial that school staff are fully aware of possible signs and symptoms of abuse and can respond to any concerns which they have. Teachers must know what actions to take in the event of concerns or of a child making a disclosure to them.

The responsibilities may include:

- creating an environment where children feel safe, valued and listened to;
- ensuring that they have thorough knowledge of policies and procedure;
- being aware of which children may be vulnerable to harm and monitoring their wellbeing or progress;
- recognising when a child may be showing signs or symptoms of abuse;
- recording concerns using the school's system for logging concerns, e.g. the Child Protection Online Management System (CPOMS);
- reporting relevant information in an appropriate way to the DSL in school;
- contributing information to any formal procedures that are in place.

## WHAT DO I DO IF I AM CONCERNED ABOUT A CHILD?

It is important that you are fully conversant with the policies and procedures within your school so that if you are concerned about any child, you know exactly what you must do.

Although children will be taught what to do to keep themselves safe as part of the curriculum, they do not always find it easy to talk about or report abuse, particularly if it is someone they know and possibly love who is their abuser; it is essential that teachers are aware of the types of abuse and the possible indicators that may be of concern.

Harm or abuse is generally defined in four ways:

- *Physical abuse*: Where someone deliberately harms or injures a child, e.g. hitting, kicking, burning or shaking a child. This may include assaulting a child with some kind of implement or weapon.
- *Emotional abuse*: Where someone makes a child feel frightened, unloved, or worthless by shouting at them, taunting them, threatening them, or verbally bullying them. Children who live in a home where there is domestic violence or a violent relationship between their adults may also be vulnerable.

- *Neglect*: Where a child is not in receipt of the care and attention that they need and deserve or are not adequately looked after. This might include not having enough food, not having a healthy diet, not having somewhere safe to sleep, not having the correct medical care, not having a satisfactory level of supervision, e.g. being left alone and vulnerable, or not having correct hygiene or the right clothes for the weather.

- *Sexual abuse*: Where someone pressurises a child to take part in sexual activity. This might be through persuading or forcing a child to look at or take part in sexual activities. It might involve encouraging unwanted touching, exposing a child in watching pornography or forcing a child or young person under the age of consent to have sex. Female genital mutilation (FGM) and child sexual exploitation (CSE) are also considered to be sexual abuse.

Being able to identify the potential signs of abuse is essential to protect the child from further harm. Some indicators may be physical, e.g. bruising, some may be behavioural, or emotional, e.g. angry outburst, sadness or withdrawn behaviour. As a class teacher you need to know your pupils well as individuals. This will enable you to be well placed to spot if their behaviour changes or if they are showing signs of unhappiness, fear or distress.

If you do identify that there are reasons to be concerned, it is critical that you pass on this information as a matter of urgency. Even if you are not completely sure, it is still important that you share any concerns with the DSL in school.

Some schools may require teachers to do this on a cause for concern proforma, other schools will utilise a computer-based recording system such as CPOMS. This allows information on a child to be recorded chronologically, safely stored, monitored and accessed quickly in the event of further concerns or investigations.

You must make sure that you are fully aware of the system being used by your school so that you can act immediately in the event of a concern. The DSL in your school will inform you of the process and procedure.

## WHAT TO DO IF A CHILD MAKES A DISCLOSURE

You must try to remain as calm and reassuring as you can. It is important not to show anger, shock, or distress. It may have taken a great deal of courage for the child to speak, and they should feel that they did the right thing by telling you. Here are some guidelines that might help you in this situation:

- *listen* carefully and without interrupting;

- *do* be supportive and reassure the child that they have done the right thing by telling you;

- *do not* interview the child but do establish enough information for you to take appropriate action and make a meaningful referral;
- *do not* ask lots of questions;
- *do* ask open questions;
- *do not* ask leading questions;
- *do not* promise to keep what they tell you secret;
- *do* accurately record what was said by the child (verbatim) and by you as soon as possible and sign and date it;
- *do* bring it to the immediate attention of the DSL – do not wait until break time. If that person is not available, you should report it to their deputy or to an appropriate member of the school's senior leadership team. In the unlikely event that no-one is available you may need to report directly to the police or to the local education authority safeguarding team;
- if in doubt seek advice.

### REFLECTIVE QUESTIONS

- What can you say to be supportive and reassuring to the child who makes a disclosure?
- Why is it important that you only ask open questions, not leading questions, and why do you avoid asking too many questions?
- What would you say to a child who asked you not to share the information they shared with you?

## ACTION YOU THEN NEED TO TAKE

- You need to report any information you have been given as soon as possible after you have been told about the abuse. This will mean that the details remain clear and fresh in your mind. It will allow action to be taken as promptly as possible. You may find it helpful to make notes as soon after your conversation with the child as possible. Try to keep these as accurate as you can. If a child has used certain words or descriptions, the guidance is to record these verbatim, which means using the same words even if they are not terms you would normally use.
- Remember that you need to treat the information you have been given sensitively and with confidentiality. You should not discuss it with other staff members or

colleagues. Being the recipient of a disclosure can be very distressing. No-one likes to think about a child they know being abused. If you are finding the situation worrying or if you are struggling to cope with the knowledge you have, then you can discuss this with the school's DSL. They may be able to support you themselves or may be able to signpost you to another person or an outside agency who can offer guidance, e.g. a counsellor or a medical professional.

# THE CHALLENGES FOR TEACHERS OF IMPLEMENTING SAFEGUARDING POLICY AND PROCEDURES

Implementing safeguarding policy and procedures can be challenging for a variety of reasons and could potentially have some negative impact on teacher emotional health and wellbeing. However, safeguarding involves the welfare and safety of children and young people, and it is a critical responsibility for teachers.

Some challenges include:

1. the complexity of policies and procedures;
2. the infrequency or availability of training;
3. the identification of signs and symptoms for concern;
4.. the time constraints;
5. knowing when to report concerns;
6. maintaining confidentiality;
7. emotional impact of the information shared;
8. seeking help and support for yourself if required.

The safeguarding of children should always be a priority across the school community, and it should be embedded in the ethos and culture of the school. The provision of high-quality induction and continuous comprehensive training updates, as well as clear protocols and a supportive environment, can empower teachers to implement policies effectively and protect the welfare of the students.

> **ACTION LEARNING SET**
>
> It is not uncommon for your first experience with safeguarding to be when a child discloses something to you. They have talked to you about a situation or incident when

> they or someone they may know is at risk of harm or has been harmed. It is important that you follow your school's safeguarding policy.
>
> It is important to consider how you will ensure your school policies are used. With your mentor or another appropriate expert colleague in school, explore how the school policies are used to protect and support every child in school.

## HOW CAN I KEEP MYSELF SAFE IN SCHOOL?

As a teacher you are expected to always behave professionally. Being able to determine what is professional or unprofessional behaviour is therefore critical if you are to be successful and if your practice and conduct is not to be called into question. You need to be able to recognise which situations or circumstances might make you vulnerable to having allegations made against you.

Sometimes, it is possible to put yourself in a vulnerable position because you are trying to help or want to appear supportive. An example of this might be if a child falls on the playground and grazes their leg so requires first aid. Think about what might make you vulnerable in this situation. Are you a trained first aider? Would the child need to remove items of clothing for you to attend to the graze? Who else is nearby and could support? Think about how you could protect yourself in such a situation. It is generally good common sense.

Guidelines that you should follow:

- your behaviour should be open and transparent;
- you must adopt high standard of personal conduct;
- avoid being alone with a pupil in a classroom with a closed, window-less door;
- never give an individual pupil a gift or treat that is not part of the school's reward system for all;
- never give your personal mobile phone number or other contact details to a pupil;
- be aware of the dangers of social media and ensure that you are not inadvertently sharing personal details and information;
- your behaviour both inside and outside school must never compromise your position within the school.

> **EVIDENCE-INFORMED RESEARCH**
>
> Schools will have a code of conduct which clearly outlines their expectations of your professional conduct. You could also refer to the *Guidance for Safer Working Practice* (DCSF, 2009) which gives very detailed information on what constitutes good practice for those working with children and young adults (DCSF, 2009).

## PHYSICAL CONTACT – IS IT ALLOWED?

As primary school teachers there are going to be times where you find it necessary to have physical contact with pupils. There may be rare occasions when this involves using what we refer to as *reasonable force* to intervene if a pupil is likely to cause danger to themselves, others or to cause severe disruption. The DfE (2013, p. 8) guidance, *Use of Reasonable Force*, provides that teachers can use *reasonable* force to:

- remove disruptive children from the classroom where they have refused to follow an instruction to do so;
- prevent a pupil behaving in a way that disrupts a school event or a school trip or visit;
- prevent a pupil leaving the classroom where allowing the pupil to leave would risk their safety or lead to behaviour that disrupts the behaviour of others;
- prevent a pupil from attacking a member of staff or another pupil;
- stop a fight in the playground;
- restrain a pupil at risk of harming themselves through physical outbursts.

This is something that is not entered into lightly and should only be utilised by those who have undertaken certified training such as 'Team Teach'.

The DfE (2013, p. 8) advice which applies to schools states: 'It is not illegal to touch a pupil. There are occasions when physical contact, other than reasonable force, with a pupil is proper and necessary.' The guidance gives clear examples of times when contact might be what it terms 'proper and necessary':

- *Holding the hand of the child at the front/back of the line when going to assembly or when walking together around the school;*
- *When comforting a distressed pupil;*
- *When a pupil is being congratulated or praised;*

- To demonstrate how to use a musical instrument;
- To demonstrate exercises or techniques during PE lessons or sports coaching; and
- To give first aid.

DfE, 2013, p. 8

## WELLBEING: DEFINING WELLBEING

'Wellbeing' is a well-known term but has different meanings for different people. Ryff (2014) explores wellbeing, or the felt experience of health, happiness and flourishing, predicting several outcomes considered desirable, which include better health and more positive social behaviour and relationships.

According to the DfE (2021), one third of teachers leave within the first five years of qualifying. Schools continue to be faced with the challenge of retaining skilled staff each year. ITT providers and schools aim to work collegiately to identify the pressures of the role to create supportive environments for teachers.

## YOUR DUTY AS AN EDUCATOR

Educators have a legal duty of care to ensure the safety and welfare of students in their care. The Children Act 1989 and its subsequent amendments in the Children Act 2004 set out the legal framework for child protection and the welfare of children. It places a duty on local authorities and schools to work together to promote the welfare of children and protect them from harm.

The most important thing to do is to get to know your students (see Chapter 9 on Pupil Behaviour for more information). Building a trusting relationship enables you to identify signs of risk or harm early on. Greeting your students with a welcome greeting is one strategy that supports the relationship. A good morning handshake with a child establishes a professional and well-natured connection in the morning. Where both parties are engaged, this opens an opportunity for you to have a check in with the child.

Observing your pupils is an important part of understanding your role. Observation is key to building positive relationships with your students and helps build a positive classroom environment as, once you start to really observe a child, you get to know the children. According to Montessori (1964), observation enables you to be aware of where the child is at and what they need, which means you are able to prepare the environment to meet the needs of the child. It is during purposeful observation that we, as the adult, witness the child forming relationships, learning knowledge and regulating their own behaviours.

Your training provider will support you and offer advice on how best to observe pupils when you begin to visit placement schools.

The extract below from a trainee's ongoing reflective development record identifies the frustrations that can be felt by an adult when a child's behaviour is difficult to interpret.

> *I am so frustrated, I am logging cause for concerns about Child A all the time, I've tried to talk to the DSL and my mentor, but they don't seem to understand my frustration. It is really getting me down. It seems like nothing gets done. The home circumstances really impact on their behaviour and engagement in class. It feels like no-one wants to help. A friend has suggested that I talk to the mental health lead in school.*
>
> Extract from ECT's reflective journal, week 9 in the autumn term

### REFLECTIVE QUESTIONS

Consider the importance and perseverance of the trainee here.

Why is it vital that they log each concern?

### EVIDENCE-INFORMED RESEARCH

The United Nations Convention of the Rights of the Child (UNCRC, 1989) is highly relevant to safeguarding and wellbeing in primary schools as it serves as an international framework that outlines the rights and protections that children are entitled to. The UNCRC provides a comprehensive framework for promoting the wellbeing and safeguarding of children in school. It guides policies, practices and actions to ensure that children's rights are respected and that they can learn and thrive in a safe and nurturing environment.

Read the extract below from a trainee's ongoing reflective development record as they move through the programme.

> *I ended up talking to the mental health lead in school, they helped me to talk to the DSL, now I understand more about the DSL role. I've also been reading about ACES (adverse childhood experiences) and attachment. This has helped me to understand*

*my class better and improved my classroom practice. I feel so much more confident now. I even contributed to my first PEP (personal education plan) for the child in my class who lives with foster parents.*

Extract from ECT, final week of the spring term

> **ACTIVE LEARNING SET**
>
> Look back across the extracts, consider difference in language used and the confidence the trainee now has in their use of terminology and their level of participation in these essential meetings.

# MAINTAINING YOUR PUPILS' WELLBEING

## WHOLE-SCHOOL APPROACH

A school environment that prioritises the emotional needs of both teachers and students leads to a positive community where everyone benefits. When teachers feel they are supported, they are better equipped to provide the emotional care and guidance children need.

## WITHIN YOUR CLASSROOM

Observing experienced teachers is a valuable and essential component of teacher training programmes as it offers the opportunity for experiential learning and exposure to different learning styles. It also affords trainees exposure to pedagogical knowledge and reflective practice. Observing experienced teachers bridges the gap between theoretical knowledge and practical application. It equips trainees with a diverse set of skills and strategies while promoting reflective and adaptive teaching practices. It is an integral part of preparing educators to be effective in the classroom and to support the learning and wellbeing of their pupils.

## CREATING AN EMOTIONALLY SAFE ENVIRONMENT FOR PUPILS

Emotional safety is considered a critical component of a positive learning environment, with research evidencing the impact on psychological wellbeing, and academic and social outcomes (Shean and Mander, 2020). According to Parry-Langdon (2008), children with emotional difficulties are more likely to be excluded from school and the possibility of leaving with poor or no qualifications increases.

Teachers are best placed to create an environment that has a positive impact on a student's emotional wellbeing, which Clark et al. (2018) suggest can have a positive impact for five or more years.

Integrating emotional literacy into the curriculum helps students identify and name their emotions This practice supports students in learning to understand and manage how they feel, as well as how they respond to the emotions of others. Begin with the emotional vocabulary used within your setting and consider ways where a range of emotion words can be explored and discussed (for more information see Chapter 9).

## CONCLUSION

Ensuring the safety, security and wellbeing of pupils and educators is of paramount importance in any educational setting. This chapter has addressed the comprehensive approach that primary schools must adopt to safeguard their pupils and educators, creating an environment conducive to learning, growth and development. Prioritising safeguarding and promoting wellbeing within your environment will not only foster a positive and nurturing community, but will also enable pupils and educators to thrive within a secure environment.

The chapter has identified how we can create safe and secure environments for all young children while protecting your own self and sense of wellbeing throughout the training year/s and your early career.

Throughout this chapter you have read extracts and reflections from a trainee across their training year. They reviewed their understanding of safeguarding, procedure and the impact of wellbeing on the children and themselves. The accounts demonstrate how the trainee's understanding of what safeguarding involves in school deepens as the year progresses and the importance of recognising the impact of this on all involved.

### REVIEW OF CHAPTER OBJECTIVES

Within this chapter you have considered:

- what is meant by safeguarding and wellbeing and the challenges around these terms;
- what is meant by the terms 'safeguarding' and 'child protection';
- your role and responsibilities in relation to safeguarding young children;

- the importance of an awareness of current legislation in safeguarding children;
- how to support pupils' wellbeing;
- that promoting safe environments and opportunities for teacher and student to grow emotionally and mentally will benefit the whole community.

## FURTHER READING AND RESOURCES

Department for Education (DfE) (2023a) *Keeping Children Safe in Education*. London: DfE. Available at: https://assets.publishing.service.gov.uk/government/uploads/system/uploads/attachment_data/file/1161273/Keeping_children_safe_in_education_2023_-_statutory_guidance_for_schools_and_colleges.pdf [accessed 21 December 2023].

Unicef (1989) *A Summary of the United Nations Convention on the Rights of the Child*. Available at: www.unicef.org.uk/wp-content/uploads/2019/10/UNCRC_summary-1_1.pdf [accessed 21 December 2023].

## REFERENCES

Boyd, G. (2019) Safeguarding children, in Fitzgerald, D. and Maconochie, H. (eds.), *Early Childhood Studies: A Student Guide*. London: Sage, pp. 193–207.

Clark, A. E., Flèche, S., Layard, R., Powdthavee, N., and Ward, G. (2018) *The Origins of Happiness: The Science of Well-being Over the Life Course*. Princeton, NJ: Princeton University Press.

Department for Children, Schools and Families (DCSF) (2009) *Guidance for Safer Working Practice for Adults who Work with Children and Young People*. Updated from original guidance in document published by the DCSF. Available at: https://cscp.org.uk/wp-content/uploads/2021/03/Guidance-for-safer-working-practice-for-adults-who-work-with-children-and-young-people-DCSF.pdf [accessed 21 December 2023].

Department for Education (DfE) (2013) *Use of Reasonable Force: Advice for Headteachers, Staff and Governing Bodies*. London: DfE. Reviewed 2015. Available at: https://assets.publishing.service.gov.uk/media/5a819959ed915d74e6233224/Use_of_reasonable_force_advice_Reviewed_July_2015.pdf [accessed 21 December 2023].

DfE (2019) *ITT Core Content Framework*. London: DfE. Available at: https://assets.publishing.service.gov.uk/government/uploads/system/uploads/attachment_data/file/974307/ITT_core_content_framework_.pdf [accessed November 2023].

DfE (2021) *Promoting and Supporting Mental Health and Wellbeing in Schools and Colleges*. Available at: www.gov.uk/guidance/mental-health-and-wellbeing-support-in-schools-and-colleges [accessed 8 November 2023].

DfE (2023a) *Keeping Children Safe in Education*. London: DfE. Available at: https://assets.publishing.service.gov.uk/government/uploads/system/uploads/attachment_data/file/1161273/Keeping_children_safe_in_education_2023_-_statutory_guidance_for_schools_and_colleges.pdf [accessed 21 December 2023].

DfE (2023b) *Working Together to Safeguard Children*. London: DfE. Available at: https://assets.publishing.service.gov.uk/media/65803fe31c0c2a000d18cf40/Working_together_to_safeguard_children_2023_-_statutory_guidance.pdf [accessed 21 December 2023].

Montessori, M. (1964) *The Montessori Method*. New York: Schocken.

National Education Union (NEU) (2023) *Education, The Law and You*. Available at: https://neu.org.uk/latest/library/education-law-and-you [accessed 21 December 2023].

Parry-Langdon, N. (2008) *Three Years On: Survey of the Development and Emotional Wellbeing of Children and Young People*. London: ONS.

Ryff, C. D. (2014) Psychological well-being revisited: Advances in the science and practice of eudaimonia. *Psychotherapy and Psychosomatics*, 83, pp. 10–28.

Shean, M. and Mander, D. (2020) Building emotional safety for students in school environments: Challenges and opportunities, in Midford, R., Nutton, G., Hyndman, B. and Silburn, S. (eds.), *Health and Education Interdependence: Thriving from Birth to Adulthood*. New York: Springer, pp. 225–248.

# SECTION 2
## INITIAL TEACHER TRAINING: KNOWLEDGE AND UNDERSTANDING

# 7

# THE CURRICULUM IN THE PRIMARY SCHOOL

## ANNA PARK AND LEWIS MORGAN

**Learn that and Learn how to –
The Knowledge and Application Model**

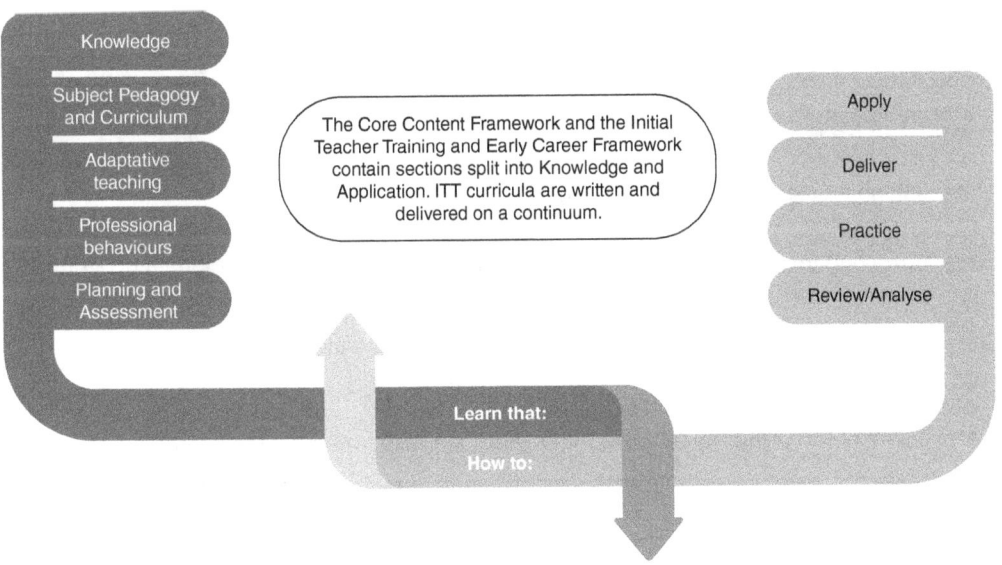

## FRAMED BY THE CCF – FOR FULL LINKS TO THE ITTECF, SEE PAGE 337

Subject and Curriculum
(Standard 3 – 'Demonstrate good subject and curriculum knowledge')

| Learn that ... | Learn how to ... |
| --- | --- |
| 1. A school's curriculum enables it to set out its vision for the knowledge, skills and values that its pupils will learn, encompassing the national curriculum within a coherent wider vision for successful learning.<br><br>3. Ensuring pupils master foundational concepts and knowledge before moving on is likely to build pupils' confidence and help them succeed.<br><br>5. Explicitly teaching pupils the knowledge and skills they need to succeed within particular subject areas is beneficial. | Deliver a carefully sequenced and coherent curriculum, by:<br><br>• Receiving clear, consistent and effective mentoring in how to identify essential concepts, knowledge, skills and principles of the subject.<br><br>• Discussing and analysing with expert colleagues the rationale for curriculum choices, the process for arriving at current curriculum choices and how the school's curriculum materials inform lesson preparation. |

## CHAPTER OBJECTIVES

On reading this chapter you will consider:

- how changes in our educational landscape brought about the national curriculum we use today;
- how each school develops its curriculum in a unique way;
- how a curriculum is sequenced to develop learning in small and cumulative steps;
- how you can bring the national curriculum to life in how you plan and teach.

## KEY VOCABULARY

Curriculum

Intent

Implementation

Impact

Deep dive

Regulatory framework

Statutory

# INTRODUCTION

In this chapter, we will be developing your understanding of what a curriculum is, what it is for and how we arrived at the national curriculum that has been in use since 2014. Using case studies and examples, you will learn that schools take the content of the national curriculum and use this as a minimum entitlement for all children. In this chapter, we demonstrate how schools bring this curriculum to life in a way that offers all children deep and rich learning experiences. By the end of this chapter, you will have a greater understanding of whole-school planning and a child's overall learning experience.

# WHY DO WE HAVE A CURRICULUM?

The original meaning of curriculum stems from the Latin word *currere* meaning 'to run' or 'a racecourse'. The curriculum is exactly that for teachers. It is a roadmap or 'racecourse' for teachers to help navigate their students through their learning. This road map is a structured and coherent plan that outlines the intended content to help pupils make progress and flourish. It provides teachers with a set of subjects, learning objectives and assessment criteria to ensure that a high-quality education is provided to children and that this is consistent and fair. Its aim is to provide a well-rounded education that nurtures the whole student, including their cognitive, social, physical and emotional growth. It aims to provide and equip students with the skills and understanding for them to progress academically and prepare them for further education and work.

# WHAT IS THE PRIMARY NATIONAL CURRICULUM IN ENGLAND 2014?

The primary national curriculum that is in use today was introduced in 2014, but the first national curriculum was implemented under the Education Reform Act of 1988. Before this date, governments did not regulate on a national level what content would be taught in schools. Teachers and schools were given the autonomy to decide the content of their subject delivery. This led to the quality of education and outcomes for pupils being inconsistent from classroom to classroom, school to school. The debate that raged as a result of this inconsistency was that standards nationally could not be accurately measured, basic skills of reading, writing and maths were overlooked, and the education system did not fit the needs of a modern society (Shaw and Shirley, 2018).

The 1988 Education Reform Act brought in a standardised common primary curriculum, the notion of key stages and standardised testing in English and maths. This 1988 national curriculum was also divided into three *core subjects* (maths, science and English) and the *foundation subjects*.

The national curriculum continued to be placed under political scrutiny and subject to debate from 1988 onwards. In 2014, the curriculum that we operate within today was published. This document slimmed down expectations in several subjects, altered expectations in many others and placed a deeper focus on spelling and grammar.

The national curriculum is a statutory document – this means that it has been given legally binding status. Schools are required to deliver its contents and are judged on their efficacy in doing so. It is important that you are aware of how the curriculum is regulated and the frameworks through which pupil outcomes are monitored.

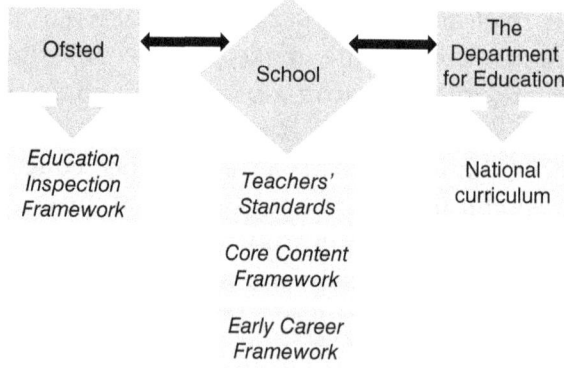

*Figure 7.1 The regulatory framework around schools in England*

## THE DEPARTMENT FOR EDUCATION (DFE)

The DfE is responsible for education and children's services. The national curriculum and documentation to support the delivery of the national curriculum originate within this department.

## THE NATIONAL CURRICULUM (2014)

This is a statutory document setting out which subjects are taught and the standards children are expected to reach in primary and secondary schools. It is to be understood as a minimum entitlement and schools are expected to meet – if not surpass – the requirements within this document.

## OFSTED

The Office for Standards in Education (Ofsted) inspects schools in England, as well as childcare, further education and social care settings. It reports to parliament and is separate from the Department for Education. Inspection reports and judgements are public documents.

### THE OFSTED *EDUCATION INSPECTION FRAMEWORK* (2023A)

This document sets out the framework through which each school and setting will be inspected and judged. They reach judgements on:

- the quality of education;
- behaviour and attitudes;
- personal development including spiritual, moral, social and cultural development;
- safeguarding pupils;
- leadership and management;
- provision for pupils with special educational needs.

The quality of education judgement is crucial for this chapter. In recent years Ofsted have shifted emphasis away from scrutinising data contained within the SATS results (and other results) and have focused on how schools are providing wider opportunities for pupils in all aspects of learning across the subjects set out in the national curriculum.

### THE *TEACHERS' STANDARDS* (DFE, 2021)

These define the minimum level expected of all teachers from the point of being awarded qualified teacher status (QTS). There is an emphasis on the curriculum and its importance in the following standards which state that teachers should:

- promote good progress and outcomes by pupils;
- demonstrate good subject and curriculum knowledge;
- plan and teach well-structured lessons.

## THE *ITT CORE CONTENT FRAMEWORK* (CCF) (DFE, 2019B) AND THE *EARLY CAREER FRAMEWORK* (ECF) FOR EARLY CAREER TEACHERS (ECTS) (DFE, 2019A, 2024)

These frameworks support trainee learning and development in the period leading up to qualification and the early years that follow. They are evidence-informed frameworks that set out a minimum entitlement for your early experiences in teaching.

## WHAT ARE SCHOOLS FOR?

What do you think the purpose of school is? It is worth thinking about your answer to this question as you develop as a teacher because it will provide a backdrop to your educational ethos.

Consider for a moment the ways in which education is discussed in the news and political spheres. There is a perennial debate around subject outcomes – particularly English and maths – which suggests that the *purpose of education is to teach subjects*. At the same time, there is a persistent debate around whether schools tackle societal issues such as inequality or social justice, which suggests that the *purpose of education is to contribute to a strong and stable society*. Running alongside this are news items about developing a workforce that is equipped with the skills required of a productive and future-facing nation, which suggests that the *purpose of education is to develop a workforce of the future*.

Biesta (2009) suggests that there are three different functions that education performs: qualification, subjectification and socialisation. This certainly fits with the three purposes outlined above. Importantly, he argues that all three elements should be present in a strong curriculum and urges us to think of them as three overlapping parts of a Venn diagram. An impactful school curriculum is developed when staff are aware of these three overlapping elements and the impact these have on children. As you develop as a teacher, keep these three elements in mind when you plan and teach.

### REFLECTIVE QUESTIONS

When you teach, what are you teaching beyond subject knowledge?

What else are you developing in your children?

What is the curriculum *for* in your setting?

# DEVELOPING THE CURRICULUM

Ofsted uses the analogy of a game of Jenga® to describe a strong and effective curriculum. Each building block represents the knowledge and skill that the children need at their level – but it also rests on the strong layer below and provides the foundation for the layer above. In this way, a carefully sequenced curriculum will ensure that each child feels successful in every step along their time in school. If there are gaps in knowledge and skills, either through misconceptions or through curriculum design, then the Jenga® tower becomes unstable and a child's learning is insecure (Fearn and Keay, 2021).

## INTENT

Curriculum *intent* is a school's stance on the curriculum and how it can be aligned with its vision, values, ethos and community. This is a whole-school effort that draws upon the expertise of the leadership team and subject leader as well as the knowledge and skills of all staff.

Consider this section as a route map from the national curriculum to your lessons, rather like the map of the London Underground. The different lines are clearly defined, and you can see the journey from start to finish, from one stop to the next. Not only that, but you can see how all the lines interact and join to form a coherent whole. Using this analogy, we can think of the curriculum in school as the whole map, and each of the subjects as different lines.

Each school designs a unique curriculum which encompasses and grows from the national curriculum. We use the word 'design' deliberately here: school staff teams deliberately and carefully design their curriculum to deliver a learning journey that sequences knowledge and skills and allows each child to feel successful and ready for their next step.

## IMPLEMENTATION

A carefully sequenced and designed curriculum now needs to be taught and experienced by the children. This is intent turned into action. To do this well, teachers must have a good understanding of their own subject knowledge and the possible misconceptions of pupils. Teachers must also provide feedback that is clear and develops the learner. As you begin your teaching journey, this is the point at which you may find your planning and teaching begins. Initially, you might use the planning and ideas of your class teacher and learn how to make these come to life. As you develop in confidence and understanding, you will develop your skills in designing more of the intent that leads up to your moment of teaching.

It is important to remember that *implementation* feeds into *impact* – the decisions you make in delivering learning opportunities must impact on the children's learning. Keep your focus on what the children will learn, rather than what they will do. (You can read more about the importance of process over product-led curricula in Chapter 10.)

## IMPACT

You will only know if your curriculum intent and implementation is effective if it has had an impact on the children. Pupils will learn and achieve well if the intent and the implementation have been well-designed, sequenced and delivered. This may be reflected in national tests, government expectations or qualifications. It is vital that you ensure that your children have understood your objectives and can remember and apply their knowledge and skills in the future. Children will need you to design opportunities to reuse their knowledge and skills and to consolidate and build on them.

## HOW CAN THE SAME CURRICULUM FEEL DIFFERENT IN EVERY SCHOOL?

Although the national curriculum is a statutory document for the whole of England, this does not mean that it must be applied in the same way in each school, town or region. A confident school curriculum is one that is unique to the school and its location, its characteristics and its community.

Each school is in its own unique setting. This means that it can use the national curriculum as a framework within which it designs local learning experiences. Staff can work together to develop a curriculum that builds on aspects of local geography or history, for example, or that develops key features of the local community and its events and people.

## HOW IS IT PERSONALISED TO THE CHILDREN?

Bishop (1990) described how books can be *windows* (they allow us to see the experiences of others), *mirrors* (they reflect ourselves back to us) and *sliding glass doors* (they allow us to step through and be a part of a new experience). The same can be said of a curriculum. A carefully designed curriculum has the power and potential to help children learn about themselves and others and to imagine futures and possibilities that they may not have considered.

Thomson (2002) maintained that each child comes to school with a 'virtual schoolbag' full of knowledge, learning and experiences from home, their family and their community. Few of these children get the chance to completely unpack their schoolbag at school and use the rich seam of home knowledge. The curriculum they study might only ask them to unpack a narrow set of knowledge and skills from a particular cultural or societal perspective. A strong curriculum needs to acknowledge the children in your class and value the unique perspective that they can add to learning.

As you think about your curriculum and how you deliver it, the children who are learning from you need to be uppermost in your mind. How you design your lessons needs to take into consideration the virtual schoolbags of experiences that they are bringing into the classroom. Similarly, how you design your lesson needs to show each child a window, a mirror or a sliding door so that they feel included in your classroom.

### REFLECTIVE QUESTIONS

- Does your lesson plan show children a window, a mirror or a sliding door?
- How are you finding out what is in your children's virtual schoolbags?

Spend the next day of placement deliberately finding out about the lives and backgrounds of your children.

Use some of these findings in your teaching.

As you translate the national curriculum into a bespoke learning experience for your children, stop and ask yourself: 'What assumptions am I making here?' An assumption is a belief that we think everyone else has as well, or the idea that everyone else sees and experiences the world in the same way as us. It is possible, indeed probable, that you will teach children who have not been to the beach, seen snow, taken a bus, celebrated Christmas, visited a museum or had the life experiences you might expect. One cannot assume from this that these children are *lacking* in experiences: their virtual schoolbags are simply full of other and different experiences. Brookfield (1992) has written extensively on how the assumptions we make can lead us to practice in the way that we do. Reflecting on those assumptions will ultimately lead to you delivering lessons designed with your unique children in mind.

## REFLECTIVE QUESTIONS

What assumptions are you making about your children's lives, experiences and prior learning?

What will you do to focus on and eventually eliminate these assumptions?

How will your teaching change because of this?

## CASE STUDY: ART

Let us look at how art can be developed as a subject curriculum and part of a wider curriculum. St Oswald's School, West Yorkshire, led by headteacher Jonny Davies, has a curriculum that is unique to its community and setting. Seven core principles underpin the curriculum: learning to learn, exploring morals and values, taking inspiration from everything, emotional wellbeing, questioning and problem-solving, time to reflect and awe and wonder. This is the curriculum intent: it sets out the school's approach to their curriculum and learning values.

Emily Newell, Art Leader, applies these principles to her art curriculum as she considers the art knowledge and art skills that children need by the end of Year 6 - as well as the experiences that will develop their appreciation for and enjoyment of art. These knowledge areas, skills and experiences have been carefully sequenced and mapped from Year 1 to Year 6 and woven into other curriculum areas.

A progression map outlines the knowledge and skills covered each year. Every year covers painting, printing, drawing, sculpture, digital media, collage and an artist study. This allows all staff to be certain that what is taught in one year is building on learning from a previous year and prepares children for learning to come. Knowledge about art and art skills are combined in the following teaching sequence that ensures parity of delivery:

- *appreciate*: use a work of art or an artist as a stimulus;
- *investigate*: discover the skills involved in the artwork or used by the artist;
- *demonstrate*: teacher demonstrates how to use skills and materials;
- *innovate*: children develop their skills in sketchbooks and complete a creative piece;
- *appreciate and evaluate*: children respond to each other's work as a skill and as a finished piece.

Emily is passionate about how art can:

- be taught and developed as a skill. Children and staff all regularly use sketchbooks and are encouraged to appreciate the process of making art just as much as the end product;

- be taught and developed as knowledge. Children develop their knowledge about artists, artistic movements and styles and art making;
- lead to rich opportunities to reach out to the wider community. The school has worked locally with an older people's charity, art groups, primary and secondary schools and artists and musicians;
- bring the school together on a unifying project. The school celebrates a Diversity Arts Day, an arts festival, an art week and enters the Big Draw Festival;
- develop in children key areas of empathy, imagination, curiosity and enjoyment. The school holds an art and wellbeing group for pupil premium children. The responses and ideas of the child are actively encouraged;
- celebrate diversity. Through the curriculum and the Diversity Arts Day, art from around the world and from different cultural perspectives can be celebrated.

The art curriculum is seen as a vital area through which the school can channel important themes. This is an example of the curriculum being a powerful tool to develop the whole child – something we advocate for in this chapter. By thinking about art on every scale, from parts of lessons to the entire curriculum and the wider life of the school, children are given a deliberately sequenced and rich art learning experience that is woven expertly into the whole-school curriculum.

## EVIDENCE-INFORMED RESEARCH: MATHS

Maths mastery is an example of evidence-based research in action. While the maths mastery approach is not a prescribed curriculum, its principles are embedded throughout the national curriculum.

When thinking about the term 'mastery' it can be useful to use the definition from the National Centre for Excellence in the Teaching of Mathematics (NCETM): 'Mastering maths means pupils of all ages acquiring a deep, long-term, secure and adaptable understanding of the subject' (2023, n.p.). Using this approach, maths can be understood through several 'lenses', each of which is important to develop.

*Conceptual understanding*: Emphasising a deep understanding of mathematical concepts before moving to procedural fluency. Students who understand the underlying concepts are more likely to apply their knowledge to new situations. This helps to reduce cognitive overload for pupils.

*Mathematical reasoning*: Encouraging students to reason and think critically about mathematical ideas, leading to better problem-solving skills.

*Visual representation*: Using visual representations, such as diagrams, models and drawings, to support students' understanding of abstract concepts.

*(Continued)*

(Continued)

*Multiple approaches*: Allowing students to explore and solve problems using different strategies. This approach helps them develop flexibility in their thinking and enhances their ability to solve problems.

*Collaborative learning*: Encouraging students to work together on problem-solving tasks promotes communication and discussion, enhancing their understanding of mathematical concepts.

*Formative assessment*: Continuously assessing students' progress to identify areas of strength and areas that require support. Formative assessment helps teachers tailor instruction to meet individual students' needs.

In the examples below, the maths mastery approach is evident as pupils progress from the concrete stage, where they interact with physical objects, to the pictorial stage, where they use visual representations, to the abstract stage, where they work with numerical notation and symbols. This progression helps students build a deeper understanding of mathematical concepts and how to apply these concepts to real-world problem-solving. This approach aligns with the *mapping* concept of the curriculum by ensuring that teachers understand the correct route for the learning.

## ADDITION AND SUBTRACTION (KEY STAGE 1)

3+2=5

*Concrete*: Students begin counting real-life objects to physically add or subtract numbers – for example, adding together physical apples or cubes.

*Pictorial*: Students draw pictures or use bar models to represent addition and subtraction problems. They might draw apples to represent the example above or use dots or circles.

*Abstract*: Students write the addition or subtraction sentence using numbers and symbols.

## MULTIPLICATION (KEY STAGE 2)

4x3=12

*Concrete*: Students use classroom objects, like cubes, arranged in arrays or groups, showing 4x3 as four rows of three cubes. Collaborative working encourages children to discuss and reason about the best way to group the objects. This is an opportunity to assess students' understanding by listening and observing how and why objects are grouped.

*Pictorial*: Students draw diagrams or use arrays to represent multiplication problems. Students will draw four rows of three dots to represent the same example.

*Abstract:* Students write the multiplication equation using numbers and symbols.

> **REFLECTIVE QUESTIONS**
>
> Which part of the concrete, pictorial and abstract process gets left out of maths teaching? Why might this happen?
>
> What other subjects would benefit from using a concrete, pictorial, abstract procedure to help the children's understanding and knowledge?

## A DEEP DIVE INTO SCIENCE

Let us look at how the progression in knowledge and skills is developed in the science curriculum by looking at the working scientifically skill of performing a simple test.

*Table 7.1 Working scientifically: Skills by key stage*

| KS1 | Lower KS2 | Upper KS2 |
| --- | --- | --- |
| During *Years 1 and 2*, pupils should be taught: | During *Years 3 and 4*, pupils should be taught: | During *Years 5 and 6*, pupils should be taught: |
| Working scientifically | | |
| Performing simple tests | Setting up simple practical enquiries, comparative and fair tests | Planning different types of scientific enquiries to answer questions, including recognising and controlling variables where necessary |
| Materials | | |
| *Identify* and *name* a variety of everyday materials, including wood, metal, plastic, glass, metal, water and rock | Identify the part played by *evaporation* and *condensation* in *the water cycle* and associate the rate of evaporation with temperature | Know that some materials will *dissolve* in liquid to form a solution, and describe how to recover a substance from a solution<br><br>Demonstrate that *dissolving*, mixing and changes of state are *reversible changes* |

In KS1, the children need to develop a love of testing and the curiosity to test. Children need to carry out simple tests without worrying about variables and constraints. The teacher can mention these during the investigation but will not form part of the assessment or learning objectives. The need to control the test and make everything 'a fair test' can get in the way of developing a natural passion for finding things out. In the classroom, this could look like an 'I wonder …' floor book where children's ideas and questions can be gathered, or simple tests to try and find an answer. The test may not necessarily link to a topic but follow the natural curiosity of your children: this is the building block of a love for finding out and testing.

Armed with this curiosity and a growing ability to test, LKS2 now requires pupils to think about comparative and fair tests (*caution*: there are many different types of enquiry and science should not just be restricted to fair tests). As the teacher, you can now build on their ability to test and then add in the understanding about what makes a test comparative or fair and, more importantly, why we need to carry out tests. At this point children are more prepared to begin to understand why we need tests to create reliable results.

UKS2 requires pupils to build on all the knowledge of testing gained previously to plan different enquiries and tests that include variables and constraints. If pupils have never had the opportunity to just test things, adding knowledge about variables and different enquiry types could overwhelm them and they may struggle to develop a sufficient understanding as they move towards more complex testing methods.

## DISCIPLINARY AND SUBSTANTIVE KNOWLEDGE

This example also demonstrates the need for you to understand the role of *disciplinary* and *substantive* knowledge. Ofsted (2023b) explains that substantive knowledge is the established knowledge produced by science (for example, the parts of a flower or the names of planets) and disciplinary knowledge refers to what pupils learn about how to establish and refine scientific knowledge (for example, carrying out practical procedures). Ofsted identified that where science was successful not only was the substantive knowledge mapped, but the disciplinary knowledge was also mapped. This is not just isolated to science. The identification and mapping of the skills and knowledge required is what the curriculum provides for teachers.

The curriculum provides a route for you as a teacher so that you can ensure that knowledge and skills are built upon in the correct order and the pupils' foundations are strong and robust.

### REFLECTIVE QUESTIONS

When you teach science, have you checked what prior learning has taken place? How could you check this?

Can you identify disciplinary or substantive knowledge from any subject and track the progression through the national curriculum?

Why is knowing where the children have come from and where they are going important?

> **ACTION LEARNING SET**
>
> Choose a topic and objective you will be teaching in science. Can you identify the prior knowledge that your children should have gained and the future application of this knowledge?

# CONCLUSION

This chapter has explored how we have arrived at the national curriculum in use today. It has explained how it sits within the regulatory framework around schools and how it is used to monitor outcomes for children. We hope that you now have a clearer sense of the opportunities each school and each teacher has to bring this curriculum to life and offer rich learning experiences that carefully build learning and development for each child.

> **REVIEW OF CHAPTER OBJECTIVES**
>
> Within this chapter you have considered:
>
> - how changes in our educational landscape brought about the national curriculum we use today;
> - how each school develops its curriculum in a unique way;
> - how a curriculum is sequenced to develop learning in small and cumulative steps;
> - how you can bring the national curriculum to life in how you plan and teach.

# FURTHER READING AND RESOURCES

Department for Education (DfE) (2014) *The National Curriculum in England*. Available at:

https://assets.publishing.service.gov.uk/government/uploads/system/uploads/attachment_data/file/381344/Master_final_national_curriculum_28_Nov.pdf [accessed 21 December 2023].

Ofsted (2023a) *Education Inspection Framework*. London: Ofsted. Available at:

www.gov.uk/government/publications/education-inspection-framework/education-inspection-framework-for-september-2023 [accessed 21 December 2023].

# REFERENCES

Biesta, G. (2009) Good education in an age of measurement: On the need to reconnect with the question of purpose in education. *Educational Assessment Evaluation and Accountability*, 21, pp. 33–46. doi: 10.1007/s11092-008-9064-9.

Bishop, R. S. (1990) Mirrors, windows and sliding doors. *Perspectives: Choosing and Using Books for the Classroom*, 6(3).

Brookfield, S. (1992) Uncovering assumptions: The key to reflective practice. *Adult Learning*, 3(4), pp. 13–18. doi: 10.1177/104515959200300405.

Department for Education (DfE) (2019a) *Early Career Framework*. Available at: https://assets.publishing.service.gov.uk/government/uploads/system/uploads/attachment_data/file/978358/Early-Career_Framework_April_2021.pdf [accessed August 2023].

DfE (2019b) *ITT Core Content Framework*. London: DfE. Available at: https://assets.publishing.service.gov.uk/government/uploads/system/uploads/attachment_data/file/974307/ITT_core_content_framework_.pdf [accessed November 2023].

DfE (2021) *Teachers' Standards: Guidance for School Leaders, School Staff and Governing Bodies*. London: DfE. Available at: https://assets.publishing.service.gov.uk/media/61b73d6c8fa8f50384489c9a/Teachers__Standards_Dec_2021.pdf [accessed 19 December 2023].

DfE (2024) *Initial teacher training and early career framework* Available at: https://www.gov.uk/government/publications/initial-teacher-training-and-early-career-framework [Accessed March 2024].

Fearn, H. and Keay, J. (2021) *Curriculum: Keeping it simple*. Ofsted Blog Post. *Ofsted: Schools and Further Education and Skills (FES)*. Available at: https://educationinspection.blog.gov.uk/2021/12/08/curriculum-keeping-it-simple/ [accessed 21 December 2023].

NCETM (2023) What is teaching for mastery? July. Available at: www.ncetm.org.uk/professional-development/school-leaders/ [accessed 21 December 2023].

Ofsted (2018) *An Investigation into How to Assess the Quality of Education Through Curriculum Intent, Implementation and Impact*. Ref. no. 180035. Available at: https://assets.publishing.service.gov.uk/media/5fb3e55fe90e07208fd2cb85/Curriculum_research_How_to_assess_intent_and_implementation_of_curriculum_191218.pdf [accessed 21 December 2023].

Ofsted (2023b) *Finding the Optimum: The Science Subject Report*. Available at: www.gov.uk/government/publications/subject-report-series-science/finding-the-optimum-the-science-subject-report--2 [accessed 21 December 2023].

Roberts, N. and Hill, R. (2021) *School Inspections in England: Ofsted*. London: House of Commons Research Library Briefing Paper. Available at: https://assets-learning.parliament.uk/uploads/2021/12/School-Inspections-in-England-Ofsted.pdf [accessed 21 December 2023].

Shaw, S. and Shirley, I. (2018) The history of education, in Cooper, H. and Elton-Chalcraft, S. (Eds.), *Professional Studies in Primary Education*. London: Sage, pp. 3–17.

Spielman, A. (2018) Amanda Spielman Speech to the SCHOOLS NorthEast Summit (transcript). Available at: www.gov.uk/government/speeches/amanda-spielman-speech-to-the-schools-northeast-summit [accessed 21 December 2023].

Thomson, P. (2002) *Schooling the Rustbelt Kids: Making a Difference in Changing Times*. Stoke-on-Trent: Trentham.

# 8

# THE IMPORTANCE OF EARLY READING AND PHONICS

## DAVID WAUGH AND REBECCA LINFIELD

**Learn that and Learn how to –
The Knowledge and Application Model**

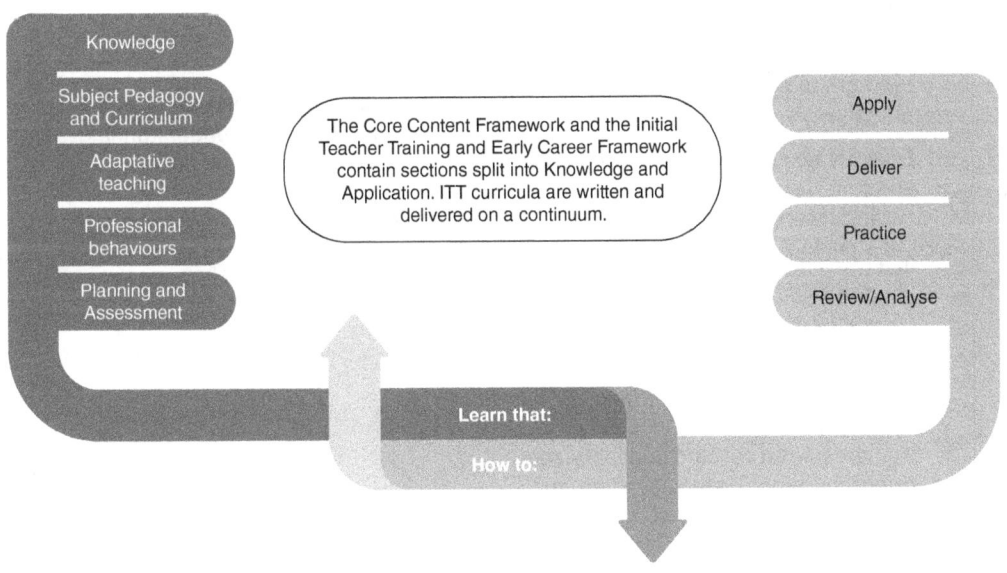

## FRAMED BY THE CCF – FOR FULL LINKS TO THE ITTECF, SEE PAGE 337

| How Pupils Learn | |
|---|---|
| (Standard 2 – 'Promote good progress') | |
| Learn that … | Learn how to … |
| 2. Prior knowledge plays an important role in how pupils learn; committing some key facts to their long-term memory is likely to help pupils learn more complex ideas.<br><br>7. Regular purposeful practice of what has previously been taught can help consolidate material and help pupils remember what they have learned. | Avoid overloading working memory, by:<br><br>• Receiving clear, consistent and effective mentoring in how to take into account pupils' prior knowledge when planning how much new information to introduce. |

| Subject and Curriculum | |
|---|---|
| (Standard 3 – 'Demonstrate good subject and curriculum knowledge') | |
| Learn that … | Learn how to … |
| 2. Secure subject knowledge helps teachers to motivate pupils and teach effectively.<br><br>5. Explicitly teaching pupils the knowledge and skills they need to succeed within particular subject areas is beneficial.<br><br>7. In all subject areas, pupils learn new ideas by linking those ideas to existing knowledge.<br><br>9. To access the curriculum, early literacy provides fundamental knowledge; reading comprises two elements: word reading and language comprehension; systematic synthetic phonics is the most effective approach for teaching pupils to decode.<br><br>10. Every teacher can improve pupils' literacy, including by explicitly teaching reading, writing and oral language skills specific to individual disciplines. | Develop pupils' literacy, by:<br><br>• Observing how expert colleagues demonstrate a clear understanding of systematic synthetic phonics, particularly if teaching early reading and spelling, and deconstructing this approach. |

## CHAPTER OBJECTIVES

On reading this chapter you will consider:

- the role that phonics plays in teaching reading;
- the alphabetic code;
- approaches to teaching phonics;
- some of the challenges you will face when teaching early reading;
- the importance of applying phonics for reading and writing;
- teaching phonics in KS2.

## KEY VOCABULARY

Common exception words

Phonemes

Graphemes

Decoding

Encoding

The alphabetic code

Systematic synthetic phonics (SSP)

Enunciation

Digraph

Trigraph

Pseudo words

# INTRODUCTION

There is a seeming preoccupation with the teaching of phonics in DfE documents. You will find this in the *Core Curriculum Framework* (CCF) (DfE, 2019) and ITTECF (DfE, 2024), *Teachers' Standards* (DfE, 2011) and *Reading Framework* (DfE, 2023). You might ask: *Why phonics?* Surely people learned to read before such emphasis was placed upon one approach. This is a question you might be asked by parents and carers, and fellow professionals.

In this chapter, you will explore some of the challenges you might face when teaching phonics and develop an understanding of why it is so important that children learn phonics in a systematic way.

What do you do when you see an unfamiliar place name? Most people use their knowledge of sound–symbol correspondences to attempt to pronounce it. For example, you may not have heard of *Diss*, but you can probably make a good attempt at saying the name because you know what sounds are typically made by D/i/ and /ss/. You know that double s makes a single sound (a *digraph*). If you saw a sign for *Chard*, you would probably automatically break the word into Ch/ar/d to pronounce it, knowing that /ch/ is a digraph and so is /ar/. Even if you were not explicitly taught phonics, you have probably developed a sophisticated knowledge of the possible sound–symbol correspondences in English. By adopting a systematic approach to teaching phonics in schools, educators hope to ensure that this knowledge is acquired early so that children are well equipped to read increasingly challenging text.

This may all seem obvious and logical, and it certainly is for languages like Finnish and Italian in which letter–sound correspondences are consistent and you can be almost certain that a letter or combination of letters will always be pronounced the same way. However, English presents a rather different challenge. For example, look at the place names below and try to pronounce them:

- Thames
- Fowey
- Leominster
- Frome.

You may be surprised to know that Fowey is pronounced 'Foy', Leominster as 'Lemster' and Frome as 'Froom'. The Thames is no doubt a familiar name, so you probably sound the *Th* as in *toy* rather than as in *this* or *think*, but how did we end up with the current pronunciation? Apparently, Thames was traditionally pronounced with a /th/ sound, but when German-born King George I saw the river for the first time, he called it 'The Tems', as he could not pronounce the 'th' sound. As no-one dared correct the monarch, everyone else began to do the same.

Children in your class are likely to have names which don't follow common spelling and pronunciation patterns. In 2023, *Chloe* and *Charlotte* were among the ten most popular girls' names, but neither has *ch* pronounced as it is first taught in phonics programmes, as in *chop* or *chip*.

> ### REFLECTIVE QUESTIONS
>
> Are you asked to spell your name? Do people get it wrong? How many different ways could your name be spelled?
>
> Which of the authors of this chapter do you think is most often mispronounced and/or misspelled?

What does all this tell us about teaching and learning phonics? Essentially, we need to know that letters and small groups of letters represent sounds when we read aloud. There are around 44 letter sounds (*phonemes*) in English, but these can be represented by many more letters and combinations of letters (*graphemes*). So, the /ie/ sound in tie can be made with igh in high, y in my, uy in buy etc. Some people have argued that these inconsistencies or variations mean that it is better to use a different approach to teaching reading, perhaps based on learning whole words. However, such an approach still necessitates learning sounds to go with letters and groups of letters. The government prescribes an approach wherein children are taught using a systematic synthetic approach in which they learn an increasingly complex set of grapheme–phoneme correspondences and apply them to sounding out words. The Education Endowment Foundation (EEF) (2020) conducted an extensive meta-analysis of research on early literacy, and this supports the use of SSP.

### EVIDENCE-INFORMED RESEARCH: APPROACHES TO PHONICS

The EEF maintained that:

> the purpose of phonics is to quickly develop pupils' word recognition and spelling. This involves developing a child's phonemic awareness, which is their ability to hear, identify, and manipulate phonemes (the smallest unit of spoken language), and to teach them the relationship between phonemes and the graphemes (a letter or combination of letters used to represent a phoneme) that represent them. There is very extensive evidence to support the use of a systematic phonics programme with pupils in Key Stage 1.
>
> (EEF, 2020, p. 21)

Before this can happen, we need to develop children's awareness of sounds and their ability to distinguish between them: their *phonological awareness*. We can do this through a range of activities and strategies – for example:

- model good listening skills;
- help children tune into sounds;
- encourage children to listen carefully to and discriminate between speech sounds;
- give children time to respond;
- encourage them to make sounds themselves;

- observe their successes and difficulties – look, listen, note;
- provide plenty of opportunities for children learning English to become familiar with the ways in which sounds are made in English.

Activities to support phonological awareness should not stop once children begin to develop *phonemic awareness* – the ability to match sounds to letters. Rather, the activities can be developed so that letter sounds are focused upon as well as sounds in the environment. For example, games like I-spy can be played with letter sounds rather than letter names (I-spy with my little eye something beginning with /mm/, /ss/, /a/ etc.). When asking children to line up or perform activities, you might say, 'Everyone whose name begins with /rr/ come and line up' or 'Stand up if your name begins with /ff/'.

When children are ready to match written letters to sounds, systematic phonics programmes provide clear guidance on the order in which grapheme–phoneme correspondences should be learned. These typically start with single letters before moving on to digraphs (two letters make one sound as in ch, ck, ou and ea) and trigraphs (three letters make one sound as in tch, dge and igh).

### ACTION LEARNING SET: SATPIN CHALLENGE

Most SSP programmes teach the letter-sound correspondences for s a t p i n first (some teach satpim). How many words can you make just using those six letters? For example, you could make *sat, pin, pit, an, in, tap.*

As a sophisticated language user, you probably found words which early readers may not have identified, such as *paint* and *pint*, because you are aware of digraphs and long vowel sounds. This kind of activity can be undertaken at different stages in children's progress through an SSP scheme, with newly learned graphemes being introduced and challenges set – for example: how many words can you make which include a consonant digraph?

However, the apparent simplicity of matching individual letters to sounds at the early stages of phonics programmes soon gives way to increased complexity. The nature of English presents challenges when teaching and learning literacy and some of these are described in the section below.

# KEY CHALLENGES

## MAKING READING FUN

At the early stages, children focus on the most frequent sounds for the letters and their ability to blend these into words is supported by simple, phonically regular reading books which accompany the programmes. Such books reinforce learning and give children an opportunity to use their burgeoning phonemic awareness to decode words. However, on their own, such books may not inspire children to enjoy reading.

It is important to share texts, including stories, poems, lists, charts and non-fiction so that children see a purpose for learning to read and find it enjoyable and useful. When reading rhyming poetry or learning songs children are tuning into the sounds of their language and developing their phonological awareness.

## COMMON EXCEPTION WORDS

A key challenge is enabling children to read texts which must, inevitably, include words with unusual grapheme phoneme correspondences and those they have not yet met as they work systematically through a programme. Many of the most common words in English fall into this category, for example:

*Table 8.1 Common exception words*

| | | |
|---|---|---|
| said | of | are |
| to | all | my |
| was | he | be |
| I | you | some |
| the | they | so |
| me | she | were |
| no | we | go |
| | | no |

Most programmes include a few common exception words to enable pupils to read texts. These words are kept to a minimum in the early stages, but without them it would be very difficult to produce meaningful text. The words may be taught as whole words, but it is important to identify the regular parts and talk about the sound–symbol correspondences. For example, *said* has two regular sounds (s and d), but a very unusual middle – can you think of any other words in which *ai* represents an /e/ sound like that in *bed*? These words are referred to as common exception or tricky words, but it should be emphasised that most such words are only 'tricky' until their unusual grapheme–phoneme correspondences have been learned.

## ALTERNATIVE GRAPHEMES AND PHONEMES

Because English is a language which has evolved from several other languages, it has inconsistencies in pronunciation and spelling. There are many *homophones* (words which sound the same but have different spellings and meanings – for example, *sea* and *see*, *pair* and *pear*); *homonyms* (words which are spelled and pronounced the same way, but have different meanings – for example, *bear* and *bear*, *match* and *match*); and *homographs* (words which are spelled the same but are pronounced differently – for example, *tear* (when crying) and *tear* (rip), *wound* (past tense of *wind*) and *wound* (injury), *wind* (turn) and *wind* (blows)). Even the word *reading* has a different pronunciation in the name of the town in Berkshire!

These words can be challenging for readers but can also be a topic for discussion as children develop as readers.

## CAPITAL AND LOWER-CASE LETTERS

Programmes teach that each lower-case letter has a corresponding capital letter; they share the letter name and represent the same sound. Pupils are taught, for example, that both 'd' and 'D' are called D and are usually pronounced /d/. Some programmes teach the names of letters only once pupils have learned to say the sounds.

## TEACHING STRATEGIES

Phonics lessons should be fast-paced and focused, providing opportunities for consolidating existing learning, learning new grapheme–phoneme correspondences (GPCs) and applying learning in practical ways. Lessons should be lively, with lots of pupil engagement. The format typically used for phonics lessons is:

- *revisit and review*: look back at what was learned in the previous lesson and ensure children have understood;
- *teach*: introduce the next topic – for example, a new grapheme–phoneme correspondence;
- *practise*: practise the new concept;
- *apply*: this might involve using a newly taught grapheme in words and sentences.

Most programmes recommend spending around five to seven minutes on each of the four elements. Of course, lessons should be part of a well-structured sequence which enables children to make rapid progress. Many phonics programmes provide lesson plans for units of work and suggest appropriate resources.

## PSEUDO WORDS

A controversial aspect of the phonics screening test, which children take in Year 1, is the inclusion of invented or pseudo words: words which children will not have met before, which are used to check if they can apply their phonemic awareness to decode. The 2023 test included pseudo words such as *heng*, *shob*, *farn* and *chesh*, each accompanied by a picture of an alien creature to demarcate them as different from the real words in the test. For most of the pseudo words there is only one way in which they might be pronounced in English, whatever the accent of the reader. However, words such as *drave* might reasonably be pronounced to rhyme with either *grave* or *have*, while the ea in 'teap' could rhyme with ea in *head* or ea in *reap*, ea in *great* etc. You may be asked by parents to justify teaching pseudo words as children prepare for the test and will need to explain that they are used to test phonemic awareness. You will also need to think carefully about the possible pronunciation of any pseudo words you create as children practice.

## UNDERSTANDING TERMINOLOGY: SUBJECT KNOWLEDGE

Sometimes trainee teachers express surprise, when they first observe a phonics lesson in KS1, that children use terms like *grapheme*, *digraph* and *split vowel digraph* confidently. They should be reassured. For those new to an SSP approach the terminology can seem daunting, but young children can grasp it and the structure of the words provides clues about meaning. For example, *phone* means sound and *graph* relates to writing, so a phoneme is a unit of sound and a grapheme is a sound written down. Di- is a prefix for two, so a *digraph* has two letters to represent one sound (ch, ou, sh), while a *trigraph* has three letters (tch, dge) and a *quadgraph* four (th*ough*, c*augh*t, W*augh*).

Many schools provide simple guidance to parents and carers so they can support their children's reading development. Some even send short video clips of the teacher sounding the GPCs currently being learned and offer advice to parents on helping their children at home.

Bear in mind that the terminology you come to take for granted may be new to others, just as the terminology associated with their jobs might be unfamiliar to you. If you are discussing approaches with parents and carers, make sure you make terminology accessible and offer simple guidance.

You will find useful glossaries which provide definitions in many textbooks, including Gill and Waugh (2017) and Jolliffe et al. (2022).

## ENUNCIATION AND ACCENT

The UK has a rich diversity of accents, which can change subtly from town to town as well as between regions. Accent refers to the way we pronounce words and differs from dialect, which refers to variations in vocabulary and phrasing. Phonics can be taught using different accents – the main variations are in the way vowel sounds are made, such as the use of a long or short sound for a in *bath*, *grass* and *path*. Accent can be a topic for discussion, and you might like to use different accents for different characters when reading to children to promote this. Some teachers modify their accents when teaching children whose accents differ from theirs, but the most important thing to do is to enunciate clearly, sounding phonemes 'cleanly' without adding a *schwa* sound (the most common sound in English as in the short /uh/ sound in *the, teacher, doctor*). This is important for parents and carers to understand if they are to support learning at home. If c is sounded as *cuh* and l as *luh*, children can end up spelling *colour* as *cl*, for example. Practise sounding the graphemes to help eliminate the schwa – it is easy for most sounds – for example, *a, e, ff, i, ll, mm, nn*, but a little more difficult for *b, c, d, g* and *p*.

> **REFLECTIVE QUESTIONS**
>
> How would you explain the importance of clear enunciation to a teaching assistant who persistently adds a schwa sound (e.g. *fuh, muh, nuh*) when working with children in your class?

## PHONICS AT KS2

Phonics does not cease to be a focus once children reach KS2 or become advanced readers at KS1. They will meet new words with unusual or unfamiliar spellings, and it is important to discuss these and provide strategies for reading and spelling them. This might include making collections of words with similar GPCs.

A range of strategies can be used to help children learn spellings. It is not sufficient simply to send them home with a list to learn for a test. Strategies might include identifying the 'tricky' parts of words and focusing on these – for example, the w in *answer*, the ui in *build*, or the kn in *know*. Groups of words can be learned together to reinforce learning – for example, *know, knit, knife, knowledge*.

We can also focus on morphology, looking at the units of meaning in words (*morphemes*) and learning their functions. Spelling becomes less challenging when words can be broken down into morphemes and an understanding of meaning is developed. Take the word *like* as a starting point: it can become *liked, liking, likely, likeable, dislike, unlike* etc. As children's knowledge of the meanings of morphemes develops, they can apply their understanding to unfamiliar words, work out meanings and find spelling easier to grasp. Try the challenge below and think about how such an exercise helps you to think about words, their meanings and their spellings.

> **ACTION LEARNING SET: CHALLENGE**
>
> Find the list of words to be learned by Year 3 to Year 4 in the English national curriculum (DfE, 2013, p. 54).
>
> How many of the words can be modified by adding a prefix and/or a suffix?
>
> How many cannot be modified?
>
> You can modify in many different ways – for example, adding s or -es to make a plural, adding -ly to turn a noun into an adverb, or adding a prefix such as un-, dis- or pre- to create antonyms (opposites) or to modify meaning in other ways.

# ENSURING CHILDREN PROGRESS

In this section, you will see how children's reading progress can be monitored, as well as some of the ways in which parents, teachers, schools and outside agencies can identify potential obstacles to learning and work together to help children overcome them.

> **CASE STUDY: SOPHIA'S EARLY READING JOURNEY – EARLY READING SUPPORT**
>
> Sophia is five and lives with her parents and younger brother, who has complex medical needs. Sophia enjoys playing outdoors, dancing and helping to take care of her brother. They are a close family and read together each evening. There is a wide range of books and poems in the family home. She attends her local primary school and is thriving in Reception class. She attended a nursery for limited hours due to her family circumstances and sibling's medical needs.
>
> Sophia transitioned very well into the Reception and now attends school full time. She often chooses to access the role-play, stage and story-telling puppet area. She
>
> *(Continued)*

(Continued)

is extremely confident and scored highly on the personal, social and emotional development early years profile.

Following the early intervention (EI) meeting with the class teacher and school SEND leader, it was decided that Sophia would have her hearing tested as this may be impacting her oral blending skills. A speech and language therapy referral was made to assess her understanding and comprehension of spoken and read language.

Throughout the spring term in Reception, Sophia made excellent progress. She is still learning to decode and beginning to utilise several different reading strategies. She now uses and applies her knowledge of phonics as one way to decode new words. She will also split a word up into individual phonemes. Sophia is now confident to track words across a page from left to right using her left hand. Her segmenting and blending skills greatly improved, and she can now read basic CVC words independently, such as:

c-a-t   m-u-m   d-a-d   p-a-n   p-i-n   d-o-g   j-u-g

Throughout the summer term Sophia made rapid progress following a medical procedure on her right ear which had greatly affected her hearing. This had not been picked up by a health visitor or her previous nursery setting. She was also assessed by an optician and now wears glasses daily.

By the end of the Early Years Foundation Stage Sophia is an enthusiastic reader and enjoys reading at home and at school. She reads to her parents and grandparents daily. It appears her home life fosters a positive attitude to reading and which has benefitted her reading progress over time.

As Sophia transitions into Year 1 it will now be crucial to encourage her enthusiasm and enjoyment of reading for her reading to progress.

Ofsted reports have consistently advocated a great emphasis on both taught systematic phonics and school curricula which are designed coherently to develop 'reading for pleasure' (Ofsted, 2022).

Sophia's ability to decode is constantly developing. She is beginning to read a larger range of digraphs and trigraphs with ease.

Sophia achieved the Literacy Early Learning Goal at the end of the Reception summer term. She reached the expected standard in comprehension, word reading and writing.

This case study provides many factors which class teachers must consider when assessing and observing a pupil in child-led 'play' in the early years. Staff members must work in partnership with parents to enhance a child's early education and reading development pathway. In this case study the inclusion of specialist SEND teams and outreach support workers and the SEND leader at the school all have a positive impact on Sophia.

> **REFLECTIVE QUESTIONS**
>
> List the key indicators and services that support and develop Sophia's success with learning to read.
>
> Plot the steps and actions that her class teacher took once she began to fall behind with phoneme recognition through her daily phonics sessions.

## PARENTAL ENGAGEMENT IN EARLY READING

Goouch and Lambrith (2011, p. 8) suggest that children who read at home will have a head start at school, 'with their knowledge of how stories work, patterns and tunes in stories, the relationship between illustration and print as well as some clear information about print drawn from reading and rereading favourite tales'. The EEF's meta-analysis (2021a) backs this up.

> **EVIDENCE-INFORMED RESEARCH: WORKING WITH PARENTS TO SUPPORT CHILDREN'S LEARNING**
>
> A meta-analysis of research on parental support by the EEF concluded:
>
> - for young children, promoting shared reading should be a central component of working with parents as a way of supporting oral language development and early literacy;
> - most schools encourage parents to read with their children in some way, but additional tips, support and resources can make home reading more effective;
> - helping parents to read in a more interactive way and prompting longer and more frequent conversations with their children are particularly important; the parent-child interactions that take place during shared reading are thought to be the key ingredient to their success;
> - shared reading is an important strategy from a very early age and continues so as children start to develop independent reading skills;
> - parents can support their children in a variety of ways – for example, by asking questions or by linking the topic of the book to real-life examples;
> - using everyday activities to reinforce literacy is important. For example, schools can encourage parents of younger children to look out for 'environmental print' with their children – looking for letters and numbers in street names and shop signs or asking children to look at food labels when out shopping.
>
> (EEF, 2021b, p. 13)

The EEF's findings provide justification for developing strong links with parents for developing children's literacy. However, not all parents are able to help in the ways described, so it is important to find ways of involving them at a level at which they are comfortable. In the case study below, Harry comes from a family where English is not the language spoken at home. As you read the case study, consider how the school might work with Harry's parents to support his development.

### CASE STUDY: HARRY'S EARLY READING PROGRESS AND DEVELOPMENT

Harry was six and had just moved to a new, one-form entry school in the January of Year 1. He relocated to the North-East of England from London, with his parents and three younger siblings. English is Harry's third spoken language, as two other languages are spoken predominantly by his parents.

His disposition and learning behaviours were closely monitored in his new school by both his class teacher and senior leaders through his pupil transition visits. Harry appeared very tired at school and greatly lacked self-confidence. He was not yet able to segment and blend CVC words alongside his peers confidently. He did know some single sounds/phonemes and could recall them very quickly verbally – using flash cards with no pictures.

It was ascertained that Harry attended Reception very sporadically at his previous setting and his attendance was an area for concern in early years. He did achieve the expected standard in communication and language in the early years profile, but he did not achieve the Literacy Early Learning Goal at the end of Reception in the summer term early years profile. To develop positive attendance habits, Harry was offered a free place at his new school's breakfast club called Books over Breakfast! Harry was then able to access a wide range of books, poems and traditional tales daily following his breakfast – to further enhance healthy, daily reading habits and foster a *love of reading*.

In addition, the two schools that he has attended adopted very different phonics schemes validated by the DfE which was also a challenge for Harry. He received very limited, daily systematic phonics teaching sessions and staff were concerned about the Year 1 phonics screening check and his ability to access basic Reception decodable texts, matched to their chosen accredited scheme.

In the first spring term, Harry was assessed in reading and the Year 1 staff team judged Harry as 'working significantly below' the Year 1 standard. However, Harry adored books and loved to access and act out poems and rhymes in the class reading corner. In provision time sessions Harry often chose the class reading corner and puppet role-play area. The Year 1 teacher observed him acting out traditional rhymes and stories – e.g. The Three Little Pigs – in his home language with great enthusiasm and with confidence. As well as traditional tales, Harry loved to explore the animal small world play area of the classroom and the mini-beast play section in particular. In his free play Harry was observed making excellent vocabulary choices for his age.

Taking Harry's needs and interests into account the Year 1 teacher and the English leader planned an English unit of work based on the text *Superworm*, by Julia Donaldson, to target a specific group of four boys including Harry. The repetition and repeating rhyming patterns in this text were easily performed and acted out by the Year 1 pupils, including Harry.

> *Superworm is super long,*
>
> *Superworm is super strong,*
>
> *Watch him wriggle,*
>
> *See him squirm,*
>
> *Hip, hip Hooray for Superworm!*

Harry joined his peers in speaking and listening tasks and oral rehearsal games. The staff observed Harry accessing the daily English lessons with great enthusiasm and developing both his oral rehearsal and fluency skills.

Alongside detailed, bespoke English planning Harry accessed systematic phonics in his new setting every morning. He quickly progressed through the phonics phases and daily sounds once he was taught in a small intervention group of four pupils. He received 1:1 catch-up tutoring in the afternoon and was given a Year 6 reading peer buddy to support his reading fluency and confidence. His 1:1 reading tutor also used Makaton signing to help deliver catch-up phonics sessions.

Before the Easter break, the Year 1 teacher held a phonics open morning which Harry and his parents attended together. Harry was given intensive support to develop his reading skills and reading for pleasure disposition, both in daily phonics sessions and daily English lessons. This detailed, multi-pronged and systematic approach ensured that Harry was able to access both Reception and Year 1 reading materials and greatly catch up with his peers by the end of the summer term.

Postscript

Harry took the phonics screening check in June of the summer term and achieved 33 out of 40 possible marks.

He passed the Year 1 Reading Standard for the national curriculum.

In Year 2 Harry went on to achieve Age Related Expectations in the Year 2 SATs.

## REFLECTIVE QUESTIONS

This case study provides many discussion points linked to early reading and the progress a child may or may not make with systematic phonics schemes, adaptation planning and specific reading intervention throughout the early years.

*(Continued)*

(Continued)

List the key factors that supported Harry's eventual success and the some of the potential obstacles which may have led him to fall behind national curriculum reading standards.

How could the school work with Harry's parents to support his development?

If you were Harry's class teacher in Year 1 what main priorities and/or reading routines would you want to establish first?

# CONCLUSION

In this chapter, you have been introduced to some of the key considerations related to early reading and phonics. The chapter has explored why phonics is the chosen method for teaching early reading and some of the challenges that phonics can pose. You have explored how you might ensure children make progress in phonics to develop their reading and how you might support parents when reading with their children at home.

### REVIEW OF CHAPTER OBJECTIVES

Within this chapter you have considered:

- the role that phonics plays in teaching reading;
- the alphabetic code;
- the different approaches to teaching phonics;
- the importance of applying phonics for reading and writing:
- teaching phonics in KS2.

# FURTHER READING AND RESOURCES

For guidance on teaching spelling, see:

Allott, K. (2023) Spelling, in Waugh, D., Jolliffe, W. and Allott, K. (eds.), *Primary English for Trainee Teachers* (4th ed.). London: Sage.

For a fascinating insight into the reasons for English spelling patterns, see:

Crystal, D. (2012) *Spell It Out: The Singular Story of English Spelling*. London: Profile.

Department for Education (DfE) (2023) *The Reading Framework: Teaching the Foundations of Literacy.* Available at: www.gov.uk/government/publications/the-reading-framework-teaching-the-foundations-of-literacy [accessed 9 November 2023].

Department for Education and Skills (DfES) (2006) *Independent Review of the Teaching of Early Reading* (Final Report by Jim Rose). Ref: 0201/2006DOC-EN. Nottingham: DfES.

Flynn, N., Powell, D., Stainthorp, R. and Stuart, M. (2021) Training teachers for phonics and early reading: Developing research-informed practice. *Journal of Research in Reading*, 44(2), pp. 301–318.

Jolliffe, W., Waugh, D. and Gill, A. (2022) *Teaching Systematic Synthetic Phonics in Primary* (4th ed.). London: Sage.

Ofsted (2022) *Research Review Series: English.* Available at: www.gov.uk/government/publications/curriculum-research-review-series-english [accessed 9 November 2023].

Waugh, D., Allott, K., Waugh, R., English, E. and Bulmer, E. (2020) *The Essential Guide to SPaG in the Primary Classroom.* London: Sage.

Waugh, D., Warner, C. and Waugh, R. (2022) *Teaching Grammar, Punctuation and Spelling in Primary Schools* (4th ed.). London: Sage. Chapters 3, 4 and 5.

# REFERENCES

Department for Education (DfE) (2011) *Teachers' Standards Guidance.* Available at: https://assets.publishing.service.gov.uk/media/61b73d6c8fa8f50384489c9a/Teachers__Standards_Dec_2021.pdf [accessed 9 November 2023].

DfE (2013) *The National Curriculum in England.* Available at: https://assets.publishing.service.gov.uk/government/uploads/system/uploads/attachment_data/file/381344/Master_final_national_curriculum_28_Nov.pdf [accessed 21 December 2023].

DfE (2019) *ITT Core Content Framework.* London: DfE. Available at: https://assets.publishing.service.gov.uk/government/uploads/system/uploads/attachment_data/file/974307/ITT_core_content_framework_.pdf [accessed November 2023].

DfE (2023) *The Reading Framework: Teaching the Foundations of Literacy.* Available at: www.gov.uk/government/publications/the-reading-framework-teaching-the-foundations-of-literacy [accessed 9 November 2023].

EEF (2021a) *Improving Literacy in Key Stage 2: Guidance Report* (2nd ed.). Available at: https://educationendowmentfoundation.org.uk/education-evidence/guidance-reports/literacy-ks2 [accessed 9 November 2023].

EEF (2021b) *Working with Parents to Support Children's Learning: Guidance Report.* Available at: https://educationendowmentfoundation.org.uk/education-evidence/guidance-reports/supporting-parents [accessed 9 November 2023].

Gill, A. and Waugh, D. (2017) *Phonics: Getting it Right in a Week.* St Albans: Critical.

Goouch, K. and Lambirth, A. (2011) *Teaching Early Reading and Phonics: Creative Approaches to Early Literacy.* London: Sage.

Jolliffe, W., Waugh, D. and Gill, A. (2022) *Teaching Systematic Synthetic Phonics in Primary* (4th ed.). London: Sage.

# 9

# PUPIL BEHAVIOUR

## ZOE PROCTOR AND MELANIE MOORE

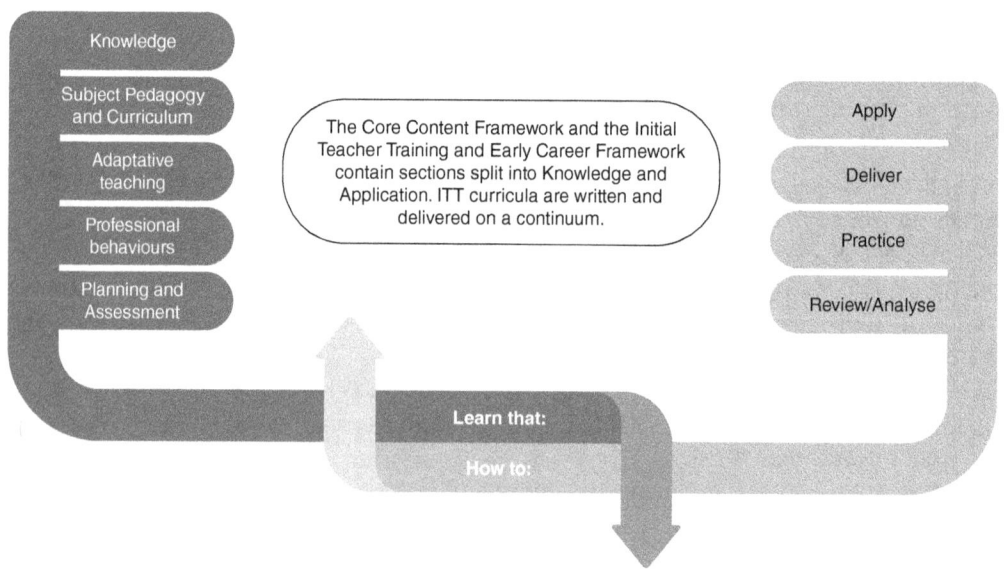

# 9 PUPIL BEHAVIOUR

## FRAMED BY THE CCF – FOR FULL LINKS TO THE ITTECF, SEE PAGE 337

Managing Behaviour

(Standard 7 – 'Manage behaviour effectively')

| Learn that ... | Learn how to ... |
|---|---|
| 1. Establishing and reinforcing routines, including through positive reinforcement, can help create an effective learning environment.<br><br>5. Building effective relationships is easier when pupils believe that their feelings will be considered and understood.<br><br>6. Pupils are motivated by intrinsic factors (related to their identity and values) and extrinsic factors (related to reward). | Develop a positive, predictable and safe environment for pupils:<br><br>• Receiving clear, consistent and effective mentoring in how to respond quickly to any behaviour ... threatens emotional safety.<br><br>And – following expert input – by taking opportunities to practise, receive feedback and improve at:<br><br>• Establishing a supportive and inclusive environment with a predictable system of reward and sanction in the classroom. |

## CHAPTER OBJECTIVES

On reading this chapter you will consider:

- what behaviour management is within a learning environment;
- the theoretical models that underpin strategies you see being used in the classroom;
- the tools required for building and maintaining positive relationships for learning;
- how a restorative approach can help with supporting behaviours.

## KEY VOCABULARY

Behaviour management

Positive reinforcement

Positive relationships/relational practice

Restorative practice

Values

(Care/trust/empathy)

# INTRODUCTION

Many years ago, as a newly qualified teacher, I was interviewed for a post as a classroom teacher and asked the following question:

> 'How do you handle discipline problems in the classroom? Can you give me an example?'

How I answered this question then and what I would say now as an experienced teacher is quite different. Consider this question now; we will revisit these considerations at the end of the chapter.

As a trainee it is likely that you have thought about how you are going to manage a class of 30 pupils. For many it is a real anxiety that can hinder progress, calling into question your very motivation for wanting to be a teacher in the first place. You may have sought out information, advice from others, or even resorted to asking the all-knowing Google, and who could blame you! If you have tried any of these methods, you will have no doubt encountered a dizzying array of information offering you a range of tips and tricks. Yet, these seemingly helpful strategies do not really tell the whole story. Many of the solutions do not contextualise the 'why', only seeking to offer solutions to situations. They offer only one piece of the complex puzzle that is *behaviour management* in a school context.

This chapter will set out where 'managing behaviour' is positioned within Standard 7 of the *ITT Core Content Framework* (CCF) (DfE, 2019, p. 26) and the Initial Teacher Training and Early Career Framework (DfE, 2024). We will discuss how many common strategies to support behaviour have evolved from evidence-informed research and how each approach connects to create a cohesive picture, which you can begin to apply in your practice in the classroom. It will also encourage you to think about your own values and the educational philosophy you hold with regards to managing behaviour. By the end of the chapter, you will have started to gather a range of tools to help you create a learning environment for *all*: building relationships, trust and using relational practice through 'visible consistency and visible kindness' (Dix, 2017, p. 3). Ultimately, it is a guide to help you navigate the nerves you will undoubtedly feel at some point during your training and indeed your ECT years of teaching. It includes lots of practical examples and will provide you with a solid foundation on which to develop the confidence you require to be the teacher you aspire to be.

# WHAT IS BEHAVIOUR MANAGEMENT IN A LEARNING ENVIRONMENT?

Managing behaviour, whether you are a trainee, or an experienced professional, is complex. There are times when you believe you have it sorted, then out of the blue something changes. Reasons for this change might range from a playground incident, a new pupil joining the class, an incident for a child at home, or simply a non-uniform day! The illusion that you have cracked the managing behaviour conundrum is shattered! The very nature of teaching means that you are working with individual personalities who have unique needs, and this presents its own challenges but is also central to how rewarding teaching is. That said, you do need pedagogical knowledge aligned to key strategies to support you in navigating the highs and lows of managing a class.

There are many old sayings in education about how to manage behaviour and by reading this chapter hopefully you *will not* succumb to any of these.

Instead, focus on the belief that managing behaviour is, at its heart, creating and fostering good relationships – which you can do by intentionally teaching and modelling good practice to the pupils. Striving to do this every day you will create a setting where pupils can and will thrive.

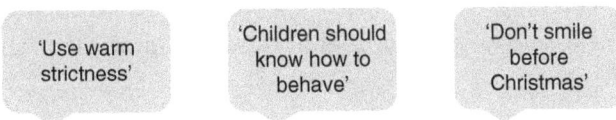

*Figure 9.1 Sayings to avoid*

# WHAT ARE THE EXPECTATIONS OF CLASSROOM BEHAVIOUR?

As teachers, we have an important role to play in modelling, shaping and nurturing the pupils that we teach. Alongside our responsibility to teach knowledge and skills, we are also responsible for helping to develop the *whole child*. We want our pupils to become responsible, self-regulating adults who can confidently take control of their lives in a way which is productive and purposeful.

Although most pupils achieve this goal through the process of natural growth, maturity and development, some pupils need to explicitly learn the boundaries of what is acceptable and unacceptable behaviour. The role of the teacher is crucial in developing this (Glazzard et al., 2022). Expectations need to be clearly identified and, when not met, dealt with in a supportive manner that is consistent, proportionate and fair (Whitaker, 2021).

*Challenging* or *poor* behaviour can come in many different forms and often constitutes what is known as *low-level* classroom disruption (Bennett, 2010). Pupils may display behaviour outwardly – for example, through physical and verbal aggression or changes in their interactions with others – that do not meet expectations. It is worth noting that not all poor behaviours are so overt or obvious. Some more covert behaviours might include eye-rolling or shrugging, refusal to complete tasks, defacing books, name calling or shouting out. The reasons for pupils exhibiting such behaviours can be varied and numerous but, in most cases, it is an attempt to communicate an unmet need, and is influenced by a range of biological and environmental factors (Glazzard et al., 2022). Pupils' behaviour is shaped by a myriad of factors, both positive and negative, and includes the effects of parenting, community influences, peers, friendships groups, social media and hormonal changes, as well as cultural expectations.

All these factors contribute to, and impact on, relationships and the way a pupil might react to complex interactions and expectations within a school setting. Where a learning environment causes stress for a pupil their responses are going to be varied and may result in behaviour that does not meet the expectations of the school policy, teachers, carers and even that of the pupil themselves.

Figure 9.2 below demonstrates how a pupil might respond to an external or internal stress.

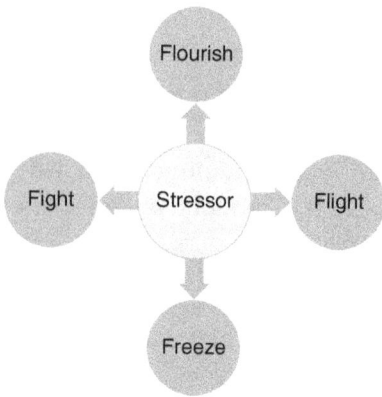

*Figure 9.2 Possible responses to stress*

As a trainee when you see behaviour that does not meet expectations it can be shocking and leave you unsure as to how to proceed. At this point, it is tempting to take the behaviour personally and you may feel an emotional and defensive response, perhaps labelling the pupil as challenging, *naughty* or *disengaged with learning*. You might also start to believe the child is inherently 'bad' and disruptive, without giving them the opportunity to demonstrate positive behaviours. Undoubtedly this leads to a further breakdown of communication and trust between a pupil and teacher. Sensing that they are not liked will have an impact on an individual's self-esteem, exacerbating and escalating the problem further. Instead, it is important to focus on the behaviours being displayed, rather than on the individual pupil. It is the behaviour, rather than the child that is undesirable.

## CASE STUDY: MANAGING AND RESPONDING TO LOW-LEVEL DISRUPTIVE BEHAVIOUR

Sara is on her second school placement on her undergraduate BA Hons degree with QTS; she has an eight-week placement in Year 5. During her initial delivery of short teaching episodes, Ben, a pupil in her class, continually starts conversations with the pupils around him. He does this mainly when Sara is talking and when other pupils are answering questions. When the majority of his peers are sat working independently, he continues to initiate conversations. Consequently, he disrupts the learning and other pupils become frustrated with him.

During the discussion and feedback time between Sara and her mentor they discuss this behaviour and how it's impacting on the teaching and learning. The mentor identifies a range of strategies to help reduce these distracting behaviours.

The following day he models using these strategies for Sara as he delivers a learning sequence to the same class.

These include:

- planning one paired task opportunity for discussion in the lesson;
- making expectations of turn-taking clear to all pupils;
- specifically asking Ben to contribute at key times during open discussion;
- using a visual cue to determine independent quiet working;
- using eye contact if Ben began talking when others were speaking;
- introducing a strategy to encourage active listening and turn-taking (having listener and the speaker turn-taking cards).

*(Continued)*

(Continued)

Once Sara observed her mentor modelling these strategies, she is able to 'have a go' at several of them herself while her mentor observes and reviews her next lesson. After the observation, Sara and her mentor deconstruct how effective each of the strategies had been in reducing the low-level disruptive behaviour.

They also speak to Ben and discuss how his behaviour has modified throughout the last few days and sessions.

*Follow up:*

We should always take a positive discipline approach (Dreikurs et al., 1982: Rogers, 2015) where we model and teach pupils to become responsible, respectful and resourceful members of the classroom community with a focus on building relationships.

Speak to your mentor in your placement school and ask about their school policy on managing low-level disruption.

## REFLECTIVE QUESTIONS

Why was it important that the mentor modelled for Sara before she was expected to 'have a go' at delivering these teaching strategies?

What steps must Sara take to continue on this positive journey?

How can those strategies be adapted if needed?

Glazzard et al. (2022, p. 279) invite the teacher to consider what they call, 'a principled approach to behaviour management' which includes a belief that:

- all pupils are inherently good;
- all behaviours are an attempt to communicate something;
- adults in the classroom significantly affect the quality of the atmosphere for the pupils;
- power and control are not effective ways to shape pupils' behaviour.

Every child needs to know that they are valued and that they are worthy of time, effort and respect, regardless of the behaviours they present. As a teacher, it is you that has the power to set the tone and culture within your classroom to ensure every child has the opportunity to succeed.

# THEORETICAL MODELS THAT UNDERPIN STRATEGIES YOU SEE BEING USED IN THE CLASSROOM

## THE IMPORTANCE OF REFLECTION

Reflecting on behaviours you see in the classroom will support your growing knowledge and help demonstrate your understanding beyond an emotional response. Using a *reflective model* to support your thinking is beneficial. A commonly used model was devised by Schön (1991) and prompts you to reflect on your actions both in the moment and after the behaviours.

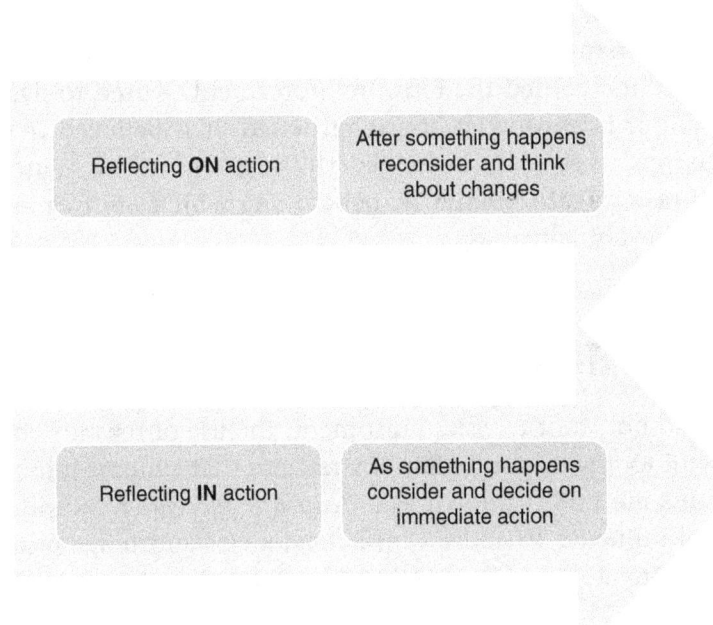

*Figure 9.3  The Schön reflective model (adapted from Schön, 1991)*

The relevance of this model for trainee teachers is the ability to reflect in action and not rely on hindsight.

Gather examples of how pupils reacted to certain situations and your subsequent actions; sharing these with your peers, expert tutors and mentors will support you in understanding how to best act in the moment and in future. The adapted Schön model (1991) can support you with these reflections.

# WHAT ARE THE PERSONAL AND PROFESSIONAL VALUES ASSOCIATED WITH MANAGING BEHAVIOUR?

Many trainees if asked about behaviour management strategies will undoubtedly answer that they are based on the use of rewards and sanctions (Bennett, 2010). Desirable, compliant behaviours are celebrated and rewarded; undesirable behaviours are met with punishment or sanction, for example, missing a breaktime or names being placed on 'red' on a board. For many schools, the use of rewards and sanctions are the cornerstone to their behaviour policy and to managing behaviour. As a trainee it is important you are fully aware of the expectations of that policy.

The use of rules and sanctions as an approach to managing behaviour is not a new one; Behaviourism is a field of psychology that has been applicable to educational theory for many decades. However, it was the psychologist B. F. Skinner (1904–1990) who first coined the term 'reinforcement' – used to describe when a desired behaviour is reinforced or strengthened. It is believed that the more a behaviour is positively acknowledged the greater the incidence that this behaviour will occur again. Similarly, behaviours which are not reinforced or strengthened will eventually cease.

# EXTRINSIC MOTIVATORS

As most pupils do not want to risk punishment, the use of rewards and sanctions can be one useful tool within a toolkit of strategies that support minor behaviour lapses. Using this method is known as an *extrinsic motivator*. Simply put, it is a form of external influence to address misbehaviour or encourage positive behaviours. Extrinsic motivators can be tangible – for example, where a sticker becomes a reward and a missed breaktime a consequence – or less tangible through verbal praise or constructive criticism. A consequence of only having extrinsic methods to support behaviour management in the classroom, however, might be pupils eventually being *desensitised*.

Consider the following scenario: Sam is a child in your class who is asked to tidy up the maths resources after a practical session.

'No, I don't want to,' he replies.

One approach using extrinsic motivators would be to use a consequence for refusal – for example, missing a breaktime.

> **REFLECTIVE QUESTIONS**
>
> Will this consequence change Sam's behaviour in the short term?
>
> Why?
>
> Consider the long term.
>
> Will this consequence prevent the behaviour reoccurring?
>
> Why? Why not?
>
> What other approach could be adopted?

The behaviourist viewpoint focuses very much on the consequences of the behaviour, a *reactionary model*. Arguably, just using this model is overly simplistic in its approach as it does not consider the motivations, feelings, or circumstances of the child displaying the behaviour. It assumes that the pupil is making rational and purposeful decisions, that there are no extenuating circumstances, that they have the ability to express their frustrations appropriately. Furthermore, for some pupils, they can become trapped in a constant cycle of punishment (Whitaker, 2021). For these pupils, the fear of punishment no longer acts as a deterrent, it no longer has power. This can result in further escalations of behaviour so, rather than the behaviour ceasing, incidents increase in their intensity and frequency. Tragically, for some pupils they grow to accept that punishment is just an inevitable part of the school day.

By only using the reward and sanction approach, teachers are at risk of just reacting to the symptoms of challenging behaviour rather than considering the cause, only seeing the situation in a stark right-or-wrong context. Teachers have turned the act of 'naming and shaming' (Dix, 2017) using visible punishments into an art form – name on the board, traffic lights, ticks, moving up and down on elaborate displays of mountains. Dix (2017) argues that we should strive for recognition as reward rather than elaborate hierarchies of reward and punishment. He advocates that teachers should instead take an *intrinsic motivation* approach.

# INTRINSIC MOTIVATORS

## TOOLS FOR BUILDING AND MAINTAINING POSITIVE RELATIONSHIPS FOR LEARNING

> *Behaviour does not just need managing it needs understanding and responding to with relational pedagogy.*
>
> Glazzard et al. (2022, p. 279)

As trainees and ECTs we need to consider what motivates a child by first thinking about why pupils do not want to complete a task or why they are displaying certain behaviours in the first place. Armed with this knowledge, we can steer pupils onto a different path. One such way is to consider how to harness a child's intrinsic values. This would mean showing the value of doing something for the sake of personal satisfaction, because it feels good or because it is a worthwhile pursuit. Intrinsic motivators can be developed using praise or by encouraging the child to take pride in their learning and behaviour. To identify a pupil's intrinsic motivation teachers should ask themselves reflective questions and take time to consider the triggers or antecedents for behaviour. By doing this, teachers take a preventative stance in managing behaviour rather than a reactionary one (Coe et al., 2020).

## EVIDENCE-INFORMED RESEARCH

Evidence shows us that in the short term, extrinsic motivators, such as rewards, can have a negative impact on intrinsic motivation. For example, if there is not a reward pupils may be less likely to complete a task or change a behaviour. Extrinsic motivators are useful when dealing with minor misbehaviour but have little to no impact on sustained behaviour change (Whitaker, 2021). Therefore, an intrinsic approach, developing the whole child, knowing your pupils (Coe et al., 2020) and encouraging them to be self-motivated can have the most impact on behaviour (Sammons et al., 2016).

The guidance report *Improving Behaviour in Schools* (Moore et al., 2019) states that there are three strategies that need to be implemented by individual teachers and schools to help minimise behaviour incidents.

1. The first is *proactive* strategies; these are implemented at a classroom level which, when successfully administrated, reduces the number of incidents of undesirable behaviour in the first place and allows a greater effort to be placed on the teaching and learning in the classroom.
2. The second is *reactive* strategies; these are used for pupils who require additional support which is tailor-made to help them meet the expected behaviour standards.
3. The third strategy is *implementation*. This covers how the first two approaches are consistently implemented and is considered a crucial component to successful school-wide behaviour management policy.

Teachers should convey care, empathy and warmth towards their students and avoid negative emotional behaviours, such as sarcasm, shouting or humiliation. Moreover, there is empirical evidence to suggest that an empathetic approach is associated with higher achievements along with other positive pupil outcomes. Evaluations of practice show that when teachers work on improving the warmth and support in their classrooms, pupil outcomes improve (Coe et al., 2020).

# SUPPORTING PUPILS' BEHAVIOUR: BUILDING RELATIONSHIPS

Relationships in primary classrooms are built, maintained and repaired as part of your day-to-day responsibility as a teacher. You will maintain high expectations of behaviour through regular reflection. Pupils look to teachers for an emotional connection. The work of Golding (2015) discusses the phrase 'connection before correction', meaning we build relationships before making judgements on pupils' behaviour choices. The work also makes it clear that you can only use effective extrinsic strategies if you have fostered a mutually respectful relationship with pupils. Where this is missing there may be a deficit within the relationship which can result in non-compliance and often challenging behaviour.

# PUPIL SELF-REGULATION

Encouraging pupils themselves to understand their own behaviours and reflect on them can also support the building of mutually respectful relationships between pupils and teachers. The work of psychologist Carl Rogers (1961) maintains relevance to educational theory as it places an emphasis on the importance of individual agency and personal growth. Pupils with a developed sense of self-regulation (Mujis et al., 2018) learn to gain agency over their actions and take responsibility. Those who don't develop agency will not accept responsibility for their behaviour and future actions will be repeated. The implication of this could be damage to a child's self-concept. They 'feel bad about themselves' and as a result abdicate responsibility to others – for example, 'you made me angry' or 'the lesson was boring'.

The following Action learning set will support you in recognising how established and mutually respectful relationships promote *connections* and *self-regulation* in the classroom.

> ### ACTION LEARNING SET
>
> Arrange with your mentor to observe an expert colleague.
>
> As you observe the lesson use the following prompts.
>
> How did the class teacher:
>
> - make use of the school or setting system of rewards and sanctions;
> - give manageable specific and sequential instructions during the lesson;
>
> *(Continued)*

(Continued)

- check that pupils understand instructions before a task begins;
- use consistent language and appropriate non-verbal signals for standard classroom directions;
- use early and least-intrusive interventions as an initial response to low-level disruption;
- provide positive praise for work and behaviour.

After the observation discuss and deconstruct with the class teacher. Reflect on the preparation that has been done behind the scenes where expert teachers make this look easy. You might observe this through the teacher's *unconditional positive regard* (Rogers, 1961) and the ways in which they encourage personal resilience in their learners, how they plan learning with structure and set and maintain routines in the classroom. Teachers' high expectations are value-driven, involve mutual respect and the desire to understand their learners.

# THE POWER OF MUTUAL RESPECT

## POSITIVE CONNECTION-MAKING

Authentic relationships are motivating in themselves for learners. Think about the power of eye contact and smiling in creating connection. When observing colleagues, you may see examples of connection-making through non-verbal cues like nods or a hand on the shoulder, teacher and pupil positioning in the room and being at the pupil's level. A sense of humour, forgiveness and the use of second chances can also be a form of promoting mutual respect.

Social constructivist approaches to managing behaviour enable teachers to consider and involve the child in developing mutually acceptable behaviours. Pupils are active participants in their learning, and this should be applied to developing expected behaviour also. A pupil's awareness of their own social and emotional learning – allowing them to express and self-manage their own emotions and respond to other's emotions – plays a key factor in this (Glazzard et al., 2022; Roffey, 2017).

Whitaker (2021) advocates that teachers develop an accepting and empathetic classroom environment. The examples below give ideas of what each approach might include.

- *Genuineness*

    Modelling and supporting actions and decisions that build trust.

    Championing honesty and transparency.

- *Acceptance*

    Allowing pupils' to feel understood, in time building self-esteem and trust.

- *Empathy*

    Identifying with others and their feelings and considering the perspectives of peers.

- *Self-actualisation*

    Modelling *being our best selves*, not always getting things right, accepting mistakes and understanding that mistakes lead to 'having another go'.

# HOW A RESTORATIVE APPROACH CAN HELP WITH SUPPORTING BEHAVIOURS

Creating a learning environment where the pupils are listened to and there is time to respond to questions and discuss ideas is important when managing behaviour. Restorative practice is an approach that takes a humanistic and social constructivist stance, encouraging a viewpoint of behaviour management being done with pupils and not done to pupils (McCold and Watchel, 2001). Strategies that exemplify creating mutually respectful relationships also include: greeting pupils on arrival, asking them about their weekend or engaging with them on the playground. Restorative practice features both elements of support and challenge and is essential in teaching pupils to manage conflict resolution (Zehr, 2015) and maintain relationships in the classroom. It is not based on arbitrary consequences that are punitive in nature, but on care and kindness proactively applied.

Strategies that may be unique to the classrooms you visit during your training will reflect the conscious choices individual teachers have made to seek connections and build and maintain relationships. Examples of these might be:

- the use of show and tell time to promote pupil voice;
- adapted curriculum plans to engage with the pupils' interests;
- a worry box, to allow pupils to share concerns with you and, if appropriate, their peers.

As psychologist Karen Treisman aptly tells us 'Every interaction can be an intervention' (Treisman, 2020) and a teacher should never underestimate the power of small 'quality moments' for supporting behaviour.

As you observe the positive effects that caring and interaction have on relationships between staff and pupils you will begin to adopt these strategies. Careful modelling by expert tutors, class teachers and mentors will support this. Developing this practice as your own will in turn have a positive impact on the learning environment, self-esteem of pupils (and you as the teacher!) and lead to a reduction in undesirable behaviour and negative impact on the learning environment.

Combining whole-school policies with ideas of your own that involve both extrinsic and intrinsic motivators is the key to success.

## CASE STUDY: RESTORATIVE PRACTICE AND RELATIONAL PEDAGOGY

Approaches to behaviour are school context-dependent but in principle should be reasonable, proportionate and necessary.

Ameena is often out of her seat in her Year 2 classroom. She is an enthusiastic learner with lots of energy and ideas. She walks out of the KS1 classroom and into the shared area with EYFS during a lesson. She responds to a range of classroom behaviour strategies in the moment, but this is not sustained. The class teacher and support assistant used the following strategies to support Ameena with her behaviour.

At the start of each session the expectations were made clear to Ameena:

- routines were reinforced – for example, settling down tasks and transitions between areas of the classroom and sessions in the day;
- other adults and pupils were asked to politely explain that they were working and needed to concentrate;
- her peers explained to her that by walking away from her place and moving around the classroom she was distracting herself and others;
- adults listened to Ameena's ideas about why she'd moved away from her seat and what would support her to sit down and stay sat down when needed;
- a timer and visual timetable were used to reinforce key expectations;
- pre-arranged breaks were established (after she had completed her tasks) and in a quieter part of the classroom.

At all times Ameena was praised for meeting her expectations using consistent, kind and fair language.

Over the half term Ameena began to see how her behaviour was affecting her learning and that of her peers. With consistent use of these restorative approaches, she reduced the times she would get up from her place.

Restorative practice is promoted by the school as an approach to meet the needs of all stakeholders in a school community. The case study demonstrates that the school follows the approaches used in relational practice to ensure that they use child-centred behaviour management strategies (Dix, 2017; Whitaker, 2021). It is essential to follow a school's behaviour policy as it lays out agreed practice and consistency is proven to be effective in behaviour management and changes of behaviours (EEF, 2019).

# TIPS

Strive for a balanced and values-driven approach between extrinsic and intrinsic motivators:

- observe effective practitioners and implement successful strategies in your own practice;
- reflect on approaches you have previously taken when supporting difficult or poor behaviours;
- explicitly plan for learning behaviours in interactions;
- apply policy and guidance consistently;
- consider how to build and maintain effective relationships with pupils.

## EVIDENCE-INFORMED PRACTICE

Current government guidance on behaviour (DfE, 2022, p. 13) states that:

> All pupils deserve to learn in an environment that is calm, safe, supportive, and where they are treated with dignity. To achieve this every pupil should be made aware of the school behaviour standards, expectations, pastoral support and consequence processes. Pupils should be taught they have a duty to follow the school behaviour policy and uphold the school rules.

EEF (2019) guidance states that successful management of behaviour relies on far more than a setting of standards to draw upon when pupils misbehave. Ellis and Tod (2014) suggest that to meet these standards pupils must have a set of learning behaviours and that it is these that impact on behaviour development and regulation.

*(Continued)*

(Continued)

'Learning behaviour can be thought of as a behaviour that is necessary in order for a person to learn effectively in the group setting of the classroom' (EEF, 2019, p.16).

Three strands of learning behaviours are identified: emotional, social and cognitive developmental. Relationships pupils have with themselves, others and the curriculum can result in changes in learning behaviours. When pupils improve their learning behaviours this impacts on academic achievement and cognitive ability. Pupils who are aware of their own behaviour can self-regulate and deploy coping skills and will be less likely to misbehave in school. However, teachers are responsible and need to be alert to opportunities to support, teach and reinforce these learning behaviours.

Although teaching learning behaviours alongside behaviour management is effective there will also be some pupils that require additional support for behaviour. Challenging and disruptive behaviour is a recognised need in the SEND Code of Practice (DfE/DoH, 2015) within the category of social, emotional and mental health (SEMH). DfE guidance (2017) on mental health for pupils promotes building resilience in learners and the creation of an affirming place to trust and talk openly with adults within an educational setting (DfE, 2017, p. 8). Where a child is identified as having this need then as a trainee teacher you will be well supported in your management of the learning environment.

For more information on supporting pupils with SEND, see Chapter 12.

## REFLECTIVE QUESTIONS

Refer back to the key question and think about how you have developed your original answer?

'How do you handle discipline problems in the classroom?'

Compare your initial thoughts with what you know now after reading this chapter.

# CONCLUSION

Consistency, high expectations and strong, mutually respectful relationships promote positive behaviour choices at both whole-school and classroom level. This approach will prevent the relationship between teacher and pupil being one based on managing behaviour with only discipline in mind. An approach based on the idea of obeying rules and making use of punishment as a driver should instead be replaced with a drive to understand and support behaviour to maximise the opportunities to learn (Coe et al., 2020).

This chapter has set out where managing behaviour (DfE, 2019, p. 26) is positioned within CCF/ITTECF Standard 7. It has discussed how many common strategies to support behaviour have evolved from evidenced-informed research and how each approach connects to create a cohesive whole picture, which you can begin to apply in your practice in the classroom. It also encouraged you to think about your own values and the educational philosophy you hold with regards to managing behaviour. You will have started to gather a range of tools to help you create a learning environment for *all*: building relationships, trust and using relational practice through 'visible consistency and visible kindness' (Dix, 2017, p. 3). It has included lots of practical examples to help you identify with and empathise with managing behaviours. It has provided you with a solid foundation on which to develop the confidence you require to be the professional teacher you aspire to be.

> **REVIEW OF CHAPTER OBJECTIVES**
>
> Within this chapter you have considered:
>
> - what behaviour management is within a learning environment;
> - the theoretical models that underpin strategies you see being used in the classroom;
> - the tools required for building and maintaining positive relationships for learning;
> - how a restorative approach can help with supporting behaviours.

# FURTHER READING AND RESOURCES

Bates, B., Bailey, A. and Lever, D. (2019) *A Quick Guide to Behaviour Management*. London: Sage.

Colquhoun, K. (2023) *A Practical Guide to Pupil's Wellbeing*. Melton: John Catt Education.

# REFERENCES

Bennett, T. (2010) *The Behaviour Guru: Behaviour Management Solutions for Teachers*. London: A&C Black.

Coe, R., Rauch, C. J., Kime, S. and Singleton, D. (2020) *Great Teaching Toolkit: Evidence Review. Evidence Based Education*. Cambridge: Cambridge Assessment International Education. Available at: https://evidencebased.education/great-teaching-toolkit-evidence-review/ [accessed 19 December 2023].

DfE (2017) *Supporting Mental Health in Schools and Colleges: Summary Report*. Available at: https://assets.publishing.service.gov.uk/media/5a82186fed915d74e3401b34/Supporting_Mental-Health_synthesis_report.pdf [accessed November 2023].

DfE (2019) *ITT Core Content Framework*. London: DfE. Available at: https://assets.publishing.service.gov.uk/government/uploads/system/uploads/attachment_data/file/974307/ITT_core_content_framework_.pdf [accessed November 2023].

DfE (2022) *Behaviour in Schools*. Available at: www.gov.uk/government/publications/behaviour-in-schools--2 [accessed November 2023].

Department for Education and Department of Health (DfE/DoH) (2015) *Special Educational Needs and Disability Code of Practice: 0 to 25 Years. Statutory Guidance for Organisations Which Work with and Support Children and Young People who Have Special Educational Needs or Disabilities*. London: DfE/DoH.

Dix, P. (2017) *When the Adults Change, Everything Changes: Seismic Shifts in School Behaviour*. Carmarthen: Crown House.

Dreikurs, R., Grunwald, B. and Pepper, F. (1982) *Maintaining Sanity in the Classroom* (2nd ed.). New York: Harper and Row.

Education Endowment Foundation (EEF) (2019) *Improving Behaviour in Schools: Guidance Report*. Available at: https://d2tic4wvo1iusb.cloudfront.net/production/eef-guidance-reports/behaviour/EEF_Improving_behaviour_in_schools_Report.pdf [accessed November 2023].

Ellis, S. and Tod, J. (2014) *Promoting Behaviour for Learning in the Classroom: Effective Strategies, Personal Style and Professionalism*. London: Routledge.

Glazzard, G., Glazzard, J. and Green, M. (2022) *Learning to be a Primary Teacher*. St Albans: Critical.

Golding, K. (2015) Connection before correction: Supporting parents to meet the challenging of parenting who have been traumatised within their early parenting environments. *Children Australia*, 40(2), 152–159.

McCold, P. and Watchel, T. (2001) Restorative justice in everyday life, in Strang, H. and Braithwaite, J. (eds.), *Restorative Justice and Civil Society*. Cambridge: Cambridge University Press.

Moore, D., Benham-Clarke, S., Kenchington, R., Boyle, C., Ford, T., Hayes, R. and Rogers, M. (2019) *Improving Behaviour in Schools: Evidence Review*. London: EEF.

Mujis, D., Quigley, A. and Stringer, E. (2018) *Metacognition and Self-regulation*. London: EEF. Available at: https://dera.ioe.ac.uk/id/eprint/31617/1/EEF_Metacognition_and_self-regulated_learning.pdf [accessed December 2023].

Roffey, S. (2017) The ASPIRE principles and pedagogy for the implementation of social and emotional learning and the development of whole school well-being. *International Journal of Emotional Education*, 9(2), 59–71.

Rogers, B. (2015) *Classroom Behaviour* (4th ed.). London: Sage. [Available in Australia through Footprint Books, Sydney.]

Rogers, C. (1961) *On Becoming a Person: A Therapist's View of Psychology*. Boston, MA and New York: Houghton Mifflin.

Sammons, P., Lindorff, A. M., Ortega, L. and Kington, A. (2016) Inspiring teaching: Learning from exemplary practitioners. *Journal of Professional Capital and Community*, 1(2), 124–144.

Schön, D. A. (1991) *The Reflective Practitioner*. Aldershot: Ashgate.

Treisman, K. (2020) Every Interaction is an intervention, 9 April. Available at: www.youtube.com/watch?v=8pBkXbCP3Q4 [accessed November 2023].

Whitaker, D. (2021) *The Kindness Principle: Making Relational Behaviour Management Work in Schools*. Carmarthen: Independent Thinking Press.

Zehr, H. (2015) *The Little Book of Restorative Justice: Revised and Updated*. London: Simon & Schuster.

# 10

# DELIVERING SEQUENCES OF LEARNING: UNDERSTANDING THE PRINCIPLES OF PLANNING

## SOPHIE NELSON AND LOUISE BROOKE

**Learn that and Learn how to –
The Knowledge and Application Model**

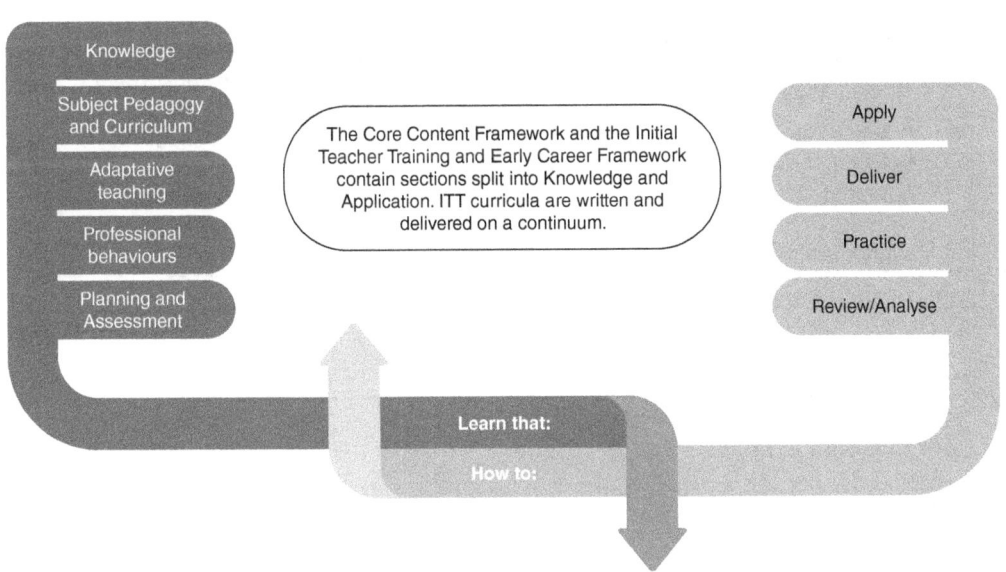

## FRAMED BY THE CCF – FOR FULL LINKS TO THE ITTECF, SEE PAGE 337

| Subject and Curriculum | |
|---|---|
| (Standard 3 – 'Demonstrate good subject and curriculum knowledge') | |
| Learn that ... | Learn how to ... |
| 3. Ensuring pupils master foundational concepts and knowledge before moving on is likely to build pupils' confidence and help them succeed.<br><br>7. In all subject areas, pupils learn new ideas by linking those ideas to existing knowledge, organising this knowledge into increasingly complex mental models (or 'schemata'); carefully sequencing teaching to facilitate this process is important. | Deliver a carefully sequenced and coherent curriculum, by:<br><br>• Discussing and analysing with expert colleagues the rationale for curriculum choices, the process for arriving at current curriculum choices and how the school's curriculum materials inform lesson preparation. |

| Classroom Practice | |
|---|---|
| (Standard 4 – 'Plan and teach well structured lessons') | |
| Learn that ... | Learn how to ... |
| 2. Effective teachers introduce new material in steps, explicitly linking new ideas to what has been previously studied and learned.<br><br>8. Practice is an integral part of effective teaching; ensuring pupils have repeated opportunities to practise, with appropriate guidance and support, increases success. | Plan effective lessons, by:<br><br>• Observing how expert colleagues break tasks down into constituent components when first setting up independent practice (e.g. using tasks that scaffold pupils through metacognitive and procedural processes) and deconstructing this approach. |

## CHAPTER OBJECTIVES

On reading this chapter you will:

- learn that planning is a critical component of effective teaching and learning;
- understand what is meant by a *sequence of learning*;
- explore the importance of prioritising process over product;
- learn practical approaches to support lesson planning.

> **KEY VOCABULARY**
>
> Planning            Memory
>
> Learning            Preparation
>
> Sequence            Knowledge

# INTRODUCTION

## WHY IS PLANNING IMPORTANT?

Although it is widely understood that planning is an essential component of a teacher's role, like many aspects of teaching, the principles and expectations of lesson planning have evolved over time. Prompted by concerns for teacher workload and retention, and an emphasis upon the principles of cognitive science, most recently, this has included a shift from teachers producing individual lesson plans to planning sequences of learning, and a far greater number of schools subscribing to pre-prepared, fully resourced schemes of work. It is understandable then, that we might question the purpose of planning, and the inevitable time and labour this demands – especially if it may seem that our expert colleagues in school do not need to engage in this process. It is thus, important for us to begin this chapter by exploring the current position of planning in schools and, most crucially, *why* engaging in this process is critical to ensuring that high-quality teaching and learning takes place in the classroom.

## PLANNING: THE CURRENT LANDSCAPE

In 2016, the Independent Teacher Workload Review Group published the report *Eliminating Unnecessary Workload Around Planning and Teaching Resources* (DfE, 2016). This was commissioned by the DfE, following consultation regarding teachers' workload (DfE, 2015), and the recommendations were later adopted in the *School Workload Reduction Toolkit* (DfE, 2018).

Within the report, the importance of planning as central to effective teaching and learning is emphasised: 'Planning is critical and underpins effective teaching, playing an important role in shaping students' understanding and progression. It is the area of work where teachers can bring their passion for a subject and their desire to make a difference together' (DfE, 2016, p. 5).

This statement highlights the multifaceted nature of lesson planning; not only does a teacher need to consider the desired outcomes of a learning episode, the pupils' prior learning and how they will monitor progress towards these goals; they must also consider how they will motivate and engage pupils, the extent to which content is contextually appropriate and the unique needs of the pupils in their class.

The report, and subsequent recommendations in the *School Workload Reduction Toolkit* (DfE, 2018), goes on to outline the following 'Principles for planning':

a. Planning a sequence of lessons is more important than writing individual lesson plans.
b. Fully resourced schemes of work should be in place for all teachers to use each term.
c. Planning should not be done simply to please outside organisations.
d. Planning should take place in purposeful and well-defined blocks of time.
e. Effective planning makes use of high-quality resources.

(DfE, 2016, pp. 6–9; DfE, 2018, 02 slide.3)

With many schools adopting these principles, this chapter will enable you to understand what we mean by a *sequence of learning*, consider what informs the decisions teachers make when constructing a learning sequence and reflect upon how we respond to pre-prepared schemes, to ensure that our lessons are tailored to the pupils in our setting.

## WHY DOES IT SEEM LIKE MY EXPERT COLLEAGUES DO NOT PLAN?

Planning is a craft which is honed over time; experienced teachers, through years of practice, have become experts! That is not to say that they *do not* plan; rather, because of their 'extensive and qualitatively better schema' (Hattie and Yates, 2014, p. 7), they can draw upon a bank of strategies and solutions which have been chunked and automated in their long-term memory over time. Lovell (2020) asserts that 'new teachers are overwhelmed because they are surrounded by new information, which takes up a considerable amount of working memory capacity' (p. 21).

## DEVELOPING EXPERTISE: A SNAPSHOT OF PRACTICE

If we consider a frequently used pedagogical approach such as questioning, in just one exchange the teacher must:

- formulate a question;
- determine how pupils will respond;

- listen and assimilate the pupil's answer;
- formulate a response, drawing on both subject knowledge and emotional intelligence to avoid demotivating or discouraging the pupil should the answer be incorrect;
- build upon the response as a learning point in relation to the overarching lesson objective;
- all while maintaining the attention of the whole group or class.

For an expert teacher, the process of initiating and responding to questions in the classroom is supported by their experience; they can simultaneously draw upon subject knowledge, anticipated misconceptions, effective question structures and classroom management techniques in order to manage this process with ease. For a trainee, this is a much more complex task, but thorough lesson planning can alleviate this load. By planning questions, considering how this will be executed (and associated classroom management strategies), anticipating misconceptions and ensuring subject knowledge is secure, the burden upon working memory can be alleviated. When we consider the complexities of an entire learning episode, this 'thinking process at the heart of teaching' (DfE, 2016, p. 6) is crucial to facilitating successful lessons. What is important to note is that trainees cannot jump immediately to being experts; they require repeated guided practice (Lemov, 2015) and experienced teachers have had years of this. Be patient, an expert does not emerge overnight!

### ACTION LEARNING SET

Observe your class teacher initiating questioning with the class.

What strategies do they use to pose questions and receive responses?

How do they maximise learning by building upon pupil responses?

How do they ensure that they maintain the engagement of the whole class?

## WHAT DO WE MEAN BY A *SEQUENCE OF LEARNING?*

The *ITT Core Content Framework* (CCF) (DfE, 2019) is underpinned by the principles of cognitive science; our understanding of the limited capacity of the working memory and the necessity for pupils to assimilate and accommodate new knowledge into existing schema to process and retain information has influenced the way in which we view our lessons. While we may still teach subjects in 60-minute blocks of time, we understand that very few concepts can be taught and understood within this time frame. Instead of viewing individual lessons in isolation, we understand that 'when something complicated is expected to be covered in one or two lessons, it is very unlikely that expertise can be developed' (Myatt, 2018, p. 52). It is helpful, then, to consider learning as a sequence of carefully planned episodes, in which expertise is developed gradually over time. Hattie and Yates (2014) suggest that if teachers view their lessons in this way, they 'focus more [on] the learning process and less on the result' (p. 112) and this 'process over product' approach is further advocated in the *Education Inspection Framework* (DfE, 2023) which states that inspectors will not review individual lesson plans, but will consider the extent to which teaching is carefully sequenced towards clearly defined end points.

## PLANNING A SEQUENCE OF LEARNING: A STEP-BY-STEP APPROACH

### STEP 1: ZOOM OUT: A PANORAMIC VIEW

#### THE BIG PICTURE

Building upon the reference to the *Education Inspection Framework* (DfE, 2023) in the previous section, if our learning episodes are the small chunks of learning leading towards *clearly defined end points*, then we must engage in backwards planning, by *beginning with the end* (Lemov, 2015). This step involves zooming out to establish the big picture by asking ourselves what we want learners to know by the end of a teaching sequence. Glazzard and Green (2022) refer to this as the *composite knowledge*.

If teachers have clarity about what expertise looks like, then they can present content – the *component knowledge* (Glazzard and Green, 2022), with gradual and increasing complexity – 'methodically asking how one day's lesson builds off the previous day's, how it prepares for the next day's, and how these all fit into a larger sequence of objectives that lead to mastery' (Lemov, 2015, p. 133).

> **REFLECTIVE QUESTIONS**
>
> During this stage you might ask yourself:
>
> - what knowledge, concepts or procedures do I want pupils to learn?
> - what are the small steps that they will need to take to get there?

- what do the pupils already know?
- how will I ensure that existing schema are secure?
- how will I build upon pupils' prior knowledge, ensuring that pupils can assimilate and accommodate new knowledge into existing schema?

The process over product-led approach emphasises the planning and step-by-step approach taken to supporting children through the learning. It does not rely on a finished *product* or one piece of *work*, but a *culmination of knowledge*.

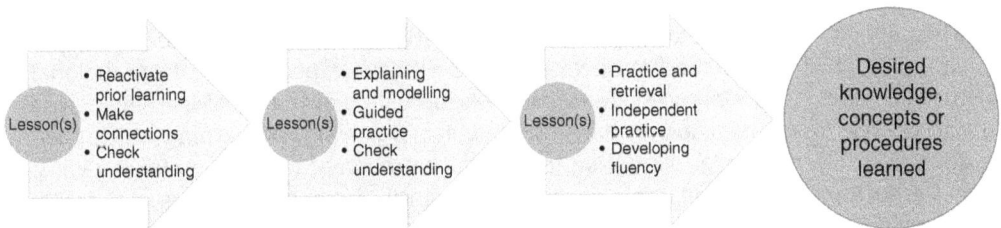

*Figure 10.1 Process over product-led approach to planning*

## CONSIDERING CONTEXT

In addition to considering the introduction of new content in relation to pupils' prior learning, with the intent of bridging the gap between current and target knowledge (Hattie, 2012), teachers may also consider how the context of the school will inform the decisions upon which a sequence of learning is constructed. In Chapter 7, you read about the 'virtual schoolbags' (Thomson, 2002) pupils bring to the classroom, which are influenced by their learning and experiences from their homes, families and communities. In planning sequences of lessons, or delivering sessions from pre-prepared schemes, it is important to consider pupils' 'cultural capital' (Bourdieu, 1973); getting to know the children and the community they live in will enable you to tailor your lessons to better meet their needs. Glazzard and Green (2022) suggest that a school's curriculum should 'confront prejudices head on and provide students with rich experiences which extend their cultural and linguistic knowledge' (p. 35).

> ### CASE STUDY: A CONTEXTUALLY RELEVANT SEQUENCE OF LEARNING
>
> At a primary school in Wakefield with predominantly White British pupils, leaders have taken steps to addressing rising racial tension in the community by developing a cross-curricular sequence of learning based on *Windrush Child* by Benjamin Zephaniah (2020).
>
> This unit of work explores the themes of migration and immigration, developing reading skills – a high-priority area for pupil outcomes in the setting – and historical knowledge and understanding, while promoting 'acceptance of and engagement with the fundamental British values of democracy, the rule of law, individual liberty and mutual respect and tolerance of those with different faiths and beliefs' (DfE, 2023).
>
> Teachers and leaders at the school articulate their commitment to challenging prejudice and discrimination and convey their vision for the curriculum to be personalised to the community which they serve – preparing pupils to be educated, global citizens, who make a positive contribution to society.
>
> While upholding these values, there is also a meticulous focus upon the knowledge and skills which pupils need to develop, in line with the expectations of the national curriculum. In history, progression frameworks, providing oversight of learning across age phases, enable teachers in the school to plan sequences of learning which build upon prior learning as a foundation for the introduction of new concepts and skills; this reduces cognitive load, frees up working memory resources and fosters the transfer of knowledge to new contexts (Kalyuga, 2011). Within the planning for this learning sequence, consideration is made for the teaching of generative knowledge, including substantive knowledge of abstract concepts such as religion, conflict and society, and chronological knowledge which enables pupils to organise their learning into coherent narratives. This generative knowledge is balanced with disciplinary knowledge regarding how historians study and make judgements about the past. 'Books create belonging. They help us see each other and understand one another. They shine a light on the world. It's vital that the books we read in our formative years reflect the rich diversity of the society we live in' (Elliott et al., 2021, p. 3).
>
> High-quality text *Windrush Child* (Zephaniah, 2020) is used within this sequence of learning as a vehicle to expand pupils' understanding of other cultures and to develop empathy towards the experiences of people from different backgrounds. This illustrates how a school can integrate the *core knowledge* stipulated by the national curriculum with enhancements which reflect the context of the school community and the unique needs of the pupils within it.

## STEP 2: ZOOM IN: SHARPEN YOUR FOCUS

In the initial stages of teacher training, and within the early stages of your career, collaboration among your peers in school remains the most powerful way of making plans, forming common conceptions of what pupils should learn, sharing convictions about obstacles and achievement, and joining together to judge the effects of the plans on pupil achievement. 'Planning is everywhere. In the end, it's almost impossible to execute at a high level if your planning isn't also thoughtful, consistent, and focused on the most important tasks' (Lemov, 2015, p. 131).

To enable your pupils to master a concept, or achieve a desired outcome, your lesson objectives should build from one another over time. Unit planning involves carefully looking at each learning episode, while simultaneously keeping how it can be connected to the previous and upcoming lessons in the forefront of your mind.

Teachers should be explicit in their guidance, purposeful planned activities and scaffolding, breaking learning objectives down into bitesize chunks, referencing relevant aspects of the national curriculum or early years foundation stage (EYFS) framework. These smaller, detailed components support pupils' understanding through continual practice, leading to steady improvement. This provides pupils with deeper layers of meaning and understanding and, in turn, splits complex information into manageable chunks that are within their cognitive capacity, minimising cognitive overload (Ayres and Sweller, 2014). Over time, support and scaffolding can be gradually reduced as pupils master the content, allowing pupils to gain independence and apply their learning in different contexts.

Your carefully crafted learning objectives should state clearly what skill, knowledge and understanding pupils will gain during a learning episode. While they are set out in the curriculum framework, they need to be broken down and expressed in terms children can understand, allowing for pupils to comprehend what they are being taught and, crucially, understand what is expected from them during the lesson (Glazzard and Green, 2022).

There are several factors to consider when designing an effective learning objective. Each objective should be:

- Manageable: An objective should be of a size and scope that can be taught in a single lesson.

- Measurable: Setting an explicit, measurable goal beforehand helps you hold yourself accountable.

- Made first: An objective should be designed to guide the activity, not to justify how a chosen activity meets one of several viable purposes. The objective comes first.

- Most important: An objective should focus on what's most important on the path to college, and nothing else. It describes the next step straight up the mountain.

(Lemov, 2015, pp. 137–139)

> **REFLECTIVE QUESTIONS**
>
> Consider the following learning objective and its suitability within a Year 6 English lesson:
>
> Learning objective: I can consider shades of meaning when selecting verbs which advance the action.
>
> - How does it meet the criteria detailed above?
> - Is the objective measurable and attainable?
> - Is it realistic for your learners, focusing on what is most important for their progress?
> - What would you need to know in order to judge the suitability of this learning objective?

### COGNITIVE LOAD THEORY

In addition to planning the introduction of new material, we must also contemplate how to aid pupils in transferring details they have already been presented with to their long-term memory, freeing up their short-term memory by understanding, categorising and articulating new information. Research into cognitive load theory supports the view that practitioners must ensure pupils' working memory, which has a limited capacity to hold information, is not overloaded (Sweller et al., 2019).

As we know the brain stores and organises information into schemata, or networks; this makes it more likely that the new information we present to our pupils will be preserved if it can be connected freely to existing knowledge. Activating pupils' pre-existing knowledge can help learners understand how to attach any new material to an existing schema, and an interconnected schema can also help learners transfer the data from short-term to long-term memory. When information is so ingrained in your mind that it can be easily recalled with little effort, then it is claimed that it has reached a state of automaticity – 'a most desirable place to be' (Hattie and Yates, 2014, p. 147).

For further information on cognitive load, please see Chapters 11 and 12.

### SUCCESS CRITERIA

Beyond the lesson planning itself, pupils need to visualise what success actually looks like within the parameters you have set. By the end of a lesson, pupils should be clear of the learning intention and be able to demonstrate what they have learned. Success criteria, designed against your learning outcomes, can be used to assess how successful the lesson has been and enables both teachers and students to know that the desired learning has been achieved. Hattie (2008) propounds the view that, when shared, success criteria make learning visible and this transparency empowers pupils to monitor their own progress. Such criteria provide students with clear benchmarks and standards against which they can evaluate their own strengths and areas for development.

---

### ACTION LEARNING SET

Think about the lesson you are planning.

- Thinking about the big picture, what do you want your pupils to remember and understand at the end of the learning sequence? How does this connect to their prior learning?
- Once your learning objective has been defined, what will be the indicators of success? How will your lesson activities support you in your ongoing assessment of pupils?
- How does your planning support your desired outcome? How does this overarching outcome link to pupils' prior knowledge and their next steps?
- How will this lesson activate pupils' prior knowledge, while simultaneously preparing them for future learning?
- What will the lesson outcomes be and what will success look like?

---

## STEP 3: COMPOSITION: AVOIDING SATURATION

### OPTIMISING COGNITIVE LOAD

Kirshner et al. (2006) suggest that 'If nothing has changed in the long-term memory, nothing has been learnt' (p. 77); it is impossible then, for us to plan an effective learning episode without consideration of the pedagogical approaches (often referred to as *signature pedagogies*) we will employ, which are informed by our understanding of how children learn and are often dependent on the subject and age phase we are teaching. Just as a photographer arranges the visual elements in their shot – considering balance, perspective and saturation levels which elevate or enhance their main subject – so too must teachers consider *how* they will implement and achieve their chosen focus, carefully selecting strategies to optimise cognitive load.

## METACOGNITION

The process of learning how to learn is known as *metacognition*. Children are known to reach the highest standards when they are empowered to define their goals, supported in planning how to reach them, and explicitly taught how to self-monitor and evaluate their learning. Metacognitive strategies are used by effective learners all the time and have a lifelong impact on their future progression.

## ENGAGEMENT AND MOTIVATION

> *Securing children's interest in a subject emerges from being exposed to teachers who are enthusiastic, interesting and passionate about what they are teaching.*
>
> (Glazzard and Stones, 2021, p. 39)

While we must utilise our understanding of how children learn alongside subject and age phase pedagogy when planning episodes of learning, we cannot ignore teachers' ability to influence pupil motivation and engagement. It is not sufficient to take a pre-prepared lesson plan and assume that this will capture the children's attention. As a teacher, you must consider *how* you will motivate pupils to learn; this can, but does not always, rely on an elaborate hook for learning. Creating a meaningful purpose for the learning, using age-appropriate songs and games, or simply being transparent about how the lesson builds towards the overall learning outcome can also ensure that pupils are engaged and motivated in your lessons.

The sequence of learning in Table 10.1 demonstrates the planning for three, sequential learning episodes in history, for Year 6 pupils.

*Table 10.1 Example sequence of learning*

| Day 1 | | | |
|---|---|---|---|
| Learning objectives | Planned learning experiences and resources | Vocabulary | Questioning |
| I can study a significant turning point in British history<br><br>I can develop a chronologically secure understanding of World War II and understand how our knowledge of the past is constructed from primary and secondary sources | Explain the sequence and chronology of key events from 1918-39, focusing particularly on those that led to the breakout of war<br><br>Pupils sequence event cards of the early stages of WWII<br><br>Detail the arguments for and against appeasement, guiding pupils to table an open forum debate<br><br>Pupils to create their own responses summarising reasons for and against appeasement | Chronological, allies, home front, appeasement, conflict, rationing, resistance | Why did Britain have to go to war in 1939? |

| Day 2 | | | |
|---|---|---|---|
| Learning objectives | Planned learning experiences and resources | Vocabulary | Questioning |
| I can critique and infer the context of a historical source of evidence<br><br>I can undertake an evacuation enquiry | Provide pupils with historical data, graphs detailing evacuation statistics and photographs of evacuation<br><br>Together, critique and appraise biased or misleading propaganda<br><br>Using a range of sources, work with pupils to pose questions relating to what the data seems to be telling us<br><br>Does the extent of evacuation give an indication of how the war was progressing?<br><br>Can we correlate any data with what we know to have been major events in the WWII timeline?<br><br>Pupils compare British child evacuees to the experiences of the many recipients of those evacuated from Germany via Kindertransport | Evacuation, blitz, air raid, civilians, billeting, propaganda | Why was it necessary for children to be evacuated?<br><br>Were the experiences of evacuees all the same?<br><br>Can you predict when the propaganda posters were produced? |

| Day 3 | | | |
|---|---|---|---|
| Learning objectives | Planned learning experiences and resources | Vocabulary | Questioning |
| I can infer the feelings of evacuees using a range of primary and secondary sources<br><br>I can appraise the effectiveness of artefacts | Using the National Archives, newspaper clippings, photographs, testimonials, radio interviews and firsthand accounts, pupils investigate the question: 'Just how happy were evacuees?'<br><br>Discuss why many images showed children and parents smiling, setting aside any concerns of mistreatment or homesickness<br><br>Pupils use their findings to present the different experiences of children evacuees and the families who took them in, providing a written account of what evacuation was really like beyond potentially biased historical sources | Conflict, bias, source, testimonial, host, archive, primary, secondary | Why do you think evacuation was necessary during the war?<br><br>Just how happy were evacuees?<br><br>What role do you think schools played in the lives of evacuated children?<br><br>Do you think children in the countryside welcomed evacuees from the cities, or were there challenges? |

## STEP 4: ADAPTATIONS: ADJUST YOUR VIEW

While your school may already have comprehensive, accessible and fully resourced schemes of work at their fingertips – often an invaluable aid to the workload and wellbeing of staff – we must ensure reasonable adjustments are made to the existing planning, adapting lesson sequences to consider the demographic of your setting, the personal interests of your pupils and the needs of specific groups and individuals in your care. Personalising planning in this way, within learning episodes and across a sequence of lessons, enables practitioners to be responsive to the needs of their learners.

At first as a trainee and ECT, as you are still learning about how children's knowledge, skills and understanding progress, making these adaptations will not yet be second nature. However, as you hone your craft, you will inevitably become more confident to modify planning as opposed to sticking rigidly to what is stated, getting through the quantity of the content without pausing to reflect on the quality of learning where children know and remember more.

If the majority of students in your class do not achieve the learning objective, it indicates that the lesson's pitch or pace needs alteration; it may need to be retaught in a different way to ensure progress can be made. Glazzard and Green (2022) affirm there is 'little point in moving on to the next stage of a lesson if your learners have developed misconceptions' (p. 182). If misconceptions arise, these must be acted upon and responded to swiftly by:

- providing your learners with further worked examples
- re-teaching a skill or a concept in a different way
- re-explaining something with greater clarity
- asking people who have understood to demonstrate their understanding to the rest of the class
- further breaking down your instruction step by step
- using pre-teaching
- providing children with concrete resources (manipulatives)

Glazzard and Green (2022, pp. 182–184)

It is important to remember that not all students in your class will be working at the same rate, nor will their starting point be the same. As such, it is important to adapt schemes of learning inclusively, understanding that learning 'does not happen in neat, linear sequences' (Clarke et al., 2003). Table 10.2 demonstrates how the previous Year 6 sequence of learning might be adapted.

*Table 10.2 Example sequence of learning demonstrating adaptations*

| Day 3 | | | |
|---|---|---|---|
| Learning and resources | Planned learning experiences | Vocabulary | Questioning |
| I can infer the feelings of evacuees using a primary sources of evidence | Using newspaper headlines, photographs, audio testimonials and snippets from the diary entries of evacuees, pupils investigate the question: 'Just how happy were evacuees?'<br><br>Pupils use their findings to work in teams role playing experiences of children evacuees and the families who took them in, providing an account of what evacuation was really like beyond potentially biased historical sources | Primary, source, bias, propaganda, evacuee | What was evacuation really like?<br><br>How would you feel if you were told you had to leave your home and go to a different place during a time of danger?<br><br>Can you imagine what it would be like to leave your home and school to live in a rural area with strangers? |

## EVER-EVOLVING LESSON PLANNING

At its core, effective teaching is appreciating when and how you need to change your instruction for an entire class, group, or individual, using lesson plans dynamically as an ever-evolving guide.

Do we expect teachers to be subject specialists and pedagogy experts, or simply the latter? Should teachers know both what to teach and how to deliver it best? Or should teachers be told prescriptively what to teach and simply be left to deliver it?

## CASE STUDY: SINGLE FORM PRIMARY SCHOOL IN LEEDS

At a single form-entry primary school in Leeds, leaders have taken steps to alleviate workload and support the wellbeing of their teachers by implementing pre-prepared schemes of work.

The school has embraced well-placed schemes as a framework that can and must be adapted to meet the needs of the individuals working their way through it. Planning is used as an overview, allowing continual evaluation and revision. Rather than being prescriptive, subject leaders alongside subject specialists understand that one size doesn't fit all. They are skilled in quality assuring planning and, as well as ensuring consistency and fidelity to particular schemes, pedagogical decisions take place within

*(Continued)*

(Continued)

and across their Trust so that individual staff have opportunities to collaborate and share resources. Schemes of work, giving objectives and outcomes with the flexibility to adapt and change, are seen here as a foundation for teachers to build upon and develop without having to plan everything from scratch.

The school places a significant emphasis on maintaining a healthy work-life balance for their teachers. As their teachers are reflective and given autonomy to adapt and supplement existing planning to suit their children, the school articulate that their quality of lessons has increased year on year. Leaders and senior staff recognise the importance of developing leadership at all levels, as the structure of these schemes of work also supports the subject knowledge and expertise of ECTs and middle leaders. Moreover, teachers at the school articulate that they are particularly invaluable for support and non-specialist staff teaching a subject.

By fostering a sense of ownership and flexibility in lesson planning, their teachers effectively tailor the curriculum to meet the unique needs of their students while still adhering to the national curriculum expectations. Regular staff meetings and well-structured professional development opportunities allow teachers to express their ideas, collaborate and exchange best practices.

To combat and pre-empt potential misconceptions, pre-teaching and post-teaching interventions are cleverly timetabled each week and staff are adept in continuous diagnostic assessment. Within lessons, both teachers and support staff, when necessary, readily provide further explanations, additional modelling and scaffolded, worked examples. If the task is too complex, lessons are adapted and learning is slowed to an appropriate pace. Setting the highest expectations, staff also respond to specific groups of learners who are finding tasks too easy by moving them on to more challenging content, providing pre-planned additional challenges, individual interventions, or the use of assistive technology to support learning. Moreover, staff use carefully designed lesson structures so that all children have the opportunity to access quality first teaching, and support staff deployment is varied.

This exemplifies how a strong focus on teacher wellbeing, coupled with carefully crafted schemes of work, can create an environment where educators flourish and their pupils thrive.

## STEP 5: MEASURING SUCCESS: CHIMPING

In the same way that a photographer may continuously review photos after taking them in order to make necessary adjustments (known colloquially as *chimping*), it is impossible for us to ensure that pupils make adequate progress during a sequence of learning or learning episode without regularly checking pupil understanding and responding to feedback. Wiliam (2017) observes that teachers 'rarely plan in detail how they are going to find out where students are in their learning' (p. 83) and yet this is of vital importance to ensure that lessons are adapted to reflect pupils' current stages of understanding.

For more information on assessing learning and considerations when including assessment in your planning, see Chapter 14.

# CONCLUSION

Whether you are teaching from pre-prepared resources or creating your own sequences of learning from scratch, this chapter has explored the vital thinking process which must take place when preparing your lessons to ensure effective teaching and learning in your classroom. While planning is a complex process, the steps within this chapter offer considerations which will support you to sequence learning episodes over varying periods of time and ensure that the learning reflects the unique context and needs of the pupils in your setting.

> **REVIEW OF CHAPTER OBJECTIVES**
>
> Within this chapter you have considered:
>
> - planning as a critical component of effective teaching and learning;
> - what is meant by a sequence of learning;
> - the importance of prioritising process over product;
> - practical approaches to support lesson planning.

# FURTHER READING AND RESOURCES

Education Endowment Foundation (EEF) (2021) *Metacognition and Self-regulated Learning*. https://educationendowmentfoundation.org.uk/education-evidence/guidance-reports/metacognition [accessed 20 November 2023].

# REFERENCES

Ayres, P. and Sweller, J. (2014) The split-attention principle in multimedia learning, in Mayer, R. E. (ed.), *The Cambridge Handbook of Multimedia Learning* (2nd ed.). Cambridge: Cambridge University Press, pp. 206–226.

Bourdieu, P. (1973) *Cultural Reproduction and Social Reproduction*. London: Routledge.

Clarke, S., Timperley, H. and Hattie, J. A. C. (2003) *Unlocking Formative Assessment: Practical Strategies for Enhancing Students' Learning in the Primary and Intermediate Classroom* (1st New Zealand ed.). Auckland: Hodder Moa Beckett.

Department for Education (DfE) (2015) *Workload Challenge: Analysis of Teacher Consultation Responses*. Available at: https://assets.publishing.service.gov.uk/government/uploads/system/

uploads/attachment_data/file/401406/RR445_-_Workload_Challenge_-_Analysis_of_teacher_consultation_responses_FINAL.pdf [accessed 29 December 2023].

DfE (2016) *Eliminating Unnecessary Workload Around Planning and Teaching Resources*. Available at: https://assets.publishing.service.gov.uk/government/uploads/system/uploads/attachment_data/file/511257/Eliminating-unnecessary-workload-around-planning-and-teaching-resources.pdf [accessed 29 December 2023].

DfE (2018) *School Workload Reduction Toolkit*. Available at: www.gov.uk/guidance/school-workload-reduction-toolkit [accessed 29 December 2023].

DfE (2019) *ITT Core Content Framework*. London: DfE. Available at: https://assets.publishing.service.gov.uk/government/uploads/system/uploads/attachment_data/file/974307/ITT_core_content_framework_.pdf [accessed November 2023].

DfE (2023) *Education Inspection Framework*. Available at: www.gov.uk/government/publications/education-inspection-framework/education-inspection-framework-for-september-2023 [accessed 29 December 2023].

Elliott, V., Nelson-Addy, L., Chantiluke, R. and Courtney, M. (2021) *Lit in Colour: Diversity in Literature in English Schools Research Report*. London: Penguin.

Glazzard, J. and Stones, S. (2021) *Evidence Based Primary Teaching*. Exeter: Learning Matters.

Glazzard, J. and Green, M. (2022) *Learning to be a Primary Teacher: Core Knowledge and Understanding* (2nd ed.). St Albans: Critical.

Hattie, J. (2008) *Visible Learning: A Synthesis of Over 800 Meta-Analyses Relating to Achievement*. London: Routledge.

Hattie, J. (2012) *Visible Learning for Teachers: Maximizing Impact on Learning*. London: Routledge.

Hattie, J. and Yates, G. C. Y. (2014) *Visible Learning and the Science of How We Learn*. London: Routledge.

Kalyuga, S. (2011) Cognitive load theory: How many types of load does it really need? *Educational Psychology Review*, 23(1), 1–19.

Kirschner, P., Sweller, J. and Clark, R. (2006) Why minimal guidance during instruction does not work: An analysis of the failure of constructivist, discovery, problem-based, experiential, and inquiry-based teaching. *Educational Psychologist*, 41(2), 75–86.

Lemov, D. (2015) *Teach like a Champion 2.0: 62 Techniques that Put Students on the Path to College*. Hoboken, NJ: Jossey-Bass.

Lovell, O. (2020) *Sweller's Cognitive Load Theory in Action*. Melton: John Catt.

Myatt, M. (2018) *The Curriculum: Gallimaufry to Coherence*. Melton: John Catt.

Sweller, J., van Merrienboer, J. J. G. and Paas, F. (2019) Cognitive architecture and instructional design: 20 years later. *Educational Psychology Review*, 31(2), 261–292.

Thomson, P. (2002) *Schooling the Rustbelt Kids: Making the Difference in Changing Times*. Stoke-on-Trent: Trentham.

Wiliam, D. (2017) *Embedded Formative Assessment: Strategies for Classroom Assessment that Drives Student Engagement and Learning* (2nd ed.). Bloomington, IN: Solution Tree Press.

Zephaniah, B. (2020) *Windrush Child*. London: Scholastic.

# 11

# ADAPTIVE TEACHING

## ALISON GRIFFITHS

**Learn that and Learn how to –
The Knowledge and Application Model**

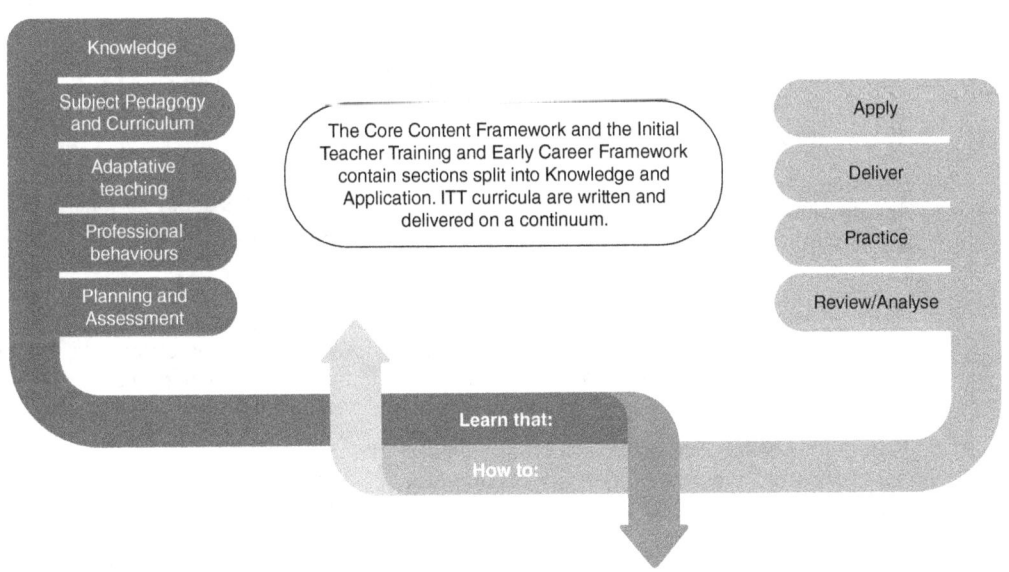

## FRAMED BY THE CCF – FOR FULL LINKS TO THE ITTECF, SEE PAGE 337

**High Expectations**

(Standard 1 – 'Set high expectations')

| Learn that … | Learn how to … |
|---|---|
| 2. Teachers are key role models, who can influence the attitudes, values and behaviours of their pupils.<br><br>3. Teacher expectations can affect pupil outcomes; setting goals that challenge and stretch pupils is essential. | Communicate a belief in the academic potential of all pupils, by:<br><br>• Receiving clear, consistent and effective mentoring in how to set tasks that stretch pupils, but which are achievable, within a challenging curriculum. |

**Adaptive Teaching**

(Standard 5 – 'Adapt teaching')

| Learn that … | Learn how to … |
|---|---|
| 1. Pupils are likely to learn at different rates and to require different levels and types of support from teachers to succeed.<br><br>2. Seeking to understand pupils' differences, including their different levels of prior knowledge and potential barriers to learning, is an essential part of teaching.<br><br>3. Adapting teaching in a responsive way, including by providing targeted support to pupils who are struggling, is likely to increase pupil success.<br><br>4. Adaptive teaching is less likely to be valuable if it causes the teacher to artificially create distinct tasks for different groups of pupils or to set lower expectations for particular pupils.<br><br>5. Flexibly grouping pupils within a class to provide more tailored support can be effective, but care should be taken to monitor its impact on engagement and motivation, particularly for low attaining pupils.<br><br>6. There is a common misconception that pupils have distinct and identifiable learning styles. This is not supported by evidence and attempting to tailor lessons to learning styles is unlikely to be beneficial. | Provide opportunity for all pupils to experience success, by:<br><br>• Observing how expert colleagues adapt lessons, whilst maintaining high expectations for all, so that all pupils have the opportunity to meet expectations and deconstructing this approach.<br><br>• Discussing and analysing with expert colleagues how to balance input of new content so that pupils master important concepts. |

# 11 ADAPTIVE TEACHING

## CHAPTER OBJECTIVES

On reading this chapter you will consider:

- what we mean by the term 'adaptive teaching';
- key deliverable strategies for adaptive teaching;
- how to make connections when adapting curriculum planning and assessment;
- how you can directly begin to adapt your teaching in the classroom to meet the needs of all learners.

## KEY VOCABULARY

Responsive teaching

Scaffolding

High expectations

Differentiation

## INTRODUCTION

As a teacher, you are a role model who can influence the way that children view themselves as learners. Learning is built from a foundation of high expectations, the way that you view your children is central to the way you adapt your teaching. In this chapter you will learn what is meant by *adaptive teaching* and the principles that underpin this. Like a lot of education terminology, what it means to be an adaptive teacher might seem on the surface to be straightforward, but getting to grips with the nuance of what is involved is complex, requiring practice, evaluation and time. The sections that follow will explain some of the strategies you could use in your classroom to ensure that your teaching is responsive to the needs of all your young learners. We will emphasise the connections between curriculum, planning and assessment, shining a spotlight on the importance of maintaining high expectations of all of your children. As the Programme for International Student Assessment (PISA) report finds (OECD, 2016), adaptive instruction is one of the approaches that positively correlated to improvements in performance. This chapter is designed to unpack why that might be, providing you with a foundation from which you can reflect on your own practice and that of expert colleagues you are working with and providing approaches you can begin to employ in your classroom or settings.

# ADAPTIVE TEACHING OR DIFFERENTIATION

Before beginning to consider what adaptive teaching is, it is worth spending a moment considering what it is not.

> ## CASE STUDY: RORY
>
> Rory is a student teacher in a large inner-city Year 2 classroom. He has been asked by the supervising teacher to plan a maths lesson that requires him to create three different worksheets, one for each of the maths ability groups that have been identified from the results of the most recent end of term assessment.
>
> After a brief introduction and revision of prior learning about time, Rory has decided to ask the group from the highest ability (the yellow group) to use their knowledge of time to solve word problems; the middle ability group (the blue group) will be asked to read the time using the 24-hour clock; and the lower ability group (the red group) will be asked to draw hands on analogue clocks and write the time in words underneath. They will be supported by a teaching assistant to keep them on track as they can often become disruptive.
>
> During the lesson, some of the children in the lower ability group completed the task very quickly and were given additional times to draw; they became restless and needed the teaching assistant to step in to manage their behaviour. The higher ability group, in contrast, struggled with what was being asked of them and also became restless. The middle ability group finished quickly, but Rory was unsure about what he should do to extend their learning.

> ## REFLECTIVE QUESTIONS
>
> - From the case study, pick out what you see as being moments where Rory took his pupils' needs into account.
> - Why do you think they became restless?
> - What do you see as being the problems associated with this approach?
> - Does this connect to your experiences as a learner in the classroom?

This case study provides an example of what we are *not* talking about when we discuss adaptive teaching. While Rory, with the support of his teacher, has identified that his children have different prior experiences and knowledge to bring to their learning, he has chosen to structure the lesson to cater for three broad ability groups, each having different learning outcomes and tasks. This approach, which might be familiar to you from your own education, is traditionally referred to as *differentiation* or *differentiated teaching*.

In your reflections, you might have noted that this approach, based upon grouping according to perceived ability across the breadth of a particular subject, may overlook specific strengths that the child may bring to that particular area of learning. In my time as teacher, I have worked with children who struggle with solving multiplication problems but shine when being asked to tell the time and vice versa. The children in the lower ability group were also not given the opportunity to engage in the higher-order thinking that the teacher expected from some of their higher-achieving peers. While this might be justifiable for a single lesson, as Burris et al. (2006) identify in relation to maths education, when differentiated objectives and activities of this kind are assigned to ability groups over time, a ceiling is placed upon what students are able to achieve. Most significantly, you may also have considered the impact that fixed-ability grouping has upon the way that the children view themselves as learners. As Deunk et al. (2018) ask: how will you ever grow as a learner if you do not see yourself as having the same capacity for learning as your peers?

In contrast to the divergence that is often at the heart of a differentiated approach to teaching, adaptive teaching involves the whole class in working towards a common outcome or objective. However, rather than assuming a one size fits all approach or planning for fixed-ability groups, the adaptive teacher is flexible in their approach, mediating learning in light of the knowledge they have of the prior learning, experiences and motivations that individual pupils bring with them. In this way, teaching adaptively requires a teacher to draw upon their knowledge of learning and learners to choose the most relevant teaching strategies, methods and content, the goal being to create an inclusive learning environment where all pupils can flourish.

## DISTINGUISHING BETWEEN DIFFERENTIATED AND ADAPTIVE TEACHING

While the principles behind differentiation in the early 21st century were identified as being a key component of high-quality teaching, there is now a move to reconsider the impact that the classroom application of differentiated teaching practices has had on the education and wellbeing of children. Marking this change in thinking has been a change the terminology we use to describe it, the word 'differentiation' replaced by 'adaptive teaching' in key policy documentation such as the *Core Content Framework* (CCF) and ITTECF (DfE, 2024). While both adaptive teaching and differentiation require the teacher to know their pupils – and as you look into the research around this the terms are used somewhat interchangeably – there are some significant differences that might help you to understand and reflect upon the practice in your classroom or setting.

Table 11.1 Distinguishing between differentiated and adaptive teaching

| Differentiated teaching | Adaptive teaching |
| --- | --- |
| • Different learning objectives for the lesson. These might be expressed in a range of different ways and might include statements of *must, could, should* or may even draw culinary inspiration using *extra spicy, spicy and medium*.<br>• A range of pre-planned resources used that have been designed to cater for the needs of groups of learners.<br>• Potential for a ceiling to be placed upon learning, with the children perceived as being lower ability never able to access high-level thinking of their peers. | • One set of learning objectives for the whole class with the teacher providing focused support as needed for individuals and groups of learners.<br>• Starting points for learning considered to ensure that all pupils can be successful.<br>• Targeted catch-up when needed for individuals and groups.<br>• Emerging needs are catered for by tweaking the lesson in the moment. |

### REFLECTIVE QUESTIONS

- Using the table above as a guide, to what extent do you feel that your practice is adaptive?
- What do you feel might be the opportunities and challenges of adopting this as an approach?

# GETTING TO KNOW YOUR PUPILS

When I listen to primary school teachers talking about the individual children in their classes I am often struck by what teachers know about them.

### CASE STUDY: SARA

Read the comments a class teacher made about Sara who is a child in their class.

*Well, what can I say about Sara - she's amazing ... I've loved working with her this year. You'll love her. She's always there in class, always sitting up straight and listening, she's a real pleasure. She's struggled a little with her spelling through, didn't do too well on the test but we can work on that. I think Mum would help her at home, but she is working nights at the moment and just hasn't got the time to help. Gran, who looks after her, doesn't speak much English so can't really help either. When it comes to maths though, she's a whiz, she's strong. I've seen it in her times tables, she's ahead of a lot of the others, really quick with really good recall. I know if I ask her a question she'll be there with the answer. She's on track overall but exceeding in maths.*

## REFLECTIVE QUESTIONS

- What data/evidence has the teacher used to generate this story about Sara?
- Now think about a child that in your class. What story would you tell about them and their learning? What sources of information have you drawn upon to inform this story?
- Which of these sources of information do you think are the most influential in informing the way that you teach that child?

Schools are evidence-rich places and teachers have access to a range of data about their pupils to draw upon to inform the way that they view, and often talk about, their pupils. When you are beginning to get to know your pupils it is essential that you spend time talking to others to gain a picture of the children you are working with. However, you should also be mindful that the information that you gather from these more informal sources might be unhelpful and could present a picture of the child that affects the relationship that you form with them. Try to keep an open mind about the stories that teachers might tell about the children; remember that just because they behave in a certain way for one teacher does not mean that the same will be true of your interactions with them. When thinking about adapting your teaching, it is also particularly important to look beyond the potential biases in the information that you have about the child if you are to maintain high expectations of what all your pupils might achieve.

In thinking critically about the stories that you are being told, and to ensure that you are creating as full a picture as possible about the children in your class, it is useful to ensure that you draw data from a range of different sources. The data that you gather might be sorted into two main categories.

*Table 11.2 Data types: Quantitative and qualitative*

| Quantitative | *Objective data.* Includes the results of summative assessments and tests and predicted outcomes. It may also include attendance data, free school meal eligibility and data that relates to English as an additional language (EAL) and ethnicity. |
|---|---|
| Qualitative | *Subjective data.* Gleaned from a range of sources which might include observations of the pupils, previous teacher's comments, conversations with parents or caregivers, the way you perceive their motivation and interests. This may also include your formative assessment of their learning. |

Both sets of data are highly relevant in informing the way that you view your learners and, for the purpose of adapting your teaching, both qualitative and quantitative approaches should work in harmony to ensure that you maintain appropriately high expectations of all your pupils while also being aware of the potential barriers that they might face in accessing learning.

### EVIDENCE-INFORMED RESEARCH: MAINTAINING HIGH EXPECTATIONS OF ALL

As we have outlined above, teaching in a way that is adaptive will ask you to move from organising learning according to broad levels of ability, to instead ask that you maintain *high expectations of all your pupils*. Building on the seminal work of Rosenthal and Jacobson (1968/2003), Rubie-Davies (2015) shows us that if a teacher believes that a child is capable that child is more likely to do well academically. However, if a teacher has low expectations for a pupil, it can negatively affect the child's performance. On the one hand, for Rubie-Davies (2015), low-expectation teachers present less cognitively demanding tasks, spend more time reinforcing and repeating information, accept a lower standard of work and over-emphasise rules and procedures. On the other hand, when students are given greater challenge they make more progress, with the children of high-expectation teachers showing larger achievement gains than those of low-expectation teachers.

We will unpack what this means in practice in the sections that follow, but how would you know if you are an adaptive teacher who has high expectations?

> ### REFLECTIVE QUESTIONS
>
> Consider the following characteristics of high-expectation teachers that have been adapted from the work of Rubie-Davies (2015).
>
> - You foster a sense of belief in your children by using language that values challenge and provides sincere and focused praise.
> - You are enthusiastic about what you are teaching and have cultivated a classroom culture that promotes a love of learning.
> - You avoid making ill-informed judgements about your pupils and go into your classroom with the assumption that all children have the potential to do well.
> - You know what success looks like for each of your children and build in opportunities for them to see this for themselves.
> - You expect high-quality work from everyone.
> - You praise effort rather than ability.
> - You understand the way that the goals that you set are challenging.
>
>   1. To what extent do you feel that your practice shows high expectations?
>   2. Talk to an expert colleague about the challenges that you might face in maintaining high expectations of all children in your classroom.

## EFFECTIVE CURRICULUM PLANNING

Adaptive teaching is located at the point where the curriculum and the knowledge that you hold about your children converges. It is at this point where you, as adaptive teacher, make the important pedagogical choices about what you need to teach and how you will teach it with a view to reducing complexity and removing unnecessary distractions. Mansworth (2021) advocates that when thinking about planning the curriculum adaptively we need to *Teach to the Top*. By this she means that when planning and teaching adaptive teachers need to keep their aspirations high for all children, regardless of the perceptions they might have of prior attainment. As we teach to the top, we allow children to experience meaningful success, an important driver that contributes to their overall motivation to want to keep on learning.

As a trainee or early career teacher, the choices that you make about what should be taught will most likely be based upon the curriculum plans given to you by the school or be taken from a commercially published scheme. However, the way you choose to implement these plans in your classroom should be based upon what you know about your children. As a human being, and not a form of computer-generated artificial intelligence, you should realise by now that being a teacher is more than delivering plans created elsewhere. Instead – in recognition that learning, as well as engaging the body and the brain, is also deeply affective – teaching adaptively requires careful curriculum planning if you are to be responsive to the needs of your children on that specific day, at that specific time and in that specific place (Wiliam, 2017). You can read more about planning sequences in Chapter 10.

As you observe expert colleagues in school you might not appreciate the subtle ways in which they are constantly reflecting and evaluating the application of the content of their lesson, making adaptions to ensure that what is planned meets the needs of their young learners. For experienced practitioners, adapting their teaching often becomes part of what they do, an automatic process that is carried out without them consciously thinking about it. To help you as an early career teacher to understand this, you should observe, an expert colleague teaching from a given plan. As you observe, have a copy of the plan to hand and note where their teaching diverges from what is written down. After the lesson, you should speak to the teacher about their pedagogical choices to find out what evidence informed these.

### ACTION LEARNING SET

Consider the last time you observed an expert colleague deliver a lesson:

- the way that they made use of published materials such a PowerPoints or worksheets;
- the way that they made connections to the prior learning or experiences of the children;
- how they built in additional practice or removed unnecessary explanations;
- how they adapted their questions to provide challenge and stretch for specific children as needed.

## ADAPTIVE TEACHING AND ESTABLISHING PRIOR KNOWLEDGE

Understanding the prior knowledge that pupils bring to their learning is one of the most influential factors in promoting individual achievement (Hattie and Yates, 2014). As well as knowing your children as humans, the more information that you as a teacher hold about their prior learning, the better prepared you can be to build upon it. Eliciting your children's prior knowledge has two main purposes:

- to enable you to make informed choices about what pupils will need to be taught next to ensure progress through the curriculum;
- to prepare in advance a range of targeted approaches for individual and groups designed to support them to meet the stated learning outcomes.

You can explore prior learning in a range of ways which might include reviewing of previous curriculum plans, observation of lessons, speaking to expert colleagues, looking in pupils' books or talking to the children themselves. The different data sources identified in Table 11.2 can be valuable in effective strategic curriculum planning. Remember, the better you become at planning proactively, identifying potential barriers that children might face in accessing the learning, the less likely it will be that you will need to adapt your teaching in the moment.

## SUPPORTING CHILDREN WITH COMPLEX NEEDS

As an adaptive teacher, you should be aware of your responsibility to follow the Equalities Act (2010) which outlines the legal responsibility your school has in ensuring that pupils with additional needs are not subject to any detriment or disadvantage, and they have full access to education in line with their peers. As you will read in Chapter 12, you should also be aware of the *SEND Code of Practice* (DfE/DoH, 2015) which explains the legal requirements on teachers and puts in place guidelines for schools to follow. When considering adapting your teaching however, it is important to recognise that you are not on your own; when supporting pupils who have more complex needs you will need to work closely with expert colleagues such as the special needs (disability) coordinator, inclusion manager or designated safeguarding lead (DSL) in your school. They will have identified strategies that are tailored to the needs of the child which will support you in adapting your teaching appropriately.

## ADAPTIVE TEACHING AND FORMATIVE ASSESSMENT

So, you have got to know your pupils, carried out your research about prior learning, have worked on your subject and knowledge. The final step in preparing to teach adaptively is ensuring that you have built opportunities into the lesson when you might get a feel for what the children are learning. Here is where the careful use of formative assessment is essential. There are a range of strategies you might employ to do this. Some possible approaches are listed below:

- focused observation of groups of individuals;
- live marking while your pupils are working independently;

- low-stakes testing at points in the lesson such as multiple-choice or quick quizzes;
- targeting questions;
- embedding performances which might include a PE demonstration that exemplifies the skill being taught.

Regardless of the approach that you choose, it is important that you consider how you will use the form of assessment that you have chosen and what you will do in response.

## THE POWER OF THE HINGE QUESTIONS

Particularly valuable are *hinge questions* which Fletcher-Wood (2018) identifies as being valuable in that they enable the teacher to know within a lesson whether it is appropriate to move on, to recap, or completely reteach a concept before moving on. Hinge questions have some specific characteristics.

- The planning of the question prior to the lesson is essential.
- The question should be asked when you move from explanation to independent work or from one concept to another at a point when you have time to address the issues.
- Everyone in the class *must* respond to the question within two minutes.
- The teacher must be able to assess the results within less than a minute.

> ### REFLECTIVE QUESTIONS
>
> Using Fletcher-Wood's (2018) example, which of the following do you think is true?
>
> A hinge question is …
>
> a) a powerful formative assessment tool;
> b) a sophisticated way to use multiple-choice questions;
> c) a useful way to elicit evidence of students' achievement;
> d) a way to read students' minds.
>
> The correct answer would be c.
>
> - What makes this an appropriate hinge question?
> - What might you do if you got the answer wrong?
> - Think about a lesson you have taught recently, why and when might you have used a hinge question to elicit where the children are in their thinking?

# ADDRESSING MISCONCEPTIONS

Teachers are wizards and often the success of your lesson will depend upon the way in which you transform misconceptions into learning opportunities. Children do not come into school as empty vessels ready to be filled with knowledge, rather they have their own set of ideas about how the world around them works. These ideas may have been generated through informal play, the media they engage with (TikTok has a lot to answer for), from stories they have read or even misunderstandings that have arisen from previous teaching. It is necessary for us to be aware of potential misconceptions and adapt our teaching to ensure that they are addressed as they provide the foundation for future learning.

## CASE STUDY: MISCONCEPTIONS

I recently taught a workshop session designed to debunk a variety of *neuromyths* to a group of trainees. As part of the session, we spent a large amount of time challenging the misconception that many trainees have that children have preferred learning styles (visual, auditory and kinaesthetic) that should guide the way the teacher differentiates their lessons.

While this is a theory that prevailed in schools up to around 2019, it has since been challenged and while we encourage trainees to adopt a range of ways of presenting information to their pupils, assuming that there is one preferred way that an individual learns is a misconception that could lead to poor classroom practice.

A trainee stopped at the end of the workshop to speak to me about the content of the session. They reported that while they found the content very interesting, and they completely agreed that children should not be labelled as having a preferred learning style, as a kinaesthetic learner themselves, they found listening to the content difficult and would have preferred moving around a bit more to help them learn.

## REFLECTIVE QUESTIONS

- Where do you feel the trainee gained this misconception about their own learning?
- What do you think might be needed to challenge this misconception?
- How may you use some of these principles in your own teaching?

We need to be mindful of the way that we manage the children's misconceptions as we want to ensure that children feel the classroom is a safe space for sharing ideas. After all, you need to hear what they are telling you about their understanding if you are to know how to best respond. It is also important to plan activities that allow your pupils to confront their misconceptions head on. This might involve presenting children with discrepant events or outcomes that are unexpected given existing understanding. The use of *concept cartoons* can be particularly valuable in providing a stimulus for children to discuss their misconceptions, providing a visual representation of a specific phenomenon along with a range of viewpoints for the children to discuss and debate.

As a teacher, you should be prepared to offer credible and plausible alternatives and, where appropriate, allow pupils to test these out, experiencing for themselves the correct way of thinking. It is here that we need to stress the importance of the subject knowledge of the teacher. The more secure that you are with the content of what you are teaching the better prepared you will be to identify and challenge misconceptions. For the primary practitioner particularly, this can be challenging; you are after all expected to be knowledgeable across the curriculum. Doing your research ahead of planning is essential. Look at the long-term plans that will be available from your school's website, talk to expert colleagues about the content of the curriculum, read around the concepts that you will be teaching. Most of all, be honest about your subject knowledge. As a teacher, you will have misconceptions about certain concepts and ideas that you will be teaching and only by preparing effectively before planning will you be able to identify where these might be.

# APPROACHES TO SCAFFOLDING

Another concept essential to adapting teaching is that of *scaffolding*, which was first used by Wood et al. (1976). It is a metaphor that refers to the temporary support provided for learners by experienced others that are gradually removed or 'faded out' as learners become increasingly independent. McLeskey's (2019) work identifies scaffolding as a high-leverage practice that if used effectively makes a significant difference to all children, but is particularly impactful for those with SEND. There are many strategies that you might draw upon to scaffold learning, but the important thing to remember is that scaffolding should not become a permanent feature of the learning landscape in your classroom. Rather, as an adaptive teacher you need to scaffold flexibly, removing or adapting support when you assess that a child is able to meet the learning outcomes or intention with increased independence.

## SCAFFOLDING: VISUAL APPROACHES

These support pupils in knowing what the day will look like in the form of a visual timetable. You might develop task planners that outline for children the equipment that might be needed for a task or provide a checklist of the steps for success. As a minimum, regardless of the age group you are teaching, you should include carefully chosen images in your teaching that provide a visual context for learning. However, be mindful that these should not provide a distraction from the content of what is being taught; keep images purposeful and connected, asking yourself what they add to learning.

## SCAFFOLDING: VERBAL APPROACHES

It is essential to recognise the centrality of spoken language in the primary classroom. As a teacher, it is imperative that you are clear in your communication and when thinking about a lesson you should also be mindful about your language choices, gestures and intonation, tailoring these to what you know about your intended audience. However, it is important to remember that you are not working in a vacuum and need to be responsive to the verbal and non-verbal feedback that you receive from your learners, ensuring that any praise you give is meaningful and specific to their needs. As part of your verbal repertoire, remember that it is important to give appropriate thinking time when asking pupils to respond verbally. Using *Think, Pair, Share* can be valuable as it gives pupils time to formulate an answer themselves, share it with a peer to orally rehearse and to create a sense of safety before sharing it with a wider audience.

## SCAFFOLDING: WRITTEN APPROACHES

According to the Education Endowment Foundation (EEF), these scaffolds will be designed to support with independent written tasks and may include word banks or vocabulary maps, writing frames or sentence starters. Another example would be the ubiquitous *What a Good One Looks Likes* (WaGOLL), or even multiple versions of the WaGOLL for discussion and debate. The written notes that you make on the whiteboard or working wall could also provide a scaffold for learners; thinking carefully about what you choose to keep on display for learners as they work independently should be part of your planning process. Also, remember that children have their own work to look back on which could provide a valuable source of support for independent work.

# BEWARE: POTENTIAL DANGERS!

So, you are ready to begin to become even more responsive to the need of your learners – but, be warned … there are some dangers ahead that you need to be mindful of.

Adaptive teaching should not be overly cumbersome; while you need to recognise that children have individual needs, you should not be tasked with creating 30 individual lesson plans. Rather, look for broad patterns in the data that you hold about your children, find out about their prior learning and read about the potential misconceptions that you might come across. Preparation is key here. It also comes with the warning that this might call for the creation of groups of children to provide targeted support and that is fine. However, remember that groups should be formed according to the learning needs of children in that specific lesson and should not become part of your classroom organisation.

You should also be aware of the dangers of a range of pervasive myths that continue to haunt education despite being debunked. An example of this was seen in the case study above in relation to learning styles. This is a myth that has been robustly disproved and while you would be advised to use a range of strategies, resources and approaches in your teaching, limiting a child to a particular way of learning because you have identified them as being visual, auditory or kinaesthesic is not an example of adaptive teaching. Myths that relate to the brain, referred to as neuromyths, seem to be particularly sticky in education (Howard-Jones, 2014); as an adaptive and responsive teacher you are urged to proceed with caution, reading around initiatives before adopting them fully in your classroom.

All of this might seem to be overwhelming. You might have a clear intention of becoming an adaptive teacher, but wonder how any individual can be expected to remember and apply the strategies that have been covered in this chapter. Our advice here would be to not panic but instead to pick one or two strategies or approaches to think about and begin to embed them across your practice. We are not going to pretend that it is easy, but, with practice and patience, you will become more open and responsive to the needs of the children that you are working with.

## CONCLUSION

In this chapter you have learned what is meant by adaptive teaching and the principles that underpin this. We emphasised connections between curriculum, planning and assessment, shining a spotlight on the importance of maintaining high expectations for all children. We identified how adaptive instruction is one of the approaches that positively correlates to improvements in performance. This chapter unpacked why that might be, providing you with a foundation from which you can now reflect on your own practice and that of expert colleagues you are working with. We have explained some of the strategies you can now use in your classroom to ensure that your teaching is responsive to the needs of all your young learners.

> **REVIEW OF CHAPTER OBJECTIVES**
>
> Within this chapter you have considered:
>
> - what is meant by the term 'adaptive teaching';
> - key deliverable strategies for adaptive teaching;
> - how to make connections when adapting curriculum, planning and assessment;
> - how you can now directly begin to adapt your teaching in the classroom to meet the needs of all learners.

## FURTHER READING AND RESOURCES

Bath Spa University (n.d.) *Student and Tutor Resources*. Available at: www.bathspa.ac.uk/projects/learning-sciences-in-teacher-education/resources/ [accessed 2 August 2023].

Trabelsi, G. (2022) *Adaptive Teaching: A Comprehensive Approach to Accommodation Teaching in the Inclusive Classroom*. Printed by author.

## REFERENCES

Burris, C. C., Heubert, J. P. and Levin, H. M. (2006) Accelerating mathematics achievement using heterogeneous grouping. *American Educational Research Journal*, 43(1), 137–154. https://doi.org/10.3102/00028312043001105

Department for Education and Department of Health (DfE/DoH) (2015) *Special Educational Needs and Disability Code of Practice: 0 to 25 Years. Statutory Guidance for Organisations Which Work with and Support Children and Young People who Have Special Educational Needs or Disabilities*. London: DfE/DoH.

Deunk, M. I., Smale-Jacobse, A. E., de Boer, H., Doolaard, S. and Bosker, R. J. (2018) Effective differentiation practices: A systematic review and meta-analysis of studies on the cognitive effects of differentiation practices in primary education. *Educational Research Review*, 24, 31–54. https://doi.org/10.1016/j.edurev.2018.02.002

Fletcher-Wood, H. (2018) *Responsive Teaching: Cognitive Science and Formative Assessment in Practice*. London: Routledge.

Hattie, J. and Yates, G. (2014) *Visible Learning and the Science of How We Learn*. London: Routledge, Taylor & Francis Group.

Howard-Jones, P. (2014) Neuroscience and education: Myths and messages. *Nature Reviews. Neuroscience*, 15. https://doi.org/10.1038/nrn3817

Mansworth, M. (2021) *Teach to the Top: Aiming High for Every Learner*. Melton: John Catt.

McLeskey, J. (Ed.) (2019) *High Leverage Practices for Inclusive Classrooms*. London: Routledge.

OECD (2016) *PISA 2015 Results (Volume II): Policies and Practices for Successful Schools*. OECD. https://doi.org/10.1787/9789264267510-en

Rosenthal, R. and Jacobson, L. (2003) *Pygmalion in the Classroom: Teacher Expectation and Pupil's Intellectual Development* (newly expanded ed). Carmarthen: Crown House.

Rubie-Davies, C. M. (2015) *Becoming a High Expectation Teacher: Raising the Bar*. London: Routledge.

Wiliam, D. (2017) *Embedded Formative Assessment: Strategies for Classroom Assessment that Drives Student Engagement and Learning* (2nd ed). Bloomington, IN: Solution Tree Press.

Wood, D., Bruner, J. S. and Ross, G. (1976) The role of tutoring in problem solving. *Journal of Child Psychology and Psychiatry*, 17(2), 89–100. https://doi.org/10.1111/j.1469-7610.1976.tb00381.x

# 12

# INCLUSIVE EDUCATION: WORKING WITH PUPILS WHO HAVE SPECIAL EDUCATIONAL NEEDS AND/OR DISABILITIES (SEND)

## JONATHAN GLAZZARD

**Learn that and Learn how to –
The Knowledge and Application Model**

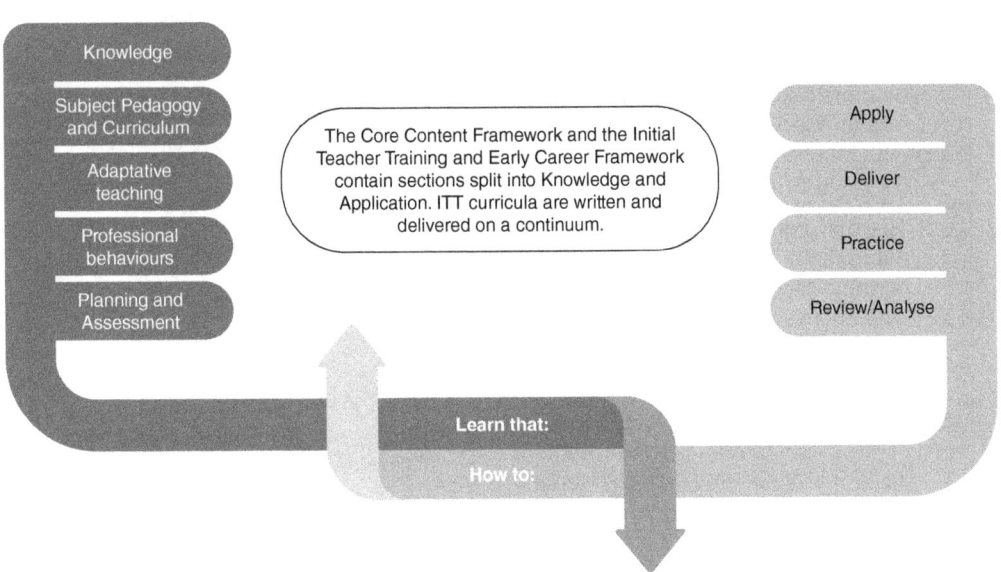

# FRAMED BY THE CCF – FOR FULL LINKS TO THE ITTECF, SEE PAGE 337

| Adaptive Teaching (Standard 5 – 'Adapt teaching') ||
|---|---|
| Learn that … | Learn how to … |
| 1. Pupils are likely to learn at different rates and to require different levels and types of support from teachers to succeed.<br><br>2. Seeking to understand pupils' differences, including their different levels of prior knowledge and potential barriers to learning, is an essential part of teaching.<br><br>3. Adapting teaching in a responsive way, including by providing targeted support to pupils who are struggling, is likely to increase pupil success.<br><br>4. Adaptive teaching is less likely to be valuable if it causes the teacher to artificially create distinct tasks for different groups of pupils or to set lower expectations for particular pupils.<br><br>5. Flexibly grouping pupils within a class to provide more tailored support can be effective, but care should be taken to monitor its impact on engagement and motivation, particularly for low attaining pupils.<br><br>6. There is a common misconception that pupils have distinct and identifiable learning styles. This is not supported by evidence and attempting to tailor lessons to learning styles is unlikely to be beneficial.<br><br>7. Pupils with special educational needs or disabilities are likely to require additional or adapted support; working closely with colleagues, families and pupils to understand barriers and identify effective strategies is essential. | Develop an understanding of different pupil needs, by:<br><br>• Receiving clear, consistent and effective mentoring in supporting pupils with a range of additional needs, including how to use the SEND Code of Practice, which provides additional guidance on supporting pupils with SEND effectively.<br><br>And – following expert input – by taking opportunities to practise, receive feedback and improve at:<br><br>• Identifying pupils who need new content further broken down.<br><br>• Making use of formative assessment.<br><br>• Making effective use of teaching assistants and other adults in the classroom under supervision of expert colleagues.<br><br>• Planning to connect new content with pupils' existing knowledge or providing additional pre-teaching if pupils lack critical knowledge.<br><br>• Building in additional practice or removing unnecessary expositions.<br><br>• Reframing questions to provide greater scaffolding or greater stretch.<br><br>• Applying high expectations to all groups, and ensuring all pupils have access to a rich curriculum |

| How Pupils Learn<br>(Standard 2 – 'Promote good progress') ||
|---|---|
| Learn that … | Learn how to … |
| 4. Working memory is where information that is being actively processed is held, but its capacity is limited and can be overloaded.<br><br>6. Where prior knowledge is weak, pupils are more likely to develop misconceptions, particularly if new ideas are introduced too quickly.<br><br>7. Regular purposeful practice of what has previously been taught can help consolidate material and help pupils remember what they have learned.<br><br>8. Requiring pupils to retrieve information from memory, and spacing practice so that pupils revisit ideas after a gap are also likely to strengthen recall.<br><br>9. Worked examples that take pupils through each step of a new process are also likely to support pupils to learn. | Avoid overloading working memory, by:<br><br>• Receiving clear, consistent and effective mentoring in how to take into account pupils' prior knowledge when planning how much new information to introduce.<br><br>And – following expert input – by taking opportunities to practise, receive feedback and improve at:<br><br>• Breaking complex material into smaller steps (e.g. using partially completed examples to focus pupils on the specific steps).<br><br>Build on pupils' prior knowledge, by:<br><br>• Discussing and analysing with expert colleagues how to sequence lessons so that pupils secure foundational knowledge before encountering more complex content.<br><br>• Discussing and analysing with expert colleagues how to identify possible misconceptions and plan how to prevent these forming.<br><br>Increase the likelihood of material being retained, by:<br><br>• Observing how expert colleagues plan regular review and practice of key ideas and concepts over time. |

## CHAPTER OBJECTIVES

On reading this chapter you will consider:

- the special educational needs and disabilities (SEND) code of practice;
- further approaches to support learners using adaptive teaching;
- working in partnership with colleagues and parents/carers to meet pupils' needs.

> **KEY VOCABULARY**
>
> - Special educational needs
> - Adaptive teaching
> - Differentiation
> - Inclusion

## INTRODUCTION

This chapter focuses on inclusive education for pupils with special educational needs and/or disabilities (SEND). It further addresses the concept of adaptive teaching and contrasts this with traditional approaches to differentiation. The chapter covers the *SEND Code of Practice* (DfE/DoH, 2015) and considers the implications of this for trainee teachers, teachers and early career teachers. The chapter outlines some important adaptive teaching strategies and considers how to work effectively with teaching assistants, the special educational needs coordinator (SENCO), external professionals and parents and carers.

## WHAT DO WE MEAN BY SPECIAL EDUCATIONAL NEEDS AND INCLUSION?

According to the *Code of Practice*:

> *A child or young person has SEN if they have a learning difficulty or disability which calls for special educational provision to be made for him or her.*
>
> *A child of compulsory school age or a young person has a learning difficulty or disability if he or she has a significantly greater difficulty in learning than the majority of others of the same age or has a disability which prevents or hinders him or her from making use of facilities of a kind generally provided for others of the same age in mainstream schools or mainstream post-16 institutions.*
>
> (DfE/DoH, 2015, pp. 15–16)

Teachers are not qualified to provide medical diagnoses of specific special educational needs such as autism, dyslexia, or mental health. These diagnoses must be made by suitably qualified professionals. However, teachers can use the definitions above to identify whether it is likely that pupils may have a special educational need and/or disability. Decisions about whether children have a special educational need or disability should always be made in collaboration with parents or carers and, where appropriate, pupils. Involving parents and pupils in decision-making processes is a fundamental principle of the *SEND Code of Practice* (DfE/DoH, 2015).

It is important to understand that pupils with SEND do not necessarily have impaired cognition, although they may have other needs which require additional or special educational provision. It is sometimes assumed that all pupils with SEND have impaired cognition, but they may have a *specific learning difficulty* (for example, dyslexia) or they may experience no difficulties at all with cognition. Some pupils with specific types of SEND demonstrate knowledge and understanding at a level significantly above their chronological age and this is why it is problematic to group pupils with SEND together and teach them accordingly.

## RATES OF LEARNING

If pupils with SEND can learn the same curriculum content as their peers, they are better off doing so. Sometimes, this will require teachers to implement specific adaptations to enable them to access the same curriculum content as their peers. Most pupils with SEND should be working towards achieving the national curriculum goals that are specified for all pupils at the end of Key Stages 1 and 2. They should be following the same trajectory as other pupils because the national curriculum is an entitlement for all pupils. Most pupils with SEND in mainstream education will be learning the national curriculum with specific adaptations in place to enable them to keep up with their peers. Further information on adaptive teaching can be found in Chapter 11.

There may be instances when some pupils with SEND need to follow an alternative curriculum to their peers; in these cases, there should always be a clear rationale. Most pupils with SEND who require a different curriculum will be placed in alternative provision and often they will have highly complex needs.

Some pupils with SEND require subject-specific interventions to enable them to learn the same curriculum as their peers. These interventions are designed to enable them to catch up as rapidly as possible so that gaps in learning between pupils are closed. Although it is important to understand that pupils learn at different rates, pupils who are working at earlier stages of development may require additional and repeated practice and opportunities for overlearning. These strategies will be addressed later in this chapter.

## THE *SEND CODE OF PRACTICE*

The *SEND Code of Practice* (DfE/DoH, 2015) provides statutory guidance for early years settings, schools and local authorities in relation to supporting pupils with SEND. This section focuses on the responsibilities of schools and teachers.

The *Code of Practice* covers provision for children and young people with special educational needs and/or disabilities from the age of birth to 25. This ensures that support is provided to individuals with SEND throughout their education and during their transition into adult life. Many young people with SEND have not achieved good educational and life outcomes, not because they lack the capacity to achieve these outcomes, but because they have been subjected to low expectations in school and they have not been adequately supported during adult life. Consequently, this impacts on progress into further or higher education, employment, or training. The *Code* seeks to reverse this by ensuring that the support continues after they leave school and therefore its ambition is for young people with SEND to leave productive, independent and fulfilling adult lives.

The *Code* states that schools must:

- endeavour to ensure that a child with SEN gets the support they need – this means doing everything they can to meet children and young people's SEND;
- ensure that pupils with SEND engage in the activities of the school alongside pupils who do not have SEND;
- designate a SENCO to lead the provision for pupils with SEND;
- prepare a SEND information report.

(DfE/DoH, p. 92)

The *Code* also places several other duties on schools. Schools must ensure that there is a clear process to identifying pupils with SEND and a member of the governing body must have strategic oversight of SEND provision. In addition, schools must fulfil their legal duties in relation to the Equality Act 2010 which requires leaders to ensure that reasonable adjustments have been provided for pupils with disabilities.

The *Code* places a requirement on schools and local authorities to ensure that:

- pupils' needs are identified early;
- pupils and parents are involved in decision-making, including contributing to setting goals and reviewing progress;
- there is effective collaboration between education, health and social care services.

The responsibility for pupils with SEND rests with the teacher. The *Code* is clear that teachers are responsible for children's education. Teaching assistants may form part of a package of support for the child but must never replace a qualified teacher. Evidence from research suggests that pupils make more progress when interventions are delivered by qualified teachers and pairing children with teaching assistants who then work with them individually can result in a dependency effect (Sharples et al., 2015).

The *Code* identifies *four broad areas of need*. These include:

- communication and interaction needs (for example, speech, language and communication needs, autistic spectrum conditions);
- cognition and learning needs (moderate learning difficulties, specific learning difficulties, profound and multiple learning difficulties);
- social, emotional and mental health needs (SEMH);
- sensory and physical needs (for example, visual impairment, hearing impairment, multisensory impairment).

In addition, the *Code* sets out a *graduated approach*. This is a process for responding to the identification of SEND. Once a SEND has been identified the school places the child on *SEN support*. It is at this stage that the graduated approach is implemented, including a four-stage cycle which is summarised below.

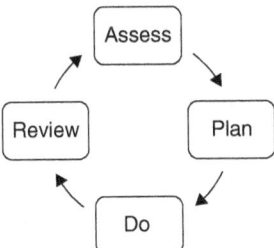

*Figure 12.1 The graduated appoach (SEND Code of Practice, DfE/DoH, 2015)*

- *Assess*: The school assesses the child's needs in partnership with children and parents/carers.
- *Plan*: The school plans how to meet these needs.

- *Do*: Interventions are implemented to precisely target the child's needs.
- *Review*: The impact of the interventions is evaluated, and the cycle is repeated.

It is important to note that the school does not receive additional funding to provide resources at this stage. If the child's needs are persistent and severe, the school can ask the local authority to carry out a *statutory assessment* of the child's needs. The outcome of this assessment will determine whether the local authority agree to issue an education and health care plan (EHCP). If this is issued, the plan will outline the child's needs and the provision that is required to address these needs and it is at this stage that the local authority may agree to provide additional funding. However, in most cases, local authorities will expect that schools have implemented several cycles of the graduated approach at SEN support before they agree to carry out a statutory assessment.

## PERSPECTIVES ON INCLUSION FOR PUPILS WITH SEND

*Inclusion* should not be confused with *integration*. Integration was introduced in 1981, following the publication of the Warnock Report (DES, 1978). At the time of the publication of her report, many children with special educational needs were being educated in special schools. Warnock recommended that, where possible, these pupils should be taught in regular mainstream schools. However, many children with special educational needs were placed in mainstream schools but not adequately supported.

So, how is inclusion different to integration? Inclusion necessitates a deep cultural change within schools (Corbett, 1999; Graham and Harwood, 2011) to make schools more able to respond to difference. It places an onus upon schools to examine the environmental, curricular and pedagogical factors which limit achievement (Erten and Savage, 2012), resulting in radical reform of pedagogy and value systems (Mittler, 2000). It requires schools to be proactive in meeting pupils' diverse needs and therefore to adapt teaching, policies and the environment to ensure that pupils with SEND can access education.

## TEACHING PUPILS WITH SEND

High-quality teaching for pupils with SEND benefits all pupils. It is the first response that schools should adopt in addressing pupils' SEND needs. Most pupils with SEND do not require specialist teachers. They will make progress if teachers establish a culture of high expectations and implement specific adaptations to support their learning.

Key adaptations to support pupils with SEND:

- pupils with SEND are more likely to learn if they are fully included in lessons and if they have opportunities to participate fully in the life of the school;
- they will also make more progress if they are taught by a teacher (Sharples et al., 2015);
- frequent opportunities to revisit subject content will benefit all pupils;
- breaking subject content down into small steps will also benefit all pupils;
- reducing distractions and not overloading the working memory will ensure that all pupils can focus on their learning.

It should not be assumed that all pupils with SEND have cognition and learning difficulties and it is important not to assume that delayed learning is caused by a SEND. This is particularly important for pupils who have English as an additional language (EAL) who may be experiencing delays in learning because they are still developing proficiency with the English language.

# BUILDING ON PRIOR KNOWLEDGE

When children learn something new, they develop schemas. Schemas are mental representations. As they progress through the curriculum, the simple schemas that they have developed need to be modified and they become more complex. This process results in *cognitive dissonance*. This is when the new knowledge does not 'fit' with their prior knowledge and it needs to be accommodated. Once the process of accommodation takes place, the schema becomes more complex and knowledge deepens.

## AN EXAMPLE OF DEVELOPING COMPLEX SCHEMA

When teachers explicitly connect new knowledge to existing knowledge, children can then start to use their existing knowledge to make sense of new knowledge. See the example below.

- In the early stages of reading, children learn the phoneme associated with the grapheme 'ch' in words such as [**ch**-i-p], [**ch**-o-p] and [**ch**-ur-ch]. They develop a simple schema for this grapheme.
- As they progress through the synthetic phonics curriculum, they learn that the same grapheme represents different phonemes in words such as the phoneme /k/ in **ch**emist and the phoneme /sh/ in **ch**ef.

- Simple schema that they originally developed for the grapheme 'ch' now need to be extended to incorporate the phonemes /k/ in **ch**emist and /sh/ in **ch**ef.
- Pupils make progress when schemas become modified and become more complex.
- It is also important to remind pupils about the simple schema that they initially developed when they learned the simple alphabetic code [**ch**-i-p and **ch**-o-p] before teachers start to disrupt this schema.

The example illustrates the process of learning and highlights the importance of linking new knowledge to existing knowledge.

## HIGH-QUALITY TEACHING FOR PUPILS WITH SEND: STRETCH AND CHALLENGE

All children rise to high expectations. If expectations are low and lessons and tasks are not challenging, pupils will not develop more complex schema. Setting tasks which provide a suitable level of challenge will ensure that pupils can make progress through the curriculum, thus enabling them to know more, remember more and do more. Effective ways of providing suitable challenge in lessons are identified below:

- requiring pupils to answer questions in full sentences where appropriate;
- asking pupils to elaborate when they give a response by providing more detail;
- asking pupils to explain their answers: *Why* do you think that? *How* do you know?
- requiring pupils to complete some independent work during lessons;
- expecting the whole class, where appropriate, to work on the same subject content, but implementing specific adaptations to enable some pupils to learn that same content.

### ADAPTIVE TEACHING FOR PUPILS WITH A RANGE OF NEEDS

Adaptive teaching is a key strand of the *ITT Core Content Framework* (CCF) (DfE, 2019) and ITTECF (DfE, 2024) and has been covered in detail in Chapter 11. The following sections briefly outline further important adaptive teaching strategies. They can be used with all pupils but many benefit pupils with SEND more widely.

#### PRE-TEACHING

Some pupils will benefit from being introduced to subject content prior to the actual lesson. Examples might include:

- being introduced to subject concepts, principles and facts;
- learning subject-specific and unfamiliar vocabulary and being introduced to a text.

Introducing pupils to content prior to the actual lesson helps to reduce cognitive load in the lesson and gives them a 'head start'.

## CHUNKING: BREAKING DOWN COMPLEX MATERIAL

*Chunking* is the practice of breaking down larger aspects of knowledge into smaller components. Each lesson is designed to focus on introducing pupils to a small component of knowledge rather than requiring pupils to learn too much content within a single lesson. Chunking knowledge into smaller components benefits all pupils because it reduces cognitive load. Another approach to chunking is to break tasks down into a series of smaller steps. Teachers then model each step and pupils practise that aspect of content before they move on to the next step. Structuring complex tasks into smaller steps makes tasks more manageable for all pupils.

## SCAFFOLDING AND FADING

*Scaffolding* provides pupils with support before they are required to complete a task independently. There are different approaches to scaffolding that teachers can use. A teacher might model new subject content in a lesson and work through several examples with pupils before asking them to work on that subject content independently. Another approach is to use *I do, we do, you do*:

- *I do*: The teacher demonstrates explicitly the subject content.
- *We do*: The teacher and the pupils work on the subject content together. Alternatively, the teacher might pair pupils up and ask pupils to work together on the subject content (peer scaffolding).
- *You do*: The scaffolding is gradually removed and pupils are required to work on the subject content independently.

Teachers need to decide when it is appropriate to fade out the scaffolding. They may implement a short formative assessment opportunity in the lesson to check whether pupils have understood the content. This might take the form of a question which pupils must answer or a quick task so that pupils can demonstrate that they have understood.

The part of the lesson where pupils and teachers or pupils and pupils work on subject content together is the part of the lesson where the scaffolding takes place, and this stage of the lesson is particularly valuable for pupils with SEND because they have opportunities to practise the subject content with others before they are required to work independently.

### DUAL CODING

*Dual coding* is the practice of presenting information in different formats, for example, supporting a spoken explanation in a lesson with a diagram or combining written text with visual information. The working memory processes language-based information in one chamber and visual information is processed in a different chamber. Both types of information can be processed concurrently because the processing takes place in separate processing chambers; this prevents cognitive overload. Where visual information supports understanding of spoken or written information, this is helpful for all pupils, but particularly helpful for pupils with SEND.

### OVERLEARNING

Pupils with SEND, like most pupils, will benefit enormously from repeated exposure to the same subject content. This enables them to develop fluency and enables them to learn the subject content to automaticity. Revisiting subject content in different ways will help to maintain pupils' interest.

### USING CONCRETE RESOURCES

Some pupils with SEND may find abstract subject concepts (for example, division in mathematics) difficult to understand. Using *concrete* manipulatives will help pupils to develop critical subject knowledge. Examples of concrete resources include counters, cubes, place value apparatus and other practical equipment in different subjects.

### RETRIEVAL PRACTICE

Regular *retrieval practice* is important for all pupils. Long-term memory stores knowledge but if we do not work with that subject content again, it is filed away and can be forgotten. Regular opportunities to retrieve knowledge from long-term memory benefits all pupils.

### USING WORKED EXAMPLES

All pupils benefit from worked examples, but for pupils with SEND *worked examples* provide them with an important scaffold to build their confidence. Examples include:

- worked examples which outline the steps through a mathematical problem;
- examples to show what a finished piece of writing should look like;

- using the visualiser to model how to complete a task;
- demonstrating how to complete a practical task.

## SPACED OR DISTRIBUTED LEARNING

When subject content is spaced out over time and revisited after a gap, this supports long-term retention of knowledge. Spacing out learning over time will ensure that subject content is revisited, and will activate the knowledge that is stored in the long-term memory.

## REGULAR PURPOSEFUL PRACTICE

All pupils benefit from direct opportunities to practise subject content. Through *regular purposeful practise* pupils develop automaticity. Consider the knowledge gained when adults learn to drive a car. Adults do not become effective drivers unless they have many frequent opportunities to practise their driving skills. Eventually, because of repeated practice, driving becomes automatic, and drivers do not need to think so hard about how to drive a car. All pupils need opportunities to regularly practise their skills and therefore it is important that teachers use the technique of fading out scaffolding so that pupils can practise the subject content independently.

## REDUCING COGNITIVE LOAD

*Reducing cognitive load* in lessons by limiting subject content is extremely beneficial for pupils with SEND because it allows them to focus on a single component of knowledge. Introducing multiple components of knowledge in a lesson will result in cognitive load and the working memory will not be able to process the information efficiently. Learners with SEND benefit from reducing the amount of subject content (intrinsic load) and reducing sensory and other distractions (extraneous load). Autistic pupils may find exposure to noise or visual information in the classroom distracting; reducing background noise is also extremely important for pupils with hearing impairments. Light and temperature can also be distracting and cause some autistic pupils to become easily distressed.

# GROUPING PUPILS

Placing pupils in fixed attainment groups based on attainment can lead to a range of negative impacts, although it might be argued that attainment groups make it easier to meet pupils' learning needs. Pupils' attainment is not fixed because the brain is malleable and influenced by environmental factors. Through exposure to high-quality teaching and through investing effort into learning, pupils' attainment can increase and therefore groupings should be sufficiently flexible so that teaching can be responsive as pupils know more, remember more and can do more. Ability groups can also have a detrimental impact on the self-esteem of pupils in low attainment groups. In addition, there is a danger that all pupils with SEND and those with EAL may be placed in low-attaining groups despite not all experiencing delays in cognition and learning. It seems reasonable to suggest that pupils should be given opportunities to change groups frequently as they make progress and it is reasonable to argue that pupils should not be placed in a single attainment group for all subjects, given that their attainment may vary between subjects. Mixed attainment grouping arrangements provide opportunities for pupils with different levels of attainment to work together and, therefore, for peer scaffolding to take place. A combination of attainment groups and mixed attainment groups may also be appropriate.

### EVIDENCE-INFORMED RESEARCH

Existing research has demonstrated that ability grouping can result in:

- misallocation of pupils to groups and a lack of fluidity in groups;
- poor-quality teaching for pupils in lower-attaining groups;
- differential pedagogy which can result in a widening of the achievement gap;
- reduced teacher expectations;
- negative pupil perceptions about themselves.

(Francis et al., 2017)

### REFLECTIVE QUESTIONS

- What are your views on attainment groups versus mixed attainment grouping?
- What are the arguments for and against attainment groups?

# DEPLOYMENT OF SUPPORT STAFF

Pupils with SEND should not always be asked to work with teaching assistants. It is important that all pupils learn from a teacher and teaching assistants should be seen as part of a package of support. One of the problems which Sharples et al. (2015) identified was that pupils with SEND often become dependent on their teaching assistants and, in some cases, teaching assistants focused on task completion rather than promoting understanding and independence.

> **EVIDENCE-INFORMED RESEARCH: EFFECTIVE DEPLOYMENT OF TEACHING ASSISTANTS**
>
> Schools deploy teaching assistants to improve outcomes for students with SEND. However, research demonstrates that:
>
> - the ineffective deployment of teaching assistants does not lead to improved student outcomes;
> - students with the highest levels of SEND often make the least progress due to ineffective deployment arrangements;
> - when they are well-trained and used in structured settings with high-quality support and training, teaching assistants can make a noticeable positive impact on student learning.
>
> (Sharples et al., 2015)

> **ACTION LEARNING SET**
>
> In school, talk to a teaching assistant about their roles and responsibilities. Ask them to explain, from their perspective, how they prefer teachers to work with them. Arrange to shadow them when they are working directly with pupils with SEND and make a note of specific pedagogical approaches that they use to support the development of pupils' knowledge.

# WORKING WITH PARENTS AND CARERS

The *Code of Practice* (DfE/DoH, 2015) explicitly requires schools to develop effective partnerships with parents or carers. Schools should involve them in setting targets and reviewing progress and parents and carers must be involved in all decisions which affect their child. Regular communication with parents and carers will ensure that your approaches to supporting pupils with SEND are informed by their unique knowledge of their child. The SENCO will also be a critical point of contact for parents or carers.

## WORKING WITH EXTERNAL AGENCIES

There have been several high-profile cases where agencies have not worked together effectively. If information is not shared between education, health and social care and other organisations it is likely that pupils will not make the progress that they could have made. Many pupils with SEND are also supported by other services. The SENCO is largely responsible for liaising with different agencies. However, professionals from other services (for example, the local authority learning support team or the educational psychology service) may be responsible for directly working with specific pupils and their parents. In some cases, they will carry out specialist assessments to determine the child's needs and they will write reports which outline their findings and recommendations. Class teachers will be required to read these and to address the advice that has been provided by the specialist services that are supporting the child.

## THE ROLE OF THE SENCO

The *Code of Practice* (DfE/DoH, 2015) outlines the roles and responsibilities of the SENCO. The SENCO is responsible for the leadership and management of SEND provision. The role of the SENCO is a strategic role, but it will also involve operational aspects, including ensuring that resources are available to meet pupils' needs.

Duties typically include:

- being a point of contact for pupils with SEND and their parents/carers;
- being a point of contact for external professionals, including those representing the health and social care sectors and liaising with professionals from the local authority;
- chairing formal review meetings for pupils with EHCPs;
- facilitating smooth transitions when pupils move between schools;
- advising and training teachers and teaching assistants;
- writing the SEND policy;
- producing the SEND information report which outlines the SEND provision in the school. This must be published on the school website;

- deploying resources appropriately – for example, ensuring that interventions are in place and monitoring the SEND budget;
- producing reports for the governing body;
- monitoring the implementation of the graduated approach, including monitoring the quality of provision and teaching for pupils with SEND;
- dealing with complaints;
- advising the senior leadership team.

> **ACTION LEARNING SET**
>
> Meet with the SENCO and discuss the following:
>
> - the school's approach to identifying SEND;
> - the range of pupils' needs in the school;
> - the range of interventions which are implemented through the school.

## SUPPORTING PUPILS WITH SEND AS AN EARLY CAREER TEACHER

It is impossible to anticipate the range of SEND needs that you will have to address in your classroom during your time as an early career teacher. You will not leave your initial teacher training phase knowing everything and you will need to be prepared to research pupils' needs further when you are employed. Remember, you do not need to be an expert! The SENCO will support you in meeting pupils' needs, although it is not their responsibility to plan your lessons. It is important to establish positive relationships with parents and carers and to maintain an ongoing dialogue with them. You can join organisations to help you develop your knowledge, including the National Association for Special Educational Needs (NASEN). In addition, you need to develop effective working relationships with teaching assistants and be prepared to learn from them. Many teaching assistants are highly experienced. The key thing to remember is that you need to be determined to do your very best for all pupils and work with 'good faith and effort' (Cole, 2005), even though you will not know everything.

> ### CASE STUDY: SUPPORTING EMOTIONAL REGULATION SKILLS
>
> A school in the North East of England had a significant intake of pupils who displayed social and emotional regulation difficulties. The school invested in a nurture classroom for pupils aged four to seven and it provided a separate nurture classroom for pupils aged seven to 11. Several members of staff were appointed to run the nurture provision and they were required to undertake a professional qualification. Children who displayed social and emotional regulation difficulties were identified for placement in the nurture classroom. These pupils were taught separately in the nurture provision until they were ready to be included in their usual classroom. In the nurture provision, teaching focused on developing key skills including developing listening and concentration skills, cooperation, resilience, manners and anger management. Teaching also focused on developing pupils' self-esteem and confidence. Pupils were taught foundational subject knowledge from the national curriculum. Some pupils spent two terms in the nurture provision before they were deemed ready to be included in their usual classroom.

# CONCLUSION

This chapter has outlined the key principles of the *SEND Code of Practice* (DfE/DoH, 2015). It has provided a comprehensive overview of adaptive teaching and provided you with a further bank of adaptive teaching strategies. The approaches that have been outlined in this chapter benefit all pupils – not just pupils with SEND. Pupils with SEND do not therefore always require different pedagogical approaches. They require exposure to high-quality teaching and strategies such as overlearning, repeated practice and chunking, which are beneficial to everyone.

> ### REVIEW OF CHAPTER OBJECTIVES
>
> Within this chapter you have considered:
>
> - the *Special Educational Needs and Disabilities Code of Practice*;
> - approaches to support learners using adaptive teaching;
> - working in partnership with colleagues and parents/carers to meet pupils' needs.

# FURTHER READING AND RESOURCES

The National Association for Special Educational Needs (NASEN) is a charitable organisation that supports those working with, and for, children and young people with SEND and learning differences. The website below provides information to support your growing knowledge.

https://nasen.org.uk/

The Mentally Healthy Schools website below identifies quality-assured mental health resources, information and advice for schools and further education settings.

https://mentallyhealthyschools.org.uk/

# REFERENCES

Cole, B. (2005) Good faith and effort? Perspectives on educational inclusion. *Disability and Society*, 20(3), 331–344.

Corbett, J. (1999) Inclusive education and school culture. *International Journal of Inclusive Education*, 3(1), 53–61.

Department for Education (DfE) (2019) *ITT Core Content Framework*. London: DfE. Available at: https://assets.publishing.service.gov.uk/government/uploads/system/uploads/attachment_data/file/974307/ITT_core_content_framework_.pdf [accessed November 2023].

Department for Education and Department of Health (DfE/DoH) (2015) *Special Educational Needs and Disability Code of Practice: 0 to 25 Years. Statutory Guidance for Organisations Which Work with and Support Children and Young People who Have Special Educational Needs or Disabilities*. London: DfE/DoH.

Department for Education and Science (DES) (1978) *Special Educational Needs: Report of the Committee of Enquiry into the Education of Handicapped Children and Young People* (Warnock Report). London: HMSO.

Erten, O. and Savage, R. S. (2012) Moving forward in inclusive education research. *International Journal of Inclusive Education*, 16(2), 221–233.

Francis, B., Archer, L., Hodgen, J., Pepper, D., Taylor, B. and Travers, M.-C. (2017) Exploring the relative lack of impact of research on 'ability grouping' in England: A discourse analytic account. *Cambridge Journal of Education*, 47(1), 1–17.

Graham, L. J. and Harwood, V. (2011) Developing capabilities for social inclusion: Engaging diversity through inclusive school communities. *International Journal of Inclusive Education*, 15(1), 135–152.

Mittler, P. (2000) *Working Towards Inclusive Education: Social Contexts*. London: David Fulton.

Sharples, J., Webster, R. and Blatchford, P. (2015) *Making Best Use of Teaching Assistants: Guidance Report*. London: EEF.

# 13

# DIVERSITY AND INCLUSIVE EDUCATION

## MAHNAZ SIDDIQUI

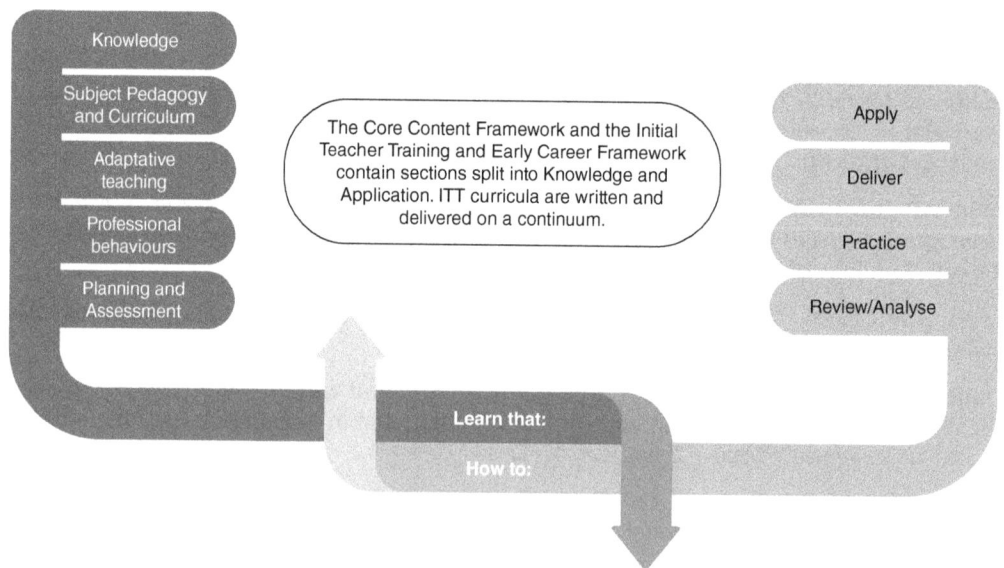

Learn that and Learn how to –
The Knowledge and Application Model

## 13 Diversity and Inclusive Education

### FRAMED BY THE CCF – FOR FULL LINKS TO THE ITTECF, SEE PAGE 337

| High Expectations (Standard 1 – 'Set high expectations') ||
|---|---|
| Learn that ... | Learn how to ... |
| 3. Teacher expectations can affect pupil outcomes; setting goals that challenge and stretch pupils is essential.<br><br>5. A culture of mutual trust and respect supports effective relationships. | Demonstrate consistently high behavioural expectations, by:<br>• Receiving clear, consistent and effective mentoring in how to create a culture of respect and trust in the classroom that supports all pupils to succeed (e.g. by modelling the types of courteous behaviour expected of pupils). |

| Subject and Curriculum (Standard 3 – 'Demonstrate good subject and curriculum knowledge') ||
|---|---|
| Learn that ... | Learn how to ... |
| 1. A school's curriculum enables it to set out its vision for the knowledge, skills and values that its pupils will learn, encompassing the national curriculum within a coherent wider vision for successful learning. | Deliver a carefully sequenced and coherent curriculum, by:<br>• Discussing and analysing with expert colleagues the rationale for curriculum choices, the process for arriving at current curriculum choices and how the school's curriculum materials inform lesson preparation. |

| Adaptive Teaching (Standard 5 – 'Adapt teaching') ||
|---|---|
| Learn that ... | Learn how to ... |
| 2. Seeking to understand pupils' differences, including their different levels of prior knowledge and potential barriers to learning, is an essential part of teaching.<br><br>3. Adapting teaching in a responsive way, including by providing targeted support to pupils who are struggling, is likely to increase pupil success. | And – following expert input – by taking opportunities to practise, receive feedback and improve at:<br>• Applying high expectations to all groups, and ensuring all pupils have access to a rich curriculum. |

| Professional Behaviours (Standard 8 – 'Fulfil wider professional responsibilities') ||
|---|---|
| Learn that ... | Learn how to ... |
| 2. Reflective practice, supported by feedback from and observation of experienced colleagues, professional debate, and learning from educational research, is also likely to support improvement. | And – following expert input – by taking opportunities to practise, receive feedback and improve at:<br>• Contributing positively to the wider school culture and developing a feeling of shared responsibility for improving the lives of all pupils within the school. |

Being an anti-prejudiced educator is part of the *ITT Core Content Framework* (CCF) (DfE, 2019) and the Initial Teacher Training and Early Career Framework (ITTECF) (DfE 2024) and an ambitious curriculum (above and beyond the minimum expectations of the CCF/ITTECF).

> **CHAPTER OBJECTIVES**
>
> On reading this chapter you will consider:
>
> - knowing why it is essential to become an anti-prejudiced educator;
> - having awareness of your own biases and stereotypes;
> - exemplifying dialogic practices to diversify and decolonise the curriculum (DtC) through social, moral, spiritual and cultural development (SMSC);
> - setting personal next steps.

> **KEY VOCABULARY**
>
> Anti-racism/anti-prejudiced
> Bias
> Black Asian global majority (BAGM)
> Decolonising the curriculum (DtC)
> Diversity
> LGBTQIA+ (lesbian, gay, bisexual, transgender, queer, intersex, asexual and other identities). Stonewall (2023) uses the language LGBTQ-inclusive education for primary school
> Prejudice
> Race
> Stereotype
> Intersectionality
> Cultural capital
> Protected characteristic

# INTRODUCTION

This chapter seeks to explore issues of inclusion and diversity with a focus on being an anti-prejudiced educator. First, in order to be committed with the intentions of this chapter, knowing why it is essential to be anti-prejudiced will be explored. Race, religion, ethnicity, language, gender and sexual orientation can be barriers to learning and data proves there are discrepancies of attainment between specific groups of pupils (DfE, 2023a). Closing this attainment gap for all pupils via an equitable education is important for every educator (Choudry, 2021). An inclusive and anti-discriminatory school culture will support teachers to implement practices to enable all pupils to have positive learning experiences; this requires a teacher to take conscious action to reflect on their current position, knowledge and understanding of their own biases and stereotypes.

Addressing how to be actively anti-prejudiced will take time and some honest consideration of one's own biases and stereotypes of marginalised groups of people. The journey will begin with a reflection of an individual teacher's needs. This process can mean that personal views and beliefs will be challenged, and it may cause some discomfort to consider alternative perspectives. As a trainee teacher, consciously setting personal targets for teaching placements will be the next step to being an anti-prejudiced educator. Finally, suggestions will be offered for diversifying and decolonising the curriculum at classroom level via *spiritual, moral, social and cultural* development (SMSC). This is part of adaptive practice to teach in a responsive way to increase pupil success. Treating everyone the same is not adaptive practice and does not provide equity or liberation. The image below explains how practice needs to be adapted to offer equity and to liberate; the barriers need to be removed.

*Figure 13.1 Equality, equity and liberation (reproduced by kind permission of Interaction Institute for Social Change; artist: Angus Maguire)*

# WHY BECOMING AN ANTI-PREJUDICED EDUCATOR IS ESSENTIAL

The Equality Act (2010) makes it unlawful to discriminate against, harass or victimise someone on the basis of a protected characteristic. These include:

- age
- disability

- gender reassignment
- marriage and civil partnership
- pregnancy and maternity
- race
- religion or belief
- sex
- sexual orientation.

The Equality Act (2010) superseded the previous Race Relations Act (2000) which had been amended following the racially motivated murder of Stephen Lawrence in 1993. It is important to read more about what happened to Stephen Lawrence and the flawed investigation to be an actively anti-racist teacher. MacPherson's independent review (Home Office, 1999, p. 49) reported that institutionalised racism played a significant part in the flawed investigation by the Metropolitan Police. Institutional racism was defined as: 'The collective failure of an organisation to provide a professional service to people because of their colour, culture or ethnic origin. It can be seen ... in processes ... which [discriminate] through unwitting prejudice, ignorance, thoughtlessness and racist stereotyping.'

As an anti-racist teacher, it is important to understand what institutional racism is. In simple terms, institutional racism is embedded in policies and accepted practices of an institution, and structural racism relates to the wider society in which an institution belongs. This relates to that society's history and culture and excludes minority groups. This chapter will address what a teacher can do at classroom level and with support of a school culture that consciously recognises structural racism and advocates anti-discriminatory practices.

### ACTION LEARNING SET

On placement, locate the school's equal opportunity policy.

What are the school's equality objectives?

Do any of these relate to any protected characteristics?

What is school policy following a prejudiced incident?

MacPherson (Home Office, 1999) defined a racist incident as one perceived to be racist by the victim and this applies to any act of discrimination where the word 'racist' can be replaced with *prejudiced* (Equaliteach, 2023).

In addition to the Equality Act (2010), the statutory national curriculum's inclusion statement (DfE, 2013, 4.2) stipulates that it is a teacher's lawful duty to not discriminate against the protected characteristics and they should respond to the needs of individuals and groups of pupils to overcome potential barriers. Every child has human rights (civil, economic, social and cultural) whatever their ethnicity, gender, religion, language, abilities or any other status (UNCRC, 1989).

# DIVERSITY

Every class will be diverse in different ways, including pupils in your class with protected characteristics. There may be pupils with specific learning needs, different racial identities, adverse childhood experiences (ACEs), English as an additional language (EAL) and the list continues. A pupil should not be defined by their differences, and it is the role of the teacher to have high expectations of all pupils to enable them to access their entitled education. A pupil can have multiple aspects of diversity. It is important to recognise this and *intersectionality*, where social categorisations (gender, race, low *socioeconomic status* (SES)) co-exist. Ideally, each aspect of diversity requires a teacher to be a specialist, but, as with medicine, this would involve deep research and further training. Schools should have designated specialists or draw upon outside expertise to train staff in the latest research-informed best practices, to be inclusive of narratives on age, gender, race, disability, sex and sexual orientation (protected characteristics that relate best to what schools can address) (Kara, 2021).

> ### EVIDENCE-INFORMED RESEARCH: EVIDENCE OF EDUCATIONAL ACHIEVEMENT GAPS
>
> #### THE DATA
>
> Governments and educational authorities collect and regularly publish data on pupil achievement and attainment to monitor disparities between different pupil groups, including those with protected characteristics (DfE, 2022, 2023a; UK Government, 2018). For example, the UK government (2018) revealed significant attainment gaps between White British and some ethnic minority groups, with Black Caribbean and Gypsy/Roma pupils facing some of the largest disparities. Government attainment and progress statistics data (DfE, 2022) for Key Stage 2 revealed that girls outperformed boys in reading and writing, while boys made more progress in mathematics. Choudry (2021) brings together relevant research related to particular groups of
>
> *(Continued)*

(Continued)

pupils, highlighting key issues pertinent to them, and offers best practice regarding addressing gaps.

**POTENTIAL BARRIERS**

Several factors contribute to these attainment gaps, including socioeconomic inequality, educational resources and support, bias and stereotypes and cultural relevance. SES often intersects with protected characteristics, and children from disadvantaged backgrounds may face additional barriers to educational success, including economic barriers that impact their access to resources, quality education and learning support. The quality and availability of educational support, both in school and at home, can vary, affecting academic performance. Unconscious bias and stereotypes can influence teacher expectations and perceptions of pupils, impacting opportunities and support. Pupils at risk of being bullied include those with differences in race, ethnicity, gender or sexual orientation, and schoolwork can be affected by this; if left unaddressed bullying can have devastating effect on individuals and their mental health (NSPCC, 2023; DfE, 2017).

Finally, the curriculum and teaching methods may not always be culturally relevant, affecting engagement and motivation among certain groups. Engagement and motivation to learn are influenced by pupils having a sense of belonging, worth and value.

### ACTION LEARNING SET

Find out more about your placement class.

From discussions with your school mentor and information you are permitted to access, list any pupils with potential barriers to learning based on diversity and protected characteristics.

This activity in itself will make you more aware of the different needs of your class.

# OVERCOMING BARRIERS

## EQUITABLE FUNDING

The pupil premium (PP) grant is funding to improve educational outcomes for disadvantaged pupils in state-funded schools in England (DfE, 2023b). In the financial year 2023–24, pupil premium spending will increase to almost £2.9 billion. The intention is to support all schools to use this funding effectively based on research evaluated by the Education Endowment Foundation (EEF). This can help to address and overcome barriers based on protected characteristics and SES.

> **ACTION LEARNING SET**
>
> Find out what your placement school is prioritising with regards to pupil premium funding.
>
> Do any priorities relate to the protected characteristics?
>
> What does the EEF state regarding any initiatives?

## ADDRESSING BIASES AND STEREOTYPES

Addressing personal biases and stereotypes and learning more about being actively anti-prejudiced will provide a teacher with transferable skills to support with inclusion of a range of diversities. Everyone will start this process from a unique place and, depending on personal experiences, will have specific knowledge of different aspects of diversity already. All educators are constantly learning.

The first part of becoming an anti-prejudiced educator involves being aware of personal biases and stereotypes. A *stereotype* (cognitive bias) is a generalised view of a group of people and can be negative or positive. Prejudice refers to a negative view of the stereotype and bias is when a prejudice favours or is against a person or group. This can be unconscious or conscious.

Engage in the following activities to support your reflection.

> **REFLECTIVE QUESTIONS**
>
> Identity: who are you?
>
> Write your name in a circle.
>
> Draw arrows pointing outward and at the end of these, write words or phrases that describe what you consider to be key aspects of your identity.
>
> Draw arrows pointing inward and for these write what others might say to describe you.
>
> You may wish to include your name, nationality, ethnicity, race, religion and beliefs, culture and any of the nine protected characteristics from the Equality Act (2010).
>
> *(Continued)*

> (Continued)
>
> Consider where you grew up, information about your carers/parents, your core beliefs and values, who influenced you, your education.
>
> Definitions to help:
>
> *Race*: According to critical race theory (CRT) race is a social construct (Dixson and Anderson, 2018). However, it is a term used to define people based on physical attributes. Show Racism the Red Card (SRtRC) (2023) defines racism as treating people differently or unfairly because of differences in their skin colour (sometimes known as race), religion, nationality or culture.
>
> *Culture*: Embraces the customs/traditions, beliefs, arts and languages of a particular group or nation and can include ethnicity, race, religion (faith or non-faith).
>
> *Ethnicity*: Ethnicity is a social construct and relates to groups of people who share similar cultures (Suyemoto et al., 2020).
>
> Use this information to create a timeline of your education and learning to date, identifying significant episodes. Were there any barriers to learning or obstacles along the way that made your journey more difficult? These barriers could include bullying, a specific learning need, gender expectations or be related to SES.

The purpose of this activity is to make you start to think about who you are. If you consider your identity chart and timeline, who you are at home will influence your teacher persona. This will impact on your journey to be an anti-prejudiced teacher and the pedagogical choices you choose to implement. Most importantly, it will affect how you engage and communicate with your pupils and all stakeholders within the school setting. Your beliefs and values will influence your behaviours in the classroom.

Did you consider your racial identity and how this has shaped your life? If you consider yourself to be a white educator, did you recognise *white privilege* within your identity and learning journey? Recognising white privilege is integral to the anti-bias work of white educators (Collins, 2018). White privilege, very simply, is to not be discriminated against because of skin colour. Deeper reading is required to fully understand this terminology.

Where do your values and beliefs originate from? (This can be called *perceived wisdom* and may include biases that have been inherited from parents, carers and wider family culture.) Have you ever challenged any family member because of different viewpoints or use of language that you may find offensive? This could relate to any protected characteristic. Challenging your perceived wisdom is one of the first steps to identifying any biases or stereotypes you may have.

When a bias refers to a negative view of a stereotype it can lead to displaying prejudiced attitudes and small acts of prejudice; unchallenged, these can lead to discrimination. With regards to employment discrimination, recent government data reveals that there is an underrepresentation of Black Asian global majority (BAGM) teachers in the UK (DfE, 2023c). BAGM, 'global majority', 'Black and brown people' are current UK terms to describe *race and ethnicity.* 'Black Asian minority ethnic' (BAME) is now a dated term. Ethnic minority/minority ethnic, still used in some documentation, does not acknowledge that the *minority* group could be global majority. Institutes need to be mindful of the data when recruiting trainee and qualified teachers.

Violent threats are in the section below genocide, demonstrating how prejudiced attitudes can escalate to deliberate mass killings of specific groups/peoples. Hope not Hate (2019) states that hate crimes, including threatening behaviour and harassment, committed against someone because of their disability, transgender identity, race, religion or belief, or sexual orientation should be reported to the police. In primary, pupils can be educated about how different people have been discriminated against without going into disturbing facts. Pupils can be made aware of the persecution of marginalised groups through age-appropriate stories – for example, *Star of Fear, Star of Hope* by Jo Hoestlandt (1995) is a moving picture book telling the story of friendship and fear during the holocaust. An anti-discriminatory teacher will actively consider curriculum choices to offer a diverse education to prevent pupils developing stereotypes and what Ngozi (2013) calls 'single stories' of people.

> **REFLECTIVE QUESTIONS**
>
> Biases and Stereotypes – Neighbourhood (adapted from SRtRC, 2023)
>
> Who would you rather live next door to? Look at the list below and order the different neighbours from those that you would most prefer to be your neighbours and those that you would least prefer to be.
>
> A gay man
>
> A footballer
>
> A tattooed motorbike rider
>
> A student who has lots of friends
>
> A Christian who attends church
>
> *(Continued)*

> (Continued)
>
> A teenage parent
>
> Someone with a learning difficulty
>
> A hoody wearer
>
> A vegetarian
>
> A Black person
>
> A guitarist in a band

If you do this activity alone, consider your rationale and how this may relate to any biases or stereotypes that you may have identified. Would you share your honest thoughts with friends or family? The original idea was for trainee teachers to work in groups, discussing and sharing their choices. The group would then discuss their most/least preferred neighbours with the whole group, offering reasoning.

Once everyone has offered their responses the facilitator can reveal that the neighbour is in fact the same person. This will then highlight how everyone is unique with varied and complex elements to our identities. To judge or label someone based on one of their characteristics of their identity does not take account of their full diverse individuality. This activity demonstrates how biases and stereotyping may have influenced choices.

> ## REFLECTIVE QUESTIONS
>
> Next step targets
>
> Project Implicit (2011) has developed *hidden bias tests* to measure unconscious bias. These could help you to further identify your own conscious/unconscious biases. Visit the Project Implicit website (implicit.harvard.edu/implicit/takeatest.html) and take tests related to protected characteristics.
>
> Being consciously aware of personal biases and stereotypes, demonstrates readiness to actively engage in educating yourself about them:
>
> - ask yourself: who do you choose to sit next to on a bus, or in the classroom?
> - examine the diversity of your friendship groups, including those on social media (think of all the protected characteristics);

- in class, notice how pupils are seated/grouped;
- notice who asks/answers questions (is there a dominance related to any protected characteristic?).

Whatever you discover, take conscious action to find out more.

For example:

- offer to support local refugee support charities and visit www.ourmigrationstory.org.uk/ to find out more about Britain's migration history;
- arrange to visit a place of worship new to you (conformist/non-conformist);
- find out more LGBTQ-inclusive education at www.stonewall.org.uk/lgbtq-inclusive-education-everything-you-need-know;
- find out more about how to promote disability inclusion at https://neu.org.uk/advice/equality/disability-equality.

## OVERCOMING BARRIERS BY DIVERSIFYING AND DECOLONISING THE CURRICULUM (CULTURAL RELEVANCE)

Decolonising the curriculum (DtC) has its basis in CRT. CRT is an understanding that society is shaped by structural racism. It offers a framework to consider how racial inequality presents itself in policies and practices, discriminating against minoritised groups and those who speak different languages (Bradbury, 2020). DtC at school level is about diversifying the curriculum to include non-Eurocentric viewpoints and to celebrate different perspectives in education. For cultural relevance, it is important that children's home languages are celebrated, valued and respected as part of a decolonised curriculum. Pupils should feel proud of their language as it is a part of their identities, which links to having that sense of belonging, motivation and confidence. EAL is an umbrella term for all children that have been identified as having another language at home. This includes fluent bilingual children who are British born and children who are new arrivals to the country who may or may not have English as a language and who have arrived for different reasons such as: parents studying in the UK, economic migrants or asylum seekers. DtC includes embedding anti-racist practices that benefits all children and those with EAL.

## AMBITIOUS CURRICULUM CHOICES

Inspections will be looking for a curriculum intent that is ambitious and designed to enable all learners, including those that are disadvantaged or with SEND, to acquire what they call the knowledge and cultural capital to succeed (Ofsted, 2019). The aims of the national curriculum (DfE, 2013) help to define knowledge and cultural capital by stating that to be educated global citizens with an appreciation of human creativity and achievement, pupils need to be introduced to the best of what has been thought and said.

Schools have the power to be the architects of their curricula in terms of how the statutory national curriculum and early years framework are implemented. It is up to ambitious leadership to decide what knowledge is considered worthy of being included in their broad and balanced decolonised curricula, to empower socially mobile, global citizens of the future. Curriculum choices, resources and pedagogical practices will support representing our diverse world. Ofsted (2023) will be inspecting personal development of pupils, which includes SMSC development.

## SMSC DEVELOPMENT

SMSC development is a broad concept that brings together many aspects of personal development (Ofsted, 2023). It includes, the spiritual development of pupils demonstrated by their ability to be reflective about their own beliefs (religious or otherwise) and perspective on life, knowledge of, and respect for, different people's faiths, feelings and values-teaching. Personal, social, health and economic (PHSE) education, religious education (RE) and citizenship education can be taught as part of SMSC. Explicitly teaching for diversity through SMSC supports an inclusive environment.

## LGBTQ-INCLUSIVE EDUCATION

In primary, integrating LGBT content into the curriculum needs to be carefully considered and age appropriate. Schools can foster a sense of belonging and respect for diversity, combat discrimination and prejudice, and help questioning pupils feel represented and valued. Including LGBT content through SMSC development using children's literature can enable teachers to feel more confident in diversifying their curriculum.

> ### CASE STUDY: SMSC AND RE
>
> Following an observation of an RE lesson, PGCE trainee Amy realised how important it is to teach RE to Year 1 pupils using dialogic enquiry and lived experiences to avoid othering and teaching from a Christian perspective. She planned the use of videos sharing lived experience of Muslim children, lived experience from a

pupil in the class and a persona doll to help explain specific subject knowledge related to Islam.

The persona doll was an initial hook to help to support with specific language associated with Islam and the videos helped to share lived experiences of children to reinforce and help explain, for example, aspects of Muslim worship. Then a Muslim pupil who was keen and willing to share their personal family cultures and traditions was drawn upon to support the class in developing a better understanding of Islam related to the intended learning for the lesson.

When planning the lesson, the trainee was aware that enquiry-based dialogic pedagogy needs careful consideration to support safeguarding issues regarding bullying and racism. Permission from parents was sought regarding the Muslim pupil sharing stories related to their Islamic faith. Creating a classroom culture of open discussion supports the building of trust between teacher and pupil.

The trainee concluded that by using lived experiences, the persona doll and dialogic approaches, the class were highly engaged with the learning, curious and questioning. It was also noted that she needed to have deep subject knowledge of the intended learning and subject-specific vocabulary. To be able to use a persona doll effectively requires careful consideration and planning. If the doll is used with a script, expert advice should be sought regarding accuracy and cultural sensitivity.

This case study highlights how trainee teachers can be active change agents, by implementing different pedagogical choices. Teachers who question their own internalised bias and who develop an inclusive and diverse approach to their educational provision can minimise alienation and microaggressions (for example, questions such as: 'But where are you really from?') that BAGM children often experience. Pupils will be motivated to learn if they feel a sense of belonging within your class. To feel valued and connected to the class and school community, their physical and psychological needs need to be met (Maslow, 1987, cited in Bates, 2019).

## TEACHING FOR DIVERSITY THROUGH DIALOGIC APPROACHES

Dialogic approaches are a good way to build tricky conversations and discussions into your practice when teaching SMSC development. The facilitator needs to be knowledgeable of the purpose of the discussion and able to confidently navigate pupils' talk. Flexibility within dialogic approaches enables a skilled facilitator to ask powerful questions to challenge pupils' opinions about specific topics and if conducted in a safe and trusting environment all pupils can express themselves.

## CASE STUDY: SMSC DEVELOPMENT AND PHSE

When Martha was in her second-year placement Year 3 class, she was asked to plan a PHSE lesson using children's literature (*What Makes Us Unique* by Dr Jillian Roberts) as a philosophy for children (P4C) stimulus. Martha planned from the PHSE Association (https://pshe-association.org.uk/key-stage-1-2) health and well-being core theme and the objective that she created was to 'appreciate that each person is unique and has valuable contributions to make'.

Part of the structure of P4C (a dialogic, oracy pedagogy) is a preparation starter task to engage the children in some initial talk (SAPERE, 2016, 2022). Pupils had to find peers with attributes that might make them different from each other. Martha had designed 'Find someone who …' questions. One question was, 'Find someone who was not born in Liverpool'. Martha had not expected a child to get upset because numerous children had approached him to find out. This child was of Chinese heritage, British born and Liverpudlian. Having his peers question his identity caused him upset and most likely made him realise that his racial difference was why they asked him. At the time Martha, a White British trainee, did not exacerbate the distress the child was feeling and instead talked to other children about how she was not born in Liverpool and that no one had asked her.

Martha received feedback from the class mentor regarding the overall successful implementation of this P4C approach. Pupils had been engaged in rich discussions around difference and positive contributions. However, the pupils' behaviour had been more challenging in this lesson and the mentor advised her to develop behaviour management for future active oracy lessons.

In a further discussion with a university tutor, Martha declared that she had found the above incident challenging; both tutor and Martha realised how important having courageous conversations is for both trainee teachers and school mentors, and how confidence and further training is needed to address tricky issues skilfully and sensitively.

This case study highlights the positives of dialogic approaches and includes a challenge for a trainee with regards to discussing racial difference. One of the EEF (2015) findings was that teachers and pupils generally reported that P4C had a positive influence on pupils' confidence to speak, listening skills and self-esteem. Perceived outcomes included how pupils from disadvantaged backgrounds gained more from this approach than high achievers because it did not directly relate to academic achievement and those with EAL gained more vocabulary from listening to others and taking part in discussions. Schools may choose to train teachers in P4C as an initiative to overcome barriers to learning, using PP funding.

# CONCLUSION

Becoming an anti-prejudiced educator will support schools in diversifying and decolonising their curricula for inclusion. Schools' leaders need to develop a culture that strongly believes in the importance of social justice and anti-discriminatory practices. By diversifying and decolonising the curriculum – knowing why this is important and the impact that curriculum design has on achievement, inclusion (sense of belonging), motivation – is the duty of every teacher. The journey begins with addressing one's own biases and stereotypes that can prevent unconscious and conscious prejudiced practices, considering all curriculum choices for diversity, setting next personal steps and continuing to learn of those issues about which you have less knowledge and understanding.

Being a diverse and inclusive educator takes time, effort and commitment (Thomas, 2022). There is not a simple tick list to becoming and being anti-discriminatory; it is a constant part of a teacher's practice. This chapter emphasises the importance of self-reflection and awareness development which will help you to actively consider some solutions with regards to your classroom practices and embedding SMSC development and dialogic approaches into curriculum choices. Pupils need to see themselves represented in the narratives told and literature choices, to improve school experiences.

> ### REVIEW OF CHAPTER OBJECTIVES
>
> Within this chapter you have considered:
>
> - knowing why it is essential to become an anti-prejudiced educator;
> - having awareness of your own biases and stereotypes;
> - exemplifying dialogic practices to diversify and decolonise the curriculum (DtC) through social, moral, spiritual and cultural development (SMSC);
> - setting personal next steps.

# FURTHER READING AND RESOURCES

## READING

Brett, A. and Brassington, J. (2023) *Pride and Progress: Making Schools LGBT+ Inclusive Spaces*. London: Corwin.

Choudry, S. (2021) *Equitable Education*. St Albans: Critical.

Dellenty, S. (2019) *Celebrating Difference: A Whole-school Approach to LGBT+ Inclusion*. London: Bloomsbury.

Kara, B. (2021) *Diversity in Schools*. London: Corwin.

Pinkett, M. and Roberts, M. (2019) *Boys Don't Try? Rethinking Masculinity in Schools*. London: Routledge.

Thomas, A. (2022) *Representation Matters: Becoming an Anti-racist Educator*. London: Bloomsbury.

## ONLINE RESOURCES

Diverse children's literature

https://misterbodd.wordpress.com/2019/08/14/i-see-me-inclusive-books-ks2/ and www.anewchapterbooks.com/

HOPE Not Hate: This group's mission is to work tirelessly to expose and oppose far-right extremism. It champions and promotes democracy and the rule of law

https://hopenothate.org.uk/

National Education Union (NEU): Resources and guidance on removing barriers to inclusion and abolishing ablism, disablism and discrimination https://neu.org.uk/advice/equality/disability-equality

NEU: Framework for developing an anti-racist approach

https://neu.org.uk/latest/library/anti-racism-charter-framework-developing-anti-racist-approach

NEU: Anti-racism framework for initial teacher education/training www.ucet.ac.uk/downloads/14636-Anti-Racism-ITET-framework.pdf

Our Migration Story: Learn about Britain's migration history

www.ourmigrationstory.org.uk/

Runnymede Trust: For reliable and impartial evidence on racial inequalities in the UK www.runnymedetrust.org/about/about-us

Show Racism the Red Card (SRtRC)

www.theredcard.org/

Stonewall: Building LGBTQ-inclusive spaces

www.stonewall.org.uk/build-workplace-works-lgbtq-people

Stonewall: Guidance on inclusive education

www.stonewall.org.uk/lgbtq-inclusive-education-everything-you-need-know

# REFERENCES

Bates, B. (2019) *Learning Theories Simplified* (2nd ed.). London: Sage.

Bradbury, A. (2020) A critical race theory framework for education policy analysis: The case of bilingual learners and assessment policy in England. *Race Ethnicity and Education*, 23(2), 241–260. doi: 10.1080/13613324.2019.1599338

Choudry, S. (2021) *Equitable Education*. St Albans: Critical.

Collins, C. (2018) What is white privilege, really? *Learning for Justice*, 60(Fall). Available at: www.learningforjustice.org/magazine/fall-2018/what-is-white-privilege-really [accessed 31 July 2023].

Department for Education (DfE) (2013) *The National Curriculum for England. Key Stage 1 and 2 Framework Documents*. Available at: https://assets.publishing.service.gov.uk/government/uploads/system/uploads/attachment_data/file/425601/PRIMARY_national_curriculum.pdf [accessed 7 July 2023].

DfE (2017) *Preventing and Tackling Bullying: Advice for Headteachers, Staff and Governing Bodies*. Available at: https://assets.publishing.service.gov.uk/government/uploads/system/uploads/attachment_data/file/1069688/Preventing_and_tackling_bullying_advice.pdf [accessed 7 July 2023].

DfE (2019) *ITT Core Content Framework*. London: DfE. Available at: https://assets.publishing.service.gov.uk/government/uploads/system/uploads/attachment_data/file/974307/ITT_core_content_framework_.pdf [accessed November 2023].

DfE (2022) *Key Stage 2 Attainment, Academic Year 2021/22*. Available at: https://explore-education-statistics.service.gov.uk/find-statistics/key-stage-2-attainment [accessed 9 August 2023].

DfE (2023a) *Key Stage 2 Attainment, Academic Year 2022/23*. Available at: https://explore-education-statistics.service.gov.uk/find-statistics/key-stage-2-attainment [accessed 2 August 2023].

DfE (2023b) *Schools, Pupils and Their Characteristics, Academic Year 2022/23*. Available at: https://explore-education-statistics.service.gov.uk/find-statistics/school-pupils-and-their-characteristics [accessed 2 August 2023].

DfE (2023c) *School Teacher Workforce*. Available at: www.ethnicity-facts-figures.service.gov.uk/workforce-and-business/workforce-diversity/school-teacher-workforce/latest#by-ethnicity-and-role [accessed 2 August 2023].

DfE (2024) *Initial teacher training and early career framework* Available at: https://www.gov.uk/government/publications/initial-teacher-training-and-early-career-framework [Accessed March 2024].

Dixson, A. D. and Anderson, C. R. (2018) Where are we? Critical race theory in education 20 years later. *Peabody Journal of Education*, 93(1), 121–131, doi: 10.1080/0161956X.2017.1403194

EEF (2015) *Annual Report, 2014/15*. London: EEF.

Equaliteach (2023) *Embedding Anti-racism into School Culture: A Group Workshop for Headteachers in Liverpool*. Equaliteach, Liverpool John Moore University Centre for Educational Leadership and Liverpool City Council.

gov.uk (n.d.) Equality Act 2010. Available at: www.legislation.gov.uk/ukpga/2010/15/contents [accessed 8 November 2023].

Hoestlandt, J. (1995) *Star of Fear, Star of Hope*. London: Bloomsbury.

Home Office (1999) *The Stephen Lawrence Inquiry*. Available at: www.gov.uk/government/publications/the-stephen-lawrence-inquiry [accessed 11 August 2023].

HOPE not Hate (2019) *Hate Crime*. Available at: https://hopenothate.org.uk/2019/09/09/hate-crime/ [accessed 8 November 2023].

Interaction Institute for Social Change (IISC) (2016) *Illustrating Equality vs Equity, Artist: Angus Maguire*. Available at: https://interactioninstitute.org/illustrating-equality-vs-equity/ [accessed 22 August 2023].

Kara, B. (2021) *Diversity in Schools*. London: Corwin.

Ngozi Adichie, C. (2013) *Ted Talk: The Danger of a Single Story*. Available at: www.ted.com/talks/chimamanda_ngozi_adichie_the_danger_of_a_single_story [accessed 11 August 2023].

NSPCC (2023) *Bullying and Cyberbullying: Effects of Bullying*. Available at: www.nspcc.org.uk/what-is-child-abuse/types-of-abuse/bullying-and-cyberbullying/#effects [ accessed 12 July 2023].

Ofsted (2019) *Education Inspection Framework*. Available at: www.gov.uk/government/publications/education-inspection-framework [accessed 2 August 2023].

Ofsted (2023) *Education Inspection Framework*. Available at: www.gov.uk/government/publications/school-inspection-handbook-eif/school-inspection-handbook-for-september-2023#evaluating-personal-development [accessed 11 August 2023].

Project Implicit (2011) *Implicit Association Test*. Available at: https://implicit.harvard.edu/implicit/takeatest.html [accessed 4 August 2023].

Roberts, J. (2016) *What Makes Us Unique*. Victoria, BC: Orca.

SAPERE (2016) *Handbook to Accompany the Level 1 Foundation Course* (5th ed.). Sheffield: SAPERE.

SAPERE (2023) *P4C Teacher Training: Philosophy for Children*. Available at: www.sapere.org.uk/ [accessed 3 July 2023].

Show Racism the Red Card (SRtRC) (2023) https://theredcardhub.org/ and https://dormston.dudley.sch.uk/wp-content/uploads/2020/09/Homophobia-workshop-materials.pdf [accessed 7 July 2023].

Stonewall (2023) *Schools and Colleges*. Available at: www.stonewall.org.uk/schools-colleges [accessed 8 November 2023].

Suyemoto, K. L., Curley, M. and Mukkamala, S. (2020) What do we mean by 'ethnicity' and 'race'? A consensual qualitative research investigation of colloquial understandings. *Genealogy*, 4(3), 81. Available at: https://doi.org/10.3390/genealogy4030081 [accessed 30 December 2023].

Thomas, A. (2022) *Representation Matters: Becoming an Anti-racist Educator*. London: Bloomsbury.

UK Government (2018) *Ethnicity, Gender, and Social Mobility*. Available at: https://assets.publishing.service.gov.uk/government/uploads/system/uploads/attachment_data/file/705788/Ethnicity__gender_and_social_mobility_-_main_report.pdf [accessed 2 August 2023].

UNCRC (1989) *United Nations Convention on the Rights of a Child*. Available at: www.unicef.org.uk/what-we-do/un-convention-child-rights/ [accessed 20 July 2023].

# 14

# ASSESSMENT AND PROGRESSION

## RACHEL SIMPSON

**Learn that and Learn how to –
The Knowledge and Application Model**

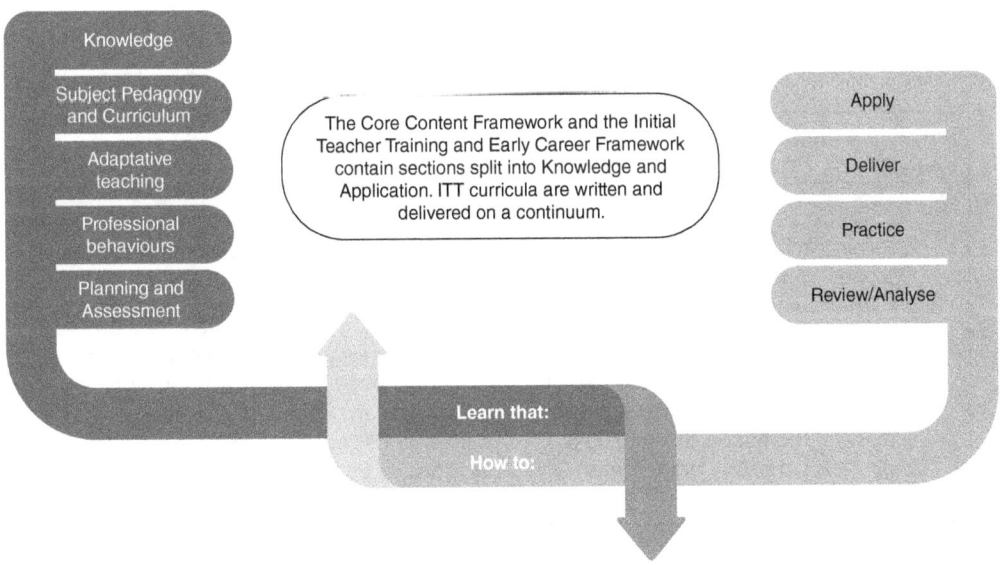

## FRAMED BY THE CCF – FOR FULL LINKS TO THE ITTECF, SEE PAGE 337

| Assessment (Standard 6 – 'Make accurate and productive use of assessment') ||
|---|---|
| Learn that … | Learn how to … |
| 1. Effective assessment is critical to teaching because it provides teachers with information about pupils' understanding and needs.<br>3. Before using any assessment, teachers should be clear about the decision it will be used to support and be able to justify its use.<br>4. To be of value, teachers use information from assessments to inform the decisions they make; in turn, pupils must be able to act on feedback for it to have an effect.<br>5. High-quality feedback can be written or verbal; it is likely to be accurate and clear, encourage further effort, and provide specific guidance on how to improve. | Avoid common assessment pitfalls, by:<br><br>• Discussing and analysing with expert colleagues how to plan formative assessment tasks linked to lesson objectives and think ahead about what would indicate understanding. |

| How Pupils Learn (Standard 2 – 'Promote good progress') ||
|---|---|
| Learn that … | Learn how to … |
| 1. Learning involves a lasting change in pupils' capabilities or understanding.<br>2. Prior knowledge plays an important role in how pupils learn; committing some key facts to their long-term memory is likely to help pupils learn more complex ideas. | Increase likelihood of material being retained, by:<br><br>• Observing how expert colleagues plan regular review and practice of key ideas and concepts over time (e.g. through carefully planned use of structured talk activities) and deconstructing this approach. |

## CHAPTER OBJECTIVES

On reading this chapter you will consider:

- different types of assessment in primary education;
- why assessment is critical to pupils' progression of knowledge and understanding, and your development as a teacher;

- how to plan and use assessments and feedback according to different purposes as a trainee teacher, including considering pupils' roles in assessment;
- what progress looks like, by considering the integral role of assessment in planning, teaching and adaptive practice.

### KEY VOCABULARY

Formative assessment

Summative assessment

Pupil progress

Feedback

Misconceptions

Core Content Framework

Initial Teacher Training and Early Career Framework (ITTECF)

# INTRODUCTION

As a trainee and a teacher in the future, you will make decisions. Many of these decisions will be aiming to answer the questions:

- What should the pupils learn?
- Why should they learn this?
- How should they learn this?
- What should come next in the learning sequence?

The answers to these questions will depend largely upon the school's curriculum, but the most effective teaching and learning experiences will also depend upon your awareness of each pupil's knowledge, understanding and ability to apply their skills. How will you find out this information about your pupils? Unlocking this information is considered to be at the heart of effective teaching and learning experiences, and thoughtfully planned assessment opportunities will be your set of keys.

This chapter will help you to develop your knowledge and understanding of assessment in primary education, and its place in enabling pupils' progression in their learning experiences. The crucial role of assessment regarding pupil progress will be considered by exploring different types of assessment, according to different purposes. The chapter aims to equip you as a trainee to make the most effective decisions about assessment. Therefore, the discussion of different assessment strategies alongside reflective tasks will enable you to develop assessment skills as a trainee and apply these to your teaching context. A case study of a trainee's assessment practices in her school-based learning centre (SBLC) will provide examples of assessment practice on an ITT programme.

# WHAT IS ASSESSMENT IN PRIMARY EDUCATION AND WHY IS IT IMPORTANT FOR PUPIL PROGRESSION?

As a trainee, you will need to engage with the idea of assessment in primary education. To help with this, it is important for you to understand your feelings about assessment currently. This short task will help to gauge your starting point.

## ACTION LEARNING SET

One thing we all have in common is that we have been assessed in some way. Therefore, it is possible that we all have strong views of assessment! A simple understanding of the term assessment could be: *a measure of my attainment, performance, achievement, or progress compared to others, compared to myself, or compared to a 'standard'.*

These measures can be made using different assessment tools, for example:

- written tests – essays, short answers, multiple choice;
- written work (not in test form) – portfolios, PowerPoint presentations;
- oral presentations or discussions;
- practical demonstrations – use of a particular skill or equipment, conducting an experiment;
- products – artwork, technology products, musical performance.

Think of an example of an assessment you have experienced (at school, college, university or elsewhere). Note down your responses to the following questions:

- What was being assessed? (the focus of the assessment)
- Why was it being assessed? (the purpose of the assessment)
- How was it assessed? *(the assessment tool)*

Most people choose a high-stakes summative example to answer this question (you will find the definition of 'summative' later in the chapter). This may be because their examples of assessment had some lasting effect – either a practical effect or an emotional effect. Perhaps you chose an example of assessment that led to a great success for you and provided a pivotal turning point in your life; perhaps you chose an example that had the opposite effect.

The idea of assessment is often considered to be challenging in education, particularly by trainees. This may be because society often focuses on high-stakes assessment, such as end of age phase testing. However, if we view assessment as an integral part of the planning, teaching and evaluating learning cycle, with a focus particularly on formative assessment, then it starts to become less daunting.

As a trainee, developing your understanding of effective assessment processes will be integral to your journey into teaching. The three questions above about assessment will be important ones for you to consider throughout this chapter and beyond, as you plan assessments that are meaningful, informative and positive experiences for both you as the teacher and your pupils.

## WHAT ARE THE TYPES OF ASSESSMENT?

For many decades, assessment in education has been categorised under two distinct headings: formative assessment (assessment *for* learning) and summative assessment (assessment *of* learning).

Assessment for learning, or formative assessment, can be understood as: 'The process of seeking and interpreting evidence for use by learners and their teachers to decide where the learners are in their learning, where they need to go and how best to get there' (Assessment Reform Group, 2002, p. 1). This definition explains that formative assessment informs the planning and teaching of future learning experiences, aiming to move pupils' learning forward. It can also be diagnostic, providing information about pupils' prior knowledge and misconceptions before beginning a learning activity (diagnosing strengths and areas of need) to inform planning. Many teachers include a formative assessment opportunity in each learning activity, and it can also be planned into topics at key points to inform the next steps in the learning sequence.

Assessment of learning, or summative assessment, is an assessment which provides evidence of a learner's knowledge, understanding and skills at a given point in time. These 'summaries of learning' may be used for reporting and public accountability (Black and Wiliam, 2009). The national curriculum (DfE, 2013) was implemented in England as part of the 1988 Education Act, alongside statutory assessment tests (SATs) for primary schools in 1991. SATs are examples of standardised summative assessments, testing aspects of English and mathematics for all pupils at the end of Key Stages 1 and 2 in state schools in England. The phonics screening check in Key Stage 1 is another example of statutory testing.

The government in England provides summative assessment and reporting guidance and schools have to respond to these requirements – this guidance can change annually according to different priorities in education. Schools will also administer and keep records of their own summative *teacher assessments*. These may use published assessment materials or resources devised by the school to assess pupils' achievements in primary subjects. It is important to note that assessment tools other than a written test can be used for summative assessments.

There is sometimes confusion about these two assessment terms so here is an example to help. You are teaching an electricity topic to Year 6 pupils. You give them a written test of ten questions, based on learning outcomes taken from your electricity lessons so far. Would this be an example of formative assessment or summative assessment? Take a moment to think about your response.

The answer depends upon how you plan to use the pupils' responses and the results of the test. For example, the test may come at a mid-point in your electricity topic. The teacher may help the pupils to reflect on their answers and identify their next steps for learning if they are struggling with a particular learning outcome. They will have time and opportunity to improve their understanding, knowledge and skills. This example would be categorised as formative assessment and would help to move the learning forward. Alternatively, the test may come at the end of the topic. The pupils do not receive their tests back and there is not an opportunity for them to improve their understanding, knowledge and skills based on these results. These results are reported to parents in the end of year school report, therefore providing a summary of learning and being classed as a summative assessment.

This example of an electricity test shows that it is the purpose of an assessment that defines it as formative or summative, rather than the assessment tool – in this case a written test.

In Standard 2 ('Promote good progress') the CCF/ITTECF explains that 'Learning involves a lasting change in pupils' capabilities or understanding.' It also discusses that 'Prior knowledge plays an important role in how pupils learn; committing some key facts to their long-term memory is likely to help pupils learn more complex ideas.' Well-planned use of formative and summative assessment will help you as a trainee to ensure that your pupils are making progress in their learning and provide evidence of this lasting change.

## REFLECTIVE QUESTIONS

Assessment in education is a widely researched and strongly debated topic. Read the evidence-informed research below to help you to reflect upon these questions:

- How is assessment linked to helping pupils make good progress?
- Do you think all assessments can and should be used for formative purposes?
- In what ways do you think a summary of learning (summative assessment) is useful?

## EVIDENCE-INFORMED RESEARCH: FORMATIVE ASSESSMENT AND ITS ROLE IN PUPIL PROGRESSION

The potential use and impact of formative assessment has been investigated by researchers in the field of education for several decades. A seminal piece of work was completed by Paul Black and Dylan Wiliam in 1998. Their study, *Inside the Black Box* (Black and Wiliam, 1998), reviewed 250 published studies of formative assessment strategies being used in the classroom. Most of these studies focused on real-life classroom experiences (for example, a case study of a few teachers in one school using a particular formative assessment strategy).

Many more studies into the use and potential impact of formative assessment followed this publication (for example: Black et al., 2004; Black and Wiliam, 2009; Christodoulou, 2017). Black and Wiliam's (2009, 2012) research suggests that the following five elements of formative assessment are considered to be the most influential in helping pupils to make progress in their learning:

- clarifying and understanding learning intentions and criteria for success;
- engineering effective classroom discussions, questions and tasks that elicit evidence of learning;
- providing feedback that moves learning forward;
- activating pupils as instructional resources for each other;
- activating pupils as owners of their own learning.

*(Continued)*

(Continued)

The first element listed suggests that high-quality formative assessment is directly linked to high-quality lesson planning, based on a teacher's strong subject knowledge (Harlen and James, 1997), and this aligns with Ofsted's *Education Inspection Framework* (Ofsted, 2019). It is crucial for the aspects of learning that will be formatively assessed to align with the learning intentions and success criteria of the lesson, and for the assessment criteria to be understood by both the teacher and the pupils (Sadler, 1989). To achieve progress, a learning experience should provide opportunities for pupils to be challenged and make mistakes. Smith and Cowie (2015) suggest that mistakes are viewed as powerful when they are considered as constructive points in the learning process and lead to future learning, enabling progress to be made. Hattie (2012) discusses the importance of making pupils' learning more visible, and a way to achieve this is for the formative assessment to focus on what the pupils are supposed to be *learning*, rather than what they are *doing* in a lesson.

You may have noted that all five elements listed above have a strong focus on each pupil's ownership of the formative assessment processes, alongside the teacher's role. This makes sense – for a pupil to make progress in their learning, they need to have an idea of their current understanding, any misconceptions and their next steps. Therefore, formative assessment requires the development of positive assessment attitudes, habits and skills (of both the teachers and the pupils), embedded in classroom practice (Black et al., 2004). Effective strategies to develop such habits have been documented in assessment-related literature, for example the Embedding Formative Assessment Programme, evaluated by Speckesser et al., (2018).

Is such an investment in embedding quality formative assessment practices worthwhile for a teacher? The Education Endowment Foundation's (EEF) Toolkit evaluates the potential impact of aspects of teaching on learning outcomes, using systematic reviews of high-quality research studies (EEF, 2021). It concludes that the use of feedback (a main component of formative assessment) has a very high impact for a very low cost based on extensive evidence. The use of feedback strategies in assessment will be discussed later in this chapter.

## CAN SUMMATIVE ASSESSMENT SERVE A FORMATIVE PURPOSE?

The aim of assessment used for summative purposes is to elicit an accurate understanding of a pupil's knowledge, understanding and/or skills (Black and Wiliam, 2009). The results are commonly used for reporting purposes, and as indicators of the quality of education in a school. Many assessment-related debates in education currently focus on the aim of all assessments to have some formative purpose, by providing feedback to pupils based on assessments with an intended summative purpose (Black et al., 2004; Wiliam, 2013). The Primary Science Teaching Trust's (2020) *Teacher Assessment in Primary Science* model takes the connection between formative and summative assessment a step further, by demonstrating how all formative assessment opportunities can be used to a create a summary of the pupils' learning – serving a summative purpose. However, Harlen and James (1997) suggest that although formative assessment outcomes can inform summative judgements, there should be a clear distinction between formative and summative assessments due to their different purposes.

> **ACTION LEARNING SET**
>
> Observe the different opportunities for assessment in your SBLC and make a note of:
>
> - what is being assessed (knowledge, understanding or skills);
> - the purpose of the assessment (formative or summative);
> - the assessment tools (for example: written work; oral presentation; practical demonstration; multiple choice test);
> - how the assessment is used to support pupils' progression in their learning.
>
> So far, we have discussed some of the key terminology linked to types of assessment. These terms will be referred to in the next section as we consider strategies to help you to plan purposeful assessment for your pupils.

How can assessment be used effectively in primary education?

> **REFLECTIVE QUESTIONS**
>
> The following questions will help you to reflect on the ideas presented in this section:
>
> - Why do I think it is important to have strong subject and pedagogical knowledge when planning assessments?
> - Can I recognise some purposeful assessment strategies?
> - What might be the challenges of the some of the assessment strategies for me as a trainee, and how might I overcome these challenges?

As a trainee and a future teacher, you will aim to maximise all learning opportunities. These will incorporate well-planned assessments. To ensure your assessments achieve their intended purpose and have the greatest impact on the pupils, you can consider the following five factors.

# THE USE OF FEEDBACK IN ASSESSMENT PRACTICES

High-quality feedback is believed to be essential for pupil progress. As a trainee you will spend a lot of time using feedback to help your pupils to move forward – examples of feedback include written feedback such as marking comments after a lesson, or oral feedback during a lesson. The following evidence-informed research will help you to understand some key points about effective feedback, to help you make the best decisions about your feedback practices. As you read about the research below, consider how it links to Standard 6 of the CCF/ITTECF:

- pupils must be able to act on feedback for it to have an effect;
- high-quality feedback can be written or verbal; it is likely to be accurate and clear, encourage further effort, and provide specific guidance on how to improve.

### EVIDENCE-INFORMED RESEARCH

Formative assessment is an iterative process, allowing pupils to improve their work in response to feedback. This aligns with influential psychologist Piaget's (1936) theory of cognitive development: that learning is actively constructed rather than passively received. Hattie and Timperley (2007) conclude that the purpose of feedback is to help pupils to understand how to reduce the difference between the desired learning goal and current performance. Sadler (2010) argues that solely receiving feedback has little impact on learning, as it may be misinterpreted or ignored. The EEF (2016) support this in their review of the effectiveness of marking, stating that pupils will only benefit from marking if time is given for them to consider and respond to the marking comments.

Therefore, teachers are encouraged to focus on developing high-quality teacher-pupil dialogue, as well as pupils' abilities to self- and peer assess (Black and Wiliam, 2009) to give pupils ownership of feedback (Wiliam, 2020).

Providing feedback in a timely way and with pupil ownership should enable pupils to understand the feedback, respond to it and apply its main messages to their subsequent learning. Your SBLC will give you guidance about feedback and marking in their school's assessment policy – this may differ from school to school.

## ASSESSING WITH ACCURACY

Standard 6 of the CCF/ITTECF states that it is important for teachers to: 'be clear about the decision it [assessment] will be used to support and be able to justify its use'.

This supports the next CCF/ITTECF statement: 'To be of value, teachers use information from assessments to inform the decisions they make.' Effective assessments aim to capture a pupil's learning (this could be their knowledge, understanding, or skill) of an identified learning objective accurately. For a trainee to achieve this, they need strong subject knowledge – after all, many assessments rely on human judgement (Harlen and James, 1997). For example, if a trainee plans to assess Key Stage 1 pupils' history knowledge about significant historical events, people and places in their own locality, they need to have that subject knowledge to accurately teach and assess the learning experience.

Trainees also need strong pedagogical knowledge to enable them to devise an assessment that fits its purpose. For example, if a trainee wants to assess the Key Stage 1 science learning goal – to set up and perform simple tests to observe, compare and group items – the trainee is likely to assess this through a practical task with each pupil rather than a written test.

An assessment is then valid if it achieves its intention – with accuracy, the teacher can 'use information from assessments to inform the decisions they make', as stated in Standard 6 of the CCF/ITTECF. Getting assessment judgements right is important – you will find as a trainee that schools have supportive systems and processes such as opportunities for teachers to assess and moderate work together, and the joint development of assessment criteria.

## ASSESSING TO ENABLE PUPIL PROGRESS

Standard 2 ('Promote good progress') of the CCF/ITTECF states: 'Learning involves a lasting change in pupils' capabilities or understanding.' Assessment plays an important role in this because it is the tool used to find out if this lasting change has happened in full, partially, or not yet for each pupil. This lasting change can be explained as pupils making progress in their learning. Pupil progress can be viewed on different timescales – for example, progress within a lesson, progress made from the beginning to the end of a sequence of lessons, or progress made from year to year. Rosenshine's (2012) 'Principles of instruction' advise teachers to check for pupils' understanding at very regular points in the learning experience, and the tools used at these check points could be informed by formative assessment principles. How can a trainee ensure that the lasting change in a pupils' knowledge, understanding and/or skills has occurred? Rosenshine (2012) recommends that pupils undertake weekly and monthly reviews, 'providing extensive practice in order to develop well-connected and automatic knowledge' (p. 19). The five principles of formative assessment can be embedded in these reviews to maximise their effectiveness.

As a trainee, you will mostly be considering pupil progress for the group of pupils in your SBLC class, at the point in time when you are undertaking your teaching placement. You will follow the school's assessment policy and the advice of your expert mentor. However, it is important for you to understand that teachers assess and monitor pupils' progress from year to year to ensure each pupil makes expected progress during their time in primary education.

## ASSESSING PUPILS' PRIOR KNOWLEDGE AND MISCONCEPTIONS

The CCF/ITTECF (Standard 2, 'Promote good progress') states: 'Prior knowledge plays an important role in how pupils learn; committing some key facts to their long-term memory is likely to help pupils learn more complex ideas.' Formative assessment plays a key role in accessing the pupils' prior knowledge: ideally, this knowledge and any misconceptions should be established before planning a series of lessons (through whole-class discussions, a written set of questions, individual tasks such as a practical experiment). It is also a common way to start a lesson; accessing pupils' understandings of prior learning intentions can ensure that the lesson builds upon these understandings and addresses misconceptions. Assessment of pupils' prior knowledge relies on the questions you will ask the pupils in your lessons; carefully planning the wording of these questions will help the pupils to share their understandings with you.

## INCLUSIVE ASSESSMENT

As you would expect, pupils make progress at different rates in their learning, justifying the need for a teacher's adaptive practice. This is explored in CCF/ITTECF Standard 5, Adaptive Teaching. Adaptations to enable learning success for each pupil will be reflected in your lesson planning and this should also be considered in your assessment activities. Each assessment task needs to be accessible for each pupil, therefore pupils may be given different assessment questions, different tasks to match their individual learning goals or resources to support their specific learning needs.

## WHAT DOES ASSESSMENT LOOK LIKE IN PRACTICE FOR A TRAINEE ON AN ITT PROGRAMME?

Read the following case study of trainee Charlotte to find out how a trainee developed the use of assessment during an ITT programme.

## CASE STUDY: SCAFFOLDING ASSESSMENT-RELATED TASKS FOR TRAINEES

Charlotte is a PGCE Primary Education trainee who completed a series of assessment tasks during a PGCE programme in SBLCs, supported by an expert mentor. Tasks were scaffolded in this sequence to enable trainees to build up their understanding of effective assessment in practice:

Intensive training and practice (ITaP):

1. observe and critically reflect upon assessment practices in individual lessons led by the expert mentor (including the use of questioning to elicit understanding);
2. plan, teach and evaluate individual lessons, including the use of formative assessment strategies;
3. discuss strategies to support a pupil with misconceptions in mathematics with the expert mentor; use the strategies with the pupil and assess the pupil's progress.

Main teaching placement tasks:

1. plan, teach and evaluate sequences of lessons in all subjects, including the use of formative and summative assessment strategies;
2. keep formative assessment records for three pupils in English, mathematics and science;
3. keep formative assessment records for a pupil with SEND;
4. carry out age-related internal assessments in English (reading) and mathematics;
5. write summative reports for four pupils, including a pupil with SEND, in English, mathematics and science.

These are some of Charlotte's reflections about the use of assessment strategies during the teaching placement:

*Pupils' ownership of assessment criteria (English)*: The pupils are aware of the success criteria and have a copy of it in their English books when producing their own written pieces of work. These remind them of the learning expectations they need to meet in specific tasks, such as including empty words, short sentences and onomatopoeia throughout their suspense-writing narratives.

*Peer assessment (mathematics)*: I modelled how I wanted the pupils to peer assess each other's work using their green pupil-marking pens and the answer sheet. I highlighted the importance of looking at the whole mathematical process and working out, not just the final answer. Errors can arise from mistakes or wrong answers within the working out process, so it was important the pupils were aware of this and able to both recognise and rectify them in their own and each other's work. After the lesson ended, I went through the pupils' books with a red pen to ensure peer assessment was completed correctly and that each pupil had met the learning objective.

*(Continued)*

(Continued)

*Use of summative assessment outcomes to support future pupil progression (English):* The Year 5 NFER SPAG and reading tests gave me an insight into the strengths and weaknesses each pupil had in English, helping me to develop targets for them to achieve towards the end of the year and in Year 6.

*Timely oral feedback, including use of peers (art):* I had individual discussions with pupils about the specific patterns or colours they had chosen to express their emotions. During whole-class feedback and discussion towards the end of the lesson, pupils looked at each other's artwork and offered their thoughts according to the success criteria.

### ACTION LEARNING SET

When you are in your SBLC:

- observe how expert colleagues plan regular review and practice of key ideas and concepts over time (for example, through the use of structured talk activities) (CCF/ITTECF, Standard 2);
- discuss and analyse with expert colleagues how to plan formative assessment tasks linked to lesson objectives and think ahead about what would indicate understanding (CCF/ITTECF, Standard 6);
- consider ways to adapt assessments to enable access for all pupils.

## CONCLUSION

This chapter has explained some key aspects of assessment in primary education and its place in enabling pupils' progression in their learning. It explored different types of assessment, according to different purposes. Different assessment strategies were discussed, with ideas for you to take into your ITT context to help you to make effective decisions about assessment. The importance of meaningful feedback, with pupil ownership, was highlighted.

As a trainee, you will find that assessment practices vary between schools, but all schools will have an assessment policy and support you to develop your assessment strategies for productive outcomes.

> **REVIEW OF CHAPTER OBJECTIVES**
>
> Within this chapter you have considered:
>
> - different types of assessment in primary education;
> - why assessment is critical to pupils' progression of knowledge and understanding, and your development as a teacher;
> - how to plan and use assessments and feedback according to different purposes as a trainee teacher, including considering pupils' roles in assessment;
> - what progress looks like, by considering the integral role of assessment in planning, teaching and adaptive practice.

# FURTHER READING AND RESOURCES

Dylan Wiliam Center (including a series of videos considering different aspects of formative assessment)

https://dylanwiliamcenter.com/webinars/

Education Endowment Foundation (EEF) (2021) *Teaching and Learning Toolkit*. Available at: https://educationendowmentfoundation.org.uk/education-evidence/teaching-learning-toolkit [accessed 19 December 2023].

# REFERENCES

Assessment Reform Group (2002) *Assessment for Learning: 10 Principles*. Available at: http://assessmentreformgroup.files.wordpress.com/2012/01/10principles_english.pdf&gt [accessed 30 December 2023].

Black, P. and Wiliam, D. (1998) *Inside the Black Box: Raising Standards Through Classroom Assessment*. London: King's College London.

Black, P. and Wiliam, D. (2009) Developing the theory of formative assessment. *Education Assessment, Evaluation and Accountability*, 21, 5–31.

Black, P. and Wiliam, D. (2012) Assessment for learning in the classroom, in Gardner, J. (Ed.), *Assessment and Learning*. London: Sage, pp. 11–32.

Black, P., Harrison, C., Lee, C., Marshall, B. and Wiliam, D. (2004) Working inside the black box: Assessment for learning in the classroom. *Phi Delta Kappan*, 86(1), 8–21.

Christodoulou, D. (2017) *Making Good Progress: The Future of Assessment for Learning*. Oxford: Oxford University Press.

Department for Education (DfE) (2013) *The National Curriculum for England. Key Stage 1 and 2 Framework Documents*. Available at: https://assets.publishing.service.gov.uk/government/

uploads/system/uploads/attachment_data/file/425601/PRIMARY_national_curriculum.pdf [accessed 30 December 2023].

DfE (2019) *ITT Core Content Framework*. London: DfE. Available at: https://assets.publishing.service.gov.uk/government/uploads/system/uploads/attachment_data/file/974307/ITT_core_content_framework_.pdf [accessed November 2023].

Education Endowment Foundation (EEF) (2016) *A Marked Improvement? A Review of the Evidence on Written Marking*. Available at: https://educationendowmentfoundation.org.uk/public/files/Publications/EEF_Marking_Review_April_2016.pdf [accessed 30 December 2023].

Education Endowment Foundation (EEF) (2021) *Teaching and Learning Toolkit*. Available at: https://educationendowmentfoundation.org.uk/education-evidence/teaching-learning-toolkit [accessed 19 December 2023].

Harlen, W. and James, M. (1997) Assessment and learning: Differences and relationships between formative and summative assessment. *Assessment in Education: Principles, Policy and Practice*, 4(3), 365–379.

Hattie, J. (2012) *Visible Learning for Teachers*. London: Routledge.

Hattie, J. and Timperley, H. (2007) The power of feedback. *Review of Educational Research*, 77, 81–112.

Ofsted (2019) *Education Inspection Framework*. Available at: www.gov.uk/government/publications/education-inspection-framework/education-inspection-framework [accessed 30 December 2023].

Piaget, J. (1936) *Origins of Intelligence in the Child*. London: Routledge & Kegan Paul.

Primary Science Teaching Trust (PSTT) (2020) *The TAPS Pyramid: School Self-evaluation Tool*. Available at: https://taps.pstt.org.uk/whole-school/self-assessment/ [accessed 30 December 2023].

Rosenshine, B. (2012) Principles of instruction: Research-based strategies that all teachers should know. *American Educator*, Spring, 12–20.

Sadler, R. (1989) Formative assessment and the design of instructional systems. *Instructional Science*, 18, 119–144.

Sadler, R. (2010) Beyond feedback: Developing student capability in complex appraisal. *Assessment and Evaluation in Higher Education*, 35, 535–550.

Smith, P. and Cowie, H. (2015) *Understanding Children's Development: Basic Psychology*. London: John Wiley & Sons.

Speckesser, S., Runge J., Foliano, F., Bursnall, M., Hudson-Sharp, N., Rolfe, H. and Anders, J. (2018) *Embedding Formative Assessment: Evaluation Report*. Available at: https://educationendowmentfoundation.org.uk/public/files/EFA_evaluation_report.pdf [accessed 30 December 2023].

Wiliam, D. (2013) Assessment: The bridge between teaching and learning. *Voices from the Middle*, 21(2), 15–20.

Wiliam, D. (2020) Research into practice: The case of formative classroom assessment, in Gorard, S. (Ed.), Getting Evidence into Education: Evaluating the Routes to Policy and Practice. London: Routledge, pp. 119–135.

# 15

# EDUCATION, SOCIAL JUSTICE AND DISADVANTAGE

## AMANDA NUTTALL

**Learn that and Learn how to –
The Knowledge and Application Model**

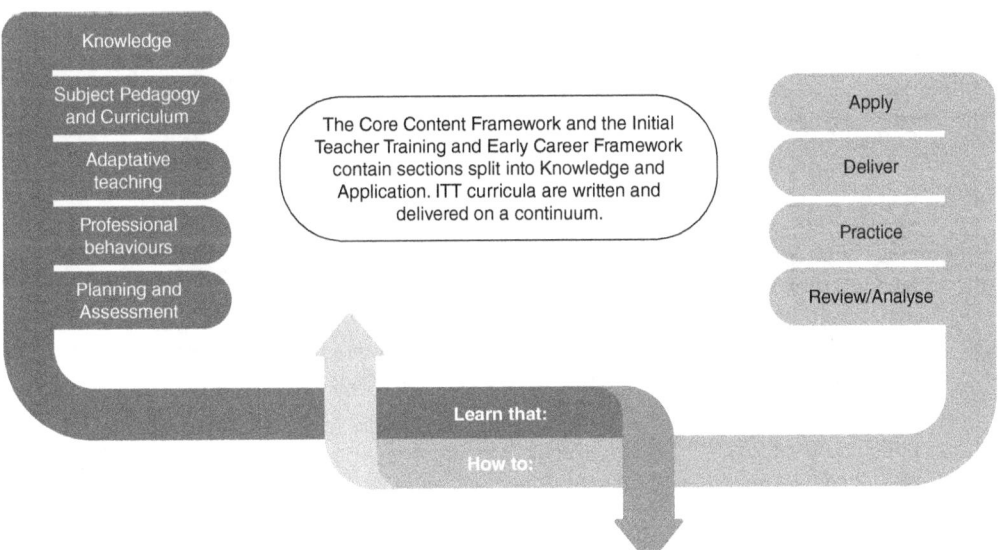

## FRAMED BY THE CCF – FOR FULL LINKS TO THE ITTECF, SEE PAGE 337

**Adaptive Teaching**

(Standard 5 – 'Adapt teaching')

| Learn that ... | Learn how to ... |
|---|---|
| 2. Seeking to understand pupils' differences, including their different levels of prior knowledge and potential barriers to learning, is an essential part of teaching. Learning involves a lasting change in pupils' capabilities or understanding. | Develop an understanding of different pupil needs, by: <br><br>• Receiving clear, consistent and effective mentoring in supporting pupils with a range of additional needs, including how to use the *SEND Code of Practice*, which provides additional guidance on supporting pupils with SEND effectively. <br><br>And – following expert input – by taking opportunities to practise, receive feedback and improve at: <br><br>• Working closely with the Special Educational Needs Co-ordinator (SENCO) and special education professionals and the Designated Safeguarding Lead (DSL) under supervision of expert colleagues. |

**Professional Behaviours**

(Standard 8 – 'Fulfil wider professional responsibilities')

| Learn that ... | Learn how to ... |
|---|---|
| 2. Reflective practice, supported by feedback from and observation of experienced colleagues, professional debate, and learning from educational research, is also likely to support improvement. <br><br>4. Building effective relationships with parents, carers and families can improve pupils' motivation, behaviour and academic success. | Build effective working relationships, by: <br><br>• Observing how expert colleagues communicate with parents and carers proactively and make effective use of parents' evenings to engage parents and carers in their children's schooling and deconstructing this approach. <br><br>And – following expert input – by taking opportunities to practise, receive feedback and improve at: <br><br>• Contributing positively to the wider school culture and developing a feeling of shared responsibility for improving the lives of all pupils within the school (e.g. by supporting expert colleagues with their pastoral responsibilities, such as careers advice). <br><br>• Knowing who to contact with any safeguarding concerns and having a clear understanding of what sorts of behaviour, disclosures and incidents to report. |

# 15 EDUCATION, SOCIAL JUSTICE AND DISADVANTAGE

## CHAPTER OBJECTIVES

On reading this chapter you will:

- understand some of the scope and key statistics of child poverty in the UK;
- learn how growing up in poverty can affect children's development;
- understand some aspects of the relationship between poverty and disadvantage and school attainment;
- consider how you approach issues of poverty and disadvantage in your role as a primary teacher.

## KEY VOCABULARY

Poverty

Disadvantage

Social justice

Attainment

Achievement

Child development

Inequality

# INTRODUCTION

Raising the educational achievement of children from low-income families has been a topic of debate for governments in Britain for many years and is a key priority in education. But many voices have expressed concern that there is a systemic lack of understanding of the relationship between family income and educational outcomes in England, and a lack of political will to address the multiple, cumulative disadvantages that children growing up in low-income families experience. Writers such as Stephen Ball argue that the education system in the UK – but particularly in England – replicates and, at times, exacerbates social and structural inequalities that already exist in society (e.g. Ball, 2013, 2018). The *attainment gap* at all stages of schooling between the least and most well-off pupils is not only large, but is rapidly increasing following the impact of Covid-19 (Farquharson et al., 2022) and this gap in England is one of the largest when compared internationally (OECD, 2023). Thirteen years of austerity measures have led to reductions in school funding as well as broader services and facilities for children and young people, including mental health support and early childhood family support. But as a society we seem to lack consistency in how we view the 'problem' of poverty and educational outcomes.

Is it due to the actions of individuals and a lack of engagement and aspiration of pupils, families and communities?

Or should we look to wider social, cultural and economic factors that lead to life-long experiences of disadvantage?

In this chapter we will unpack some of what is meant by poverty and disadvantage and go on to examine the distinct relationship between family income and educational attainment. We will conjoin these relationships with notions of social justice and consider what this means for you in your role as a primary teacher.

## CHILD POVERTY IN ENGLAND

How we understand a problem determines the solutions we offer to that problem. Several authors in the UK have criticised how we, as a society in general, often perceive children and families who experience poverty. For example, Emery et al. (2022) take issue with the way in which children living in poverty are often viewed as 'a homogeneous, uniform collection of students who simply need to be taught better and work harder' (p. 4). So, how do you understand child poverty?

There is no single best or commonly accepted measure of poverty. Poverty is complex and related to multiple factors, including income, costs and outgoings, as well as what is culturally and socially considered to be a minimum standard of living. One of the most commonly used measures of poverty is from the Joseph Rowntree Foundation (JRF), which defines a *poverty line* at 60 per cent of the median household income after housing costs (2023). This means that a family whose income is 60 per cent or less of the average in their geographical and contemporary area would be considered to experience relative poverty. There are then further measures of poverty, including absolute poverty, deep poverty and destitution, where an individual is consistently unable to meet their basic and essential needs such as housing, clothing, food and hygiene.

When we talk about poverty – and child poverty – we often imagine children and families living in terrible circumstances, struggling with daily life. We may believe that child poverty is a feature of developing countries, where children may not have access to clean water and adequate food, or start to work in their early years, or live in inadequate and unhygienic houses. These images of poverty have been frequently shown to us through media, social media and international fundraising organisations. But the reality is that, in the UK, child poverty is prevalent. According to the Child Poverty Action Group (CPAG, 2023), in 2021–22 there were 4.2 million children living in poverty in the UK, which is 29 per cent of all children or nine in a classroom of 30. There are additional complexities: children in large families (three or more siblings) are more likely to experience poverty, as are those in lone-parent families and children from Black and minority ethnic groups.

The causes of poverty are complex. In contrast to popular opinion and media representation, worklessness is not the main cause of poverty; in fact, 72 per cent of children growing up in poverty live in a household where at least one person works (CPAG, 2023). Some of the causes of poverty (and many of these are interrelated factors) include:

- low-paid and insecure employment;
- low levels of education and lack of education opportunities;
- ineffective benefit access;
- high costs of housing, essential goods and services;
- discrimination;
- lack of family support;
- unstable relationships;
- abuse or trauma at any stage in life.

The effects of growing up in poverty are far-reaching. It seems obvious that poverty restricts options and opportunities as it limits spending power of families and prevents individuals from purchasing items or participating in experiences, such as sports, holidays and other leisure activities that are considered the 'norm' in society. But poverty also restricts access to the basics: to secure housing, secure heating, transport, a well-balanced diet and hygiene products. If we think beyond 'spending power', poverty also causes poor physical and mental health, increases the likelihood of involvement in crime or violent behaviour, can lead to drug or alcohol abuse, limits academic outcomes and often becomes cyclical; children who grow up in poverty are more likely to experience poverty as an adult and have children themselves who also grow up in poverty (JRF, 2023).

> **REFLECTIVE QUESTIONS**
>
> Think about children's daily experiences at school.
>
> What kind of effects might poverty have on their day?
>
> What resources might they have difficulty in accessing?
>
> What experiences might they not have compared to their peers?
>
> How might this impact on their engagement with the curriculum and their attainment in each subject?
>
> How might it affect their friendships and their wellbeing?

> **EVIDENCE-INFORMED RESEARCH: EFFECTS OF POVERTY**
>
> The effects of poverty are far-reaching. Cognitive effects mean children's academic results are significantly low at every stage and age of schooling (Doherty and Nuttall, 2023). The impact of poor-quality housing and homelessness – often hidden problems – on children's development is particularly acute. Damp conditions, overcrowding, lack of heating and unsafe conditions all lead to increased risk of illness, accidents and poor mental health in children (Cross et al., 2022). Three-year-olds in households with incomes below about £10,000 are 2.5 times more likely to suffer chronic illness than children in households with incomes above £52,000. Infant mortality is 10 per cent higher for infants in the lower social group than the average. There is a higher risk of unemployment and a higher probability of being involved in crime. Children in those communities are much more likely to be victims of accidents in the home and are nine times less likely than those living in affluent areas to have access to green space, places to play and to live in environments with better air quality (Doherty and Nuttall, 2023).
>
> Psychological impacts of poverty include increased mental illness, poor self-image, lack of confidence and difficulty in building and maintaining friendships (Mazzoli Smith and Todd, 2019). The reality for many children and families is waking up every day facing uncertainty and insecurity, coping with marginalisation and discrimination. Poverty is a blight to a healthy, thriving childhood. It adversely affects educational, social and health outcomes and aspirations they have for their futures (CPAG, 2023).

## THE EFFECTS OF POVERTY ON CHILD DEVELOPMENT

Healthy child development in the first years of life is crucial to later life chances. We know that the first 1,001 days of a child's life – from conception to age two – are a key determinant of their social, emotional and physical health as an adult (Wave Trust, 2013). Brain development is most rapid during the first few years of a child's life, with around 80 per cent of brain cell development having taken place by age three. Due to its plasticity, the brain grows through a combination of stimulation and maturation, accommodating new experiences and interactions. Its specialist functions allow motor, language, visual and auditory processing to take place and these 'bricks and mortar' are the foundations for all learning (Langston and Doherty, 2012). Research from neuroscience is unequivocal that brain growth is enhanced through early sensory, social and emotional experiences (Doherty and Hughes, 2014). The early years are also the prime window for language acquisition. Young children need a rich environment of spoken language to build vocabulary and allow them to express their feelings and thinking. Language development at age two is strongly associated with school readiness and the early communication environment in the home provides the strongest influence on language (Gross, 2012).

This further emphasises the quality of interactions with parents and carers. What takes place in the home learning environment builds neural circuits as part of brain architecture and it is the quality of the home learning environment that is recognised as the most significant factor in terms of outcomes at age five (Gerhardt, 2014). In other words, it is what parents and carers do at home: the activities and experiences that provide stimulation and create stretch and challenge for the child's mind and body. It is well-established that social and emotional domains are highly significant in children's engagement with school and their academic achievement (Wood, 2022). Various dimensions of social and emotional learning (SEL) help children to succeed in school in multiple ways, including:

- regulating emotions;
- managing stress;
- cooperating with others;
- setting and achieving goals;
- becoming more self-aware;
- building self-confidence.

Early adverse childhood experiences (ACEs) increase the risk of reduced outcomes across all developmental domains (Brooks, 2019). Severe deprivation disrupts normal brain processing and functioning and increases the risks of attentional, emotional, cognitive and behavioural disorders. They are associated with emotional disorders including impulse control, low levels of enthusiasm and low self-esteem. They include problems with memory, general learning difficulties and cognitive delay, which lead to poor academic achievement.

## THE IMPACT OF COVID-19 ON DISADVANTAGED YOUNG LEARNERS

Poverty has always been a constant challenge for schools, but social and economic effects of the global pandemic have intensified both the scale and the impact of poverty for many children and families. At the time of writing, we are already aware that the pandemic response has led to a significant increase in the number of children and young people being referred for specialist mental health support and that these referrals tend to be classed as more urgent and more severe than they were pre-pandemic (Huang and Ougrin, 2021). Overall school attendance has fallen, with a particular rise in *persistent absentees* (McDonald et al., 2023). And these kinds of patterns tend to be more significant in schools that serve disadvantaged communities.

At the same time, gaps in progression and attainment in learning have widened. The attainment gap between disadvantaged and more well-off pupils widened during the pandemic, meaning that the impact of the pandemic on disadvantaged pupils was greater than it was for their better-off peers. In the primary curriculum, this widening seems to have been worse in maths than in reading or writing (Twist et al., 2022). Academic literature, organisations' research reports and media reports have all highlighted a clear difference in pupils' level of engagement with and access to remote learning during the pandemic. Research by the Institute of Fiscal Studies (IFS) (Andrew et al., 2020) demonstrated that during 'lockdown' primary pupils spent an average of four and a half hours a day on home learning, representing a 25 per cent reduction in learning compared to their pre-pandemic school days. But children from better-off families not only were more likely to have access to online lessons and tutorials with their teachers, but also spent 30 per cent more time on home learning than those from poorer families. This equated to a difference of 15 full school days for children who did not return to full-time on-site schooling until September 2020. If we consider that even one extra hour of instructional time *per week* can significantly raise achievement, then we can see the potential scope of long-term consequences for many disadvantaged pupils.

## GOVERNMENT INTERVENTION

Children from poorer backgrounds were also more likely to experience significant impact due to the loss of their school environment and access to resources. With a sudden and unprecedented to shift to remote learning, inequalities in family circumstances and home environments became more prominent. Not only did pupils from better-off families access more time in remote learning but they also had access to more individualised learning, such as through private tutors; they had a better home set-up for remote learning and secure internet access; and their parents felt more able to support them (Andrew et al., 2020). Although the

Department for Education (DfE) pledged significant funding to support the most affected pupils through *catch-up* programmes and a *recovery curriculum*, the impact for disadvantaged pupils has been negligible. Analysis of attainment and progression data demonstrates that, post-pandemic, disadvantaged pupils are making progress at the same rate as their better-off peers. This means that the gaps which widened during the pandemic are not reducing but are staying the same. As a result, disadvantaged pupils in 2023 are likely to have *worse* educational outcomes than similar pupils in the years before the pandemic (Twist et al., 2022).

## SOCIAL JUSTICE

Why is all of this important? When we talk about the ways in which individuals and/or particular groups access and experience education we are often drawn to notions of *social justice*. Social justice is an ambiguous and contested term and one that is often not defined or articulated clearly, particularly in relation to education (Cochran-Smith and Lytle, 2009). Relating to our knowledge and understanding of some of the impact of poverty on children's school experiences, here we consider social justice as related to inclusion, diversity and marginalisation – recognising cultural, social and economic contexts that impact an individuals' ability to engage with and be successful in education.

At the start of your teaching career, it's important that you develop an understanding of issues related to social justice and your role as a teacher. This is not just because you will need to consider pupils' progress and attainment and how individual needs affect these (as seen in the references to the CCF/ITTECF at the start of this chapter), but you will also need to critically reflect on the progress and attainment of particular groups of pupils that you work with and the impact you can (and sometimes cannot) have on these groups. England has multiple, wide social, gender and race divisions in educational attainment. As we have already seen, despite many policies designed to tackle inequality, the gap between the most and least well off is great and the relationship between school achievement and family background continues to be strong (Littler, 2018; Reay, 2022).

## DEFICIT DISCOURSE

One very striking feature of England's education policy environment is the insistence that gaps in educational attainment can be narrowed, and indeed removed entirely, within the schooling system – despite the persistence of inequities and years of austerity measures leading to rising levels of wage inequality, child poverty and increased marginalisation of vulnerable and non-White groups (Ivinson and Thompson, 2020). Indeed, politicians and policy-makers are keen to blame individuals for their educational failings – for example, Ofsted Chief Inspector Amanda Spielman's criticism of families' lack of engagement and schools prioritising feeding poor pupils rather than educating them during the Covid-19 pandemic response (Weale, 2021) and former Education Secretary Damian Hinds blaming 'strife at home and parents being disengaged' for the continued gap in attainment between disadvantaged pupils and their better-off peers (Hinds, 2019). Nuttall and Beckett (2020) critique school improvement programmes which purport to help disadvantaged groups do better academically, access higher education or increase employability through superficial and short-term interventions. For example, schools may have career 'aspiration' programmes to introduce disadvantaged pupils to potential high-earning professional careers. This is based on the assumption that these pupils do not already have high aspirations and that their lack of attainment in education is due to their unwillingness to engage with academic study. This could be termed as a 'deficit discourse', where poor educational outcomes for particular groups of pupils are inappropriately located in the individual rather than their circumstances.

### EVIDENCE-INFORMED RESEARCH: 'OTHERING' PUPILS WHO EXPERIENCE POVERTY

Burn and Childs (2018) criticise externally driven and policy-focused improvement strategies in which disadvantaged pupils are viewed as deficient in some way compared to White, middle-class ideals. They consider that pupil premium (PP) funding, although beneficial in many ways, is a very blunt tool and positions pupils as in need of extra money to improve them in some way. In literature this is referred to as an 'othering' agenda, whereby professionals – including teachers – misinterpret the complex influence and impact of structural inequity. Rather than blaming existing inequities for pupils' low attainment, teachers are pressed to implement compensatory interventions intended to 'fix' the deficiencies of disadvantaged pupils by improving their academic performance (Nuttall and Beckett, 2020). A different approach would be to start with a more contextualised understanding of what is at issue. Beckett and Wrigley (2014) identify how 'contextual intelligence' underpins authentic interventions which are more likely to meet the needs of particular groups and which are designed to build connections with pupils' interests and lived experiences (Nuttall, 2016).

At the most basic level, it is clear that different schools with different communities, demographics and histories need differing ways of tackling attainment gaps. This involves careful reflection on the purposes of schooling (including giving thought to the moral purpose of education), which then leads to intelligent and sustainable reform at all levels and for all learners (Nuttall and Podesta, 2020). Anyon (2014) provokes teachers to question: how can school interventions truly benefit disadvantaged pupils when their educational outcomes cannot lead to a funded college place or secure employment which provides a living wage, or secure housing? She argues that genuine socially just policies and practices in education are intrinsically linked to national (and international) social and economic reforms.

Providing economic and social opportunity for the vulnerable and marginalised groups in society creates conditions in which schools and teachers can make a meaningful difference for all pupils.

## ACTION LEARNING SET

Introduced in 2011, PP funding is allocated depending on the number of children in each cohort who access free school meals (FSM). For each pupil the school receives £1,345 (primary) or £955 (secondary). Schools are held accountable by Ofsted who expect to see positive impact on academic attainment of these children in receipt of funding.

The use of FSM is a commonly accepted proxy indicator for poverty in England but it is a blunt tool: it treats disadvantage as a binary – that is, disadvantaged or not ... and therefore presumably advantaged. This measure cannot capture the complexity of poverty or how combinations and accumulations of multiple vulnerabilities affect individuals or groups of pupils and their families.

A further complication for primary schools is that all KS1 children are eligible for FSM so many parents do not indicate to school administrators that they are in receipt of benefits that would mean their child[ren] are eligible for PP funds. The complexity of negotiating out of work and in work benefit systems also means that many children do not access FSM despite being entitled to do so.

Find out some more about the use of PP funding in your school.

Can you see any patterns in the proportion of children who receive PP in each year group?

What kinds of interventions does the school use PP funding for?

How does school track the effects of these interventions?

What are the implications for you as a trainee and ECT? What will you prioritise?

# THE ROLE OF THE TEACHER

So far in this chapter we have considered some of the ways in which we understand and respond to pupils who experience poverty and disadvantage. Now let's consider *your* position some more. Why did you choose to be a teacher? Teaching is often cited as a values-oriented enterprise: it may feel as if, as a teacher, your role is to focus on educational attainment, but teachers' work goes beyond the academic to encompass students' emotional and social development, their understandings of their place in the world and their interactions with society around them (Boylan and Woolsey, 2015). Many teachers and trainee teachers report that they chose teaching as a profession because they felt they could 'make a difference' to children, young people, their families and their communities, and such attitudes are often positioned as *moral domains* of teaching (Sanger and Osguthorpe, 2011). Putting social justice and equity at the centre of a teacher's role means enabling them to recognise some of the ways in which individuals or groups of pupils experience multiple disadvantages and inequalities, and how these may also affect their families and local communities. But it also means that, as teachers, we have a moral responsibility to ask critical questions and try to actively challenge some of the policies and practices in our classrooms and schools that reproduce inequality (Burn and Childs, 2018; Mazzoli Smith and Todd, 2019).

## CASE STUDY: UNDERSTANDING LOW ATTAINMENT OF PUPILS IN POVERTY

Doherty and Nuttall (2023) report a case study where concerns about the attainment and engagement of a small group of disadvantaged White-British boys in an inner-city primary school came under scrutiny. The class teacher in this case moved away from focusing on attainment data alone and investigated different questions about this group of young boys which centred on their broader social and emotional dimensions, asking how they responded to different learning experiences, how they managed various social aspects of their school day, and constructing a rich description of their home lives which brought together information from multiple agencies.

Central to this work was the prioritising of the boys' voices, a significant step change to previous interventions which were applied to 'raise standards' and improve attainment in English and maths in the short term.

Following this investigatory work, a set of interventions was designed by the teacher and the school leadership team to attempt to address some of the complex interplay between the realities of students' lived experiences, including insecurities in housing, poor health and wellbeing linked to poverty, drug and alcohol addictions, criminal activity, domestic violence and their engagement and attainment at school. While it was essential not to make a 'deficit reading' (Thompson et al., 2016) of these kinds of issues, it became clear that attention needed to be paid beyond the bounds of daily classroom practice and this led to action within the local community. For example, this school, along with others in its local partnership, engaged with a national campaign against domestic violence to encourage children and their families to become involved in this movement; built active relationships with local children's centres to offer wider support for families, including access to play therapies; and developed relationships with community policing and fire service to tackle juvenile anti-social behaviours and to build more positive relationships with local services.

> **REFLECTIVE QUESTIONS**
>
> Think about the interventions you have seen happening at your placement school or read about in case studies and literature. How is the kind of intervention work reported above different?
>
> Interventions often focus on improving attainment in reading, writing and maths.
>
> Why might it be important to think about pupils' broader life experiences when planning interventions?
>
> What might be missed or overlooked if we only focus on academic progress and attainment?

# CONCLUSION

Children's early learning experiences up to the age of three are crucial, but for families who experience multiple cumulative disadvantages such as stress, insecure housing, marginalisation from mainstream education and limited access to physical and cultural resources it is harder to provide stimulating and social experiences for young children. Some pupils are then at a distinct disadvantage compared to their better-off peers as they begin school without the positive cultural and social resources which give them an understanding of and secure access to schooling systems and expectations. These inequalities continue throughout school life, as pupils who experience poverty are more likely to have interrupted schooling, experience the debilitating effects of tiredness or malnutrition, be stigmatised by their peers and have less access to cultural and social experiences and resources.

Some of the research, reports and statistics we have covered in this chapter exemplify how attainment gaps are only part of a broader picture of social, cultural and economic inequalities related to many factors within and outside the context of an individual classroom or school. So, how do we, as individual teachers, challenge these systemic issues? You have already made a good start by engaging with this chapter! As a teacher, you have opportunity to ask critical questions and to challenge deficit discourses. You can build strong and respectful relationships with children and families, helping you to build a rich understanding of disadvantaged and marginalised communities. You can continue to engage with research in this area and design and implement meaningful and contextualised responses to improve pupils' outcomes. But, most of all, you can commit to embedding what the author and educator bell hooks (1994) calls the 'love ethic' in your teaching: being caring and considerate of all the different starts in life that children have, and will, experience.

> ## REVIEW OF CHAPTER OBJECTIVES
>
> Within this chapter you have learned:
>
> - to understand some of the scope and key statistics of child poverty in the UK;
> - how growing up in poverty can affect children's development;
> - to understand some aspects of the relationship between poverty and disadvantage and school attainment;
> - to understand how you approach issues of poverty and disadvantage in your role as a primary teacher.

## FURTHER READING AND RESOURCES

Thompson, I. and Ivinson, G. (eds.) (2020) *Poverty in Education Across the UK: A Comparative Analysis of Policy and Place*. Bristol: Policy Press.

## REFERENCES

Andrew, A., Cattan, S., Costa-Dias, M., Farquharson, C., Kraftman, L., Krutikova, S., Phimister, A. and Sevilla, A. (2020) *Learning During the Lockdown: Real-time Data on Children's Experiences During Home Learning*. London: IFS.

Anyon, J. (2014) *Radical Possibilities: Public Policy, Urban Education, and a New Social Movement* (2nd ed.). London: Routledge.

Ball, S. J. (2013) *The Education Debate* (2nd ed.). Bristol: Policy Press.

Ball, S. (2018) The tragedy of state education in England: Reluctance, compromise and muddle: A system in disarray. *Journal of the British Academy*, 6, 207–238. https://doi.org/10.5871/jba/006.207

Beckett, L. and Wrigley, T. (2014) Overcoming stereotypes, discovering hidden capitals. *Improving Schools*, 17(3), 217–230.

Boylan, M. and Woolsey, I. (2015) Teacher education for social justice: Mapping identity spaces. *Teaching and Teacher Education*, 46, 62–71. https://doi.org/10.1016/j.tate.2014.10.007

Brooks, R. (2019) *The Trauma and Attachment-aware Classroom: A Practical Guide to Supporting Children who have Encountered Trauma and Adverse Childhood Experiences*. London: Jessica Kingsley.

Burn, K. and Childs, A. (2018) Responding to poverty through education and teacher education initiatives: A critical evaluation of key trends in government policy in England 1997–2015, in McNamara, O. and McNicholl, J. (eds.), *Poverty Discourses in Teacher Education*. London: Routledge, pp. 14–30.

Child Poverty Action Group (CPAG) (2023) *Child Poverty Facts and Figures*. Available at: https://cpag.org.uk/child-poverty/child-poverty-facts-and-figures [accessed 31 December 2023].

Cochran-Smith, M. and Lytle, S. L. (2009) *Inquiry as Stance: Practitioner Research in the Next Generation*. New York: Teachers College Press.

Cross, S., Bywaters, P., Brown, P. and Featherstone, B. (2022) Housing, homelessness and children's social care: Towards an urgent research agenda. *British Journal of Social Work*, 52(4), 1988–2007. https://doi.org/10.1093/bjsw/bcab130

Doherty, J. and Hughes, M. (2014) *Child Development: Theory and Practice 0–11* (2nd ed.). London: Pearson.

Doherty, J. and Nuttall, A. (2023) The effects of disadvantage on children's life chances and educational outcomes, in Hayes, L. (ed.), *The Early Years Handbook for Students and Practitioners: An Essential Guide for Levels 4 and 5* (2nd ed.). London: Routledge.

Emery, C., Dawes, L. and Raffo, C. (2022) The local matters: Working with teachers to rethink the poverty and achievement gap discourse. *Education Policy Analysis Archives*, 30(122), 1–18.

Farquharson, C., McNally, S. and Tahir, I. (2022) Education inequalities. *IFS Deaton Review of Inequalities*. https://ifs.org.uk/inequality/chapter/education-inequalities

Gerhardt, S. (2014) *Why Love Matters: How Affection Shapes a Baby's Brain* (2nd ed.). London: Routledge.

Gross, J. (2012) *Time to Talk: Implementing Outstanding Practice in Speech, Language and Communication*. London: Routledge.

Hinds, D. (2019) Education Secretary challenges misconceptions of disadvantage, June. Available at: www.gov.uk/government/speeches/education-secretary-challenges-misconceptions-of-disadvantage [accessed 31 December 2023].

hooks, b. (1994) *Teaching to Transgress: Education as the Practice of Freedom*. London: Routledge.

Huang, H. and Ougrin, D. (2021) Impact of the Covid-19 pandemic on child and adolescent mental health services. *BJPsych Open*, 7(5), E145.

Ivinson, G. and Thompson, I. (2020) Policy, education and poverty across the UK, in Thompson, I. and Ivinson, G. (eds.), *Poverty in Education Across the UK: A Comparative Analysis of Policy and Place*. Bristol: Policy Press, pp. 11–36.

Joseph Rowntree Foundation (JRF) (2023) *UK Poverty 2023: The Essential Guide to Understanding Poverty in the UK*. Available at: www.jrf.org.uk/report/uk-poverty-2023 [accessed 31 December 2023].

Langston, A. and Doherty, J. (2012) *The Revised EYFS in Practice: Thinking Reflecting and Doing!* London: Bloomsbury.

Littler, J. (2018) *Against Meritocracy: Culture, Power and Myths of Mobility*. London: Routledge.

Mazzoli Smith, L. and Todd, L. (2019) Conceptualising poverty as a barrier to learning through 'Poverty proofing the school day': The genesis and impacts of stigmatisation. *British Educational Research Journal*, 45(2), 356–371. https://doi.org/10.1002/berj.3506

McDonald, B., Lester, K. J. and Michelson, D. (2023) 'She didn't know how to go back': School attendance problems in the context of the Covid-19 pandemic. A multiple stakeholder qualitative study with parents and professionals. *British Journal of Educational Psychology*, 93(1), 386–401. https://doi.org/10.1111/bjep.12562

Nuttall, A. (2016) The 'curriculum challenge': Moving towards the 'Storyline' approach in a case study urban primary school. *Improving Schools*, 19(2), 154–166.

Nuttall, A. and Beckett, L. (2020) Teachers' professional knowledge work on poverty and disadvantage, in Beckett, L. (ed.), *Research-Informed Teacher Learning: Critical Perspectives on Theory, Research and Practice*. London: Routledge.

Nuttall, A. and Podesta, E. (2020) School reform in England. *Oxford Research Encyclopedia of Education*. Oxford: Oxford University Press. https://doi.org/10.1093/acrefore/9780190264093.013.848

Organisation for Economic Co-operation and Development (OECD) (2023) *Education at a Glance 2023: OECD Indicators*. Paris: OECD. https://doi.org/10.4135/9781529714395.n163

Reay, D. (2022) From worse to worse: Why is it so difficult to change English education for the better? *Forum*, 64(1), 9–18. https://doi.org/10.3898/forum.2022.64.1.01

Sanger, M. N. and Osguthorpe, R. D. (2011) Teacher education, preservice teacher beliefs, and the moral work of teaching. *Teaching and Teacher Education*, 27(3), 569–578. https://doi.org/10.1016/j.tate.2010.10.011

Thompson, I., McNicholl, J. and Menter, I. (2016) Student teachers' perceptions of poverty and educational achievement. *Oxford Review of Education*, 42(2), 1–16.

Twist, L., Jones, E. and Treleaven, O. (2022) *The Impact of Covid-19 on Pupil Attainment: A Summary of Research Evidence*. Available at: www.nfer.ac.uk/publications/the-impact-of-covid-19-on-pupil-attainment-a-summary-of-research-evidence/#:~:text=Key%20Findings&text=There%20is%20a%20lack%20of,of%20Covid%20on%20pupil%20attainment [accessed 31 December 2023].

Wave Trust (2013) *Conception to Age 2: The Age of Opportunity*. Available at: www.wavetrust.org/Handlers/Download.ashx?IDMF=474485e9-c019-475e-ad32-cf2d5ca085b0 [accessed 31 December 2023].

Weale, S. (2021) Ofsted head: Schools' focus on food parcels may have hit learning. *Guardian*, September. www.theguardian.com/education/2021/sep/14/ofsted-head-schools-focus-food-parcels-may-have-hit-learning [accessed 31 December 2023].

Wood, P. (2022) The interpretation and use of social and emotional learning in British primary schools. *International Journal of Inclusive Education*. https://doi.org/10.1080/13603116.2022.2088870

# 16

# TEACHING CHILDREN SUSTAINABILITY

## LEIGH HOATH

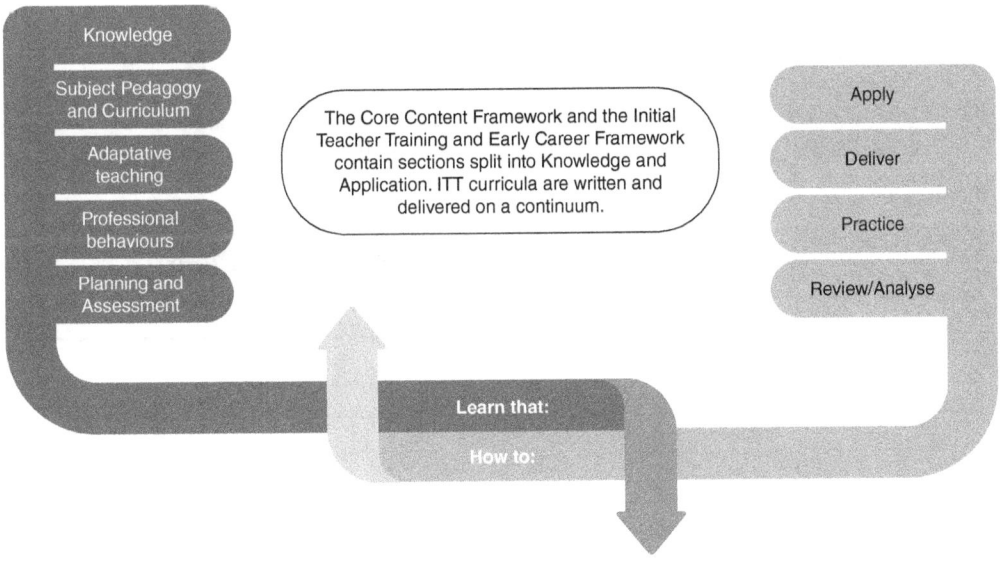

## FRAMED BY THE CCF – FOR FULL LINKS TO THE ITTECF, SEE PAGE 337

**Classroom Practice**

**(Standard 4 – 'Plan and teach well structured lessons')**

| Learn that ... | Learn how to ... |
|---|---|
| 5. Explicitly teaching pupils metacognitive strategies linked to subject knowledge, including how to plan, monitor and evaluate, supports independence and academic success. | Plan effective lessons, by:<br><br>• Observing how expert colleagues break tasks down into constituent components ... (e.g. using tasks that scaffold pupils through metacognitive and procedural processes). |

**Subject and Curriculum**

**(Standard 3 – 'Demonstrate good subject and curriculum knowledge')**

| Learn that ... | Learn how to ... |
|---|---|
| 5. Explicitly teaching pupils the knowledge and skills they need to succeed within particular subject areas is beneficial.<br><br>6. In order for pupils to think critically, they must have a secure understanding of knowledge. | Deliver a carefully sequenced and coherent curriculum, by:<br><br>• Receiving clear, consistent and effective mentoring in how to identify essential concepts, knowledge, skills and principles of the subject.<br><br>And – following expert input – by taking opportunities to practise, receive feedback and improve at:<br><br>• Providing opportunity for all pupils to learn and master essential concepts, knowledge, skills and principles of the subject. |

## CHAPTER OBJECTIVES

On reading this chapter you will consider:

- the purpose and complexities of sustainability education within the primary school setting;
- ways in which sustainability education can be meaningfully linked with existing curricula;
- different approaches and existing frameworks for teaching sustainability and education for sustainable development.

> **KEY VOCABULARY**
>
> Sustainability
>
> Climate change education (CCE)
>
> Curriculum
>
> Education for sustainable development (ESD)
>
> UN sustainable development goals (UNSDGs)
>
> Inner development goals (IDGs)

# INTRODUCTION

This chapter will outline some tricky conversations around sustainability and climate change education. Although this is not a mandatory element of the curriculum, *Core Content Framework* (CCF) (DfE, 2019) and the Initial Teacher Training and Early Career Framework (ITTECF) (DfE 2024) or any other aspect of education, it is one with a growing agenda and prevalence within schools. The purpose of this chapter is to draw upon many of the other learnings from previous chapters and demonstrate that sustainability and climate change education demands the same consideration. The content within this will position the difficulties to be overcome, the need to think carefully about how and who you are teaching and explore a lot of the existing literature in this area.

Teaching of this subject area is complex because everyone who reads it will hold different values in relation to sustainability, have a different understanding of what it is and most likely a very limited knowledge of how to teach it. This chapter will not be able to answer all of those – it rather highlights that the complexities are to be embraced as part of your teacher development, that it is a moral obligation to address and that there is not a one size fits all approach to teaching about sustainability and climate change.

# THE PURPOSE AND COMPLEXITIES OF TEACHING ABOUT SUSTAINABILITY

## THE STRATEGY PERSPECTIVE

In 2022, the Department for Education (DfE) published a strategy to make the education sector in England a world leader in sustainability and climate change action by 2030 (DfE, 2022). The strategy sets out a vision and four strategic aims: excellence in climate education and skills; achieving net zero carbon emissions; adapting the education estate to be resilient to climate impacts like flooding; and creating a better environment through enhancing biodiversity and access to nature.

The key actions identified within the strategy included:

- introducing a natural history GCSE;
- building all new schools to be net zero carbon;
- launching a National Education Nature Park to connect children with nature;
- piloting technologies like air source heat pumps to decarbonise buildings;
- implementing flood resilience measures;
- appointing sustainability leads in all schools and providing carbon literacy training;
- and setting emissions reporting frameworks.

The strength of this strategy comes from the recognition that sustainability issues cannot be addressed by just *one* focus but that a whole-school approach is required to make a difference.

Internationally, the strategy aims to promote climate education, showcase UK expertise, increase exports and jobs in green skills and launch initiatives like an international version of the National Education Nature Park – currently being developed by a consortium led by the Natural History Museum. The strategy was certainly not lacking ambition and, although very welcome by most, was seen to fall short in terms of supporting resources and at placing sustainability and climate change education at the heart of the future of education. *In short, it still does not provide school leaders and teachers with the details of what to do for the best to engage meaningfully with sustainability and climate change education.*

There are several ways in which teaching about sustainability is challenging in schools; the existing literature below offers some indication of the main reasons why this is so.

### EVIDENCE-INFORMED RESEARCH: CHALLENGES OF TEACHING SUSTAINABILITY AND CLIMATE CHANGE EDUCATION

Alongside everything else that a primary teacher is expected to know and be competent in teaching, there is a lack of teacher training, knowledge and confidence in teaching sustainability topics (Chinedu et al., 2018; Hallinger and Chatpinyakoop, 2019)

> which has also been mirrored within UK-based research such as the British Science Association's report (BSA, 2023) and Teach the Future (2021). This in turn highlights that there is a real need for more professional development for trainee, early career and experienced teachers in this area.

There is difficulty in meaningfully integrating sustainability across the curriculum and making connections between subjects (Thomas, 2004; Kagawa, 2007). We will consider later in this chapter how consideration of the curriculum is imperative when looking at how such content is taught and integrated into existing subjects.

Pupil (and teacher) misconceptions around sustainability as a concept and differences in how they understand it in reality are very problematic (Kagawa, 2007; Salas-Zapata et al., 2018). Pupils may hold ingrained and inaccurate views established from skewed headlines, parents' perspectives, naivety and the distance that is created through discussion around the fragility of the planet not being on their doorstep.

There is an increasing number of resources being produced within the UK market (Hallinger and Chatpinyakoop, 2019) with topics related to sustainability and climate change being higher on the agenda. The issues arise from the curation of *high-quality* resources and ensuring that these are appropriately pitched for pupils.

In order to best teach sustainability and climate change education it may be the case that alternative pedagogical approaches are required (Boström et al., 2018; Stanitsas et al., 2018) – new pedagogies which enable children to learn through nature-based approaches, effective use of the outdoors, enabling metacognition and self-regulation to mitigate climate anxiety. In time-poor schools, under the demands of assessment and accountability, it may be that lack of practical experiences and connection to nature (Hallinger and Chatpinyakoop, 2019) inhibit the opportunities for pupils to really connect with what it means to learn about sustainability.

> ## EVIDENCE-INFORMED RESEARCH
>
> A key finding in relation to the work by Hoath and Dave (2022) is that there is a real need for a focus on sustainability education to be adopted and driven by the school or academy trust leadership. Where there is poor institutional support from school leadership on sustainability (Velazquez et al., 2005) there is the greatest challenge in engaging with it in anything other than a superficial capacity. Sustainability needs to be a high priority in schools' strategic planning if it is to happen - a genuine challenge with the day-to-day demands of meeting pupils' needs, safeguarding, attendance and post-Covid mitigation, to name but a few.
>
> *(Continued)*

> The need to consider the differences in cultural context and priorities around the world (Hallinger and Chatpinyakoop, 2019; Raffe and Semple, 2011) is fundamental; however, this is also true of the locality within which we are teaching in the UK. Teaching approaches need to be tailored to local communities, taking into account their vulnerabilities and how to approach teaching with consideration of equality and diversity (Hoath and Dave, 2022).

> **ACTION LEARNING SET**
>
> With these challenges and issues in mind consider these two key questions:
> 1. what does sustainability mean to you?
> 2. which of the challenges described are most concerning for your own development as a trainee and early career teacher?

# WHAT DOES SUSTAINABILITY MEAN?

One of the issues with sustainability is agreeing on a definition – many consider the environmental impacts without taking into account other factors. The United Nations Brundtland Commission (1987) defined sustainability as *meeting the needs of the present without compromising the ability of future generations to meet their own need*. The more detailed exploration of this definition outlines an interplay between the environmental, societal and economic aspects of sustainability which all have links with the existing content we teach within primary school settings. It is, however, often challenging for us as teachers to unpick these links and the fundamentals of what sustainability is when it is not within our existing knowledge base. It is essential that this begins to form a thread through your teaching, along with school guidance, in order to address what has become a real environmental crisis for our population.

> **EVIDENCE-INFORMED RESEARCH**
>
> The IPCC report (2022) places the need to teach about sustainability and climate change firmly at the fore and this next section summarises some of the reasons for this imperative.
>
> - Climate change poses major threats to human wellbeing, health, food and water security, infrastructure, ecosystems and biodiversity. Educating people, especially pupils and young people, about these risks is more likely to bring about a change.

- Carbon emissions need to be rapidly reduced to limit global warming to 1.5°C and avoid catastrophic impacts. Education is needed to build awareness and enable society-wide behaviour changes as well as being focused on teaching pupils the knowledge they need to be able to understand the causes and mitigation – which is linked with the previous issue of sufficient teacher professional development.

- Adaptation is urgently required to reduce vulnerability to climate impacts. Education can empower people with the knowledge and skills for adaptation and climate resilience and achieving climate resilient development requires transformation across all parts of society and the economy. Educating all sectors and generations, starting with nurturing a love of the environment in early years settings, creates readiness for the needed transformations. This does not mean it is a school-only issue but one where education plays a pivotal role.

- Inequities exacerbate climate risks and undermine sustainable development. Education that promotes equity, justice and inclusion helps address these systemic issues. This should build upon the foundations of your reasons for teaching and the ethos of any schools you experience; however, these inequalities are very real when it comes to sustainability and climate change education and something that we must remain mindful of.

- Climate change demands new ways of thinking and acting, and education can foster the mindsets, values and competencies needed for climate solutions and sustainable lifestyles. We are aiming for a shift in societal behaviour – not just knowing more.

- Coordinated action is essential but constrained by gaps in climate literacy, science communication and access to knowledge. Quality education is key to closing these gaps.

These are the reasons why we must look to develop our own subject knowledge as teachers, to engage with effective curriculum delivery and contextualised learning and not avoid the teaching of these challenging issues any longer. We have a moral obligation to do so.

# LINKING SUSTAINABILITY WITH EXISTING CURRICULA

As you have read in Chapter 7, the teaching of the curriculum in primary schools involves far more than simply what is written on paper. As a trainee, you will be learning the best ways that you can bring this content to life for the pupils in front of you – based on their needs and context, what you are comfortable with in terms of teaching approaches and how to best link the learning that takes place. The teaching of sustainability and climate change education needs to have as credible a curriculum approach as any subject that you teach.

## APPROACHING SUSTAINABILITY AND CLIMATE CHANGE CURRICULA

Hoath and Dave (2022) outline a number of key points to consider when thinking about approaching teaching sustainability and climate change.

1. The curriculum needs to develop the knowledge, skills and attributes in learners to approach current and future environmental challenges. This means establishing their prior learning and where you are aiming for in order to establish that progress has been made.

2. Sustainability and climate change should be infused throughout, which means that there needs to be a coherent approach to linking existing curriculum content. The *ad hoc* approach of the odd lesson to teach a specific aspect does not work – meaningful integration is needed. This requires identifying connections and sequencing substantive and procedural knowledge appropriately, as supported by Anderson et al. (2014). A whole-school curriculum approach is recommended, not just individual subjects, so sustainability permeates school life; this is a school leader issue and not just down to the enthusiastic teacher willing to push the agenda forward.

3. High-quality curriculum resources that support teaching sustainability and climate change across subjects are important for implementation. As previously mentioned, there is a wealth of resources relating to sustainability and climate change education. But with any subject being taught, the curriculum followed by the context of the learners is what should inform the choice of resource. All too often when there is a lack of subject knowledge or confidence in teaching something – as we know is the case for sustainability and climate change – a trainee or experienced teacher will search for a resource which then informs how the lesson is taught. This does not address your pupils first.

4. Environmental and outdoor education provide opportunities to make connections between classroom learning and real-world sustainability issues. This has long been supported through the work of Dillon (2003) and Rickinson et al. (2004), who highlight the benefits of hands-on experience; this support continues today from many sources.

5. The curriculum should develop systems thinking, futures thinking, evaluative skills and critical thinking skills relevant to sustainability issues. This is a big ask of trainees and even more experienced teachers. However, there is a real need to break through the acceptance of what is freely available on the internet; the 'but my dad says …' mentally described by an executive head working in developing climate-adapted curricula in his schools. Most importantly, a curriculum should have the flexibility to allow local contexts and learners' lives to be connected to sustainability issues. This latter point takes into

account the inequalities mentioned previously and will be discussed further on. The curriculum needs to address social justice issues because, as the IPCC (2022) report stated, climate change exacerbates inequality.

There are obvious links with some subjects, but the idea of sustainability and climate change education is that it should be infused through a curriculum rather than shoe-horned in at every opportunity. It is about using the lens appropriately to contextualise learning for those pupils. Here are some case studies of what this might look like.

## CASE STUDY: SCHOOL CONTEXT

Coastal South East England, high area of disadvantage and coastal deprivation. There is an offshore windfarm visible minutes' walk from the school. There is an opportunity to make strong links with the science curriculum (rocks, for example, in Year 3) and geography (KS1, human and physical) in relation to what is happening in their local area and introduce that this is being influenced by climate change – that, in order to protect the locality, change is needed. At KS2 the wind farm can be used as a context for discussing energy consumption and the human demand on this. In addition, the school has established a wrapper-free Friday, when the pupils are not to bring snacks wrapped in plastic.

Inner-city London, five-form entry primary school. The pupils have little green space around their school. The extension of the Ultra-Low Emission Zone (ULEZ) is being written about in English in persuasive writing to ask other cities to do the same. Some data around the reduction in the number of cars coming into the zone is used for calculations in maths. The school has also introduced a Climate Ambassadors Club which looks at activities the school pupils can undertake to contribute to sustainability and addressing climate change. They opt for litter picking and more recycling bins around school.

An academy trust in Yorkshire sets sustainability and climate change education at the heart of its curriculum and ethos. It has a strong commitment to ensuring its pupils develop an understanding and care for nature and the environment. The schools are varied in size and demographic due to being inner-city as well as some rural. Every school has a board of pupils who present to the Trustees; the leadership team focuses on developing 'green non-negotiables' and their stance is environmentally ethical.

## REFLECTIVE QUESTIONS

Thinking of the examples above, what are the vulnerabilities that need to be taken into account with what you have read?

With the additional activities being undertaken, what are the pros and cons of each?

## FURTHER CONSIDERATION

With the examples we should consider the extent to which they take into account the sensitivities around the pupils in the class. It is essential that when initiatives such as wrapper-free days are introduced that they do not highlight pupils who may get their food from food banks, for example, and do not have an option as to what their food comes wrapped in. Or, for those in inner-city London, that initiatives do not isolate those who cannot afford newer, less polluting cars and are being penalised for this through the ULEZ approach. Infusing issues of social inequality and climate justice throughout the curriculum using appropriate resources will help to mitigate this. We return here to the previous point about the curriculum being not just 'content led', but more around how we teach within the context and environment our pupils and their families live in – and that there is not a one size fits all. Through adopting pedagogical approaches that connect to pupils' lives and communities, addressing local social issues related to climate impact, we can make a better difference through what and how we teach. The other important element of the activities we often see taking place in schools is that they are tokenistic – while litter picking, bug hotels and recycling have a sense of helping pupils, and sometimes teachers, feel that they are doing something worthwhile, these activities do little do bring about a change in understanding, knowledge or agency that is required in order to address the environmental issues that are currently being faced. Integration into the school culture – demonstrated more fully in the third example – holds the greatest potential to address education in relation to the climate and sustainability crises.

## CURRICULUM AND PEDAGOGY INTERPLAY

It is impossible to write about curriculum without discussing pedagogy, as this section has highlighted. There are a number of principles of pedagogy for sustainability and climate change education that again mirror developments when learning to teach any subject area.

A starting point should be for you to consider your confidence in content knowledge and adopt scaffolding approaches if needed (Ofsted, 2019) – think about who and what can support your teaching in a way that best suits what and who you have in front of you. Throughout this chapter it has been suggested that sustainability and climate change teaching should align closely to the curriculum subject/s; in the same way, using subject-specific pedagogies should be adopted (Hattie, 2009). As with curriculum – there is not a one size fits all. I have written of the need to contextualise what is taught and this is further supported by Cantell et al. (2019), who advocate adopting pedagogies that connect to students' lives, identities and motivations.

## PRACTICAL ADVICE FOR TRAINEES AND EARLY CAREER TEACHERS

Teaching within the classroom is where you develop most expertise; however, with the need to embrace a greater appreciation of the natural environment, this will inevitably lead to more teaching time outside. It is important that as teachers we employ pedagogies suitable for outdoor settings beyond the classroom (Dillon, 2003; Rickinson et al., 2004).

Something mentioned earlier within this chapter was the need to teach this content – which can bring about climate anxiety and a range of emotions in our pupils. Allowing time for reflection on experiences (Higgins and Christie, 2018), creating a culture in your classroom of self-regulation and metacognition and creating opportunities for peer discussion, deliberation and collaborative problem-solving (Warburton, 2003) is key. The way our curriculum is sequenced is critical here; you can read more on developing sequences of learning in Chapter 10. It is also crucial that we consider the pupils within our schools; all children will have differing levels of understanding and socioeconomic differences within the families of those we teach must also always be taken into consideration. Read more information on promoting social justice in education in Chapter 15.

## APPROACHES AND FRAMEWORKS TO TEACHING SUSTAINABILITY AND EDUCATION FOR SUSTAINABLE DEVELOPMENT

### SUSTAINABILITY EDUCATION OR EDUCATION FOR SUSTAINABLE DEVELOPMENT (ESD)?

These two terms are often used interchangeably, and it is perhaps pedantic to consider the differences. It is worth considering how you can think about these in relation to your teaching and how you can then apply these differences to what you are doing within the classroom. UNESCO (2014, p. 33) defines ESD as something which 'allows every human being to acquire the knowledge, skills, values and attitudes that empower them to contribute to sustainable development', going on to suggest that it also 'requires innovative, participatory teaching and learning methods that empower and motivate learners to take action for sustainable development'. ESD consequently 'promotes skills like critical thinking, … imagining future scenarios, and making decisions in a … collaborative way'. These points can be considered *learning outcomes* – the things you want to be able to see when progress has been made: the differences we will see in our pupils in years to come and ultimately in society.

Sustainability education, however, could be seen to focus more on the how we get to this point. What are the learning intentions, the knowledge, the thinking and the action which will ensure that pupils have greater depth of understanding about what they need to know in order to bring about those changes? The importance of getting the knowledge 'right' in relation to these areas is paramount – without understanding the relationships between our actions, the elements and the planet then there will be no real change. What is important is that you are clear as to what you are teaching, and what you are teaching it for.

There are a number of frameworks that can be used to structure some of the teaching of sustainability within schools which should be considered carefully before adoption.

## THE UNITED NATIONS SUSTAINABLE DEVELOPMENT GOALS (UNSDGS)

The UNSDGs are 17 goals with 169 targets behind them which cover a wide range of issues. They are country targets with a view to making a collective approach in challenging the problems they cover. There is some criticism that with there being so many they are vague and unfocused which makes practical implementation challenging. Some schools adopt these and try to demonstrate where they are teaching about or addressing them. This was never how they were intended for use and could therefore be considered somewhat problematic. There are nuances around the content which should be highlighted, such as conflicting goals or having unintended consequences. For example, economic growth goals could increase resource use and emissions. The biggest question to be asked is if it is better for schools and teachers to address learning of these whole-world issues through the SGDs than not teaching them at all.

Linking back to the earlier section in the chapter where it is important to consider the context of your learners and their vulnerabilities and inequalities, it is worth noting that one of the concerns regarding the SGDs is that they are western-centric; they have been criticised as reflecting western perspectives and not fully incorporating voices and views from the Global South which has the potential to exacerbate power imbalances and may therefore not reflect your pupils' backgrounds.

In order to bring about the changes needed to address the global crises we are facing, one of the key messages within this chapter has been around ensuring pupils understand cause and mitigation fully in order to effect change. There has been discussion that the SDGs focus on symptoms rather than root causes of unsustainability – like overconsumption, injustice and globalisation – and avoid challenging the status quo. I am not suggesting that it is solely our role as teachers to do this, but rather ask you to reflect on the approach you use to frame teaching of sustainability. Bendell (2022, p. 17) argues 'it is time for replacing Sustainable Development as the overarching framework for international cooperation with alternative frameworks that are better suited for our new era of increasing crises and disasters'; so it is reasonable to question their validity for a teaching and learning framework used in a way that was never intended.

## A MULTI-FACETED WHOLE-SCHOOL APPROACH

One of the greatest challenges with sustainability and climate change education is that the first step should be to build a whole-school culture that makes sustainability and climate change education a priority (Hoath and Dave, 2022). This requires strong leadership to develop policies, routines and practices that bring these issues to the forefront where teachers across subjects must buy into a shared vision to develop climate-literate students. There are limited opportunities currently to engage with professional development to ensure staff have the knowledge and skills to embed sustainability perspectives in their teaching. However, it is appropriate to consider where you can start to engage pupils in shaping the school's approach in an attempt to foster young leadership, remembering that any social inequalities are exacerbated by climate change which should inform efforts to increase access and inclusion.

The curriculum requires coherent planning to develop students' climate change knowledge and competencies across subjects and ages with existing curriculum content carefully mapped to identify opportunities to incorporate climate change perspectives. Key concepts and skills then need to be sequenced appropriately as substantive knowledge. High-quality curriculum resources need to be identified or developed to support teachers. This needs to be supported by effective pedagogy which is crucial to successfully deliver the sustainability curriculum. Outdoor learning develops empathy with nature and understanding of ecosystems and should become an integral part of the ways in which content is taught, with scope for discussing students' emotions, validating and mitigating climate anxiety.

None of this is easy with barriers like time, resources and knowledge, and must be addressed through leadership prioritisation and strategic resourcing. Gradually embedding sustainability education, with ongoing improvements, is realistic given multiple pressures schools face and, with a coordinated effort, education can empower youth to take climate action and build a sustainable future. This chapter has provided you with detailed information, contextual examples, the evidence-based research and some case studies that explain the complexities involved for schools when approaching the delivery of sustainability and climate change education.

## CONCLUSION

The future of our planet is in your hands. As a new teacher, you have an unprecedented opportunity and responsibility to shape the next generation who will inherit environmental challenges like no other. Your pupils are calling for knowledge, skills and hope to create a liveable world. They need you to spark their imagination so they can envision solutions not yet created. Nurture their empathy so they walk gently on the Earth. Instil societal values so they raise their voices for justice. Guide their hands so they can act with ingenuity. Allow their anxiety so they grasp the stakes. Build their confidence so they believe in change. While curriculum evolves, make sustainability come alive through creative lessons outdoors, in gardens, on farms and in the classroom.

Our pupils need more than basic literacy and numeracy ... they need climate literacy – and you can lead the way. The future is unwritten, and we need you to inspire young writers. Teach as if life depends on it. In many ways, it does. Your time is now. Seize this challenge with courage.

> **REVIEW OF CHAPTER OBJECTIVES**
>
> Within this chapter you have considered:
>
> - the purpose and complexities of sustainability education within the primary school setting;
> - ways in which sustainability education can be meaningfully linked with existing curricula;
> - different approaches and existing frameworks for teaching sustainability and education for sustainable development.

## FURTHER READING AND RESOURCES

Hoath, L. and Dave, H. (2022) *Sustainability and Climate Change Education: Creating the Foundations for Effective Implementation.* Leeds: Leeds Trinity University and the Teacher Development Trust.

This report outlines considerations for how to think about sustainability and climate change education implementation.

Hung, C. (2023) *Climate Change Education: Knowing, Doing and Being.* London: Routledge.

This book is a well-informed and detailed outline of what it means to teach and learn about sustainability and climate change education.

## REFERENCES

Anderson, L. W., Krathwohl, D. R. and Bloom, B. S. (2014) *A Taxonomy for Learning, Teaching, and Assessing: A Revision of Bloom's Taxonomy of Educational Objectives.* London: Pearson.

Bendell J. (2022) Replacing sustainable development: Potential frameworks for international cooperation in an era of increasing crises and disasters. *Sustainability*, 14(13), 8185. https://doi.org/10.3390/su14138185

Boström, M., Andersson, E., Berg, M., Gustafsson, K., Gustavsson, E., Hysing, E., Lidskog, R., Löfmarck, E., Ojala, M., Olsson, J., Palmberg, I. and Wamsler, C. (2018) Conditions for transformative learning for sustainable development: A theoretical review and approach. *Sustainability*, 10(12), 4479. https://doi.org/10.3390/su10124479

British Science Association (2023) *Future Forum. Climate Change in Secondary Schools: Young People's Views of Climate Change and Sustainability Education.* London: BSA.

Cantell, H., Tolppanen, S., Aarnio-Linnanvuori, E. and Lehtonen, A. (2019) Bicycle model on climate change education: Presenting and evaluating a model. *Environmental Education Research*, 25(5), 717–731

Cebrián, G., Mogas, J., Palau, R. and Fuentes, M. (2022) Sustainability and the 2030 Agenda within schools: A study of school principals' engagement and perceptions. *Environmental Education Research*, 28(6), 845–866. doi: 10.1080/13504622.2022.2044017

Chinedu, C. C., Wan-Mohamed, W. A. and Ogbonnia, A. A. (2018) A systematic review on education for sustainable development: Enhancing TVE teacher training programme. *Journal of Technical Education and Training*, 10(1), 109–125.

Department for Education (DfE) (2019) *ITT Core Content Framework*. London: DfE. Available at: https://assets.publishing.service.gov.uk/government/uploads/system/uploads/attachment_data/file/974307/ITT_core_content_framework_.pdf [accessed November 2023].

DfE (2022) *Sustainability and Climate Change: A Strategy for the Education and Children's Services Systems.* Available at: www.gov.uk/government/publications/sustainability-and-climate-change-strategy/sustainability-and-climate-change-a-strategy-for-the-education-and-childrens-services-systems [accessed 31 December 2023].

DfE (2024) *Initial teacher training and early career framework* Available at: https://www.gov.uk/government/publications/initial-teacher-training-and-early-career-framework [Accessed March 2024].

Dillon, J. (2003) On learners and learning in environmental education: Missing theories, ignored communities. *Environmental Education Research*, 9(2), 215–226.

Hallinger, P. and Chatpinyakoop, C. (2019) A bibliometric review of research on higher education for sustainable development, 1998–2018. *Sustainability*, 11(8), 2401.

Hattie, J. (2009) *Visible Learning: A Synthesis of Over 800 Meta-analyses Relating to Achievement.* London: Routledge.

Higgins, P. and Christie, B. (2018) *Learning for Sustainability.* London: Routledge.

Hoath, L. and Dave, H. (2022) *Sustainability and Climate Change Education: Creating the Foundations for Effective Implementation.* Leeds: Leeds Trinity University and the Teacher Development Trust.

Intergovernmental Panel on Climate Change (IPCC) (2022) Climate Change 2022: Impacts, Adaptation and Vulnerability. Geneva: IPCC.

Kagawa, F. (2007) Dissonance in students' perceptions of sustainable development and sustainability: Implications for curriculum change. *International Journal of Sustainability in Higher Education*, 8(3), 317–338. https://doi.org/10.1108/14676370710817196

Raffe, D. and Semple, S. (2011) Policy borrowing or policy learning? How (not) to improve education systems (CES Briefing No 55). Centre for Educational Sociology, University of Edinburgh.

Rickinson, M., Dillon, J., Teamey, K., Morris, M., Choi, M.Y., Sanders, D. and Benefield, P. (2004) *A Review of Research on Outdoor Learning*. Telford: Field Studies Council.

Salas-Zapata, W. A., Ríos-Osorio, L. A. and Cardona-Arias, J. A. (2018) Knowledge, attitudes and practices of sustainability: Systematic review 1990–2016. *Journal of Teacher Education for Sustainability*, 20(1), 46–63. https://doi.org/10.2478/jtes-2018-0003

Stanitsas, M., Vareilles, É. and Kirytopoulos, K. (2018) Sustainable development in serious games: Rethinking game-based learning strategies for master's degree engineers, in MOSIM '18, 12ème Conférence Internationale de Modélisation, Optimisation et Simulation.

Teach the Future (2021) *Research with UK Teachers on the Current State and Future of Climate Education*. Available at: www.teachthefuture.uk/research [accessed 31 December 2023].

Thomas, I. (2004) Sustainability in tertiary curricula: What is stopping it happening? *International Journal of Sustainability in Higher Education*, 5(1), 33–47. https://doi.org/10.1108/14676370410517606

United Nations Brundtland Commission (1987) *Our Common Future: Report of the World Commission on Environment and Development*. Available at: www.un.org/en/academic-impact/sustainability [accessed 31 December 2023].

United Nations Educational, Scientific and Cultural Organization (UNESCO) (2014) *UNESCO Roadmap for Implementing the Global Action Programme on Education for Sustainable Development*. Paris: UNESCO. Available at: http://hdl.voced.edu.au/10707/383002 [accessed 2 October 2023].

Velazquez, L., Munguia, N. and Sanchez, M. (2005) Deterring sustainability in higher education institutions: An appraisal of the factors which influence sustainability in higher education institutions. *International Journal of Sustainability in Higher Education*, 6(4), 383–391. https://doi.org/10.1108/14676370510623865

Warburton, K. (2003) Deep learning and education for sustainability. *International Journal of Sustainability in Higher Education*, 4(1), 44–56.

# 17
# MAKING THE MOST OF PROFESSIONAL NETWORKS AND YOUR NEXT STEPS

## CATHERINE READING

# TRAINING TO BE A PRIMARY SCHOOL TEACHER

## CHAPTER OBJECTIVES

On reading this chapter you will consider:

- the different pathways for career development and progression in teaching;
- the elements of effective professional development;
- professional learning networks and how they can support teachers;
- how to make the most of your professional network and other development opportunities.

## KEY VOCABULARY

*Core Content Framework* (CCF)

*Initial Teacher Training and Early Career Framework* (ITTECF)

*Early Career Framework* (ECF)

National professional qualification (NPQ)

Professional learning network (PLN)

Continuing professional development (CPD)

# INTRODUCTION

While completing the first three years of your early career development as a beginning teacher, you will be supported with a structured programme around the *Core Content Framework* (CCF) (DfE, 2019b) and *Early Career Framework* (ECF) (DfE, 2019a). From September 2025: the *Initial Teacher Training and Early Career Framework* (ITTECF) (DfE 2024). Qualified teacher status (QTS) will be awarded on completing this training; however, you will continue developing professionally for many years.

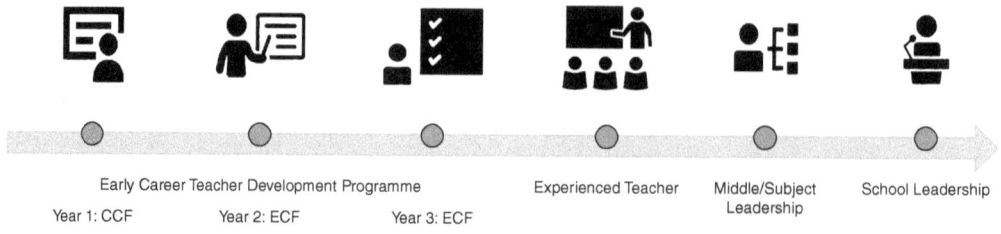

*Figure 17.1 The stages of teacher development*

The recent teacher development reforms have created a 'golden thread' of high-quality evidence underpinning the support, training and development available throughout a teacher's career. This chapter explores the career development pathways available and focuses on enhancing your professional development using networks and other opportunities.

# CAREER DEVELOPMENT AND PROGRESSION IN THE TEACHING PROFESSION

During the transition from preparation programmes into professional employment, early career teachers must develop a range of competencies over time and in different contexts. Teacher development in England offers structured opportunities for educators to enhance their skills, knowledge and careers. These opportunities are designed to improve teaching practices, promote ongoing professional growth and address the changing needs of the education system.

Following the recent *Initial Teacher Training (ITT) Market Review Report* (DfE, 2021), the national professional qualifications (NPQ) were redesigned to complement the introduction of the ECF. The Education Endowment Foundation (EEF) worked closely with the Department for Education (DfE) and was heavily involved in designing and validating the ECF and NPQs. The independent assessment of

| | | | |
|---|---|---|---|
| | Year 1 | Initial Teacher Training | Skills and knowledge are developed through the ITT Curriculum and the Core Content Framework alongside placement support and mentoring |
| | Year 2 | The Early Career Framework 1 | First year of the ECF pathway ensures that teachers in their initial stages have the necessary support and the most current skills and knowledge |
| | Year 3 | The Early Career Framework 2 | Second year of the ECF pathway builds on the year one curriculum Knowledge and skills are deepened and the aspects of subject-knowledge and curriculum are further developed |
| | Year 4+ | Subject specialist opportunities | Fundamental Leadership skills with an opportunity to specialise: Behaviour and Culture NPQ (welfare/behaviour) Leading Teacher Development (mentoring/coaching/developing staff) Leading Teaching (curriculum/phase leadership/literacy) |
| | Year 5+ | Senior leadership opportunities | Significant Leadership skills are supported by NPQ qualifications: Senior Leadership (NPQSL) New to Headship/Headship(NPQH) with specific routes for EY and SEN Executive Headship (NPQEL) |

*Figure 17.2 Professional development opportunities*

evidence means a more robust and consistent approach is used across all programmes, helping to create a more straightforward progression as teachers and leaders advance in their careers by ensuring that the content of each development programme builds on the others. A 'golden thread' of high-quality evidence underpins the support, training and development throughout a teacher's career.

There is a clear support structure and an identifiable pathway for early career development between Year 1 and Year 3. Having navigated the first phase of your development, it is time to consider the following steps on your career pathway.

## PATHWAYS FOR PROMOTION

Teachers can advance their careers in England and seek promotion through several pathways. The specific routes for promotion may vary, depending on the school, the school's governing body, or the school's academy trust. However, regardless of school setting, there appear to be common pathways for promotion:

1. *Teaching and learning responsibility (TLR) posts*: TLR posts, such as TLR1 and TLR2, are additional responsibilities or roles within a school. The roles may include leading a department, coordinating a curriculum area, or managing specific projects. Applying for TLR posts is a common way for classroom teachers to take on more responsibility and receive additional pay.

2. *Middle leadership roles*: Middle leadership positions include head of department, head of year and key stage leader. These roles involve managing a team of teachers, coordinating curriculum and overseeing the quality of teaching and learning.

3. *Senior leadership roles*: Senior leadership positions include deputy headteacher, assistant headteacher and vice principal. These roles involve significant leadership responsibilities, school management, curriculum development and staffing.

4. *Advanced skills teacher (AST)*: The AST designation recognises outstanding teachers who have demonstrated exceptional teaching skills and the ability to influence teaching practices in their schools. ASTs are often responsible for leading professional development and mentoring other teachers.

5. *National professional qualifications (NPQs)*: The NPQs prepare teachers for leadership positions. The programmes for subject specialist opportunities are leading teaching, leading literacy, leading behaviour and culture and leading teacher development. These qualifications are recognised for leadership development and may lead to promotion.

6. *Chartered teacher status (CTS)*: Chartered teacher status is a recognition for experienced teachers who have demonstrated a high level of expertise. Achieving CTS may open opportunities for more senior roles or additional responsibilities.

7. *Educational leadership programmes*: Aspiring leaders can enrol in educational leadership programmes that provide training and support for leadership positions, such as the national professional qualification for senior leadership, headship and executive leadership (NPQH).

8. *Contributions to school improvement*: Actively contributing to school improvement initiatives, such as raising student achievement, implementing effective teaching strategies and leading successful projects, can make teachers more competitive candidates for promotion.

9. *Governor or Trustee roles*: Some teachers may pursue roles as school governors or trustees within academy trusts, which can provide leadership experience and enhance their chances of advancement.

Promotion opportunities vary between schools and academies; some schools have specific policies and criteria for advancement. It is essential to seek guidance from your school's leadership team, engage in professional development and be proactive in pursuing opportunities for promotion based on your interests and career goals. Additionally, continuing professional development (CPD) and demonstrating leadership qualities are critical factors in advancing your teaching career.

> **REFLECTIVE QUESTIONS**
>
> What are your future career goals, and what steps do you plan to take to achieve them?
>
> Select one pathway and explore the demands and expectations of this role.
>
> Where do you see yourself in five years?

# CONTINUING PROFESSIONAL DEVELOPMENT FOR TEACHERS

Professional development is paramount for teachers as it is critical to enhancing their effectiveness in the classroom and shaping the quality of education (Burroughs et al., 2019). Professional development gives teachers access to the latest research and advancements in education. As our understanding of how students learn evolves, and new teaching strategies emerge, teachers must stay current to ensure that they provide their students with the best possible learning experiences. Continuous learning helps teachers refine their practices and adapt to changing educational landscapes.

> *'There are no great schools without great teachers. At the heart of great teaching and great school leadership is a shared, evidence-informed understanding of what works.'*
>
> (DfE, 2022, p. 56)

A school culture of professional development fosters a culture of reflection and self-improvement among teachers. It encourages educators to critically assess their teaching methods, identify areas for growth and seek solutions to meet the needs of their diverse student populations. This reflective process leads to more effective teaching, improved student outcomes and a more substantial commitment to the profession.

## EFFECTIVE PROFESSIONAL DEVELOPMENT

High-quality CPD for educators enhances teaching and learning, improves student outcomes and supports teachers' and education professionals' ongoing growth and development (Coe et al., 2020).

We know that teachers engage in professional development activities while balancing multiple and, at times, competing commitments and time pressures. Therefore, any activity must be well designed, selected and implemented to justify investment. Key elements that should be considered include:

1. *Relevance to teachers' needs*: High-quality CPD is tailored to meet specific needs and goals. It should consider the phase, subject area and the challenges they face in their classrooms. CPD should align with the goals and priorities of the school, ensuring that it contributes to overall school improvement.

2. *Aligned with learning objectives*: CPD should have clear learning objectives and goals, ensuring participants know what they are expected to learn and achieve.

3. *Research-based and evidence-informed*: Effective CPD incorporates the latest educational research and evidence to ensure that teachers are using strategies that have been proven to work.

4. *Sustained and ongoing*: High-quality CPD is not a one-time event but an ongoing process. It may involve a series of workshops, seminars, or courses that build on each other, allowing participants to deepen their knowledge and skills over time.

5. *Active and hands-on learning*: It provides active engagement and hands-on learning opportunities. Teachers should be able to practice and apply what they have learned in their classrooms.
6. *Collaborative and peer learning*: Peer learning and collaboration can be highly effective for sharing ideas, experiences and best practices.
7. *Feedback and reflection*: It encourages participants to reflect on their teaching practices and receive constructive feedback from peers or facilitators.
8. *Assessment and evaluation*: CPD should include assessment methods to measure the programme's effectiveness. This may involve pre- and post-assessments, classroom observations, or other evaluation tools.

> **EVIDENCE-INFORMED RESEARCH: THE MECHANISMS OF PROFESSIONAL DEVELOPMENT**
>
> A key finding of the EEF review of professional development was that the more mechanisms the programme had, the more significant the impact on pupil attainment. The more *building blocks* incorporated, the better the chance of success (EEF, 2021).
>
> The review identifies that a teacher's professional development is likely to be more effective (in improving pupils' outcomes) if it incorporates more techniques from all four of the categories it identifies.
>
> 1. *Building knowledge*
>    - managing cognitive load
>    - revisiting prior learning
> 2. *Motivate*
>    - setting and agreeing on goals
>    - presenting information from a credible source
>    - providing affirmation and reinforcement after progress
> 3. *Teach techniques*
>    - instructing teachers on how to perform a technique
>    - arranging social support
>    - modelling the technique
>    - monitoring and providing feedback
>    - rehearsing the technique
>
> *(Continued)*

(Continued)

4. *Embed practice*
   - providing prompts and questions
   - prompting action planning
   - encouraging monitoring
   - prompting context-specific repetition

The EEF report suggests that a programme featuring a mechanism from each area represents a *balanced design*. A programme may be less effective if one or more groups are missing. However, it is worth noting that this research predominantly focuses on pedagogical features of teacher development.

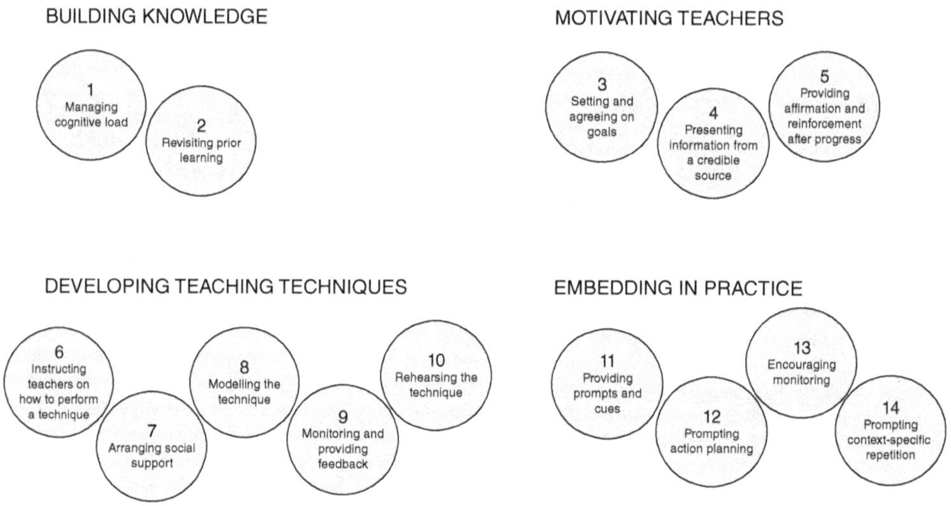

**BUILDING KNOWLEDGE**
1. Managing cognitive load
2. Revisiting prior learning

**MOTIVATING TEACHERS**
3. Setting and agreeing on goals
4. Presenting information from a credible source
5. Providing affirmation and reinforcement after progress

**DEVELOPING TEACHING TECHNIQUES**
6. Instructing teachers on how to perform a technique
7. Arranging social support
8. Modelling the technique
9. Monitoring and providing feedback
10. Rehearsing the technique

**EMBEDDING IN PRACTICE**
11. Providing prompts and cues
12. Prompting action planning
13. Encouraging monitoring
14. Prompting context-specific repetition

Figure 17.3 The mechanisms of professional development (adapted from EEF, 2021, p. 29)

## REFLECTIVE QUESTIONS

Think about a professional development programme that you have participated in.

Can you identify whether any of the 14 professional development mechanisms were present?

Can you identify where a mechanism could have been used to improve the programme?

# BUILDING CONNECTIONS THROUGH PROFESSIONAL LEARNING NETWORKS

A professional learning network (PLN) is a personalised learning environment that educators establish to connect with other professionals in the education field. With PLNs, teachers and other education professionals remain up to date in their field, share resources, exchange ideas and collaborate with others to support their ongoing professional development and learning.

Building and maintaining a PLN is a proactive approach to professional growth and development. It allows educators to stay connected, seek support and stay informed about educational changes. Teachers can continually improve their teaching practices and enrich their classrooms through collaboration, support and knowledge exchange. These networks are dynamic and integral to a teacher's ongoing development and support system.

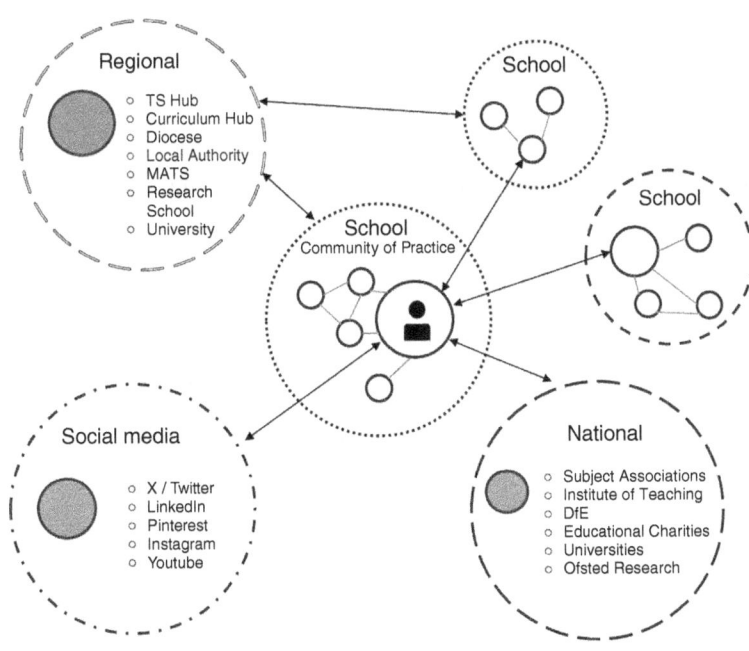

*Figure 17.4* PLNs

## INTERNAL NETWORKS

Within your school, you are part of a community of practice (CoP); there may be an established development programme, or you may feel supported by informal channels like peer mentoring and support. All schools are committed to continual improvement in the quality of teaching and learning. Moreover, most leaders understand that staff development can significantly affect school improvement (Coe et al., 2020).

## EXTERNAL NETWORKS

### LOCAL

Depending on the size and structure of your school, you may be connected to other schools through a Trust or have developed links with colleagues in the local area. These school–school links are valuable and form part of your PLN.

### REGIONAL

In your region, you will be supported by a teaching school hub and several curriculum hubs. Your school may be part of a multi-academy trust, diocese or local authority, and you may have links to a research school or university.

### NATIONAL

At a national level, you will be supported by the National Institute of Teaching and the Department for Education. You may be part of a subject association and feel part of a network of connected practitioners.

### VIRTUAL

Many teachers use social media for professional learning through different platforms such as X or LinkedIn. Online spaces are potential sources of help and support because of the large number of resources available.

---

**EVIDENCE-INFORMED RESEARCH: THE THEORY BEHIND THE PLN**

PLN is the name given to the ecosystem that connects a network of collaborators within and across schools, working together to improve the quality of teaching and learning (Brown and Poortman, 2018). A single CoP is connected to other schools as well as other experts that can support the development of the individual teacher and the school.

PLNs are rooted in *situated learning* theories, asserting that learning occurs as an apprenticeship within specific contexts (Lave and Wenger, 1991). Because teachers at any career stage have individual professional needs within their circumstances (Kennedy and McKay, 2011), teachers taking a situated approach to professional learning connect information, resources and encouragement to build a network uniquely suited to their specific needs (Trust and Prestridge, 2021).

Support shared in a PLN may include knowledge, skills, teaching resources, curricular materials and encouragement helpful for professional learning. Trust and Prestridge (2021) argue that a teacher's willingness to construct PLNs in addition to required professional development voluntarily suggests that there may be underlying reasons that justify spending extra time and effort beyond the regular demands of teaching. A PLN can be understood in terms of why a teacher constructs a support system, what they are looking for and where.

## WHAT ARE THE BENEFITS OF A PLN?

PLNs can provide teachers with many advantages, such as access to various perspectives, experiences and expertise to enrich their teaching practice. Teachers can also share their work, insights and questions with peers for constructive feedback and encouragement.

*Table 17.1 The benefits of a PLN*

| | |
|---|---|
| Continuous learning | PLNs provide access to knowledge, expertise and resources. Teachers engage with the latest trends, research and best practices, enhancing their teaching practice. |
| Resource sharing | PLNs facilitate sharing of teaching materials, lesson plans and classroom resources. This collaborative environment saves time and energy by allowing teachers to benefit from the work of others. |
| Peer support | Teachers can seek advice, share experiences and solve common challenges through their PLN. This peer support offers emotional encouragement and practical guidance. |
| Diverse perspectives | PLNs connect educators with professionals from various backgrounds and geographical locations. This diversity of perspectives helps teachers gain a broader view of education. |
| Professional growth | Teachers can acquire new skills and knowledge that can lead to personal and professional growth by engaging with peers, attending webinars and participating in discussions. |

*(Continued)*

*Table 17.1 (Continued)*

| Innovation and creativity | PLNs encourage teachers to think creatively and innovatively. The exposure to different teaching methods and ideas can inspire fresh approaches in the classroom. |
|---|---|
| Personalised learning | PLNs allow teachers to tailor their professional development to their needs and interests. They can choose resources, conversations and connections most relevant to their goals. |
| Reflection and self-improvement | Teachers can reflect on their practices and receive constructive feedback from their PLN. Self-assessment and continuous improvement are essential in a teacher's professional journey. |
| Networking and career opportunities | Building a robust PLN can lead to networking opportunities beyond the virtual world. It can open doors to speaking engagements, writing opportunities and career advancement. |

## BUILDING NETWORKS

A well-developed PLN is an invaluable teacher asset in a rapidly changing educational landscape. It fosters a culture of lifelong learning, connectivity and innovation, ultimately benefitting educators and their students.

ENGAGING WITH YOUR REGIONAL NETWORK

### CASE STUDY: CLAIRE

Claire is an assistant headteacher of a middle school in Tyneside. She reflects on her pathway to leadership via a subject specialisation in maths.

*Choosing primary science as my subject specialism during my BA Primary Education programme at university was easy – I loved science and enjoyed teaching science while on placement. However, once I took my first post, I developed a love for teaching maths. Maths had never been a strength at school; I did not understand what I was doing – more rote learning and regurgitation than anything else. In 2015, the leadership in the school were impressed with my maths teaching and asked me to attend a maths CPD session about 'maths mastery'. This was the first time I had seen the approach in action, but it fully aligned with my ethos around teaching maths.*

*I moved to teach in a middle school where the curriculum lead for maths was leaving. After teaching here for a year, I was approached to lead maths across the school. I was initially reluctant as I had no experience with KS3 maths, so I agreed to lead KS2 maths and sought support from the Great North Maths Hub (GNMH). The support from the courses I attended was invaluable, and I started drip-feeding some of the mastery approaches to maths into my school. As the approach was new to many staff who had been teaching a lot longer than me, there was some resistance initially.*

*With encouragement from my headteacher at school, I applied to train as a primary mastery specialist with the GNMH, which I consider the most valuable teaching experience in my career. I met some wonderful maths leads from schools across the North East (whom I still liaise with now) and received excellent training from the maths leads at the hub. The fully funded training, consisting of three residential trips and twilights, was invaluable for my professional development and the teachers in my school. Most importantly, we could see the approach's impact on pupils' understanding of maths.*

*The focus of becoming a primary maths specialist was to enable me to support local schools in implementing a mastery approach to maths. In addition to building my love of leading maths, I gained excellent experience leading a department and leading change across other schools.*

*The position of assistant headteacher in teaching and learning came up in my school, and I felt ready and equipped to start a new chapter. Taking the plunge into leading maths equipped me with the confidence and skills I needed to accelerate a career in school leadership.*

By connecting with the local maths hub, Claire was able to support her expertise and develop her own PLN. The expert maths input and high-quality training increased Claire's confidence and enabled the leading of this curriculum area and initiative. The confidence gained as a peer-networked maths specialist enabled her to lead maths effectively alongside other school changes. The experiences supported her development and readiness for the assistant headteacher role in teaching and learning.

Engaging with your regional professional network and curriculum hubs can benefit personal and professional growth. These networks often offer opportunities for collaboration, learning and staying connected with local professionals and experts. Here are some ideas on how to engage with them effectively.

1. *Collaborate on projects*: Collaborate with your PLN members on projects, research, or lesson planning. Sharing the workload and expertise can lead to innovative ideas and successful outcomes.

2. *Offer support and seek mentorship*: Be willing to offer support and mentorship to others, and do not hesitate to seek guidance and mentorship from experienced educators in your PLN.

3. *Utilise the expertise from the regional hubs*: Identify hubs that align with your educational interests. Look for local events, seminars, workshops, or conferences. Attend them to meet and network with professionals in your region.

Engaging with your regional professional network and curriculum hubs can help you stay connected with local professionals and contribute to the growth and improvement of your field or educational sector. It is a valuable way to exchange knowledge, build relationships and positively impact your community.

# ENGAGING WITH YOUR NATIONAL NETWORK
## SUBJECT ASSOCIATIONS

Subject associations are invaluable resources for teachers, offering a range of benefits that enhance their professional development, teaching effectiveness and overall educational impact.

Subject associations are membership organisations whose members are subject experts. Subject associations are independent of government, often charities and their mission is to further teaching and learning in a specific subject in schools, colleges and ITT in universities. Each curriculum subject has a subject association that can offer support.

Table 17.2 Subject associations and phases supported

| Subject | Subject association | 5-11 | 11-16 | 16-19 | CPD |
|---|---|---|---|---|---|
| Art and Design | Access Art | | | | |
| Computing | Computing for Schools | | | | |
| Design technology | Design and Technology Association | | | | |
| English | National Association for the Teaching of English | | | | |
| Geography | Geographical Association | | | | |
| History | Historical Association | | | | |
| Languages | Association for Language Learning | | | | |
| Maths | Association of Teachers of Mathematics | | | | |
| Music | Music Teachers' Association | | | | |
| PSHE | PSHE Association | | | | |
| Physical education | Association for PE | | | | |
| Religious education | National Association for Teachers of RE | | | | |
| Science: Biology | Royal Society of Biology | | | | |
| Science: Chemistry | Royal Society of Chemistry | | | | |
| Science: Physics | Institute of Physics | | | | |
| Science: General | Association for Science Education | | | | |
| Science: General | STEM | | | | |

## WHAT CAN SUBJECT ASSOCIATIONS DO FOR YOU AND YOUR SCHOOL?

Membership provides affordable, relevant, high-quality professional development through:

- expert advice and information;
- low-cost, high-quality teaching resources;
- access to a community of educators;
- subject courses and conferences;
- up-to-date subject knowledge and pedagogy;
- access to research;
- curriculum support;
- recognition and awards;
- advocacy.

> **ACTION LEARNING SET**
>
> Select a curriculum area that you would like to explore further.
>
> Research the subject association dedicated to your chosen area.
>
> Reflect on how the benefits might be relevant to your professional development.
>
> What opportunities are there for networking?

## ENGAGING WITH YOUR VIRTUAL NETWORK

> **CASE STUDY: MARC, SOCIAL MEDIA**
>
> Marc is an assistant headteacher at a primary school in West Yorkshire.
>
> *(Continued)*

He reflects on using social media to inform his practice and develop his PLN.

> In this early subject leadership, I invested much of my time researching the elements of an outstanding curriculum in the subjects I was leading. As this was only within a couple of years of launching the 2014 national curriculum, there needed to be more progressive thinking about most subjects other than maths. However, I found advice from subject associations invaluable and the more informal advice shared so generously on Twitter and educational blogs. Through these networks, I devised models for curriculum development, which raised standards in the subjects I lead.
>
> More recently, schools are supported more distinctly by curriculum research from Ofsted. Although these research reviews have not been without critics (especially in maths), they have provided schools with models for structuring their curricula across various subjects. These reviews are very long reads but are packed with helpful information. I have summarised them all and shared them on Twitter and my website to help make the ideas behind curriculum design more accessible.

Engaging with the subject associations, Marc utilised the advice and expertise to inform the curriculum development in school. Exploring social media, he was able to benefit from the advice and support from his PLN. Later in his career, Marc began to curate content and developed resources summarising key research and the Ofsted curriculum reviews. In this way, he has added value to the PLN and established a platform with high-quality content.

Engaging with your virtual professional network is crucial for building meaningful connections and advancing your career. Here are some steps to help you effectively engage with your virtual professional network.

1. *Select the right platforms*: Choose the platforms and tools that best suit your goals and preferences. Common options include X (Twitter), LinkedIn, educational forums, blogging platforms and more. Different platforms have different strengths and features, so use the ones that align with your objectives.

2. *Follow relevant individuals and groups*: Identify and follow educators, thought leaders and organisations relevant to your field or interests. Engage with their content and discussions. Think carefully about your online profile.

3. *Contribute to discussions*: Actively participate in discussions and conversations within your PLN. Share your insights, ask questions and provide feedback. This engagement not only benefits you but also contributes to the community.

4. *Curate content*: Curate valuable resources and content that you come across, such as articles, research papers, blogs, videos, or teaching materials. Share them with your PLN to provide value and establish yourself as a resource.

5. *Reflect and share your experience*: Regularly reflect on your teaching experiences and share your insights and lessons learned with your PLN. This can be done through blog posts, tweets, or other forms of content creation.
6. *Connect with educators in your niche*: Seek out educators who share your specific interests or teaching areas. Connecting with those with similar focus areas can lead to more in-depth and meaningful discussions.
7. *Attend webinars and virtual conferences*: Many virtual conferences and webinars are available online. Participate in these events to gain knowledge, network with professionals and stay updated on current educational trends.
8. *Balance digital and in-person networking*: While online PLNs are valuable, pay attention to the benefits of face-to-face interactions. Attend local educational events, conferences and workshops to expand your network offline.

## APPLICATION TO PRACTICE

### CASE STUDY: MARC, LEADERSHIP

Marc is an assistant headteacher at a primary school in West Yorkshire.

He reflects on his first steps towards leadership through involvement in a whole-school initiative and action research.

> During my first year of teaching, my school decided to explore the development of children's learning behaviours. As I had explored metacognition in detail for my final year dissertation, I reached out to the headteacher to express my interest in working on the project. I was offered the chance to lead the development of learning dispositions across the school, a position which was esteemed by the headteacher. I was invited to join the school's senior leadership team due to the importance the headteacher gave to the project. This was my first step into whole-school leadership.
>
> The project involved researching the impact of teaching-learning dispositions on children to develop aspects of being a 'good learner'. Across the school, we were trying to change the concept of 'good learners' from one being defined as 'well-behaved, raises their hand and has neat presentation' to one which featured, for example, good habits of paying attention, being able to learn collaboratively and wanting to make links across the learning. These areas were beyond the expertise I had developed in my dissertation and required considerable research.
>
> The most extraordinary professional development I received was being invited to visit Stonefields School in Auckland, New Zealand, which plans learner development as

*(Continued)*

> *part of its curriculum. I spent a fortnight there conducting an informal action research project where I could see first-hand how teachers and pupils actively developed the skills they needed to become effective learners.*
>
> *One of my key drivers to lead was to make a positive difference across the school. Although teaching a class brings significant responsibility for progress in many aspects of the curriculum, leading an area of whole-school development is an exciting opportunity to have an even more significant impact. Leading the development of learning behaviours enabled me to develop expertise in teaching and learning, which I could share with staff, who could implement the strategies I had researched and suggested.*

Marc could share his research and expertise with the team by engaging with a whole-school initiative. The evaluation and impact of the initiative were shared more widely, resulting in an international connection and a visit to New Zealand, expanding his PLN. Marc developed expertise in learning and teaching by leading the learning behaviours initiative, supporting his progression and readiness towards senior leadership.

Remember that a PLN is a dynamic resource that should adapt and evolve with your changing needs and interests. By actively engaging, sharing and collaborating with your PLN, you can tap into a valuable source of professional development and support throughout your career.

*Table 17.3 The evolution of your PLN*

| | |
|---|---|
| Set clear goals | Determine your specific goals for your PLN. What do you want to achieve through your network? Whether staying current in your field, improving your teaching practices, or advancing your career, having clear objectives will guide your interactions within your PLN. |
| Stay open | Embrace the diversity within your PLN. Engage with educators from various backgrounds, cultures and perspectives. This diversity can enrich your understanding and practices. |
| Evaluate and adjust | Periodically evaluate your PLN's effectiveness in helping you reach your goals. Consider adjusting your approach if certain connections or activities are outside your objectives. |
| Be consistent | Building a strong and valuable PLN takes time. Be patient and consistent in your efforts, as meaningful connections and benefits may take a while. |

### ACTION LEARNING SET

What does your PLN look like?

Identify your current connections and consider how you can build upon your network.

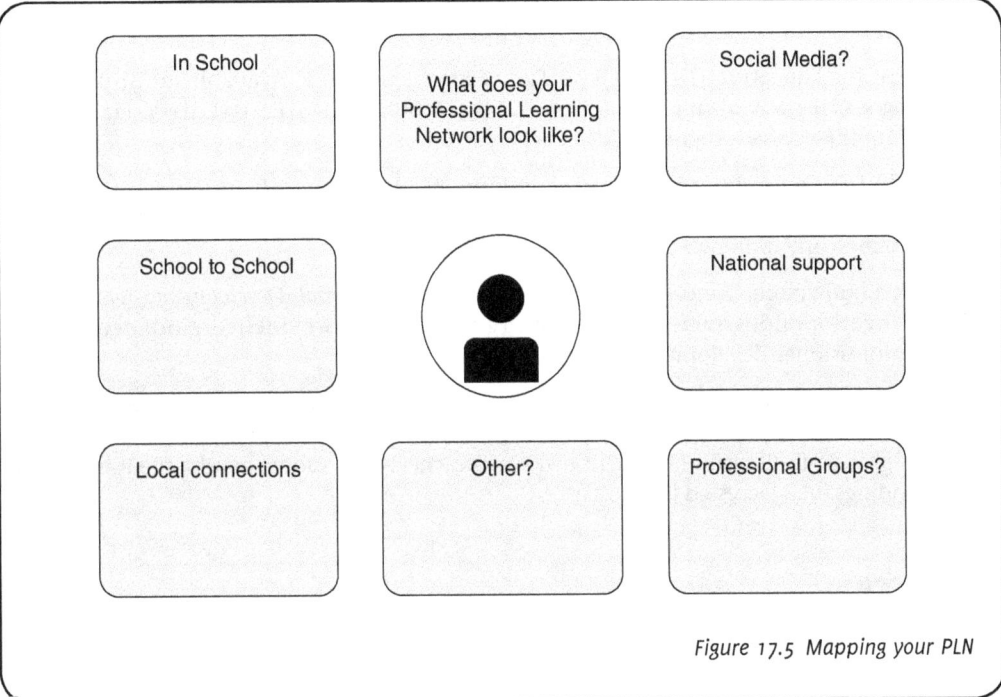

*Figure 17.5 Mapping your PLN*

# CONCLUSION

This chapter identified the diverse nature of career development and progression in the teaching profession. It emphasised the role and the importance of CPD for a practising teacher and explored the key elements that ensure effective delivery. The construct of a PLN was introduced, and examples of developing this effectively were given. Finally, the chapter explored how to make the most of a PLN and to use it effectively for your professional growth and progression.

### REVIEW OF CHAPTER OBJECTIVES

Within this chapter you have considered:

- the different pathways for career development and progression in teaching;
- the elements of effective professional development;
- PLNs and how they can support teachers;
- how to make the most of your professional network and other development opportunities.

## FURTHER READING AND RESOURCES

Department for Education (DfE) (2019a) *Early Career Framework*. Available at: https://assets.publishing.service.gov.uk/media/60795936d3bf7f400b462d74/Early-Career_Framework_April_2021.pdf [accessed August 2023].

DfE (2019b) *ITT Core Content Framework*. London: DfE. Available at: https://assets.publishing.service.gov.uk/government/uploads/system/uploads/attachment_data/file/974307/ITT_core_content_framework_.pdf [accessed November 2023].

Education Endowment Fund (EEF) (2021) *Effective Professional Development*. Available at: https://educationendowmentfoundation.org.uk/education-evidence/guidance-reports/effective-professional-development [accessed August 2023].

Ofsted (2023) *Independent Review of Teachers' Professional Development in Schools: Phase 1 Findings*. Available at: www.gov.uk/government/publications/teachers-professional-development-in-schools-phase-1-findings/independent-review-of-teachers-professional-development-in-schools-phase-1-findings#fn:2 [accessed July 2023].

## WEBSITES

| | |
|---|---|
| Access Art: | www.accessart.org.uk |
| Computing at Schools: | www.computingatschools.org.uk |
| Design and Technology Association: | www.designtechnology.org.uk |
| National Association for the Teaching of English: | www.nate.org.uk |
| Geographical Association: | www.geography.org.uk |
| Historical Association: | www.history.org.uk |
| Association for Language Learning: | www.all-languages.org.uk |
| Association of Teachers of Mathematics: | www.atm.org.uk |
| Music Teachers Association: | www.musicteachers.org |
| PSHE Association: | www.pshe-association.org.uk |
| Association for PE: | www.afpe.org.uk |
| National Association for Teachers of RE: | www.natre.org.uk |
| Royal Society of Biology: | www.rsb.org.uk |
| Royal Society of Chemistry: | www.rsc.org |
| Institute of Physics: | www.iop.org |
| Association for Science Education: | www.ase.org.uk |
| STEM: | www.stem.org |

# REFERENCES

Biesta, G. (2019) Teaching for the possibility of being taught: World-centred education in an age of learning. *English E-Journal of the Philosophy of Education*, 4, 55–69.

Brown, C. and Poortman, C. (eds.) (2018) *Networks for Learning: Effective Collaboration for Teacher, School and System Improvement*. London: Routledge.

Burroughs, N., Gardner, J., Lee, Y., Guo, S., Touitou, I., Jansen, K. and Schmidt, W. (2019) A review of the literature on teacher effectiveness and student outcomes. *IEA Research for Education*, 6, 7–17.

Coe, R., Rauch, C., Klime, S. and Singleton, D. (2020) *Evidence Review Great Teaching Toolkit*. Available at: https://evidencebased.education/great-teaching-toolkit-evidence-review/ [accessed August 2023].

Department for Education (DfE) (2016) *Standard for Teachers' Professional Development*. London: DfE. Available at: www.gov.uk/government/publications/standard-for-teachers-professional-development [accessed July 2023].

DfE (2021) *Initial Teacher Training (ITT) Market Review Report*. Available at: https://assets.publishing.service.gov.uk/media/60e45ae4e90e0764ce826628/ITT_market_review_report.pdf [accessed 31 December 2023].

DfE (2022) *Delivering World-class Teacher Development*. Policy paper. Available at: https://assets.publishing.service.gov.uk/government/uploads/system/uploads/attachment_data/file/1076587/Delivering_world_class_teacher_development_policy_paper.pdf [accessed July 2023].

DfE (2024) *Initial teacher training and early career framework* Available at: https://www.gov.uk/government/publications/initial-teacher-training-and-early-career-framework [Accessed March 2024].

Education Endowment Fund (EEF) (2021) *Effective Professional Development*. Available at: https://educationendowmentfoundation.org.uk/education-evidence/guidance-reports/effective-professional-development [accessed August 2023].

Kennedy, A. and McKay, J. (2011) Beyond induction: The continuing professional development needs of early-career teachers in Scotland. *Professional Development in Education*, 37(4), 551–569.

Lave, J. and Wenger, E. (1991) *Situated Learning: Legitimate Peripheral Participation*. Cambridge: Cambridge University Press.

Ronfeldt, M. and McQueen, K. (2017) Does new teacher induction improve retention? *Journal of Teacher Education*, 68(4), 394–410.

Sims, S., Fletcher-Wood, H., O'Mara-Eves, A., Cottingham, S., Stansfield, C., Van Herwegen, J. and Anders, J. (2021) *What are the Characteristics of Teacher Professional Development that Increase Pupil Achievement? A Systematic Review and Meta-analysis*. London: EEF. Available at: https://educationendowmentfoundation.org.uk/education-evidence/evidence-reviews/teacher-professional-development-characteristics [accessed June 2023].

Trust, T. and Prestridge, S. (2021) The interplay of five elements of influence on educators' PLN actions. *Teaching and Teacher Education*, 97(2), 103195.

# 18

# GETTING YOUR FIRST TEACHING POST AND THE ECT PROGRAMME

**LAURA WILD**

## CHAPTER OBJECTIVES

On reading this chapter you will:

- learn about the DfE *Teachers' Standards*;
- explore the entitlement of support for a trainee and an early career teacher (ECT) through the CCF and the ECF; or the ITTECF
- begin to think about how a trainee can *stand out from the crowd* when applying for their first teaching post;
- look beyond the first two years as an ECT to the role of a subject leader.

## KEY VOCABULARY

Department for Education (DfE)

Initial teacher training (ITT)

*Core Content Framework* (CCF)

Initial Teacher Training and Early Career Framework (ITTECF)

*Early Careers Framework* (ECF)

Early career teacher (ECT)

Qualified teacher status (QTS)

*Curriculum vitae* (CV)

Career professional development (CPD)

Special educational needs and disability lead (SEND lead)

Educational health care plan (EHCP)

Graduate teachers will be referred to as early career teachers (ECTs) in this chapter.

# INTRODUCTION

This chapter focuses on the DfE *Teachers' Standards* (DfE, 2021) and moves beyond the *Core Content Framework* (CCF) (DfE, 2019b) into the *Early Career Framework* (ECF) (DfE, 2019a). Key aspects that will be explored are the DfE *Teachers' Standards* (DfE, 2021), entitlement of support you will receive to achieve these, employability and subject leadership. You will examine the role that the DfE *Teachers' Standards* play in the transition from a trainee to an ECT, moving from the CCF (DfE, 2019b) to the ECF (DfE, 2019a) or the ITTECF (DfE, 2024). You will find out how you can stand out from the crowd when applying for teaching jobs and when attending interviews. Preparing for subject leadership is explored at the end of the chapter.

> **REFLECTIVE QUESTIONS**
>
> What role will the DfE *Teachers' Standards* play during your time as a trainee? Once you have graduated, achieved QTS and begun your first teaching post as an ECT, will these standards become obsolete?

# WHAT ARE THE DFE *TEACHERS' STANDARDS?*

The DfE *Teachers' Standards* 'define the level of practice at which all qualified teachers are expected to perform' (DfE, 2021, p. 6). They set a benchmark for teaching and personal conduct that you as a trainee will aspire to achieve and, as an ECT and experienced teacher, you will act upon. They provide guidance that allows teachers to evaluate their own practice and conduct and supports them in identifying areas to improve. They are important because a drive for continuous improvement enables all teachers (including ECTs) to provide the best quality of education they can.

In 2011, the Secretary of State triggered a review of the existing standards for teachers. The aim of the review was to ensure that all pupils are exposed to the best quality of education by making clear to the public and those within educational settings what is expected of a teacher. A set of *Teachers' Standards* were published by the DfE (originally in 2011; updated 2021). Adopted by educational settings, these standards are used to assess the practice and conduct of trainees, ECTs and teachers. The DfE *Teachers' Standards* apply to:

- trainees working towards QTS;
- ECTs;
- all teachers in maintained schools (including maintained special schools) (DfE, 2021).

The DfE *Teachers' Standards* document is a framework made up of three parts:

- Preamble (a summary of values and behaviours);
- Part One: Teaching (a list of eight standards, broken down into a series of shorter statements);
- Part Two: Personal and professional conduct (a list of three standards, broken down into a further series of shorter statements) (DfE, 2021).

The Preamble in the DfE *Teachers' Standards* sets out the minimum expectation of the values and behaviours required of a teacher:

*Teachers make the education of their pupils their first concern and are accountable for achieving the highest possible standards in work and conduct. Teachers act with honesty and integrity; have strong subject knowledge, keep their knowledge and skills as teachers up-to-date and are self-critical; forge positive professional relationships; and work with parents in the best interests of their pupils.*

(DfE, 2021, p. 10)

Part One: Teaching. Standard 4 from the DfE *Teachers' Standards* states that the minimum expectation of a teacher in regard to planning and teaching a lesson and evaluating its effectiveness:

4. *Plan and teach well structured lessons*

   - *impart knowledge and develop understanding through effective use of lesson time*
   - *promote a love of learning and children's intellectual curiosity*
   - *set homework and plan other out-of-class activities to consolidate and extend the knowledge and understanding pupils have acquired*
   - *reflect systematically on the effectiveness of lessons and approaches to teaching*
   - *contribute to the design and provision of an engaging curriculum within the relevant subject area(s).*

(DfE, 2021, p. 11)

The following extract from Part Two states the minimum expectation of a teacher in regard to their behaviour and conduct within the school setting. 'Teachers must have proper and professional regard for the ethos, policies and practices of the school in which they teach, and maintain high standards in their own attendance and punctuality' (DfE, 2021, p. 14).

The Preamble, Part One and Part Two of the DfE *Teachers' Standards* (DfE, 2021) provide clear statements outlining to trainees and teachers (including ECTs) what practice should be like and how they should behave as professionals. As a trainee, an ECT and eventually as an experienced teacher, you will be expected to demonstrate consistent practice, measured against each statement, to show that you are fulfilling the minimum expectation required of a teacher.

The DfE *Teachers' Standards* (DfE, 2021) can be used as a self-reflection tool to track progress. They will also be used by mentors and senior leaders in educational settings to assess achievements and the impact you have as a trainee, an ECT and, eventually, as an experienced teacher on the pupils you teach. This will include identifying areas for improvement and setting targets for development. This process is vital for you as a trainee and throughout your teaching career. It allows continuous growth and improvement in practice and conduct that ensures that you provide the best education for all pupils.

## WHAT SUPPORT IS THERE TO HELP TRAINEES ACHIEVE THE DFE TEACHERS' STANDARDS?

As you found out in Chapter 1, the CCF (DfE, 2019b) is a package of entitlement to support you as a trainee. The CCF/ITTECF is based and built upon the DfE *Teachers' Standards* (DfE, 2021, originally 2011). It provides valuable insight into the practice and behaviour you will need to grow and develop if you are to be successful in your teaching role. Initial teacher training (ITT) providers use the CCF/ITTECF to structure their curriculum design. It enables these providers to plan and deliver essential knowledge, skills and behaviour trainees need when working towards the achievement of the DfE *Teachers' Standards* (DfE, 2019b).

It is important to remember that the CCF/ITTECF is not an assessment framework; you will be assessed against the DfE *Teachers' Standards*. However, it is key for you to familiarise yourself with the CCF/ITTECF to ensure you are aware of the specific knowledge and skills for your programme. This will allow you to track your learning and progress and provide insight into your end goal.

## WHAT SUPPORT IS THERE TO HELP ECTS ACHIEVE THE DFE TEACHERS' STANDARDS?

It is important for you to understand that, once you have graduated and achieved QTS, your learning journey does not end. A teacher who strives to become the expert must continue to develop their knowledge, skills and behaviour. This will enable them to continue to provide the best education for the pupils in their care in an often-changing educational landscape. The value of career professional development (CPD) is explored in more depth in Chapter 17. As discussed in the CCF/ITTECF: 'No one is born a great teacher. Great teachers continuously improve over time, benefitting from the mentoring of expert colleagues and a structured introduction to the core body of knowledge, skills and behaviours that define great teaching' (DfE, 2019b, p. 3).

So how can this be achieved? The ECF (DfE, 2019a) is a package of entitlement of support to guide you in your continued development from trainee to teacher. It is a collection of standards akin to the CCF/ITTECF which maps out what ECTs are entitled to learn about and learn how to do when they start their first teaching post. It provides funded and structured training and support for the first two years of your teaching post including allocated time set aside for you to focus on your development (DfE, 2019b).

Figure 18.1 is an extract taken from the ECF. It shows the 'Learn that' and 'Learn how to' statements that map the essential knowledge and necessary skills you will need to demonstrate as an ECT in your practice and conduct if you are to achieve Teachers' Standard 4 – Plan and teach well-structured lessons

| Classroom Practice (Standard 4 – Plan and teach well structured lessons) ||
|---|---|
| Learn that… | Learn how to… |
| 1. Effective teaching can transform pupils' knowledge, capabilities and beliefs about learning.<br>2. Effective teachers introduce new material in steps, explicitly linking new ideas to what has been previously studied and learned.<br>3. Modelling helps pupils understand new processes and ideas; good models make abstract ideas concrete and accessible.<br>4. Guides, scaffolds and worked examples can help pupils apply new ideas, but should be gradually removed as pupil expertise increases.<br>5. Explicitly teaching pupils metacognitive strategies linked to subject knowledge, including how to plan, monitor and evaluate, supports independence and academic success.<br>6. Questioning is an essential tool for teachers; questions can be used for many purposes, including to check pupils' prior knowledge, assess understanding and break down problems.<br>7. High-quality classroom talk can support pupils to articulate key ideas, consolidate understanding and extend their vocabulary.<br>8. Practice is an integral part of effective teaching; ensuring pupils have repeated opportunities to practise, with appropriate guidance and support, increases success. | **Plan effective lessons, by:**<br>• *Using modelling, explanations and scaffolds, acknowledging that novices need more structure early in a domain*<br>• *Enabling critical thinking and problem solving by first teaching the necessary foundational content knowledge.*<br>• *Removing scaffolding only when pupils are achieving a high degree of success in applying previously taught material.*<br>• *Providing sufficient opportunity for pupils to consolidate and practise applying new knowledge and skills.*<br>• *Breaking tasks down into constituent components when first setting up independent practice (e.g. using tasks that scaffold pupils through meta-cognitive and procedural processes).*<br>**Make good use of expositions, by:**<br>• *Starting expositions at the point of current pupil understanding.*<br>• *Combining a verbal explanation with a relevant graphical representation of the same concept or process, where appropriate.*<br>• *Using concrete representation of abstract ideas (e.g. making use of analogies, metaphors, examples and non-examples).* |

(Continued)

*Figure 18.1 (Continued)*

| Classroom Practice (Standard 4 – Plan and teach well structured lessons) | |
|---|---|
| Learn that... | Learn how to... |
| 9. Paired and group activities can increase pupil success, but to work together effectively pupils need guidance, support and practice.<br>10. How pupils are grouped is also important; care should be taken to monitor the impact of groupings on pupil attainment, behaviour and motivation.<br>11. Homework can improve pupil outcomes, particularly for older pupils, but it is likely that the quality of homework and its relevance to main class teaching is more important than the amount set. | **Model effectively, by:**<br><br>• *Narrating thought processes when modelling to make explicit how experts think (e.g. asking questions aloud that pupils should consider when working independently and drawing pupils' attention to links with prior knowledge).*<br>• *Making the steps in a process memorable and ensuring pupils can recall them (e.g. naming them, developing mnemonics, or linking to memorable stories).*<br>• *Exposing potential pitfalls and explaining how to avoid them.*<br><br>**Stimulate pupil thinking and check for understanding, by:**<br><br>• *Planning activities around what you want pupils to think hard about.*<br>• *Including a range of types of questions in class discussions to extend and challenge pupils (e.g. by modelling new vocabulary or asking pupils to justify answers).*<br>• *Providing appropriate wait time between question and response where more developed responses are required.*<br>• *Considering the factors that will support effective collaborative or paired work (e.g. familiarity with routines, whether pupils have the necessary prior knowledge and how pupils are grouped).*<br>• *Providing scaffolds for pupil talk to increase the focus and rigour of dialogue.* |

*Figure 18.1* Extract from the ECF (DfE, 2019a)

*Notes*

**Learn that...** statements are informed by the best available educational research; references and further reading are provided below.

**Learn how to...** statements are drawn from a wider evidence base including both academic research and additional guidance from expert practitioners.

'Learn that' and 'Learn how to' statements, like those shown in Figure 18.1, are repeated throughout the ECF with clear links to each of the DfE *Teachers' Standards*.

You may have noticed that the ECF 'Learn that' statements are similar to the CCF/ITTECF statements. This is intentional, as it provides a coherent development path for you from trainee to ECT and beyond, enabling you to work towards and achieve the DfE

*Teachers' Standards*. The 'Learn how to' statements in the ECF, however, will expect you, as an ECT and eventually as an experienced teacher, to work with increasingly more independence and demonstrate deeper knowledge and understanding (DfE, 2019a).

The ECF (DfE, 2019a) provides guidance for colleagues in educational settings to support you, as an ECT, in achieving and maintaining the DfE *Teachers' Standards*. Like the CCF/ITTECF, the ECF is not an assessment framework (DfE, 2019a). As an ECT you will be assessed against the DfE *Teachers' Standards* (DfE, 2021). It is key, however, for you as an ECT to familiarise yourself with the ECF. This will allow you to track your development and progress so that you continue to meet, and potentially exceed, the minimum expectations of a teacher in your first two years of teaching.

The DfE *Teachers' Standards* (DfE, 2021) play a vital role in your programme of learning. They are a necessary set of standards that ensure you meet the minimum expectation of a teacher and continue to do so as you navigate through your first two years of teaching and beyond. They aim to ensure that all pupils receive a consistent and high-quality education. It is clear that once you have graduated and achieved QTS, the DfE *Teachers' Standards* do not become obsolete.

# EMPLOYABILITY

This section focuses on employability and gaining knowledge and understanding of the process of applying for a teaching post. It will encourage you to consider which graduate attributes you can take forward into your teaching role and how you can stand out from the crowd during the application and interview process.

### WHAT GRADUATE ATTRIBUTES CAN A TRAINEE TAKE FORWARD INTO A TEACHING ROLE?

When preparing to apply for your first teaching post, you should consider the attributes you have gained and how these will support you in your teaching role. Table 18.1 lists some example graduate attributes and suggests how they may be demonstrated by a trainee and an ECT.

When you apply for a teaching post you will be expected to identify your current attributes and exemplify the impact these will have on your ability to do the job. Consider creating your own table as shown in Table 18.1 to help you prepare for this.

Table 18.1 Example of graduate attributes

| Trainee | Graduate attributes | ECT |
|---|---|---|
| Complete an assignment with a national curriculum focus, e.g. What is the role of representations in primary mathematics? | Subject knowledge | Complete a mathematics lesson plan that uses representations to supports all pupils to make progress. |
| Create a timeline to map out when to complete assignments and how much time can be spent on each. | Organisation | Create a timetable to map out when to complete planning, and how much time can be spent on each subject. |
| Upload an assignment, in a timely manner onto the university system. | Meeting deadlines | Upload half-termly assessment data, in a timely manner, onto the school system. |
| Collate evidence and research for an assignment. | Independent worker | Collate evidence against the DfE *Teachers' Standards*. |
| Work with peers in a formative peer review. | Ability to work in a team | Work with the SEND lead to write an EHCP. |
| Liaise with a school partnership tutor. | Communication | Liaise with key staff when sharing a behaviour incident. |
| Work alongside a dissertation tutor. | Relationships | Work alongside the English Lead on phonics planning and delivery. |
| Follow and engage with a prominent educational professional on X (Twitter). | Grow and develop | Follow and engage with Ofsted on X (Twitter). |

## WHAT IS THE PROCESS IN APPLYING FOR A TEACHING POST?

Figure 18.2 shows an example of the process of applying for a teaching post and some of the key pieces of work you will need to complete.

To give further understanding of what is expected of you at each stage of the process outlined above, each aspect identified will now be explained. Applying for a teaching role can be competitive so look out for the top tips to help you know what to avoid and how to stand out from the crowd for certain aspects of this process.

### *CURRICULUM VITAE (CV)*

A CV is a record of personal details, qualifications, teaching and non-teaching employment, other experience and a log of any CPD. The purpose of a CV is to evidence learning and progress. This information is often asked for when applying for jobs. Table 18.2 provides an example of likely content for a teaching CV.

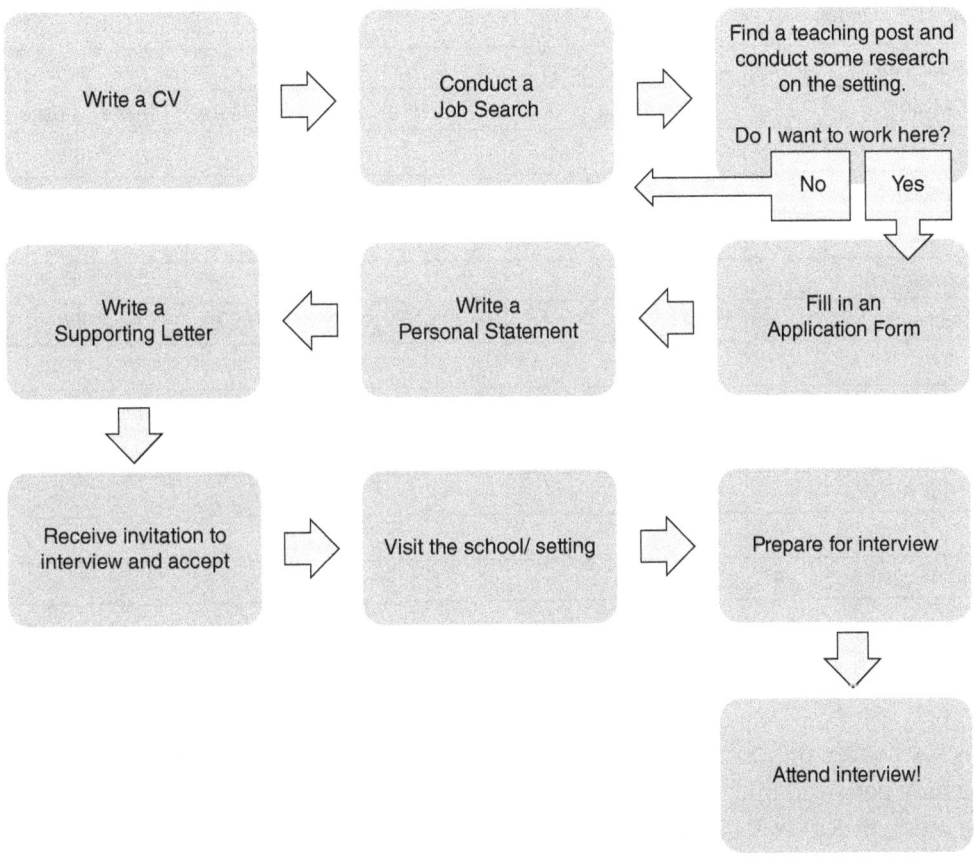

*Figure 18.2 Example application process*

Table 18.2 CV example

| Personal details | | | |
|---|---|---|---|
|  | | | |
| Qualifications | | | |
| Education and qualifications (GCSE or equivalent, A or AS, higher education) | Date | Place | Grade |
|  | | | |
| Additional education and qualifications | Date | Place | Grade |
|  | | | |
| Further qualifications | Date | Place | Grade |
|  | | | |

*(Continued)*

*Table 18.2 (Continued)*

| Employment | | | |
|---|---|---|---|
| Teaching | Date | Place | Role |
| | | | |
| Non-teaching | Date | Place | Role |
| | | | |
| Experience | | | |
| Teaching | Date | Place | Role |
| | | | |
| Non-teaching | Date | Place | Role |
| | | | |
| Other history | | | |
| | | | |
| CPD activity | | | |
| Activity | Date | | Outcome |
| | | | |

It is key to keep this document up to date. Falling into the habit of adding any changes to teaching posts and updating qualifications and CPD activities at the time of completion is the most efficient way of keeping a CV current. CVs are not always expected to be submitted as a separate document when applying for a teaching post. This is because a teaching post application form often asks for the information from a CV to be uploaded within the form itself. However, a CV is still a useful document as it will give ready access to the key information needed when applying for a teaching post and parts may even be used as evidence to demonstrate the DfE *Teachers' Standards*.

## APPLICATION FORM

An application form is an official document. The application form may have been written by the educational setting themselves or be a generic form created, for example, by a local authority. The purpose of an application form is to initially assess whether or not the applicant has the necessary attributes, knowledge and qualities to perform the teaching role. A successful application form will result in the applicant being asked to interview. Although other information may be requested, an application form usually requires the applicant to share the following information:

- personal details, e.g. name, address, contact;
- education and qualifications (GCSE or equivalent, A or AS, higher education);

- additional education and qualifications;
- further qualifications;
- employment record – teaching and non-teaching;
- experience record – teaching and non-teaching;
- other history;
- personal statement;
- references (usually two);
- equality and diversity survey.

To stand out from the crowd:

- use accurate and honest information;
- use standard English;
- use correct spelling and grammar.

Avoid:

- submitting your application late;
- leaving boxes blank.

## PERSONAL STATEMENT

A personal statement is a document written by you that describes your relevant knowledge, skills, beliefs and attitudes. The purpose of a personal statement is for you to showcase your inspiration, enthusiasm and skills when applying for a teaching post. It is a mechanism used by employers to gain knowledge and understanding of a potential employee. It informs their decision as to whether or not the applicant is a suitable fit for their setting. A successful personal statement strengthens the chance of being asked to interview. A personal statement may be written within the application form or attached as an additional document. Instructions to which is required will be given in the application guidance.

To stand out from the crowd:

- describe your beliefs and attitudes (what is your philosophy for education?);
- outline your knowledge and skills in line with the job specification criteria;

- support each statement with a classroom experience and note the impact that it had on pupils;
- when describing attributes, provide specific examples to show how these would support you to be a successful teacher in the classroom.

Avoid:

- a simple list of attributes;
- a general list of knowledge and skills;
- embellishing or exaggerating experiences; they may ask you to expand upon these in interview.

## SUPPORTING LETTER

A supporting or covering letter is a brief introduction of yourself. It should match the job specification criteria where possible and be bespoke to the educational setting being applied to. It is expected that the brief statements written in the supporting letter will be elaborated on in the personal statement.

To stand out from the crowd:

- demonstrate that you have read the school vision and describe how you see yourself aligning with their ethos;
- explain why you wish to work in their specific educational setting using knowledge you have gained from researching the school via their website and/or on a visit;
- explain what you will bring to the role;
- provide a brief reference to your attributes linked to the job specification criteria (these will be described in more depth in your personal statement).

Avoid:

- not writing one!

## SCHOOL VISIT

A school visit is an informal meeting. It is an opportunity for interview candidates to have a tour of the school and its grounds, meet the staff and ask questions. Some settings offer a school visit prior to interview but others prefer to conduct this on the interview day itself. Staff will often feedback their impressions of each interview candidate to the interview team.

To stand out from the crowd:

- arrive on time;
- be polite;
- introduce yourself;
- ask questions, listen and appear interested;
- show confidence to initiate conversation and move round the group;
- be yourself.

Avoid:

- dominating the conversation;
- relaxing too much and slipping into informality.

## INTERVIEW

An interview is a conversation triggered through a planned and structured set of questions. The interview may be face-to-face or online. In an interview there is one interviewee, but usually more than one interviewer. Interviewers usually take it in turns to ask questions while other members of the interview panel write notes of what is said against the interview criteria.

The purpose of an interview is for the interviewee to show that they are the best candidate for the job and an opportunity for them to elaborate on the details previously provided in the covering letter, application form and personal statement. Interviewees will be required to talk in depth about key aspects of the teaching role applied for, while demonstrating to the interviewers their attitude, values, knowledge and skills. Interviewers will use the encounter to judge whether the candidate will fit in their team and meet the teaching role requirements.

### CASE STUDY: HANNAH

This case study, by headteacher Hannah Williamson, explores how to answer an interview question successfully.

*(Continued)*

(Continued)

The way you answer interview questions will make you stand out from the crowd. Figure 18.3 shows the *interview triangle*. Although simple, this model displays the key elements to apply when answering a question.

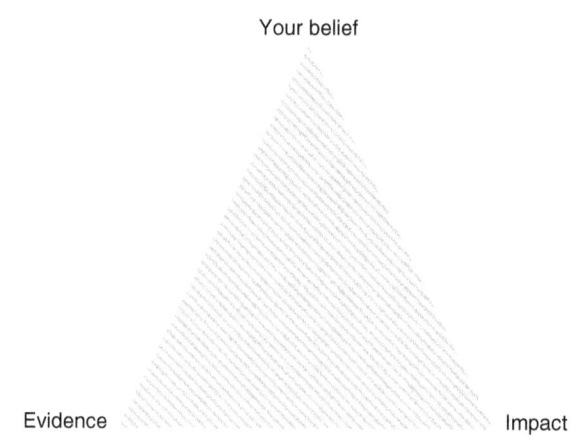

Figure 18.3 Interview triangle

Note: Figure designed by Hannah Williamson.

Belief, evidence and impact can apply to almost all questions that are asked in an interview. By using the interview triangle to structure your answer you will demonstrate knowledge and depth and cover the most essential aspects that the interviewers are looking for. Often in interviews, candidates fail to mention the impact of the work that they do which is a critical element in the interview process. This structure will ensure you avoid this.

For example, you may be asked the question 'How do you ensure children behave in your lessons?' The script below demonstrates how to best answer this question using the interview triangle.

*Belief*: I believe that behaviour management is most effective when the curriculum is engaging, expectations are high, relationships are strong and a positive approach is used.

*Evidence*: On placement I was teaching a challenging class and there was one boy I really struggled to engage. I tried to learn more about him and found that he had a love of cars. I made sure I chatted with him about that to develop our relationship. I also made him a car sticker chart to promote his best behaviour.

*Impact*: Over the course of the placement, we developed a successful relationship. He responded well to the sticker chart most of the time. The impact was that my lessons were more successful, as he was more engaged in his learning.

Now you have seen an example of the interview triangle, you can use this to plan and prepare potential answers to interview questions. Visualising the interview triangle will help you to ensure that you cover all elements to create a coherent and successful answer.

> **ACTION LEARNING SET**
>
> Consider the interview questions below and make notes about what you might say to answer them. It will be helpful to have the graduate attributes (Table 18.1), the interview triangle (Figure 18.3) and a copy of the DfE *Teachers' Standards* (DfE, 2021) to hand for this task.
>
> 1. Which behaviour management strategies do you find most effective and how would you create an effective learning atmosphere in your classroom?
> 2. Explain your understanding of the relationship between assessment and planning.
> 3. A pupil asks to speak to you in private and, in doing so, explains to you that they have something to tell you, but that you must not tell anyone. How would you respond?
> 4. What would we miss out on if we did not employ you?

To stand out from the crowd (before your interview):

- complete research of the educational setting that you are applying for;
- plan, prepare and practise answers to possible questions (use the interview triangle).

To stand out from the crowd (during your interview):

- arrive on time;
- dress smartly;
- articulate your attributes to show how you would fulfil the role;
- link your attributes to real-life examples and explain the impact this has had on the pupils;
- show your personal qualities, such as creativity, resilience and an open mindset in your answers;
- provide depth in your answers by using the interview triangle to structure your responses.

Avoid:

- being overly humble and modest – you may have prepared for the interview, but you will not be the only one. *Speak with confidence and share what you can bring to the role. This is your time to shine and share with them what you can do!*

## ADDITIONAL TASKS ON THE DAY OF INTERVIEW

Schools often ask interviewees to complete tasks on the day of interview. These tasks may be shared with the candidates prior to interview, or they may only be seen for the first time on the day. Some possible examples that an interviewee may encounter are:

- teach a lesson in your current school prior to the interview day;
- teach part of a lesson in your prospective school;
- identify strengths and areas to develop for you as a teacher after your observed lesson;
- identify what the pupils learned (or did not) in your observed lesson and suggest next steps in their learning;
- mark work, including feedback for the pupil/s;
- prioritise a list of scenarios that can happen in a school day and justify your choices. Note that there will always be a safeguarding scenario in this task. Identify it and ensure that this is your priority (for more on safeguarding see Chapter 6);
- be interviewed by the school council.

When applying for a teaching post, it is key that you take time to complete the necessary documentation. It is also necessary to allow time to prepare and practise for the interview itself. This will ensure you can consider and include all the components needed to *stand out from the crowd* and show the employer that you are the best candidate for the job.

# PREPARING FOR SUBJECT LEADERSHIP

This section looks beyond the first two years as an ECT to the role of subject leadership. It aims to capture the essence of the role and provide guidance on the qualities and skills needed to be a successful subject leader.

> **REFLECTIVE QUESTIONS**
>
> Are you born or can you learn to lead?
>
> Do I have to be an expert in the subject to be an effective subject leader?

The purpose of an effective subject leader is to assure quality first teaching and learning opportunities are in place for all pupils ensuring sustained improvement in a subject. Any teacher can be a subject leader. The role of a subject leader is the next phase in development for you after you have completed your first two years as an ECT. As a subject leader you may lead one or more subjects depending on the size and staffing structure of the educational setting. You may lead a subject that you love and are passionate about. You may have in-depth knowledge of the subject because you have studied it at a higher qualification. Alternatively, you may be allocated a subject which is not your area of expertise. However, although having prior expert knowledge can be beneficial, it is not this in-depth subject knowledge alone that ensures successful subject leadership, but the ability for you to learn and develop a specific skill set that allows you to lead and manage any subject effectively.

Below is a list of suggested qualities, knowledge and attributes that make up the skill set of an effective subject leader which you should aim to foster and develop when working towards a position of subject leadership. A prospective subject leader should look to develop:

- knowledge of the strategic direction and development of the subject within the specific educational setting, as well as more widely through evidence-informed research;
- understanding of what quality first teaching and learning looks like in the subject;
- an ability to recognise effective teaching and learning;
- specific subject knowledge sufficient to become the voice of the subject;
- effective relationships to lead and manage staff in a positive manner;
- enthusiasm and dynamism to lead colleagues through change;
- a position as a critical friend to address 'gaps' colleagues may have through bespoke CPD support;
- approaches for the efficient deployment of staff and resources;
- effective time management skills.

> **EVIDENCE-INFORMED RESEARCH**
>
> Dean (2004) recognises that to be a successful subject leader it is necessary to provide a coherent vision for a subject, to be able to stand firm against pressure and have explicit goals. They believe it is necessary to build confidence to be able to manage people and relationships and to know the strengths and limitations of yourself and those around you (Dean, 2004). In support of this, Baldwin suggests that it is vital to enable those around you and consequently necessary to understand the qualities of a good leader so you can model these characteristics in your role (Baldwin, 2018).

## HOW DOES A SUBJECT LEADER ASSURE QUALITY FIRST TEACHING AND LEARNING OPPORTUNITIES ARE IN PLACE FOR ALL PUPILS ENSURING SUSTAINED IMPROVEMENT IN THEIR SUBJECT?

To ensure successful delivery of the subject curriculum the quality of education is monitored and improved internally within an educational setting by you as the subject leader and by other senior leads. To evaluate the quality and success of a subject possible monitoring activities could include:

- the review of targets for the subject within the wider school development plan;
- scrutiny of pupil data in the subject;
- a review of subject planning;
- an audit of resources and how they are used;
- the interviewing of pupils, staff and the wider community to gauge their opinions of the subject;
- a review of pupils' work;
- lesson observations.

The subject is also monitored externally through the Office for Standards in Education, Children's Services and Skills (Ofsted) which reviews the provision and standard of learning for all children and young people in their educational settings (Ofsted, 2019b). Ofsted monitors four areas of an educational setting: quality of education; behaviour and attitudes; personal development; and leadership and management. There are four grades each area is scored against: outstanding, good, requires improvement or inadequate. A description of each grade can be found in the *School Inspection Handbook* (Ofsted, 2019b). This is the outstanding grade descriptor for quality of education:

*Outstanding (1)*

- *The school meets all the criteria for a good quality of education securely and consistently.*
- *The quality of education provided is exceptional.*

*In addition, the following apply.*

- *The school's curriculum intent and implementation are embedded securely and consistently across the school. It is evident from what teachers do that they have a firm and common understanding of the school's curriculum intent and what it means for their practice. Across all parts of the school, series of lessons contribute well to delivering the curriculum intent.*
- *The work given enables pupils, over time and across the school, to consistently achieve the aims of the curriculum, which is coherently planned and sequenced towards cumulatively sufficient knowledge and skills for future learning and employment.*
- *Pupils' work across the curriculum is consistently of a high quality.*
- *Pupils consistently achieve highly, particularly the most disadvantaged. Pupils with SEND achieve exceptionally well.*

(Ofsted, 2019b)

This outstanding grade description is a useful guide for you as a subject leader to endeavour to achieve in your subject for all pupils across the whole educational setting. To enable you to work towards this, it is useful to create a subject action plan to structure and monitor the work you do. An effective action plan could include:

- a description of the context of the subject within the specific educational setting;
- an outline of what needs to change;
- a rationale for why the change is needed;
- a list of targets to achieve;
- monitoring activities to check progress against targets and evaluate the impact of the changes;
- a timeline of activities and who will be involved;
- clear outcomes that state the short- and long-term changes (including what will be different and how this will be sustained).

As an effective subject leader not only will you enact change and development, but you must also celebrate and share the success of your subject. Recognising what is working well and where staff and pupils display outstanding practice is often overlooked, but it is an important aspect of leading a subject.

## CASE STUDY: LEARNING TO LEAD

This case study, by Dan Wheadon, former BA Primary Education student, explores the transition from trainee to subject leader. It reveals how to begin to prepare for subject leadership.

*Embarking on the journey into primary education involves various stages of growth and development, progressing from trainee to teacher and, for most, to subject leader. During my teacher training, I engaged in a Future Leaders module, a safe space to peer into the window of subject leadership and an opportunity to understand and ultimately prepare for the role. Initially, as I discovered, an undeniably multi-faceted role encompassing extensive and diverse responsibilities unique to each setting, the idea of leading a subject seemed overwhelming. However, two concepts helped me digest this mountainous responsibility.*

*First, it proved helpful to view subject leader responsibilities as one of two overarching functions: support and development. From this perspective, the expectations became much more tenable; they are things that, as teachers, we do daily. We support children, create, implement and model a classroom vision, resource, monitor and assess teaching and learning and continually try to develop our practice. As such, we possess many skills readily transferable to the context subject leader, though evidently to a different and larger audience of educational stakeholders. This simplification is by no means meant to downplay the role but by reframing it this way, for me, the subject leader mountain became less Kilimanjaro and more Scafell Pike – no leisurely stroll, but manageable.*

*But more stakeholders can mean more expectation, more accountability, more everything! Perhaps, however, fundamentally all educational stakeholders share the same goal: to improve children's learning. Thus, the second important insight for me was that subject leadership is not and should not be a solitary venture but a collaborative one where, through open communication and active engagement, trusting relationships are built, where expertise and resources are shared and where collective planning and reflection is embraced to promote a cohesive approach to subject delivery. Though I do not yet hold subject leadership responsibilities, I soon will. I will use this time to initiate collaboration, shadowing a subject leader to practically apply the knowledge from training, further understand the nature of the role and contribute to my ongoing transition from trainee to subject leader.*

It should now be clear that learning for you as an ECT does not stop at the end of your first two years. As a teacher you will need to continue to grow, develop and, if you are to move on to become a successful subject leader, you will need to build a skill set that will enable you to become effective in this role. As with your development from trainee to ECT, some of these skills may be achieved easily, whereas others may need time and support. Educational settings, with sustained and effective mentoring support, will provide the guidance you will need as an ECT as you begin your journey towards successful subject leadership; we saw that, as in Dan's case, this journey may even begin when you are a trainee. It will also rely on your own commitment to self-study and a willingness to learn.

## CONCLUSION

This chapter has provided an insight into the path that lies ahead for you in the early stages of your teaching career. It has explained what the DfE *Teachers' Standards* are and has provided an understanding in how the CCF/ITTECF and the ECF are used to support trainees and ECTs in the achievement of these standards. It aimed to equip you with an understanding of the application and interview process, including ideas on how to stand out from the crowd to secure your first teaching post. Finally, the chapter moved from the CCF/ITTECF and beyond the ECF to encourage you to begin to consider the role of subject leadership and what it takes to prepare to be successful in that role.

### REVIEW OF CHAPTER OBJECTIVES

Within this chapter you have considered:

- the DfE *Teachers' Standards*;
- the entitlement of support for a trainee and an ECT through the CCF/ITTECF and the ECF;
- how to stand out from the crowd when applying for a teaching post;
- the role and skill set for successful subject leadership.

## FURTHER READING AND RESOURCES

Bell, D. and Ritchie, R. (1999) *Towards Effective Subject Leadership in the Primary School*. Maidenhead: Open University Press.

Browne, L. (2021) *Effective School Leadership in Challenging Times: A Practice-First, Theory-Informed Approach* London: Taylor & Francis.

Dean, J. (2004) *Subject Leadership in the Primary School: A Practical Guide for Curriculum Coordinators*. London: David Fulton.

# REFERENCES

Baldwin, L. (2018) *Leading English in the Primary School: A Subject Leader's Guide* (1st ed.). London: Routledge.

Dean, J. (2004) *Subject Leadership in the Primary School: A Practical Guide for Curriculum Coordinators*. London: David Fulton.

Department for Education (DfE) (2019a) *Early Career Framework*. Available at: https://assets.publishing.service.gov.uk/government/uploads/system/uploads/attachment_data/file/978358/Early-Career_Framework_April_2021.pdf [accessed August 2023].

DfE (2019b) *ITT Core Content Framework*. London: DfE. Available at: https://assets.publishing.service.gov.uk/government/uploads/system/uploads/attachment_data/file/974307/ITT_core_content_framework_.pdf [accessed November 2023].

DfE (2021) *Teachers' Standards: Guidance for School Leaders, School Staff and Governing Bodies*. London: DfE. Available at: https://assets.publishing.service.gov.uk/media/61b73d6c8fa8f50384489c9a/Teachers__Standards_Dec_2021.pdf [accessed August 2023].

Ofsted (2019a) *Education Inspection Framework*. Available at: www.gov.uk/government/publications/education-inspection-framework/education-inspection-framework [accessed August 2023].

Ofsted (2019b) *School Inspection Handbook*. Available at: www.gov.uk/government/publications/school-inspection-handbook-eif/school-inspection-handbook [accessed August 2023].

# CONCLUSION
## MEGAN STEPHENSON AND ANGELA GILL

You have learned that combining knowledge and application is the 'golden thread' throughout your ITT curriculum. You have discovered that the *ITT Core Content Framework* (CCF), through 'Learn that' and 'Learn how to' criteria, is woven into the curriculum designed by your provider.

Chapter 1 identified the origins of the CCF/ITTECF and introduced you to the phrasing used across your initial teacher training (ITT) curriculum. It defined the key terminology that will form the basis of your ITT programme. It explored how the CCF/ITTECF has been used to create an ITT curriculum and identified and exemplified the importance of receiving carefully crafted, logically sequenced training.

In Chapter 2 the focus was on the importance of *learning about your teaching* to ensure that you continually provide high-quality learning experiences for all pupils. It explored the concept of reflective practice, and the values, attributes and competencies required to engage in this process. There was consideration of what reflective practice might look like for trainees and teachers, in both centre-based and school-based settings. A cycle of reflective practice was outlined, and advice about ways to evaluate evidence quality and teaching resources was shared. The chapter provided practical scaffolding to support trainees to embark on their reflective journey.

Chapter 3 clarified what *professionalism* means in relation to teacher identity and practice. It identified how policy frameworks and standards define professional conduct and behaviours, and explored the importance of close observation of and dialogue with your more experienced professional colleagues to help you to 'fit in' with staff and meet school expectations, while also developing your own agency and confidence.

Chapter 4 explored how to better understand, transfer and apply knowledge to the classroom. It considered how learning to be a great teacher involves building upon skills to ensure secure subject knowledge and a deep understanding of how to deliver the content. Quality teaching should be defined by its impact: a great teacher is one whose pupils learn more, with improved outcomes for all. You discovered how the first step to developing was to ascertain what you know and what you don't. The benefit of conducting learning audits was explored and a range of supportive practices highlighted to aid and inform. You reviewed how observation and feedback adds another element to the learning process and considered how progress on school-based practice is evidenced and measured on ITT programmes.

By reading Chapter 5, you will have begun to identify why wellbeing is important and where it sits within the CCF/ITTECF. You have been introduced to the benefits of journalling and created a personalised pep talk in the form of a letter addressed to the future you. You have gained insight into what you can and cannot control and know who to approach for help in a variety of situations. You have explored what makes you happy and identified your stress triggers and indicators. You have been advised to reframe stress positively to increase your resilience and your wellbeing and reassured that a little stress can be good for you, increasing blood flow and performance. Careful planning and time management are key to ensuring a good work–life balance and a high level of wellbeing.

Chapter 6 identifies that ensuring the safety, security and wellbeing of pupils and educators is of paramount importance in any educational setting. The chapter addressed the comprehensive approach that primary schools must adopt to safeguard their pupils and educators, creating an environment conducive to learning, growth and development. Prioritising safeguarding and promoting wellbeing within your environment will not only foster a positive and nurturing community but also enable pupils and educators to thrive within a secure environment. The chapter identified how we can create safe and secure environments for all young children.

Chapter 7 explored how we arrived at the national curriculum in use today. It explained how it sits within the regulatory framework around schools and how it is used to monitor outcomes for children. We hope that you now have a clearer sense of the opportunities each school and each teacher have to bring this curriculum to life and offer rich learning experiences that carefully build learning and development for each child.

In Chapter 8, you were introduced to some of the key considerations related to early reading and phonics and why teaching these aspects of the curriculum is so important. The chapter explored why phonics is the chosen method for teaching early reading and some of the challenges that phonics can pose. You have explored how you might ensure children make progress in phonics to develop their reading and how you might support parents when reading with their children at home.

Chapter 9 set out where 'managing behaviour' is positioned within the CCF/ITTECF Standard 7. It discussed how many common strategies to support behaviour have evolved from evidence-informed research and how each approach connects to create a cohesive whole picture, which you can begin to apply in your practice in the classroom. It also encouraged you to think about your own values and the educational philosophy you hold with regards to managing behaviour. It provided you with a solid foundation on which to develop the confidence you require to be the professional teacher you aspire to be.

Whether you are teaching from pre-prepared resources or creating your own sequences of learning from scratch, Chapter 10 explored the vital thinking process which must take place when preparing your lessons to ensure effective teaching and learning in your classroom. While planning is a complex process, the steps within this chapter offer considerations which will support you to sequence learning episodes over varying periods of time and ensure that the learning reflects the unique context and needs of the pupils in your setting.

Having read Chapter 11, you will have learned that, as a teacher, you are a role model who can influence the way that children view themselves as learners. Learning is built from a foundation of high expectations, the way that you view your children is central to the way you adapt your teaching. You will have begun to understand that teaching is an iterative process and as teacher you will be required to constantly assess, reflect and adapt both in planning and in the moment to respond the needs of your learners. Learning is cumulative; you need to be aware of the prior learning that your pupils bring with them and build from this. You will have learned that adaptive teaching will ask you to teach to the top, ensuring there is sufficient challenge for all.

Chapter 12 outlined the key principles of the *SEND Code of Practice*. It provided a comprehensive overview of adaptive teaching and provided you with a bank of adaptive teaching strategies. It is important to remember that the approaches that have been outlined in this chapter benefit all pupils and not just pupils with SEND. Pupils with SEND do not therefore always require different pedagogical approaches. They require exposure to high-quality teaching and strategies such as overlearning, repeated practice and chunking, which are beneficial to everyone.

By reading Chapter 13, you learned that becoming an anti-prejudiced educator will support schools in diversifying and decolonising their curriculums for inclusion. Diversifying and decolonising the curriculum, knowing why this is important and the impact that curriculum design has on achievement, inclusion (sense of belonging), motivation – these are the duties of every teacher. The chapter demonstrated that being a diverse and inclusive educator takes time, effort and commitment. It is not a simple tick list to becoming and being anti-discriminatory; it is a constant part of a teacher's practice. The chapter emphasised the importance of self-reflection and awareness development which will help you to actively consider some solutions with regards to your classroom practices.

Chapter 14 explained some key aspects of assessment in primary education, and its place in enabling pupils' progression in their learning. It explored different types of assessment, according to different purposes. Different assessment strategies were discussed, with ideas for you to take into your ITT context, to help you to make effective decisions about assessment. The importance of meaningful feedback, with pupil ownership, was highlighted. As a trainee, you will find that assessment practices vary between schools, but all schools will have an assessment policy and support you to develop your assessment strategies for productive outcomes.

Chapter 15 explored that children's early learning experiences up to the age of three are crucial, but for families who experience multiple cumulative disadvantages such as stress, insecure housing, marginalisation from mainstream education and limited access to physical and cultural resources it is harder to provide stimulating and social experiences for young children. You will have learned that some pupils are then at a distinct disadvantage compared to their better-off peers as they begin school without the positive cultural and social resources which give them an understanding of and secure access to schooling systems and expectations. The chapter demonstrated that these inequalities continue throughout school life, as pupils who experience poverty are more likely to have interrupted schooling, experience the debilitating effects of tiredness or malnutrition, be stigmatised by their peers and have less access to cultural and social experiences and resources.

Chapter 16 outlined some tricky conversations around sustainability and climate change education. Although this is not a mandatory element of the curriculum, CCF/ITTECF or any other aspect of education, it is one with a growing agenda and prevalence within schools. The purpose of the chapter was to draw upon many of the other learnings from previous chapters and demonstrate that sustainability and climate change education demands the same consideration.

The diverse nature of career development and progression in the teaching profession, was explored in Chapter 17. It emphasised the role and the importance of CPD for a practising teacher and explored the key elements that ensure effective delivery. The construct of a professional learning network (PLN) was introduced, and examples of developing this effectively were given. The chapter explored how to make the most of a PLN to use it effectively for your professional growth and progression.

Chapter 18 provided insight into the path that lies ahead for you in the early stages of your teaching career. It explained what the DfE *Teachers' Standards* are and provided an understanding of how the CCF/ITTECF and the ECF are used to support trainees and ECTs in the achievement of these standards. It aimed to equip you with an understanding of the application and interview process, including ideas on how to stand out from the crowd to secure your first teaching post. Finally, the chapter moved from the CCF/ITTECF and beyond the ECF to encourage you to begin to consider the role of subject leadership and what it takes to prepare to be successful in that role.

# APPENDIX

## THE INITIAL TEACHER TRAINING AND EARLY CAREER FRAMEWORK

In January 2024, the Department for Education announced that the Core Content Framework for ITT would be replaced from September 2025 with the Initial Teacher Training and Early Career Framework (ITTECF) (DfE 2024). This new framework is a combining of the Core Content Framework and the Early Career Framework. These frameworks have been combined to ensure that trainee and new teachers have a coherent and consistent training programme that bridges their initial teacher training and first two years in teaching. The content of the CCF continues into the ITTECF.

This appendix outlines how the ITTECF links to all chapters of this book. Of course, there is substantial cross over with the way in which the chapters link to the CCF. The links to the ITTECF are presented in a separate piece here to allow you to see links to the new framework (the ITTECF) clearly and in one place. For some chapters, notes are added with specific reference to the ITTECF.

## CHAPTER 1 AN INTRODUCTION TO THE ITT CURRICULUM

The content of this chapter links to these statements within the ITT ECF:

| How Pupils Learn (Standard 2 - Promote good progress) | |
|---|---|
| **Learn that** | **Learn how to** |
| 1. Learning involves a lasting change in pupils' capabilities or understanding.<br>2. Prior knowledge plays an important role in how pupils learn; committing some key facts to their long-term memory is likely to help pupils learn more complex ideas.<br>6. Pupils have different working memory capacities; some pupils with SEND may have more limited working memory capacity than their peers without SEND. | **Avoid overloading working memory, by:**<br>a) Taking into account pupils' prior knowledge when planning how much new information to introduce.<br>b) Breaking complex material into smaller steps (e.g. using partially completed examples to focus pupils on the specific steps).<br>c) Reducing distractions that take attention away from what is being taught (e.g. keeping the complexity of a task to a minimum, so that attention is focused on the content). |

*(Continued)*

| Subject and Curriculum (Standard 2 – Demonstrate good subject and curriculum knowledge) | |
|---|---|
| **Learn that** | **Learn how to** |
| 2. Secure subject knowledge helps teachers to motivate pupils and teach effectively.<br><br>3. Ensuring pupils master foundational concepts and knowledge before moving on is likely to build pupils' confidence and help them succeed.<br><br>10. Every teacher can improve pupils' communication and literacy, including by explicitly teaching reading, writing and oral language skills specific to individual disciplines.<br><br>11. Pupils' positive dispositions and attitudes towards mathematics are associated with positive outcomes on learning.<br><br>12. Pupils' oral language skills can be supported by teaching new words and how to use and understand words within sentences or longer texts. This can help to address speech and language difficulties, especially for children in their early school years. | **Deliver a carefully sequenced and coherent curriculum, by:**<br><br>a) Identifying essential concepts, knowledge, skills and principles of the subject and providing opportunity for all pupils to learn and master these critical components.<br><br>b) Ensuring pupils' thinking is focused on key ideas within the subject.<br><br>c) Working with experienced colleagues to accumulate and refine a collection of powerful analogies, illustrations, examples, explanations and demonstrations.<br><br>d) Using resources and materials aligned with the school curriculum. (e.g. textbooks or shared resources designed by experienced colleagues that carefully sequence content)<br><br>e) Being aware of common misconceptions and discussing with experienced colleagues how to help pupils, master important concepts. |

# CHAPTER 2 LEARNING ABOUT YOUR TEACHING

The content of this chapter links to these statements within the ITT ECF:

| How Pupils Learn (Standard 2 – Promote good progress) | |
|---|---|
| **Learn that** | |
| 6. Pupils have different working memory capacities; some pupils with SEND may have more limited working memory capacity than their peers without SEND. | |
| **Professional Behaviours (Standard 8 – Fulfil wider professional responsibilities)** | |
| **Learn that** | **Learn how to** |
| 2. Reflective practice, supported by feedback from and observation of experienced colleagues, professional debate, and learning from educational research, is also likely to support improvement. | **Develop as a professional, by:**<br><br>d) Engaging with research evidence by accessing reliable sources, seeking support for how findings can inform practice, and monitoring the impact of applications.<br><br>e) Reflecting on progress made, recognising strengths and weaknesses and identifying next steps for further improvement. |

APPENDIX

# CHAPTER 3 DEVELOPING A TEACHER IDENTITY AND CREATING PROFESSIONAL RELATIONSHIPS

The content of this chapter links to these statements within the ITT ECF:

| How Pupils Learn (Standard 2 – Promote good progress) | |
|---|---|
| **Learn that** | |
| 6. Pupils have different working memory capacities; some pupils with SEND may have more limited working memory capacity than their peers without SEND. | |
| **Professional Behaviours (Standard 8 – Fulfil wider professional responsibilities)** | |
| **Learn that** | **Learn how to** |
| 1. Effective professional development is likely to be sustained over time, building knowledge, motivating staff, developing teaching techniques, and embedding practice.<br>2. Reflective practice, supported by feedback from and observation of experienced colleagues, professional debate, and learning from educational research, is also likely to support improvement.<br>3. Teachers can make valuable contributions to the wider life of the school in a broad range of ways, including by supporting and developing effective professional relationships with colleagues. | **Develop as a professional, by:**<br>a) Engaging in professional development focused on developing an area of practice with clear intentions for impact on pupil outcomes, sustained over time with built-in opportunities for practice.<br>c) Seeking challenge, feedback and critique from mentors and other colleagues in an open and trusting working environment.<br>e) Reflecting on progress made, recognising strengths and weaknesses and identifying next steps for further improvement.<br>**Build effective working relationships, by:**<br>g) Seeking ways to support individual colleagues and working as part of a team.<br>i) Working closely with the SENCO and other professionals supporting pupils with additional needs, making explicit links between interventions delivered outside of lessons with classroom teaching.<br>l) Knowing who to contact with any safeguarding, or any pupil mental health concerns.<br>**Manage workload and wellbeing, by:**<br>m) Using and personalising systems and routines to support efficient time and task management.<br>n) Understanding the right to support (e.g. to deal with misbehaviour, or support pupils with SEND).<br>p) Protecting time for rest and recovery and being aware of support available to support good mental wellbeing. |

# CHAPTER 4 LEARNING IN CONTEXT: TRACKING YOUR KNOWLEDGE, UNDERSTANDING AND PROGRESS

The content of this chapter links to these statements within the ITT ECF:

| How Pupils Learn (Standard 2 – Promote good progress) | |
|---|---|
| **Learn that** | |
| 6. Pupils have different working memory capacities; some pupils with SEND may have more limited working memory capacity than their peers without SEND. | |
| **Subject and Curriculum (Standard 2 – Demonstrate good subject and curriculum knowledge)** | |
| **Learn that** | **Learn how to** |
| 2. Secure subject knowledge helps teachers to motivate pupils and teach effectively.<br>3. Ensuring pupils master foundational concepts and knowledge before moving on is likely to build pupils' confidence and help them succeed.<br>4. Anticipating common misconceptions within particular subjects is also an important aspect of curricular knowledge; working closely with colleagues to develop an understanding of likely misconceptions is valuable.<br>11. Pupils' positive dispositions and attitudes towards mathematics are associated with positive outcomes on learning.<br>12. Pupils' oral language skills can be supported by teaching new words and how to use and understand words within sentences or longer texts. This can help to address speech and language difficulties, especially for children in their early school years. | **Deliver a carefully sequenced and coherent curriculum, by:**<br><br>a) Identifying essential concepts, knowledge, skills and principles of the subject and providing opportunity for all pupils to learn and master these critical components.<br>b) Ensuring pupils' thinking is focused on key ideas within the subject.<br>e) Being aware of common misconceptions and discussing with experienced colleagues how to help pupils, master important concepts. |
| **Professional Behaviours (Standard 8 – Fulfil wider professional responsibilities)** | |
| **Learn that** | **Learn how to** |
| 1. Effective professional development is likely to be sustained over time, building knowledge, motivating staff, developing teaching techniques, and embedding practice.<br>3. Teachers can make valuable contributions to the wider life of the school in a broad range of ways, including by supporting and developing effective professional relationships with colleagues. | **Develop as a professional, by:**<br><br>a) Engaging in professional development focused on developing an area of practice with clear intentions for impact on pupil outcomes, sustained over time with built-in opportunities for practice.<br>b) Strengthening pedagogical and subject knowledge by participating in wider networks and as part of the lesson preparation process. |

|  | c) Seeking challenge, feedback and critique from mentors and other colleagues in an open and trusting working environment. |
|  | e) Reflecting on progress made, recognising strengths and weaknesses and identifying next steps for further improvement. |

## CHAPTER 5 YOUR WELLBEING AND SELF-CARE

The content of this chapter links to these statements within the ITT ECF:

| High Expectations (Standard 1 – Set high expectations) ||
|---|---|
| **Learn that** | **Learn how to** |
| 2. Teachers are key role models, who can influence the attitudes, values and behaviours of their pupils.<br>7. High quality teaching is underpinned by positive interactions between pupils, their teachers and their peers.<br>8. Pupils' experiences of school and their readiness to learn can be impacted by their home life and circumstances, particularly for EAL pupils, young carers, and those living in poverty. | **Communicate a belief in the academic potential of all pupils, by:**<br>c) Creating a positive environment where making mistakes and learning from them and the need for effort and perseverance are part of the daily routine.<br>**Demonstrate consistently high behavioural expectations, by:**<br>e) Creating a culture of inclusion, respect and trust in the classroom that supports all pupils to succeed (e.g. by modelling the types of courteous behaviour expected of pupils). |
| **Managing Behaviour (Standard 7 – Manage behaviour effectively)** ||
| **Learn that** | **Learn how to** |
| 3. The ability to self-regulate one's emotions affects pupils' ability to learn, success in school and future lives.<br>8. Teaching and modelling a range of social and emotional skills (e.g. how to recognise and understand feelings, manage emotions, and sustain positive relationships) can support pupils' social and emotional development.<br>9. Teaching typically expected behaviours will reduce the need to manage misbehaviour.<br>10. Pupils who need a tailored approach to support their behaviour do not necessarily have SEND and pupils with SEND will not necessarily need additional support with their behaviour.<br>11. A key influence on a pupil's behaviour in school is being the victim of bullying. | **Develop a positive, predictable and safe environment for pupils, by:**<br>g) Responding quickly to any behaviour or bullying that threatens physical or emotional safety. |

*(Continued)*

| Professional Behaviours (Standard 8 – Fulfil wider professional responsibilities) ||
|---|---|
| **Learn that** | **Learn how to** |
| 1. Effective professional development is likely to be sustained over time, building knowledge, motivating staff, developing teaching techniques, and embedding practice.<br>8. Teacher attitudes towards inclusion and SEND are a key determinant in the school experience of pupils with SEND.<br>9. Research evidence can vary in its level of reliability, which is determined by how the research was conducted and other factors that might introduce bias, such as the level of independence. High quality research communicates methods and limitations transparently. | **Manage workload and wellbeing, by:**<br>m) Using and personalising systems and routines to support efficient time and task management.<br>n) Understanding the right to support (e.g. to deal with misbehaviour, or support pupils with SEND).<br>o) Collaborating with colleagues to share the load of planning and preparation and making use of shared resources (e.g. textbooks).<br>p) Protecting time for rest and recovery and being aware of support available to support good mental wellbeing. |

# CHAPTER 6 SAFEGUARDING AND WELLBEING OF PUPILS

The content of this chapter links to these statements within the ITT ECF:

| High Expectations (Standard 1 – Set high expectations) ||
|---|---|
| **Learn that** | **Learn how to** |
| 1. Teachers have the ability to affect and improve the wellbeing, motivation and behaviour of their pupils.<br>2. Teachers are key role models, who can influence the attitudes, values and behaviours of their pupils.<br>6. High quality teaching has a long-term positive effect on pupils' life chances, particularly for pupils from disadvantaged backgrounds.<br>7. High quality teaching is underpinned by positive interactions between pupils, their teachers and their peers.<br>8. Pupils' experiences of school and their readiness to learn can be impacted by their home life and circumstances, particularly for EAL pupils, young carers, and those living in poverty. | **Communicate a belief in the academic potential of all pupils, by:**<br>d) Seeking opportunities to engage parents and carers in the education of their children (e.g. proactively highlighting successes) and consider how this engagement changes depending on the age and development stage of the pupil. |

| Professional Behaviours (Standard 8 – Fulfil wider professional responsibilities) | |
|---|---|
| **Learn that** | **Learn how to** |
| 1. Effective professional development is likely to be sustained over time, building knowledge, motivating staff, developing teaching techniques, and embedding practice.<br>3. Teachers can make valuable contributions to the wider life of the school in a broad range of ways, including by supporting and developing effective professional relationships with colleagues.<br>8. Teacher attitudes towards inclusion and SEND are a key determinant in the school experience of pupils with SEND.<br>9. Research evidence can vary in its level of reliability, which is determined by how the research was conducted and other factors that might introduce bias, such as the level of independence. High quality research communicates methods and limitations transparently. | **Develop as a professional, by:**<br>a) Engaging in professional development focused on developing an area of practice with clear intentions for impact on pupil outcomes, sustained over time with built-in opportunities for practice. |

# CHAPTER 7 THE CURRICULUM IN THE PRIMARY SCHOOL

The content of this chapter links to these statements within the ITT ECF:

| Subject and Curriculum (Standard 3 – Demonstrate good subject and curriculum knowledge) | |
|---|---|
| **Learn that** | **Learn how to** |
| 1. A school's curriculum enables it to set out its vision for the knowledge, skills and values that its pupils will learn, encompassing the national curriculum within a coherent wider vision for successful learning.<br>3. Ensuring pupils master foundational concepts and knowledge before moving on is likely to build pupils' confidence and help them succeed.<br>5. Explicitly teaching pupils the knowledge and skills they need to succeed within particular subject areas is beneficial.<br>11. Pupils' positive dispositions and attitudes towards mathematics are associated with positive outcomes on learning. | **Deliver a carefully sequenced and coherent curriculum, by:**<br>a) Identifying essential concepts, knowledge, skills and principles of the subject and providing opportunity for all pupils to learn and master these critical components.<br>**Support pupils to build increasingly complex mental models, by:**<br>f) Discussing and analysing with expert colleagues the rationale for curriculum choices, the process for arriving at current curriculum choices and how the school's curriculum materials inform lesson preparation. |

*(Continued)*

| 12. Pupils' oral language skills can be supported by teaching new words and how to use and understand words within sentences or longer texts. This can help to address speech and language difficulties, especially for children in their early school years. | |

# CHAPTER 8 THE IMPORTANCE OF EARLY READING AND PHONICS

The content of this chapter links to these statements within the ITT ECF:

| How Pupils Learn (Standard 2 – Promote good progress) ||
|---|---|
| **Learn that** | **Learn how to** |
| 2. Prior knowledge plays an important role in how pupils learn; committing some key facts to their long-term memory is likely to help pupils learn more complex ideas.<br><br>6. Pupils have different working memory capacities; some pupils with SEND may have more limited working memory capacity than their peers without SEND.<br><br>8. Regular purposeful practice of what has previously been taught can help consolidate material and help pupils remember what they have learned. | **Avoid overloading working memory, by:**<br><br>a) Taking into account pupils' prior knowledge when planning how much new information to introduce. |
| **Subject and Curriculum (Standard 3 – Demonstrate good subject and curriculum knowledge)** ||
| **Learn that** | **Learn how to** |
| 2. Secure subject knowledge helps teachers to motivate pupils and teach effectively.<br><br>5. Explicitly teaching pupils the knowledge and skills they need to succeed within particular subject areas is beneficial.<br><br>7. In all subject areas, pupils learn new ideas by linking those ideas to existing knowledge, organising this knowledge into increasingly complex mental models (or "schemata"); carefully sequencing teaching to facilitate this process is important.<br><br>9. To access the curriculum, early literacy provides fundamental knowledge; reading comprises two elements: word reading and language comprehension; systematic synthetic phonics is the most effective approach for teaching pupils to decode. | **Develop pupils' literacy, by:**<br><br>n) Demonstrating a clear understanding of systematic synthetic phonics, and the necessary prerequisite knowledge, particularly if teaching early reading and spelling. |

| 10. Every teacher can improve pupils' communication and literacy, including by explicitly teaching reading, writing and oral language skills specific to individual disciplines.<br>12. Pupils' oral language skills can be supported by teaching new words and how to use and understand words within sentences or longer texts. This can help to address speech and language difficulties, especially for children in their early school years. | |
|---|---|

# CHAPTER 9 PUPIL BEHAVIOUR

The content of this chapter links to these statements within the ITT ECF:

| Managing Behaviour (Standard 7 - Manage behaviour effectively) ||
|---|---|
| **Learn that** | **Learn how to** |
| 1. Establishing and reinforcing routines, including through positive reinforcement, can help create an effective learning environment.<br>5. Building effective relationships is easier when pupils believe that their feelings will be considered and understood.<br>6. Pupils are motivated by intrinsic factors (related to their identity and values) and extrinsic factors (related to reward).<br>8. Teaching and modelling a range of social and emotional skills (e.g. how to recognise and understand feelings, manage emotions, and sustain positive relationships) can support pupils' social and emotional development.<br>9. Teaching typically expected behaviours will reduce the need to manage misbehaviour.<br>10. Pupils who need a tailored approach to support their behaviour do not necessarily have SEND and pupils with SEND will not necessarily need additional support with their behaviour.<br>11. A key influence on a pupil's behaviour in school is being the victim of bullying. | **Develop a positive, predictable and safe environment for pupils, by:**<br>a) Establishing a supportive and inclusive environment with a predictable system of reward and sanction in the classroom.<br>g) Responding quickly to any behaviour or bullying that threatens physical or emotional safety. |

# CHAPTER 10 DELIVERING SEQUENCES OF LEARNING: UNDERSTANDING THE PRINCIPLES OF PLANNING

The content of this chapter links to these statements within the ITT ECF:

| Subject and Curriculum (Standard 3 - Demonstrate good subject and curriculum knowledge) ||
|---|---|
| **Learn that** | **Learn how to** |
| 3. Ensuring pupils master foundational concepts and knowledge before moving on is likely to build pupils' confidence and help them succeed.<br><br>7. In all subject areas, pupils learn new ideas by linking those ideas to existing knowledge, organising this knowledge into increasingly complex mental models (or "schemata"); carefully sequencing teaching to facilitate this process is important. | **Support pupils to build increasingly complex mental models, by:**<br><br>f) Discussing and analysing with expert colleagues the rationale for curriculum choices, the process for arriving at current curriculum choices and how the school's curriculum materials inform lesson preparation. |
| **Classroom Practice (Standard 4 - Plan and teach well structured lessons)** ||
| **Learn that** | **Learn how to** |
| 2. Effective teachers introduce new material in steps, explicitly linking new ideas to what has been previously studied and learned.<br><br>6. High quality classroom talk (sometimes referred to as oracy), can support pupils to articulate key ideas, consolidate understanding and extend their vocabulary.<br><br>7. Practice is an integral part of effective teaching; ensuring pupils have repeated opportunities to practise, with appropriate guidance and support, increases success.<br><br>11. Pupils' positive dispositions and attitudes towards mathematics are associated with positive outcomes on learning.<br><br>12. Pupils' oral language skills can be supported by teaching new words and how to use and understand words within sentences or longer texts. This can help to address speech and language difficulties, especially for children in their early school years. | **Plan effective lessons, by:**<br><br>e) Breaking tasks down into constituent components when first setting up independent practice (e.g. using tasks that scaffold pupils through meta-cognitive and procedural processes). |

# CHAPTER 11 ADAPTIVE TEACHING

The content of this chapter links to these statements within the ITT ECF:

| High Expectations (Standard 1 – Set high expectations) | |
|---|---|
| **Learn that** | **Learn how to** |
| 2. Teachers are key role models, who can influence the attitudes, values and behaviours of their pupils.<br>3. Teacher expectations can affect pupil outcomes; setting goals that challenge and stretch pupils from their starting points is essential.<br>7. High quality teaching is underpinned by positive interactions between pupils, their teachers and their peers.<br>8. Pupils' experiences of school and their readiness to learn can be impacted by their home life and circumstances, particularly for EAL pupils, young carers, and those living in poverty. | **Communicate a belief in the academic potential of all pupils, by:**<br>b) Setting tasks that stretch pupils, but which are achievable, within a challenging curriculum. |
| **Adaptive Teaching (Standard 5 – Adapt teaching)** | |
| 1. Adapting teaching in a responsive way, including by providing targeted support to pupils who are struggling, is likely to increase pupil success.<br>2. Pupils are likely to learn at different rates and to require different levels and types of support from teachers to succeed.<br>3. Seeking to understand pupils' differences, including their different levels of prior knowledge and potential barriers to learning, is an essential part of teaching.<br>4. Adaptive teaching is less likely to be valuable if it causes the teacher to artificially create distinct tasks for different groups of pupils or to set lower expectations for particular pupils.<br>5. Flexibly grouping pupils within a class to provide more tailored support can support learning, but care should be taken to monitor its impact on attainment, behaviour, engagement and motivation, particularly for low attaining pupils.<br>6. There is a common misconception that pupils have distinct and identifiable learning styles. This is not supported by evidence and attempting to tailor lessons to learning styles is unlikely to be beneficial. | **Provide opportunity for all pupils to experience success, by:**<br>g) Adapting lessons, whilst maintaining high expectations for all, so that all pupils have the opportunity to meet expectations.<br>h) Balancing input of new content with the revisiting of prior learning so that pupils master important concepts. |

*(Continued)*

7. Pupils with SEND are likely to require additional or adapted support; working closely with colleagues, parents/carers, and pupils to understand barriers to learning and identify effective strategies is essential.
8. High quality teaching for all pupils, including those with SEND, is based on strategies which are often already practised by teachers, and which can be developed through training and support.
9. Technology, including educational software and assistive technology, can support teaching and learning for pupils with SEND.

# CHAPTER 12 INCLUSIVE EDUCATION: WORKING WITH PUPILS WHO HAVE SPECIAL EDUCATIONAL NEEDS AND/OR DISABILITIES (SEND)

The content of this chapter links to these statements within the ITT ECF:

| Adaptive Teaching (Standard 5 – Adapt teaching) | |
|---|---|
| 1. Adapting teaching in a responsive way, including by providing targeted support to pupils who are struggling, is likely to increase pupil success.<br>2. Pupils are likely to learn at different rates and to require different levels and types of support from teachers to succeed.<br>3. Seeking to understand pupils' differences, including their different levels of prior knowledge and potential barriers to learning, is an essential part of teaching.<br>4. Adaptive teaching is less likely to be valuable if it causes the teacher to artificially create distinct tasks for different groups of pupils or to set lower expectations for particular pupils.<br>5. Flexibly grouping pupils within a class to provide more tailored support can support learning, but care should be taken to monitor its impact on attainment, behaviour, engagement and motivation, particularly for low attaining pupils. | **Develop an understanding of different pupil needs, by:**<br><br>e) Supporting pupils with a range of additional needs and using the SEND Code of Practice: 0 to 25 years, which provides guidance on effective school systems and approaches for identifying and supporting the special educational needs of pupils with SEND.<br><br>**Provide opportunity for all pupils to experience success, by:**<br><br>g) Adapting lessons, whilst maintaining high expectations for all, so that all pupils have the opportunity to meet expectations.<br>h) Balancing input of new content with the revisiting of prior learning so that pupils master important concepts.<br>i) Making effective use of teaching assistants and other adults in the classroom. |

| | |
|---|---|
| 6. There is a common misconception that pupils have distinct and identifiable learning styles. This is not supported by evidence and attempting to tailor lessons to learning styles is unlikely to be beneficial.<br>7. Pupils with SEND are likely to require additional or adapted support; working closely with colleagues, parents/carers, and pupils to understand barriers to learning and identify effective strategies is essential.<br>8. High quality teaching for all pupils, including those with SEND, is based on strategies which are often already practised by teachers, and which can be developed through training and support.<br>9. Technology, including educational software and assistive technology, can support teaching and learning for pupils with SEND. | **Meet individual needs without creating unnecessary workload, by:**<br>l) Planning to connect new content with pupils' existing knowledge or providing additional pre-teaching if pupils lack critical knowledge.<br>m) Building in additional practice or removing unnecessary expositions.<br>n) Reframing questions to provide greater scaffolding or greater stretch.<br>**Group pupils effectively, by:**<br>p) Applying high expectations to all groups, and ensuring all pupils have access to a rich curriculum. |

| How Pupils Learn (Standard 2 - Promote good progress) ||
|---|---|
| **Learn that** | **Learn how to** |
| 4. Working memory is where information that is being actively processed is held, but its capacity is limited and can be overloaded.<br>6. Pupils have different working memory capacities; some pupils with SEND may have more limited working memory capacity than their peers without SEND.<br>7. Where prior knowledge is weak, pupils are more likely to develop misconceptions, particularly if new ideas are introduced too quickly.<br>8. Regular purposeful practice of what has previously been taught can help consolidate material and help pupils remember what they have learned.<br>9. Requiring pupils to retrieve information from memory, and spacing practice so that pupils revisit ideas after a gap are also likely to strengthen recall.<br>10. Worked examples that take pupils through each step of a new process are also likely to support pupils to learn. | **Avoid overloading working memory, by:**<br>a) Taking into account pupils' prior knowledge when planning how much new information to introduce.<br>b) Breaking complex material into smaller steps (e.g. using partially completed examples to focus pupils on the specific steps).<br>**Build on pupils' prior knowledge, by:**<br>d) Identifying possible misconceptions and planning how to prevent these forming.<br>f) Sequencing lessons so that pupils secure foundational knowledge before encountering more complex content.<br>**Increase likelihood of material being retained, by:**<br>i) Planning regular review and practice of key ideas and concepts over time (e.g. through carefully planned use of structured talk activities). |

# CHAPTER 13 DIVERSITY AND INCLUSIVE EDUCATION

The content of this chapter links to these statements within the ITT ECF:

| High Expectations (Standard 1 - Set high expectations) | |
|---|---|
| **Learn that** | **Learn how to** |
| 3. Teacher expectations can affect pupil outcomes; setting goals that challenge and stretch pupils from their starting points is essential.<br>5. A culture of mutual trust and respect supports effective relationships.<br>7. High quality teaching is underpinned by positive interactions between pupils, their teachers and their peers.<br>8. Pupils' experiences of school and their readiness to learn can be impacted by their home life and circumstances, particularly for EAL pupils, young carers, and those living in poverty. | **Demonstrate consistently high behavioural expectations, by:**<br><br>e) Creating a culture of inclusion, respect and trust in the classroom that supports all pupils to succeed (e.g. by modelling the types of courteous behaviour expected of pupils). |
| **Subject and Curriculum (Standard 3 - Demonstrate good subject and curriculum knowledge)** | |
| 1. A school's curriculum enables it to set out its vision for the knowledge, skills and values that its pupils will learn, encompassing the national curriculum within a coherent wider vision for successful learning.<br>11. Pupils' positive dispositions and attitudes towards mathematics are associated with positive outcomes on learning.<br>12. Pupils' oral language skills can be supported by teaching new words and how to use and understand words within sentences or longer texts. This can help to address speech and language difficulties, especially for children in their early school years. | **Support pupils to build increasingly complex mental models, by:**<br><br>f) Discussing and analysing with expert colleagues the rationale for curriculum choices, the process for arriving at current curriculum choices and how the school's curriculum materials inform lesson preparation. |
| **Adaptive Teaching (Standard 5 - Adapt teaching)** | |
| **Learn that** | **Learn how to** |
| 1. Adapting teaching in a responsive way, including by providing targeted support to pupils who are struggling, is likely to increase pupil success.<br>3. Seeking to understand pupils' differences, including their different levels of prior knowledge and potential barriers to learning, is an essential part of teaching. | **Group pupils effectively, by:**<br><br>p) Applying high expectations to all groups, and ensuring all pupils have access to a rich curriculum. |

| | |
|---|---|
| 8. High quality teaching for all pupils, including those with SEND, is based on strategies which are often already practised by teachers, and which can be developed through training and support.<br>9. Technology, including educational software and assistive technology, can support teaching and learning for pupils with SEND. | |
| **Professional Behaviours (Standard 8 – Fulfil wider professional responsibilities)** ||
| **Learn that** | **Learn how to** |
| 2. Reflective practice, supported by feedback from and observation of experienced colleagues, professional debate, and learning from educational research, is also likely to support improvement.<br>8. Teacher attitudes towards inclusion and SEND are a key determinant in the school experience of pupils with SEND.<br>9. Research evidence can vary in its level of reliability, which is determined by how the research was conducted and other factors that might introduce bias, such as the level of independence. High quality research communicates methods and limitations transparently. | **Build effective working relationships, by:**<br>f) Contributing positively to the wider school culture and developing a feeling of shared responsibility for improving the lives of all pupils within the school. |

# CHAPTER 14 ASSESSMENT AND PROGRESSION

The content of this chapter links to these statements within the ITT ECF:

| **Assessment (Standard 6 – Make accurate and productive use of assessment)** ||
|---|---|
| **Learn that** | **Learn how to** |
| 1. Effective assessment is critical to teaching because it provides teachers with information about pupils' understanding and needs.<br>3. Before using any assessment, teachers should be clear about the decision it will be used to support and be able to justify its use.<br>4. To be of value, teachers use information from assessments to inform the decisions they make; in turn, pupils must be able to act on feedback for it to have an effect.<br>5. High quality feedback can be written or verbal; it is likely to be accurate and clear, encourage further effort, and provide specific guidance on how to improve. | **Avoid common assessment pitfalls, by:**<br>a) Planning formative assessment tasks linked to lesson objectives and thinking ahead about what would indicate understanding (e.g. by using hinge questions to pinpoint knowledge gaps). |

*(Continued)*

| How Pupils Learn (Standard 2 – Promote good progress) | |
|---|---|
| **Learn that** | **Learn how to** |
| 1. Learning involves a lasting change in pupils' capabilities or understanding.<br>2. Prior knowledge plays an important role in how pupils learn; committing some key facts to their long-term memory is likely to help pupils learn more complex ideas.<br>6. Pupils have different working memory capacities; some pupils with SEND may have more limited working memory capacity than their peers without SEND. | **Increase likelihood of material being retained, by:**<br>i) Planning regular review and practice of key ideas and concepts over time (e.g. through carefully planned use of structured talk activities). |

# CHAPTER 15 EDUCATION, SOCIAL JUSTICE AND DISADVANTAGE

The content of this chapter links to these statements within the ITT ECF:

| Adaptive Teaching (Standard 5 – Adapt teaching) | |
|---|---|
| **Learn that** | **Learn how to** |
| 3. Seeking to understand pupils' differences, including their different levels of prior knowledge and potential barriers to learning, is an essential part of teaching.<br>8. High quality teaching for all pupils, including those with SEND, is based on strategies which are often already practised by teachers, and which can be developed through training and support.<br>9. Technology, including educational software and assistive technology, can support teaching and learning for pupils with SEND. | **Develop an understanding of different pupil needs, by:**<br>c) Working closely with the Special Educational Needs Co-ordinator (SENCO) and other SEND specialists or expert colleagues.<br>d) Working closely with the Designated Safeguarding Lead.<br>e) Supporting pupils with a range of additional needs and using the SEND Code of Practice: 0 to 25 years, which provides guidance on effective school systems and approaches for identifying and supporting the special educational needs of pupils with SEND. |
| **Professional Behaviours (Standard 8 – Fulfil wider professional responsibilities)** | |
| **Learn that** | **Learn how to** |
| 2. Reflective practice, supported by feedback from and observation of experienced colleagues, professional debate, and learning from educational research, is also likely to support improvement.<br>4. Building effective relationships with parents, carers and families can improve pupils' motivation, | **Build effective working relationships, by:**<br>f) Contributing positively to the wider school culture and developing a feeling of shared responsibility for improving the lives of all pupils within the school.<br>h) Communicating with parents and carers proactively and making effective use of parents' evenings to engage parents and carers in their children's schooling. |

| | |
|---|---|
| 8. Teacher attitudes towards inclusion and SEND are a key determinant in the school experience of pupils with SEND.<br>9. Research evidence can vary in its level of reliability, which is determined by how the research was conducted and other factors that might introduce bias, such as the level of independence. High quality research communicates methods and limitations transparently. | l) Knowing who to contact with any safeguarding, or any pupil mental health concerns. |

## CHAPTER 16 TEACHING CHILDREN SUSTAINABLY

The content of this chapter links to these statements within the ITT ECF:

| Classroom Practice (Standard 4 – Plan and teach well structured lessons) | |
|---|---|
| **Learn that** | **Learn how to** |
| 5. Explicitly teaching pupils metacognitive strategies linked to subject knowledge, including how to plan, monitor and evaluate, supports independence and academic success. Questioning is an essential tool for teachers; questions can be used for many purposes, including to check pupils' prior knowledge, assess understanding and break down problems.<br>6. High quality classroom talk (sometimes referred to as oracy), can support pupils to articulate key ideas, consolidate understanding and extend their vocabulary. | **Plan effective lessons, by:**<br>e) Breaking tasks down into constituent components when first setting up independent practice (e.g. using tasks that scaffold pupils through meta-cognitive and procedural processes). |
| **Subject and Curriculum (Standard 3 – Demonstrate good subject and curriculum knowledge)** | |
| **Learn that** | **Learn how to** |
| 5. Explicitly teaching pupils the knowledge and skills they need to succeed within particular subject areas is beneficial.<br>6. In order for pupils to think critically, they must have a secure understanding of knowledge within the subject area they are being asked to think critically about.<br>11. Pupils' positive dispositions and attitudes towards mathematics are associated with positive outcomes on learning.<br>12. Pupils' oral language skills can be supported by teaching new words and how to use and understand words within sentences or longer texts. This can help to address speech and language difficulties, especially for children in their early school years. | **Deliver a carefully sequenced and coherent curriculum, by:**<br>a) Identifying essential concepts, knowledge, skills and principles of the subject and providing opportunity for all pupils to learn and master these critical components. |

# REFERENCE

Department for Education (DfE) (2024) *Initial Teacher Training and Early Career Framework*. Available at: https://assets.publishing.service.gov.uk/media/65b8fa60e9e10a00130310b2/Initial_teacher_training_and_early_career_framework_30_Jan_2024.pdf [accessed 11 March 2024].

# INDEX

Page numbers followed by "f" indicate figures; those followed by "t" indicate tables.

absence, school protocols for, 55
adaptive teaching, 187, 204, 223, 252
  chunking, 213
  data about pupils, 190–193
  and differentiated teaching, 189–190, 190t
  dual coding, 214
  effective curriculum planning, 193
  and formative assessment, 195–196
  hinge questions, 196
  misconceptions, addressing, 197–198
  overlearning, 214
  pre-teaching, 212–213
  and prior knowledge, 194–196
  reducing cognitive load, 215
  regular purposeful practice, 215
  retrieval practice, 214
  scaffolding, approaches to, 198–199, 213–214
  spaced or distributed learning, 215
  strategies, 212–215
  using concrete resources, 214
  using worked examples, 214–215
advanced skills teacher (AST), 292
adverse childhood experiences (ACEs), 263
anti-prejudiced education, importance of, 225–227
Anyon, J., 266
application form, 320–321
arrival and departure times, for staff, 55
artificial intelligence (AI), 43, 194
assessment
  with accuracy, 250–251
  evidence-informed research, 247–248, 250
  feedback, use in practices, 250–252
  formative, 195–196, 245–249
  for/of learning, 245
  idea of, 245
  inclusive, 252
  make accurate and productive use of, 242
  in practice, 252–254
  in primary education, 244–246
  and progression, 241–255
  pupil progress, 251–252
  of pupils' prior knowledge and misconceptions, 252
  in school-based learning centre, 249
  standard 2 of CCF, 251, 252
  standard 6 of CCF, 250–251
  summative, 245–249
  tools, 244
  types of, 245–246
  use of feedback in practices, 250–252
attainment gaps, 227–228, 259, 264

Ball, S., 259
Bandura, A., 83
Beauchamp, C., 53
Beckett, L., 266
Bendell J., 284
biases and stereotypes, addressing, 229–232
Biesta, G., 120
Bishop, R.S., 122
Black Asian global majority (BAGM) teachers, underrepresentation of, 231
Black, P., 247
body language, 55
Bronfenbrenner, U., 66
Brookfield, S., 123
Burn, K., 266
Burris, C. C., 189

Cantell, H., 282
career development and progression
  pathways for promotion, 292–293
  in teaching, 291–292
career professional development (CPD), 314
case study
  adaptive teaching, 188, 190–191
  advance learning partnership, 41–42
  answering interview questions, 323–325
  art as subject curriculum, 124–125
  contextually relevant sequence of learning, 174
  early reading progress and development, 144–145
  early reading support, 141–142
  initial teacher training curriculum, 21–22
  leadership, in whole-school initiative and action research, 305–306
  learning to lead, 330–331
  lesson planning, 181–182
  low-level disruptive behaviour, managing and responding to, 153–154
  misconceptions, 197
  professional learning network, 300–301, 303–304
  progression and monitoring, 71–72
  reflective teaching, 36–37

regaining control, 85–86
restorative practice and relational pedagogy, 162–163
sense of agency, developing, 57
social, moral, spiritual and cultural development
  and personal, social, health and economic education, 236
  and religious education, 234–235
supporting emotional regulation skills, 220
sustainability and climate change education, 281
teacher identity, 53–54
understanding low attainment of pupils in poverty, 268
use of assessment during ITT programme, 252–254
working with others, 58–59
centre-based learning, 20–21, 20f, 21t
chartered teacher status (CTS), 293
child abuse
  action to be taken for, 103–104
  emotional, 101
  neglect, 102
  physical, 101
  sexual, 102
child development, poverty effects on, 262–263
child disclosure, guidelines for, 102–103
Child Poverty Action Group (CPAG), 261
child poverty, in England, 260–265
Childs, A., 266
Choudry, S., 227
chunking, 213
citizenship education, 234
Clark, A.E., 110
Clarke, D., 24
classroom climate, good, 66
climate change education. *See* sustainability (and climate change education)
Coe, R., 17
cognitive bias, 229
cognitive development, 250
cognitive dissonance, 211
cognitive load
  optimising, 177
  reducing, 215
  theory, 176
cognitive overload, 17
communities of practice (CoPs), 20, 298, 299
component knowledge, 172
composite knowledge, 172
concept cartoons, use of, 198
concrete resources, 214
content knowledge, 67
contextual intelligence, 266

continuing professional development (CPD), 67
  elements of effective, 294–295
  mechanisms of professional development, 295–296, 296f
  for teachers, 293–296
*Core Content Framework* (CCF), 11–14, 120, 189, 224, 275, 290, 314
  digital approximations, 15–16
  micro-teaching, 16
  professional in, 50–53
  roles and responsibilities, 16–17
  *Teachers' Standards*, 12–13, 13f
  trainee development, support for, 12
covering letter, 322
Covid-19 impact, on disadvantaged young learners, 264
Cowie, H., 248
critical race theory (CRT), 233
cultural capital, 173, 234
culture, 230
curriculum
  adaptive teaching, 193–194
  ambitious choices, 233–236
  decolonising the curriculum, 233
  Department for Education (DfE), 118
  developing, 121–122
  disciplinary and substantive knowledge, 128
  diversifying, 233
  Early Career Framework (ECF), 120
  Education Inspection Framework, 119
  impact of, 122
  implementation, 121–122
  importance of design, 237
  integrating LGBT content into, 234
  intent, 121
  ITT Core Content Framework (CCF), 120
  linking sustainability with, 277, 279–282
  national, 117–120, 118f, 234, 245
  need for, 117
  Ofsted, 119
  personalised to children, 122–123
  planning, to develop climate change knowledge, 285
  in primary school, 117–129
  progress in phonics, 211
  school, purpose of, 120
  science, 127–128, 127t
  subject and, 223
  *Teachers' Standards* (DfE), 119
  unique setting of, 122
curriculum learning centres (CLCs), 12
curriculum vitae (CV), 318–320, 319–320t

data, pupil, 191, 192t
Dave, H., 280
decolonising the curriculum (DtC), 233
deficit discourse, 265–266

Department for Education (DfE), 11, 118, 298
  Education Endowment Foundation (EEF)
      working with, 291
  funding on disadvantaged pupils, 265
  sustainability and climate change strategy, 275
  *Teachers' Standards*, 312–317
designated safeguarding lead (DSL), 99–100, 195
Deunk, M. I., 189
Dewey, J., 32
dialogic approaches, teaching for diversity
    through, 235
differentiated teaching, 189–190, 190t
differentiation. *See* differentiated teaching
digital approximations, 15–16
disadvantage. *See* poverty
diversity, 227
  dialogic approaches, 235
  promoting in education, 231
Dix, P., 157
Doherty, J., 268
dress code, 54
dual coding, 214

*Early Career Framework* (ECF), 50–53, 120, 189,
    290, 315–316f, 317
early career teacher (ECT), 49, 313
  practical advice for trainees and, 283
  support for, aiming to achieve DfE *Teachers'
    Standards*, 314–317
  supporting pupils with SEND as, 219
Eaude, T., 51
education and health care plan (EHCP), 210
Education Endowment Foundation (EEF), 135,
    199, 229, 236, 250, 291
  review of professional development, 295–296
  Toolkit, 248
education for sustainable development (ESD),
    283–284
*Education Inspection Framework* (Ofsted),
    119, 172, 248
Education Reform Act (1988), 117–118
educational achievement gaps, 227–228
educational attainment, 265, 267
educational leadership programmes, 293
educator, child safety and welfare, duty
    in, 107–109
email protocols, 55
Embedding Formative Assessment
    Programme, 248
Emery, C., 260
emotional abuse, of child, 101
emotional regulation skills, supporting, 220
employability
  application form, 320–321
  curriculum vitae (CV), 318–320, 319–320t
  graduate attributes for teaching roles,
      317, 318t
  interview, 323–326
  personal statement, 321–322
  process of applying for teaching post,
      318–320, 319f
  school visit, 322–323
  supporting letter, 322
enactment, 69–70
English as an additional language (EAL),
    211, 216, 227, 233, 236
Equality Act (2010), 195, 208, 225–226
equality, equity and liberation, 225f
equitable funding, 228–229
Erikson, E.H., 52
ethnicity, 230
evidence
  considerations, 39–40t
  engaging with, 37–38, 40
  'Five Ws plus How' mnemonic, 39t
  quality of, evaluating, 39–40
  types of, 38–39
evidence-informed research
  ability grouping, 216
  code of conduct in schools, 106
  *Core Content Framework* (CCF), 14
  deployment of teaching assistants, 217
  educational achievement gaps, 227–228
  effects of poverty, 262
  experiencing poverty, 'othering' of
      disadvantaged pupils, 266–267
  extrinsic and intrinsic motivators, 158
  feedback, 250
  formative assessment and its role in pupil
      progression, 247–248
  high expectations, maintaining, 192
  ITaP models and frameworks, 23–24
  knowledge and understanding, 66–67
  maths mastery approach, 125–126
  mechanisms of professional development,
      295–296, 296f
  pedagogy in teaching, 19
  phonics, approaches to, 135
  pupil behaviour management, 163–164
  safeguarding and wellbeing of pupil, 108
  self-efficacy, wellbeing and control, 83
  stress, dealing with, 86–87
  subject leader, 328
  sustainability and climate change education,
      276–277, 278–279
  teacher identity and professional
      relationship, 52
  *Teaching and Learning Toolkit* (EEF), 40–41
  theory behind PLN, 298–299
  working with parents to support children's
      learning, 143
expert colleagues, 15
  observing, 73
  roles and responsibilities, 16

expert mentors, roles and responsibilities, 16
extrinsic motivators, 156–157

feedback
  and reflection, 295
  use in assessment practices, 250–252
fixed attainment groups, negative impacts of, 215
Fletcher-Wood, H., 196
flexible groupings, need for, 215–216
formative assessment, 195–196, 245, 247–248
free school meals (FSM), 267

Gill, A., 140
Glazzard, G., 154
Glazzard, J., 172, 173, 180
Golding, K., 159
Goouch, K., 143
governor/trustee roles, 293
graduate attributes
  example of, 318t
  for teaching roles, 317
graduated approach (*SEND Code of Practice*), 209–210, 209f
grapheme–phoneme correspondences (GPCs), 138
graphemes, 135
Green, M., 172, 173, 180
Grossman, P., 24
guided observations, 74

Harlen, W., 249
hate crimes, 231
Hattie, J., 172, 177, 248, 250
hidden bias tests, 232
high expectation
  maintaining, 192
  teachers, 193
Hinds, D., 266
hinge questions, 196
Hoath, L., 280
Hoestlandt, J., 231
Hollingsworth, H., 24
hooks, bell, 269
Hope not Hate, 231

inclusive assessment, 252
inclusive education
  diversity and, 222–237
  LGBTQ and, 234–235
  for pupils with SEND, 203–220
initial teacher training (ITT), 291, 314
  *Core Content Framework* (CCF), 11–14
  digital approximations, 15–16
  fidelity between centre-based and school-based learning, 20–21, 20f, 21t

initial teacher training providers (ITTPs), 11
  intensive training and practice (ITaP), 22–27
  micro-teaching, 16
  roles and responsibilities, 16–17
  sequencing, progression and alignment of, 17–19, 18f
Institute of Fiscal Studies (IFS), 264
institutional racism, 226
integration, and inclusion, 210
intensive training and practice (ITaP), 22–23, 253
  impact of, measuring, 26–27
  models and frameworks, 23–24, 23f
  weekly plan, 24–25t
intersectionality, 227
interview, 323–326
  case study, 323–325
  tasks on day of, 326
  triangle, 324f
intrinsic motivators, 157–158
IPCC report, 278

Jacobson, L., 192
James, M., 249
Jolliffe, W., 140
Joseph Rowntree Foundation (JRF), 260

*Keeping Children Safe in Education*, 98, 100
Kirschner, P., 177
knowledge
  audits, identifying, 68–70
  identifying, 68–70
  in learning process, linking new to existing, 211–212
  and understanding, 64
    interpretation of foundations, 65–66, 65f
    knowledge gaps and auditing, identifying, 68–70
    observations, 72–74
    progress tracking and monitoring, 74–75
    progression and monitoring across ITT programme, 70–71
    as trainee teacher, developing, 67
    ways for developing, 69–70

Lambrith, A., 143
Lave, J., 20
Lawrence, S., 226
leadership
  educational programmes, 293
  middle roles, 292
  and policies, 285
  preparing for subject, 326–331
  senior roles, 292
  in whole-school initiative and action research (case study), 305–306

learning
  centre-based, 20–21
  knowledge and skills, 26–27
  school-based, 20–21
  *See also specific entries*
lesson observations, 74
lesson planning, 181
LGBTQ-inclusive education, 234
LinkedIn, 298, 304
Losano, L., 51

Mansworth, M., 193
mental health support, increased referrals for, 264
metacognition, 178
micro-teaching, 16, 69–70
middle leadership roles, 292
misconceptions
  adaptive teaching, 197–198
  assessing pupils' prior knowledge and, 252
Montessori, M., 107
mutual respect, power of, 160–161

National Association for Special Educational Needs (NASEN), 219
National Association for the Teaching of English (NATE), 70
National Centre for Excellence in the Teaching of Mathematics (NCETM), 70
National Education Nature Park, 276
National Institute of Teaching, 298
national professional qualification (NPQ), 291, 292
Ngozi Adichie, C., 231
Nuttall, A., 266, 268

observations
  in classroom, 72
  expert colleagues, observing, 73
  guided observations, 74
  individual learners, tracking, 73
  initial exposure, 72–73
  knowledge gaps, identifying, 73
  lesson observations and feedback, 74
  teaching style, defining, 73
Ofsted, 119, 128, 172, 234, 248, 328
Organisation for Economic Co-operation and Development (OECD), 50–51
overlearning, 214

parents/carers, working to meet pupils' needs, 217
Parry-Langdon, N., 109
PebblePad, 72
pedagogical content knowledge, 67
pedagogical literature, 38

pedagogy
  definition of, 65–66
  quality resources and, 285
  signature, 19, 177
  for sustainability and climate change education, 282
  in teaching, 19
peer learning and collaboration, 295
peer review, 69
peer/expert feedback, 33–34
personal biases and stereotypes, addressing, 229–232
personal, social, health and economic (PHSE) education, 234, 236
personal statement, 321–322
philosophy for children (P4C) stimulus, 236
phone usage, 55
phonemes, 135
phonemic awareness, 136
phonics
  alternative graphemes and phonemes, 138
  capital and lower-case letters, 138
  children progress, ensuring, 141–142
  common exception words, 137–138, 137t
  enunciation and accent, 140
  key challenges, 137–140
  at KS2, 140–141
  making reading fun, 137
  parental engagement in early reading, 143–144
  phonological awareness, 135–136
  pseudo words, 139
  subject knowledge, 139–140
  systematic approach to teaching, 134
  teaching strategies, 138–139
physical abuse, of child, 101
physical contact, with pupils, 106–107
Piaget, J., 250
planning
  current landscape, 169–170
  developing expertise, 170–171
  expert colleagues, 170
  importance of, 169
  principles of, 169–183
  sequence of learning, 172–183
positive connection-making, 160–161
  acceptance, 161
  empathy, 161
  genuineness, 161
  self-actualisation, 161
positivity, 66
poverty
  causes of, 261
  children living in, 260–265
  and disadvantage as primary teacher, 267–268
  effects on child development, 262–263
  evidence-informed research, 262
  government intervention, 264–265

measures of, 260
'othering' of disadvantaged pupils, 266–267
pandemic impact on, 264
psychological impacts of, 262
understanding low attainment of pupils (case study), 268
pre-teaching, 212–213
prejudice, 229
Primary Science Teaching Trust, 248
'Principles of instruction' (Rosenshine), 67
prior knowledge
    formative assessment, 195–196
    purposes for establishing, 194–195
    supporting children with complex needs, 195
professional behaviours, 223
professional development opportunities, 291f
professional learning network (PLN), 297f
    benefits of, 299–300t
    building connections through, 297–301
    building networks, 300
    case study, 300–301, 303–304
    evidence-informed research, 298–299
    evolution of, 306t
    external networks, 298
    internal networks, 298
    mapping, 307f
    national network, 298, 302–303
    regional network, 298, 300–301
    in situated learning theories, 299
    virtual network, 298, 303–305
professional literature, 38
professional relationships
    being a role model, 55–57
    *Core Content Framework*, professional in, 50–53
    developing, 49–60
    *Early Career Framework*, professional in, 50–53
    professional conventions and expectations, 54–55
    seeing yourself as professional, 49–50
    sense of agency, developing, 57
    *Teachers' Standards*, professional in, 50–53
    working with others, 58–59
Programme for International Student Assessment (PISA), 187
Project Implicit, 232
promotion, pathways for, 292–293
protected characteristics, 225, 227, 229
protocols, for asking for help, 55
pupil(s)
    access to range of data about, 190–192, 192t
    misconceptions, 65
    prior knowledge and misconceptions, 252
    progress, and assessment, 251–252
    *See also* safeguarding, of pupils; wellbeing, of pupils

pupil behaviour
    building relationships, 159
    challenging or poor behaviour, 152
    classroom behaviour, expectations of, 151–154
    extrinsic motivators, 156–157
    intrinsic motivators, 157–158
    learning environment, management in, 151, 151f
    mutual respect, power of, 160–161
    personal and professional values, 156
    positive connection-making, 160–161
    positive relationships for learning, 157–158
    reflection, importance of, 155
    restorative approach, 161–163
    Schon reflective model, 155, 155f
    self-regulation, 159
    stress, possible responses to, 152f
pupil premium (PP)
    funding, 266, 267
    grant, 228

qualified teacher status (QTS), 11, 290, 312, 314
qualitative data, 192t
quality of education, 328–329
quantitative data, 192t

Race Relations Act (2000), 226
race/racism, defined, 230
reading development, example of, 211
reflective teaching, 32–33
    action planning, 35
    analysis, 35
    cycle of practice, 34f
    evaluation, 35
    implementation, 35
    reflection, 34
    review, 35
    source of feedback, 33–34
religious education (RE), 234–235
Remesh, A., 16
remote learning, disparities in engagement with, 264
research-informed decision-making, 43–44, 43–44t
resilience, 81–82
responsive teaching, 200
retrieval practice, 214
Rogers, C., 159
role model, being, 55–57
Rosenshine, B., 67, 251
Rosenthal, R., 192
Rubie-Davies, C. M., 192, 193

Sadler, R., 250
safeguarding, of pupils
    child abuse, action to be taken for, 103–104

child disclosure, guidelines for, 102–103
concerned about child, 101–104
definition of, 97–98
designated lead/officer, roles and
   responsibilities of, 99–100
factors including, 98–99
physical contact with pupils, 106–107
policy and procedures, challenges for teachers
   of implementing, 104
roles and responsibilities, 99–101
safety in school, guidelines for, 105
school governing body, roles and
   responsibilities of, 99
teachers and other school staff, roles and
   responsibilities of, 100–101
scaffolding
   fading, 213–214
   verbal approaches, 199
   visual approaches, 198–199
   written approaches, 199
schemas, 211–212
Schön, D., 32
Schon, D.A., 155
Schon reflective model, 155, 155f
school-based learning, 20–21, 20f, 21t
school-based learning centres (SBLCs),
   12, 249, 252, 254
school improvement initiatives, contributing
   to, 293
school visit, 322–323
*School Workload Reduction Toolkit*, 169–170
Secretary of State, 312
self-care, 56
   diet, exercise and sleep regimes, improving, 88
   early warning signs of illness, 84
   hobbies or interests, 83
   mental and physical health, 81
   resilience and culture of teaching, 81–82
   resting, recovery and work-life balance, 87–88
   self-help and external sources of help, 90–91
   stress behaviour, recognising, 87
   stress-busting activities, 84
   stress triggers, aware of, 84
   time management, 88–90
self-esteem, 216
self-help, 90–91
self-regulation, of pupil, 159
senior leadership roles, 292
sense of agency, developing, 57
sequence of learning
   adaptations, adjusting view, 180–181
   composition, avoiding saturation, 177–178
   demonstrating adaptations, 181t
   example of, 178–179t
   meaning of, 171–172
   measuring success, chimping, 182–183
   process over product-led approach, 173, 173f

step-by-step approach of planning, 172–183
   zoom in, sharpening focus, 174–177
   zoom out, panoramic view, 172–173
sexual abuse, of child, 102
Sharples, J., 216–217
signature pedagogies, 19, 177
Skinner, B.F., 156
Smith, P., 248
social and emotional learning (SEL), 263
social justice, 237, 265, 268
social media, and professional learning network,
   303–304
social, moral, spiritual and cultural (SMSC)
   development, 234–235
   and personal, social, health and economic
      (PHSE) education, 236
   and religious education (RE), 234–235
spaced or distributed learning, 215
special educational needs and/or disabilities
   (SEND)
   adaptive teaching strategies, 212–215
   building on prior knowledge, 211–212
   *Code of Practice*, 207–210, 217, 218
   deployment of support staff, 216–217
   emotional regulation skills, supporting, 220
   graduated approach, 209–210, 209f
   grouping pupils, 215–216
   inclusive education for pupils with, 203–220
   meaning of, 206–207
   perspectives on inclusion for pupils with, 210
   rates of learning, 207
   supporting pupils with SEND as ECT, 219
   teaching for pupils with, 210–211, 212–215
   working with external agencies, 218
   working with parents/carers, 217
special educational needs coordinator (SENCO),
   217, 218–219
Speckesser, S., 248
Spielman, A., 266
spiral curriculum, 17
spiritual, moral, social and cultural development
   (SMSC), 225
*Star of Fear, Star of Hope* (Hoestlandt), 231
statutory assessment tests (SATs), 245
stereotypes/personal biases, addressing,
   229–232
Stonewall, 224
stress
   -busting activities, 84
   behaviour, recognising, 87
   breathing techniques, 87
   dealing with, 86–87
   diet, exercise and sleep regimes, improving, 88
   regaining control, 85–86
   triggers, aware of, 84
structural racism, 226, 233
subject associations, 302–303

# INDEX

subject leadership
  assuring quality teaching and learning for all pupils, 328–330
  case study, 330–331
  preparing for, 326–331
subject/curriculum knowledge, 65
summative assessment, 245–246, 248–249
supporting letter, 322
sustainability (and climate change education)
  approaching, 280–281
  building whole-school culture for, 285
  case study, 281
  curriculum and pedagogy interplay, 282
  defined, 278
  education for sustainable development (ESD), 283–284
  evidence-informed research, 276–277, 278–279
  integration into school culture, 282
  linked with existing curricula, 279–281
  outdoor pedagogies and addressing climate anxiety, 283
  purpose and complexities of teaching about, 275–277
  social inequality and climate justice, addressing, 282
  UN sustainable development goals (UNSDGs), 284

*Teacher Assessment in Primary Science*, 248–249
teachers
  advanced skills teacher (AST), 292
  Black Asian global majority (BAGM) teachers, underrepresentation of, 231
  clarity, 67
  continuing professional development for, 293–296
  development, stages of, 290f
  high expectation, 193
  identity, 52, 53–54
  initial teacher training curriculum, 21–22
  -learner identity, 58
  role, social justice and equity at centre of, 268
  roles and responsibilities of, 100–101
  trainee, developing, 67
  *See also* early career teacher (ECT)
*Teachers' Standards* (DfE), 12–13, 13f, 119, 312–317
  document, 312–313
  professional in, 50–53
  as self-reflection tool, 314
  standard 4 from, 313, 315–316f
  support for ECTs aiming to achieving, 314–317
  support for trainees aiming to achieving, 314
  *See also* employability; subject leadership
teaching
  assistants, deployment of, 216–217
  assuring quality, 328–331

  career development and progression in, 291–292
  children sustainability, 273–286
  culture of, 81–82
  for diversity through dialogic approaches, 235
  engaging with evidence, 37–38, 40
  evidence, types of, 38–39
  graduate attributes, 317, 318t
  moral domains of, 268
  pre-, 212–213
  process of applying for post, 318–320, 319f
    (*See also* employability)
  for pupils with SEND, 210–211, 212–215
  quality of evidence, evaluating, 39–40
  reflective practice, 32–35
  resources, evaluating, 42–44, 43–44t
  social justice and, 268
  sustainability and climate change education, 276–277
  trainee expectations, 32
teaching and learning responsibility (TLR) posts, 292
*Teaching and Learning Toolkit* (EEF), 40–41, 43
terms of address, 55
Thomas, L., 53
Thomson, P., 122–123
time management, 88–90
Timperley, H., 250
trainee
  expectations, 32
  knowledge and understanding, developing, 67
  roles and responsibilities, 16
Treisman, K., 162
Trust, 298

unconscious bias, 228, 232
United Nations Brundtland Commission, 278
United Nations sustainable development goals (UNSDGs), 284

virtual professional network, 298, 303–305
visible learning, 248

Warnock Report, 210
Waugh, D., 140
wellbeing
  diet, exercise and sleep regimes, improving, 88
  early warning signs of illness, 84
  hobbies or interests, 83
  mental and physical health, 81
  of pupils
    within classroom, 109
    definition of, 107
    duty as educator, 107–109
    emotionally safe environment, creating, 109–110

    maintaining, 109–110
    whole-school approach, 109
resilience and culture of teaching, 81–82
resting, recovery and work-life
    balance, 87–88
self-help and external sources of help, 90–91
stress behaviour, recognising, 87
stress-busting activities, 84
stress triggers, aware of, 84
time management, 88–90
Wenger, E., 20
*What a Good One Looks Likes* (WaGOLL), 199

Whitaker, D., 160
white privilege, recognition of, 230
whole-school culture, for sustainability and climate change education, 285
Wiliam, D., 182, 247
working with others, 58–59
work-life balance, 87–88
Wrigley, T., 266

X (Twitter), 298, 304

Yates, G.C.Y., 172

www.ingramcontent.com/pod-product-compliance
Lightning Source LLC
Chambersburg PA
CBHW082215090526
44584CB00025BA/3701